Understanding Knowledge as a Commons

Understanding Knowledge as a Commons

From Theory to Practice

edited by Charlotte Hess and Elinor Ostrom

The MIT Press
Cambridge, Massachusetts
London, England

© 2007 Massachusetts Institute of Technology

MIT Press books may be purchased at special quantity discounts for business or sales promotional use. For information, please e-mail special_sales@mitpress.mit.edu or write to Special Sales Department, The MIT Press, 55 Hayward Street, Cambridge, MA 02142.

This book was set in Sabon by SNP Best-set Typesetter Ltd., Hong Kong and printed and bound in the United States of America.

Library of Congress Cataloging-in-Publication Data

Understanding knowledge as a commons : from theory to practice / edited by Charlotte Hess and Elinor Ostrom.
    p. cm.
Includes index.
ISBN-13: 978-0-262-08357-7 (hardcover : alk. paper)
ISBN-10: 0-262-08357-4 (hardcover)
1. Knowledge management. 2. Information commons. I. Hess, Charlotte. II. Ostrom, Elinor.
HD30.2.U53 2007
001—dc22   2006027385

10 9 8 7 6 5 4 3 2 1

This book is dedicated to the memory of Gerry Bernbom (1952–2003) who continues to be a source of inspiration and wisdom.

Contents

Preface   ix

I Studying the Knowledge Commons   1

1 Introduction: An Overview of the Knowledge Commons   3
Charlotte Hess and Elinor Ostrom

2 The Growth of the Commons Paradigm   27
David Bollier

3 A Framework for Analyzing the Knowledge Commons   41
Elinor Ostrom and Charlotte Hess

II Protecting the Knowledge Commons   83

4 Countering Enclosure: Reclaiming the Knowledge Commons   85
Nancy Kranich

5 Mertonianism Unbound? Imagining Free, Decentralized Access to
Most Cultural and Scientific Material   123
James Boyle

6 Preserving the Knowledge Commons   145
Donald J. Waters

III Building New Knowledge Commons   169

7 Creating an Intellectual Commons through Open Access   171
Peter Suber

8 How to Build a Commons: Is Intellectual Property Constrictive,
Facilitating, or Irrelevant?   209
Shubha Ghosh

9 Collective Action, Civic Engagement, and the Knowledge Commons 247
Peter Levine

10 Free/Open-Source Software as a Framework for Establishing Commons in Science 277
Charles M. Schweik

11 Scholarly Communication and Libraries Unbound: The Opportunity of the Commons 311
Wendy Pradt Lougee

12 EconPort: Creating and Maintaining a Knowledge Commons 333
James C. Cox and J. Todd Swarthout

Glossary 349
Index 353

Preface

In the spring of 2004, Charlotte Hess and Elinor Ostrom hosted a meeting titled "Workshop on Scholarly Communication as a Commons." The idea of this working session grew out of several parallel events, including the discussions at the Conference on the Public Domain organized and chaired by James Boyle at Duke University in November 2001.[1] It is also an outgrowth óf the many years of research, case studies, and theoretical work on the commons undertaken at the Workshop in Political Theory and Policy Analysis (Workshop), Indiana University. While earlier work focused primarily on the study of natural resources as commons, more recent interest has developed at the Workshop on the scholarly information and digital media as commons, the erosion of those commons through recent legislation, and the necessity of building new institutions in order to sustain those commons. An early attempt at struggling with these issues was our development of the Digital Library of the Commons,[2] which seeks to combine digital preservation of high-quality information, self-publication, and multimedia storage, while serving as the primary reference tool for interdisciplinary research on the commons.

The two-day event, funded by The Andrew W. Mellon Foundation, brought together leading interdisciplinary scholars to examine the current state of research and development of scholarly communication and the knowledge commons. Many of the participating scholars had already been thinking and writing about one of the many "commons" aspects of scholarly communication. The first objective of the meeting was to produce papers that could give other scholars as well as researchers and practitioners who create digital resources and affect digital policy, a sense of the current status of research on scholarly communication as an information commons, an idea of where it is headed, and an awareness of critical dilemmas and policy issues. We deliberately assembled a group of scholars who could address both theoretical and empirical concerns—that is, who were able to ground discussion of future research and action in a thorough synthesis of current theory and practice.

The initial focus on scholarly communication as a commons was chosen to more carefully focus the subject and to allow for the integration of study areas that have been traditionally segregated, such as intellectual property rights, computer codes and infrastructure, academic libraries, invention and creativity, open-source software, collaborative science, citizenship and democratic processes, collective action, information economics, and the management, dissemination, and preservation of the scholarly record. Other important dilemmas within the information commons, such as globalization, complexity, westernization of knowledge, indigenous knowledge and rights, and the growing problem of computer waste were kept in mind. The group also explored the question of what models and frameworks of analysis are most beneficial in building a new research agenda for this complex commons.

Some of the questions posed were: Is it possible to transfer lessons learned from the environmental movement to the knowledge-commons ecosystem? What can research on the natural-resource commons teach us about the dilemmas of scholarly communication? How can legal scholars, social scientists, and librarians and information specialists best work together to preserve the intellectual commons? Can new technologies, rules, and self-governing communities help bridge the gaps between traditional libraries, publishers, researchers, and policymakers?

The concrete goals of the meeting were to

• Identify essential "commons" of concern within the vast terrain of scholarly communication

• Reach consensus on definitions

• Map some key knowledge gaps

• Discuss and apply an analytical framework, if possible

• Draft a report to The Andrew W. Mellon Foundation outlining a new research agenda for the study of information or scholarly communication as a commons

• Identify future actions to further this agenda

The group sought to integrate perspectives that are frequently segregated within the scholarly-communication arena, such as intellectual property rights; information technology (including hardware, software, code and open source, and infrastructure); traditional libraries; digital libraries; invention and creativity; collaborative science; citizenship and democratic processes; collective action; information economics; and the management, dissemination, and preservation of the scholarly record. Since that time, our ideas have grown and developed. We have been fortunate to add a couple of new scholars in the process, and regret that a few needed to withdraw due to previous commitments.

Our understanding of this complex commons has evolved considerably since the initial meeting. While our focus was originally on scholarly communication, we came to agree with Boyle, Lynch, and others that equating the knowledge commons with the "scholarly-communication" arena was too limiting and, perhaps, parochial. It became more and more apparent that any useful study of the users, designers, contributors, and distributors of this commons could not be cordoned off to the domain of the ivory tower. Who can any longer set the boundaries between scholarly and nonscholarly information? On the other hand, we found it useful to examine some of the long-enduring knowledge commons and related institutional rules, especially in the context of exponential technological change.

Participants included

James Boyle, William Neal Reynolds Professor of Law and Faculty Co-Director of the Center for the Study of the Public Domain, Duke Law School, Durham, North Carolina

James Cox, Noah Langdale Jr. Chair in Economics; Georgia Research Alliance Eminent Scholar; Director, Experimental Economics Center, University of Arizona

Charlotte Hess, Director, Workshop Research Library, and Digital Library of the Commons, Indiana University, Bloomington

Nancy Kranich, past president of the American Library Association; former Associate Dean of Libraries at New York University

Peter Levine, Director of CIRCLE, The Center for Information and Research on Civic Learning and Engagement; a research scholar at the Institute for Philosophy & Public Policy at the University of Maryland; Steering Committee Chair of the Campaign for the Civic Mission of Schools

Wendy Pradt Lougee, University Librarian and McKnight Presidential Professor, University of Minnesota, University Libraries, Minneapolis, Minnesota

Clifford Lynch, Director of the Coalition for Networked Information (CNI), Washington, D.C.; adjunct professor at the School of Information Management and Systems, University of California, Berkeley

Elinor Ostrom, Arthur F. Bentley Professor of Political Science, Indiana University; Co-Director, Workshop in Political Theory and Policy Analysis; Co-Director, Center for the Study of Institutions, Population, and Environmental Change

Charles Schweik, Assistant Professor, Department of Natural Resource Conservation, Center for Public Policy and Administration, University of Massachusetts, Amherst

Peter Suber, Policy Strategist for open access to scientific and scholarly research literature; Director, Open Access Project at Public Knowledge; Research Professor of Philosophy at Earlham College; Author of SPARC Open Access Newsletter; Editor of Open Access News Blog

Douglas Van Houweling, President and CEO of Internet2; Professor, School of Information, University of Michigan, Ann Arbor

Donald Waters, Program Officer for Scholarly Communications, The Andrew W. Mellon Foundation

The sessions were expertly moderated by Margaret Polski, Senior Research Fellow at the Institute for Development Strategies, Indiana University (IU). Some of the attendees and active contributors to the discussions were Blaise Cronin, Rudy Professor of Information Science and Dean of the IU School of Library and Information Science; Suzanne Thorin, Dean of the IU Libraries; Jorge Schement, Pennsylvania State University Distinguished Professor of Communications; Marco Janssen, Assistant Professor of Informatics; Robert Goehlert, IU Librarian for Economics and Political Science; Harriette Hemmasi, Associate Dean, IU Libraries; Laura Wisen, Coordinator of Workshop Research Library and SLIS graduate student; and Alice Robbin, IU Professor of Information Science.

While a couple of the original participants have dropped out due to previous commitments, as noted, we have been fortunate to add two outstanding thinkers on the commons:

David Bollier, Journalist, Consultant, Senior Fellow, USC Annenberg School for Communication, The Norman Lear Center, and Co-Founder and board member, Public Knowledge

Shubha Ghosh, Professor, Dedman School of Law, Southern Methodist University, Dallas

The authors of this book would like to thank the two thorough and very helpful outside reviewers for The MIT Press.

We would also like to thank John Goodacre, Stevan Harnad, Anne MacKinnon, Ruth Meinzen-Dick, Andrew Revelle, Audun Sandberg, and Suzanne Thorin for their insightful comments. We are grateful to the contributors to this book who gave us their valuable input on chapter 1. We are also extremely grateful to Patricia Lezotte for her expert assistance with the manuscript. Finally, we wish to thank The Andrew W. Mellon Foundation for its essential support.

Notes

1. See James Boyle, ed., *The Public Domain* (Durham, NC: School of Law, Duke University, 2003) (*Law and Contemporary Problems* 66(1–2)); http://www.law.duke.edu/journals/lcp/.

2. http://dlc.dlib.indiana.edu.

I

Studying the Knowledge Commons

1

Introduction: An Overview of the Knowledge Commons

Charlotte Hess and Elinor Ostrom

Two monks were arguing about a flag. One said, "The flag is moving." The other said, "The wind is moving." The sixth patriarch, Zeno, happened to be passing by. He told them, "Not the wind, not the flag; mind is moving."
—Douglas R. Hofstadter, *Gödel, Escher, Bach*

The Purpose of This Book

This book is intended as an introduction to a new way of looking at knowledge as a shared resource, a complex ecosystem that is a *commons*—a resource shared by a group of people that is subject to social dilemmas. The traditional study of knowledge is subdivided into epistemic areas of interests. Law professors argue the legal aspects of knowledge in regard to intellectual property rights. Economists consider efficiency and transaction costs of information. Philosophers grapple with epistemology. Librarians and information scientists deal with the collection, classification, organization, and enduring access of published information. Sociologists examine behaviors of virtual communities. Physical scientists study natural laws. Every discipline, of course, has a claim on knowledge; this is the common output of all academic endeavors. The focus here is to explore the puzzles and issues that all forms of knowledge share, particularly in the digital age. The intention is to illustrate the analytical benefits of applying a multitiered approach that burrows deeply into the knowledge-commons ecosystem, drawing from several different disciplines.

Brief History of the Study of the Knowledge Commons

The exploration of information and knowledge as commons is still in its early infancy. Nevertheless, the connection between "information" in its various forms and "commons" in its various forms has caught the attention of a wide range of scholars, artists, and activists. The "information-commons" movement emerged with striking suddenness. Before 1995, few thinkers saw the connection. It was around that time that we began to see a new usage of the concept of the "commons." There appears to have been a spontaneous explosion of "ah ha" moments when multiple users on the Internet one day sat up, probably in frustration, and said, "Hey! This is a shared resource!" People started to notice behaviors and conditions on the web—congestion, free riding, conflict, overuse, and "pollution"—that had long been identified with other types of commons. They began to notice that this new conduit of distributing information was neither a private nor strictly a public resource.

An increasing number of scholars found that the concept of the "commons"[1] helped them to conceptualize new dilemmas they were observing with the rise of distributed, digital information. In the mid-1990s, articles suddenly started appearing in various disciplines addressing some aspect of this new knowledge commons. Some information scientists made inroads in new areas of virtual communities and commons (Rheingold 1993; Brin 1995; Hess 1995; Kollock and Smith 1996). Others explored commons dilemmas on the web, such as congestion and free riding (Huberman and Lukose 1997; Gupta et al. 1997). The largest wave of "new-commons" exploration appeared in the legal reviews. *Commons* became a buzzword for digital information, which was being enclosed, commodified, and overpatented.[2] Whether labeled the "digital," "electronic," "information," "virtual," "communication," "intellectual," "Internet," or "technological" commons, all these concepts address the new shared territory of global distributed information.

Study of Traditional Commons

For us, the analysis of knowledge as a commons has its roots in the broad, interdisciplinary study of shared natural resources, such as water resources, forests, fisheries, and wildlife. *Commons* is a general term that refers to a resource shared by a group of people. In a commons, the resource can be small and serve a tiny group (the family refrigerator), it can be community-level (sidewalks, playgrounds, libraries, and so on), or it can extend to international and global levels (deep seas, the atmosphere, the Internet, and scientific knowledge). The commons can be well bounded (a community park or library); transboundary (the Danube

River, migrating wildlife, the Internet); or without clear boundaries (knowledge, the ozone layer).

Commons analysts have often found it necessary to differentiate between a commons as a resource or resource system and a commons as a property-rights regime. Shared resource systems—called *common-pool resources*—are types of economic goods, independent of particular property rights. *Common property* on the other hand is a legal regime—a jointly owned legal set of rights (Bromley 1986; Ciriacy-Wantrup and Bishop 1975). Throughout this book, the more general term *commons* is preferred in order to describe the complexity and variability of knowledge and information as resources. Knowledge commons can consist of multiple types of goods and regimes and still have many characteristics of a commons.

Potential problems in the use, governance, and sustainability of a commons can be caused by some characteristic human behaviors that lead to social dilemmas such as competition for use, free riding, and overharvesting. Typical threats to knowledge commons are commodification or enclosure, pollution and degradation, and nonsustainability.

These issues may not necessarily carry over from the physical environment to the realm of the knowledge commons. There is a continual challenge to identify the similarities between knowledge commons and traditional commons, such as forests or fisheries, all the while exploring the ways knowledge as a resource is fundamentally different from natural-resource commons.

With "subtractive" resources such as fisheries, for instance, one person's use reduces the benefits available to another. High subtractability is usually a key characteristic of common-pool resources. Most types of knowledge have, on the other hand, traditionally been relatively nonsubtractive. In fact, the more people who share useful knowledge, the greater the common good. Consideration of knowledge as a commons, therefore, suggests that the unifying thread in all commons resources is that they are jointly used, managed by groups of varying sizes and interests.

Self-organized commons require strong collective-action and self-governing mechanisms, as well as a high degree of social capital on the part of the stakeholders. *Collective action* arises "when the efforts of two or more individuals are needed to accomplish an outcome" (Sandler 1992, 1). Another important aspect of collective action is that it is voluntary on the part of each individual (Meinzen-Dick, Di Gregorio, and

McCarthy 2004). *Self-governance* requires collective action combined with "knowledge and will on the one hand, and supporting and consistent institutional arrangements on the other hand."[3] *Social capital* refers to the aggregate value of social networks (i.e., who people know), and the inclinations that arise from these networks for people to do things for each other (i.e., the norms of reciprocity) (Putnam 2000). Throughout this book we will see these three elements—collective action, self-governance, and social capital—frequently in play.

Since the mid-1980s and the formation of the International Association for the Study of Common Property,[4] a large number of international, interdisciplinary studies have focused on various types of commons resources. More and more researchers began to realize that combining disciplines and pooling knowledge was the only way to arrive at deeper understandings of effective commons management. One well-known fisheries researcher illustrates the urgent need for a multidisciplinary approach in the introduction to her 1989 edited volume:

[The authors] share a belief that we can no longer afford to tackle these intractable problems in isolation from one another. All efforts are needed. All examples add something to our understanding. The making of this book had already stimulated unusual collaboration in research and our hope is that it will further the process of bringing about better communication across disciplines and between theoreticians and practitioners. (Pinkerton 1989)

To be able to understand the complex processes at work in a commons such as a fishery, researchers over the past twenty years[5] have demonstrated the necessity of examining the biological, economic, political, and social elements involved that lead to the success or failure of the resource system.

While the bulk of commons research has been aimed at natural-resource commons, particularly forests and land, fisheries, and water resources, attention to human-made resources has increased dramatically since 1995. Whether the focus is traditional or new, however, the essential questions for any commons analysis are inevitably about equity, efficiency, and sustainability. *Equity* refers to issues of just or equal appropriation from, and contribution to, the maintenance of a resource. *Efficiency* deals with optimal production, management, and use of the resource. *Sustainability* looks at outcomes over the long term. Many studies hone in on issues of property-rights regimes and the various challenges of common property. Indeed, the important distinctions between the terms "common *property*" and "common-*pool resource*" grew out of this scholarship.

One of the truly important findings in the traditional commons research was the identification of design principles of robust, long-enduring, common-pool resource institutions (Ostrom 1990, 90–102). These principles are

- Clearly defined boundaries should be in place.
- Rules in use are well matched to local needs and conditions.
- Individuals affected by these rules can usually participate in modifying the rules.
- The right of community members to devise their own rules is respected by external authorities.
- A system for self-monitoring members' behavior has been established.
- A graduated system of sanctions is available.
- Community members have access to low-cost conflict-resolution mechanisms.
- Nested enterprises—that is, appropriation, provision, monitoring and sanctioning, conflict resolution, and other governance activities—are organized in a nested structure with multiple layers of activities.

These principles were discovered after conducting a large set of empirical studies on common-pool resource governance. One of the central findings was that an extremely rich variety of specific rules were used in systems sustainable over a long time period. No single set of specific rules, on the other hand, had a clear association with success. Only after grappling with this wide diversity of robust systems was it possible to identify general principles that tended to underlie the robust institutions. The eight factors identified were those found to exist in most robust institutions—but they were absent in failed systems. These principles have inspired hundreds of studies. And they are, indeed, helpful as a possible place to start an investigation. But they are in no way prescriptive—nor are they models. Rather, they are insightful findings in the analysis of small, homogeneous systems. Whether they apply to the study of large and complex systems like the knowledge commons is a question for further research.

Knowledge as a Resource

Knowledge in this book refers to all intelligible ideas, information, and data in whatever form in which it is expressed or obtained. Our thinking is in line with that of Davenport and Prusak (1998, 6), who write that "knowledge derives from information as information derives from data." Machlup (1983, 641) introduced this division of data-information-knowledge, with data being raw bits of information, information being organized data in context, and knowledge being the assimilation of the information and understanding of how to use it. *Knowledge* as employed in this book refers to all types of understanding gained through experience or study,[6] whether indigenous, scientific, scholarly, or otherwise nonacademic. It also includes creative works, such as music and the visual and theatrical arts. Some view knowledge as polemical, in that it has "dual functions"—as a commodity and as a constitutive force of society (Reichman and Franklin 1999; Braman 1989). This dual functionality as a human need and an economic good immediately suggests the complex nature of this resource. Acquiring and discovering knowledge is both a social process and a deeply personal process (Polanyi 1958).

Further, knowledge is cumulative. With ideas the cumulative effect is a public good, so long as people have access to the vast storehouse, but access and preservation were serious problems long before the advent of digital technologies. An infinite amount of knowledge is waiting to be unearthed. The discovery of future knowledge is a common good and a treasure we owe to future generations. The challenge of today's generation is to keep the pathways to discovery open.

Ensuring access to knowledge is made easier by examining the nature of knowledge and identifying the ways in which it is a commons. This approach is in contrast to the standard economics literature. In that literature, knowledge has often been used as the classic example of a pure public good—a good available to all and where one person's use does not subtract from another's use. In the classic treatment of public goods, Paul A. Samuelson (1954, 387–389) classified all of the goods that might be used by humans as either pure private or pure public. Samuelson and others, including Musgrave (1959), placed all the emphasis on *exclusion*. Goods where individuals could be excluded from use were considered private goods. When economists first dealt with these issues, they focused on the impossibility of exclusion, but they later moved toward a classification based on the high cost of exclusion. Goods were then treated as if there were only one dimension. It was not until scholars developed a twofold classification of goods (V. Ostrom and E. Ostrom 1977) that a second attribute of goods was fully acknowledged. The new schema introduced *subtractability* (sometimes referred to as *rivalry*), where one person's use subtracted from the available goods for others, as an equally important determinant of the nature of a good. This led to a two-dimensional classification of goods (see figure 1.1).

Knowledge, in its intangible form, fell into the category of a public good since it was difficult to exclude people from knowledge once someone had made a discovery. One person's use of knowledge (such as Einstein's theory of relativity) did not subtract from another person's capacity to use it. This example refers to the ideas, thoughts, and wisdom found in the reading of a book—not to the book itself, which would be classified as a private good.

Throughout this book, we use the terms *knowledge commons* and *information commons* interchangeably. While some chapters focus specifically on scholarly and scientific communication, the issues discussed have crucial relevance that extend far beyond the ivory tower. Some aspect of knowledge in digital form is the primary focus of all the chapters, primarily because the technologies that allow global, interoperable distribution of information have most dramatically changed the structure of knowledge as a resource. One of the critical factors of digital knowledge is the "hyperchange"[7] of technologies and social networks that affects every aspect of how knowledge is managed and governed, including how it is generated, stored, and preserved.

The growing number of studies regarding various approaches to the knowledge commons indicates the complexity and interdisciplinary nature of these resources. Some knowledge commons reside at the local level, others at the global level or somewhere in between. There are

		SUBTRACTABILITY	
		Low	*High*
EXCLUSION	*Difficult*	**Public goods** Useful knowledge Sunsets	**Common-pool resources** Libraries Irrigation systems
	Easy	**Toll or club goods** Journal subscriptions Day-care centers	**Private goods** Personal computers Doughnuts

Figure 1.1
Types of goods. *Source:* Adapted from V. Ostrom and E. Ostrom 1977

clearly multiple uses and competing interests in these commons. Corporations have supported increased patents and copyright terms, while many scientists, scholars, and practitioners take actions to ensure free access to information. Universities find themselves on both sides of the commons fence, increasing their number of patents and relying more and more on corporate funding of research, while at the same time encouraging open access and establishing digital repositories for their faculty's research products.

Most of the problems and dilemmas discussed in this book have arisen since the invention of new digital technologies. The introduction of new technologies can play a huge role in the robustness or vulnerability of a commons. New technologies can enable the capture of what were once free and open public goods. This has been the case with the development of most "global commons," such as the deep seas, the atmosphere, the electromagnetic spectrum, and space, for example. This ability to capture the previously uncapturable creates a fundamental change in the nature of the resource, with the resource being converted from a nonrivalrous, nonexclusionary public good into a common-pool resource that needs to be managed, monitored, and protected, to ensure sustainability and preservation.

The Tragicomedy of the Commons

The analysis of any type of commons must involve the rules, decisions, and behaviors people make in groups in relation to their shared resource. Economist Mancur Olson's influential *The Logic of Collective Action* (1965) is still being read by students today as a basic introduction to the challenges of human organization. Collective action, voluntary groups working to achieve a shared goal, is a key ingredient in understanding commons. Olson laid the groundwork for the study of *incentives* for people to contribute to a joint endeavor and outlined the basic problem of *free riding*, where one reaps benefits from the commons without contributing to its maintenance.

The impetus for countless studies has been the model of "The Tragedy of the Commons" (Hardin 1968). Biologist Garrett Hardin created a memorable metaphor for overpopulation, where herdsmen sharing a common pasture put as many cattle as possible out to graze, acting in their own self-interest. The tragedy is expressed in Hardin's (1968, 1244) famous lines: "Ruin is the destination toward which all men rush, each pursuing his own best interest in a society that believes in the freedom of the commons. Freedom in a commons brings ruin to all." This is one of the most often cited and influential articles in the social sciences and is still taught in large numbers of university courses worldwide.

Hardin's vivid narrative contains a number of contentions that commons scholars have repeatedly found to be mistaken: (1) he was actually discussing open access rather than managed commons; (2) he assumed little or no communication; (3) he postulated that people act only in their immediate self-interest (rather than assuming that some individuals take joint benefits into account, at least to some extent); (4) he offered only two solutions to correct the tragedy—privatization or government intervention. Whether studying California groundwater basins, North Atlantic fisheries, African community forests, or Nepalese irrigation systems, scientific case studies frequently seem to answer: *Au contraire, Monsieur Hardin*! There may be situations where this model can be applied, but many groups *can* effectively manage and sustain common resources if they have suitable conditions, such as appropriate rules, good conflict-resolution mechanisms, and well-defined group boundaries.[8]

A knowledge-commons variation of the tragedy of the commons that has become quite popular in the law literature is the concept of the *anticommons*. The term was originally applied to extreme regulatory regimes in real property.[9] Adapted by Michael Heller in 1998,[10] the tragedy of the anticommons in the knowledge arena lies in the potential underuse of scarce scientific resources caused by excessive intellectual property rights and overpatenting in biomedical research.

Another frequently used model in commons analysis is the prisoner's dilemma (PD), developed in the early days of game theory in 1950 by mathematician A. W. Tucker at Stanford (Cunningham 1967, 11). The original narrative of the two-person, noncooperative, non-zero-sum game concerns two criminals who are interviewed separately about a crime. Each is given a strong incentive by the prosecutor to inform against the other. The prisoner's dilemma has remained popular perhaps because it is one of the simplest formal games to understand and can quickly illustrate the problems of collective action and irrational group behavior when trust and reciprocity have little opportunity to develop and be expressed.

All of these models—collective *in*action, tragedy of the commons, and the PD game—can be useful in helping to conceptualize some of the incentives in simple situations involving various forms of knowledge commons. The problem with them is that they have been overused as realistic models of much more complex and dynamic situations. They are frequently put forth as explaining why participants are "trapped" in perverse incentives and cannot themselves find ways of increasing trust, developing norms of reciprocity, or crafting new rules. Yet they are certainly not predictive of all situations involving a commons dilemma or any of the specific pet solutions offered to solve these problems. As study after study demonstrates, there is no one solution to all commons dilemmas.

Two Intellectual Histories

Curiously, most of the interdisciplinary work on the knowledge commons to date is not an outgrowth of the natural-resource commons literature (although the tragedy of the commons still "plays" at all the knowledge-commons theaters). Rather, it is rooted in two distinct intellectual histories: the history of enclosure and the history of openness and inclusiveness—that is, democracy and freedom.

Historically in Europe, "commons" were shared agricultural fields, grazing lands, and forests that were, over a period of 500 years, enclosed, with communal rights being withdrawn, by landowners and the state. The narrative of enclosure is one of privatization, the haves versus the have-nots, the elite versus the masses. This is the story of Boyle's (2003) "Second Enclosure Movement," featuring the enclosure of the "intangible commons of the mind," through rapidly expanding intellectual property rights. The occurrence of enclosure is an important rallying cry on the part of legal scholars, librarians, scientists, and, really, anyone who is alert to the increasing occurrence of privatization, commodification, and withdrawal of information that used to be accessible, or that will never be available in our lifetimes.

This trend of enclosure is based on the ability of new technologies to "capture" resources that were previously unowned, unmanaged, and thus, unprotected. This is the case with outer space, with the electromagnetic spectrum, and with knowledge and information. The case of distributed digital technologies is particularly complex and problematic, as many stakeholders seek to renegotiate their interests in the new digital environment. Currently there are a vast array of enclosure threats to information and knowledge—including computer code as law (Lessig 1999) and new intellectual property legislation (DMCA, TRIPS, the Copyright Term Extension Act, the Patriot Act, and so on)—that undermine free access to public, scientific, and government information.[11]

Historically in the United States, *commons* has most often referred to shared spaces that allow for free speech and the democratic process, most notably the New England town commons. This is the focus of Benkler's (2004) "commons-based production."[12] It is the narrative of digital interoperability, open science, collaboratories and scholarly networks, voluntary associations, and collective action. The U.S.-type commons underscores the importance of shared spaces and shared knowledge in fostering viable democratic societies. Libraries, as Kranich (2004) has pointed out, have been the quintessential strongholds of democracy. Traditionally, libraries have been the "protected areas" of the knowledge commons and librarians are the stewards. This narrative calls forth the urgency for all information users and providers to become stewards of the global digital commons.

Clarifying Confusion Surrounding the Knowledge Commons

Two common sources of confusion in the knowledge-commons literature require clarification. First, open access to information is a horse of a much different color than open access to land or water. In the latter case, open access can mean a free-for-all, as in Hardin's grazing lands, leading to overconsumption and depletion. With distributed knowledge and information the resource is usually nonrivalrous. As Suber points out in this book, open access in the information ecosystem means free and unfettered access, without costs or permissions. Authors who choose to make their works available for free may still retain their copyrights. In this instance, instead of having negative effects, open access of information provides a universal public good: the more quality information, the greater the public good.

Second, the knowledge commons is not synonymous with open access, although the content and the community network of the open-access movement, as Suber and Ghosh discuss in their chapters, are types of commons. Forgive us for repeating that a commons is a shared resource that is vulnerable to social dilemmas. Outcomes of the interactions of people and resources can be positive or negative or somewhere in between. Frequently, within the intellectual arena, the concept of the commons is a battle cry for free speech, universal open access, and self-governance, as a 2004 conference session illustrated:

With the Internet nurturing the sharing spirit inherent in man, commons has taken on a new meaning. Free software proved spectacularly that the commons is a viable alternative to commodification. The term Digital Commons is widely used but only loosely defined, ranging from jointly owned intellectual property to public property and the public domain. Still, it has an obvious evocative power, and the potential to reconceptualize our knowledge environment and to unite those fighting for its freedom. (Program abstract for "The Future of the Digital Commons," at the 2004 WOS3 Conference, http://wizards-of-os .org/index.php?id=1551)

This use of the word *commons* is not infrequent. It can be constructive and often provides the impetus to collective action around the commons. But a commons is not value laden—its outcome can be good or bad, sustainable or not—which is why we need understanding and clarity, skilled decision-making abilities, and cooperative management strategies in order to ensure durable, robust systems.

The Knowledge Ecosystem, Collective Action, and Self-Governance: An Overview of the Chapters in This Book

The rapidly expanding world of distributed digital information has infinite possibilities as well as incalculable threats and pitfalls. The parallel, yet contradictory trends, where, on the one hand, there is unprecedented access to information through the Internet but where, on the other, there are ever-greater restrictions on access through intellectual property legislation, overpatenting, licensing, overpricing, withdrawal, and lack of preservation, indicate the deep and perplexing characteristics of this resource.

Knowledge, which can seem so ubiquitous in digital form, is, in reality, more vulnerable than ever before. When hard-copy journals, for instance, were sold to libraries and individuals, the decentralization of multiple copies made the works robust. When journals are in digital form and licensed to libraries or individuals, the works are centralized and vulnerable to the whims or happenstance of the publisher. Users who rely on certain journals being indexed in LexisNexis or other large indexing services, are frustrated to find one day that those journals were dropped and will no longer be indexed. A vast amount of government information that used to be freely available online was withdrawn after 9/11 and not replaced. Or, cyberterrorists are too often able to infect or damage a system or steal confidential information.

On the other hand, collective-action initiatives, such as open access, and Free/Libre and Open Source Software development, are ensuring much greater accessibility and robustness of digital resources. Many questions exist as to how to develop future initiatives that will increase the security of digital knowledge while not blocking access to those who would benefit greatly from its use. Several of these issues are addressed in the chapters to follow in this book.

The book is divided into three parts. Part I, "Studying the Knowledge Commons," focuses on new ways to conceptualize and analyze knowledge as a complex, global, shared resource. In chapter 2, David Bollier reflects on the evolution of the meaning of the commons from a concept describing some historical developments to its current applications to the realm of knowledge. Although Garrett Hardin's essay brought new attention to the idea of the commons, its misconceptions tended to discredit the commons as an effective instrument of community governance. After all, if a "tragedy" of the commons is inevitable, why study it? However, in the mid-1980s, the flaws in this analysis were explored and scholarly interest in the commons began to take root. Interest in the commons grew further in the mid-1990s as the Internet engendered new types of social communities and communication in an entirely new public sphere, cyberspace. Yet even with these developments, the concept of the commons remains novel and alien to many people. Mindful of this history, Bollier helps readers develop new cognitive maps that enable them to visualize the knowledge commons in a new light. He points out the massive shift in our daily life that has resulted from being online, and how the radical changes in social and economic aspects of knowledge production have generated new problems unforeseen only a few decades ago. Now, instead of being worried about the absence of clearly defined property rights, serious thinkers are equally concerned with the imposition of private control over knowledge that many argue should be in the public domain. The challenge is how to blend systems of rules and norms related to this new commons to guarantee general access to the knowledge that empowers humans while ensuring recognition and support for those who create knowledge in its various forms.

In the third chapter, Elinor Ostrom and Charlotte Hess present the Institutional Analysis and Development (IAD) framework that has been developed over several decades by colleagues at the Workshop in Political Theory and Policy Analysis at Indiana University. The IAD framework originally emerged from our extensive research on urban public goods, including policing and education (see McGinnis 1999 for an overview, and Ostrom 2005 for an extensive exposition). It was most fully developed as we and our colleagues struggled with an understanding of complex linked social-ecological systems; we were trying to understand how diverse rules affect the likelihood of sustaining or destroying common-pool resources, including groundwater basins, irrigation systems, grazing systems, and forests. We think the framework will now be of value in understanding knowledge as a commons—in regard to both the public-good aspects of this commons and the common-pool resource aspects. Our goal is to make the framework as accessible as possible in order to heighten interest and facilitate further applications. As an illustration, the framework is loosely applied to the action arena of building a university repository, a locally produced, globally harvested complex commons.

Part II of the book, "Protecting the Knowledge Commons," contains contributions from several well-known authors concerning the problem of safeguarding the knowledge commons. These chapters draw from the tradition of guarding against enclosure of the commons. In chapter 4, Nancy Kranich looks at different types of enclosures of knowledge commons. She gives a broad review of the role of research libraries in protecting knowledge, as well as making it available to citizens, as cornerstones of democracy in the contemporary world. Kranich provides historical background to the current enclosures facing research libraries, including those caused by the skyrocketing costs of journals. To a large extent, the current budget crises are an inadvertent consequence of scholarly societies turning the publishing of their journals over to private firms in the 1980s in order to gain high-quality printed journals at a lower cost to the academic editors and universities involved. The cost of journals has risen more than three times the increase in the consumer price index since 1986! This has had further ramifications for the publication of books and the availability of printed scholarly communications, especially those located in universities facing stringent budgetary pressures. These developments, as well as amendments to copyright laws, increased government secrecy, and other enclosures, contextualize Kranich's reviews of contemporary efforts to utilize new technologies and new legal concepts to reclaim scientific and intellectual assets through diverse open-access initiatives. She also suggests ways to advance the theory and practice of sustainable knowledge commons.

James Boyle is a well-known and articulate spokesperson for the protection of the intellectual public domain. In chapter 5, he brings together two seemingly disparate thoughts. Drawing from the work of sociologist Robert Merton, he discusses the possible impact of fencing off scholarship from the general public. He postulates that greater access to cultural and scientific materials by individuals and groups outside the academy might have a remarkable impact on scholarship, culture, and possibly even science. He urges that the knowledge commons not be restricted to the scholarly community. Boyle also writes about the fencing off of ideas through copyright and licensing restrictions. He poses some interesting questions. Would the original author of a very successful series of books—he uses J. K. Rowling's Harry Potter books as an example—really be concerned that copyright protected her work for seventy years after her death rather than merely fifty years? Yes, if a corporation held the rights, they would be concerned to gain protection for as long as a government was willing to assign it. Those extra years, however, have nothing to do with creating an incentive to put in the hours of work needed to produce good books, pathbreaking research, or enticing music. At a substantial cost to the public, those extra years of protection generate profit to those who did not make the original investment in producing creative work. The chapter illustrates that knowledge is the domain of the public and that as much of it as possible needs to be freely available.

In chapter 6, Donald Waters takes on the difficult problem of safeguarding and preserving the knowledge commons by focusing in on the links that are preserved versus the links that disappear. In traditional publication, scholars use footnotes to link their statements to the authoritative source for their statement. As more and more scholars link their work to the web pages of other scholars, the problem of preserving the digital information becomes ever-more critical, especially when the average life expectancy of a web page is only a few months! Preserving electronic scholarly journals becomes a key challenge for the scientific community, given the number of citations that are currently made to what might become an ephemeral source in the future. While books and journals were never published in huge quantities in prior eras, libraries looked upon their role as one of preserving these precious resources for future ages. Waters points to the problem of free riding in creating and managing archival records. Without good archives, the scientific communication of today may be lost to the scholars of tomorrow. Waters lays out the key features that are needed to achieve the preservation of electronic knowledge in regard to legal protection, business models, and incentives to achieve this.

Part III, "Building New Knowledge Commons," draws from the intellectual history of collective action, the free exchange of ideas, and collaboration in the interest of the common good. In chapter 7, Peter Suber makes an eloquent and convincing argument for the advantages of making research and publications available online through open access. Every author has the ability to participate in building one of the richest knowledge commons by contributing peer-reviewed journal articles and their preprints, the primary literature of science. Suber concretely lays out the steps needed to understand and to participate in the open-access (OA) movement. He discusses the peculiarities of royalty-free literature, the conditions and incentives that lead authors to consent to OA, and some obstacles to an OA commons that have the flavor of a tragedy of the commons. Importantly, he discusses different funding models, since, while the user has free access, the producer faces the costs of peer review, manuscript preparation, and online dissemination, and sometimes also the costs of digitizing, copyediting, and long-term preservation. He points out the difference between open-access repositories that do not attempt to provide peer review and open-access journals that continue the important task of peer review of scholarly communication. The long-term existence of broadcast television and radio, which provide free access to users, makes Suber confident that long-term digital publishing in an open-access forum is financially feasible. It does, however, require considerable entrepreneurship in today's transition from entirely printed materials to a combination of print and electronic publication. Suber then provides a good analysis of the various categories of intellectual property. He concludes by outlining the variety of tragedies of the open-access commons that universities, publishers, scholars, and the public will need to overcome.

In chapter 8, Shubha Ghosh weaves a compelling case for understanding the role of intellectual property rights in building the knowledge commons. Focusing specifically on patents and copyrights, he examines a number of pat concepts or solutions and shows that they are not so pat. We are led through the arguments of intellectual property as constrictive, as facilitative, and as irrelevant and shown that there is a logic to all three of these positions. Ghosh then refocuses the argument from one about intellectual property as an *end* to one of intellectual property as a *means* in which it can be used as a tool in constructing the information commons. He proposes three guiding principles that can be utilized to inform intellectual property policy and to effectively design the commons: imitation, exchange, and governance. Ghosh explores important puzzles involving the separation of the market and the state, showing that these are not reasonably separated.

In chapter 9, Peter Levine demonstrates how a knowledge commons can be used effectively to stimulate students and citizens more generally to engage in research of public value, using as well as contributing to the knowledge commons. He draws on his own experience with the Prince George's Information Commons in Maryland near the University of Maryland. Levine makes a useful distinction between a libertarian commons and an associational commons. A libertarian commons is one that anyone can access if they choose. Associational commons are open to their own members but may be not be open to the public at large. Before the digital age, paper libraries were shared by associations of individuals living in communities. Levine argues that commons need protection by groups interested in their production, care, and maintenance. Thus, he argues that associational commons will be an important part of the democratic use of knowledge commons in the future. He describes the effort by the University of Maryland to develop an effective associational commons for students and citizens living in Prince George's County. By producing knowledge for the commons, students learn about public issues in a way they would not do otherwise. Levine then urges other scholars to develop associational commons of this type as a way of producing important contemporary knowledge, and as a way of training students about their own communities as well as how to produce and evaluate knowledge about communities.

In chapter 10, Charles Schweik argues that the collaborative principles around Free/Libre and Open Source Software (FOSS) development projects could potentially be applied to develop new knowledge commons in science. To make this point, Schweik first applies the institutional analysis and development framework summarized in chapter 3 to analyze the various action situations involved in the open-source software commons. He then links the various action situations faced by participants in the biophysical world, the relevant communities, and the rules-in-use affecting the action situations involved in producing and protecting software. Schweik provides a good historical overview of the effort to develop open-source software licensing agreements and of how these kinds of information-protection and information-production arrangements have blossomed. He then extends the analysis to include a broader array of artifacts beyond that of software to discuss the general problem of licensing scientific digital content. Readers who are unfamiliar with the development of open-source software will find this chapter a particularly useful history and summary of developments.

Wendy Pradt Lougee focuses chapter 11 on the profound changes occurring in the world of scholarly communication. Her discussion of the commons explores the increasingly collaborative communities within academia. Whereas university libraries used to be a separate domain from the rest of the academy, the boundaries for producing and disseminating scholarly information, as well as those surrounding the stakeholders involved in the process, have become quite blurred. In the scholarly-communication realm, the focus today is on process rather than product. Lougee looks at the traditional methods of scholarly communication and demonstrates the diversity of norms among academic disciplines. Those differences are evidenced in how particular disciplines have adapted to the digital environment, as well as in how libraries have evolved from being archives or stewards of information goods to being collaborators and potentially catalysts within interest-based communities.

Chapter 12 provides a perfect example of the blurring of the boundaries and stakeholders in the knowledge commons. Economists James C. Cox and J. Todd Swarthout describe a digital library that they, as a teaching facility, built independently of the university's library. At center stage is EconPort, an open-access, open-source digital library for students and researchers in experimental microeconomics—in essence, a new knowledge commons. Cox and Swarthout describe the content of EconPort and the educational philosophy that underlies its creation. From an economist's perspective, they present a marvelous case study of the incentives, risks, and possible negative externalities of creating and maintaining a locally based, discipline-focused digital library and experimental laboratory. They also discuss issues of preservation of such an individualized resource.

Where This Book Leads Us

In this book we are plowing a new field and, perhaps, sowing some seeds. Our hope is that the chapters herein will serve as guideposts for further research. The book brings together scholars from diverse disciplines, outlines some critical issues within the new types of commons, and presents an analytical tool that helps elucidate the complexities of the rapidly changing environments in the world of knowledge and information.

We hope the readers of this book take away a strong sense that there are indeed analytical commonalities underlying many problems of deep concern today. How do we build effective forms of collective action and self-organizing, self-governing initiatives? How do we break free from path-dependent and limiting systems and creatively design new systems that tap into the limitless capabilities of digital information technologies? How do we effectively safeguard all that is of value in the maintenance and preservation of the cultural and scientific record? Given such a new cornucopia of digital information, how do we assess priorities? How do we evaluate how we are doing? How do we monitor our progress? Who should govern the Internet? How are equity and fairness achieved? How do we protect the interests and creative freedom of authors while also ensuring wide access to new knowledge and information? How are universities going to cover the costs of purchasing journals that are skyrocketing in price? How will the rise of digital repositories affect academic publishers? How are scholarly products that are reproduced digitally going to be preserved for the centuries to come? What are appropriate and effective business models for knowledge preservation?

All of the questions above relate to ongoing challenges in organizing effective institutional arrangements to enhance the production, access, use, and preservation of diverse knowledge commons. This is a fascinating era in which to participate in these interesting questions and to develop better analytical and empirical tools with which to craft answers.

Notes

1. *Commons* is an awkward word in the English language. The same word is used for both the singular and plural forms.

2. For example, see Reese 1995; Aoki 1998; Cohen 1998; Benkler 1998; also Hess and Ostrom 2003.

3. See Wagner 2005, 176, referring to Vincent Ostrom's concept of self-governance.

4. See http://www.iascp.org. This association changed its name to the International Association for the Study of the Commons in June 2006.

5. For a history of modern commons research, see Hess 2000, 2003.

6. Adapted from the *American Heritage Dictionary of the English Language* (1969).

7. Barrett (1998, 288) defines *hyperchange* as "a combination of linear, exponential, discontinuous, and chaotic change."

8. Feeny et al. 1990; Andelson 1991; Hanna, Folke, and Mäler 1996; Bromley et al. 1992. See also *The Comprehensive Bibliography of the Commons* at http://dlc.dlib.indiana.edu/cpr/index.php.

9. The original concept was developed by Frank Michelman in "Ethics, Economics, and the Law of Property" (1982).

10. Heller 1998; see also Heller and Eisenberg 1998.

11. A great deal has been written on various types of information enclosures (see Benkler 1999; Boyle 2003; Bollier 2004; Lange 2003; Lessig 2001; Shiva 2002; David 2000).

12. Benkler (2004, 1110) writes that "production is 'commons-based' when no one uses exclusive rights to organize effort or capture its value, and when cooperation is achieved through social mechanisms other than price signals or managerial directions."

References

American Heritage Dictionary of the English Language. New York: Houghton Mifflin, 1969.

Andelson, Robert V., ed. 1991. *Commons without Tragedy: The Social Ecology of Land Tenure and Democracy.* London: Center for Incentive Taxation.

Aoki, Keith. 1998. "Neocolonialism, Anticommons Property, and Biopiracy in the (Not-So-Brave) New World Order of International Intellectual Property Protection." *Indiana Journal of Global Legal Studies* 6(1):11–38.

Barrett, Derm. 1998. *Paradox Process: Creative Business Solutions . . . Where You Least Expect to Find Them.* New York: AMACOM.

Benkler, Yochai. 1998. "Overcoming Agoraphobia: Building the Commons of the Digitally Networked Environment." *Harvard Journal of Law and Technology* 11(2):287–400.

Benkler, Yochai. 1999. "Free as the Air to Common Use: First Amendment Constraints on Enclosure of the Public Domain." *New York University Law Review* 74:354–446.

Benkler, Yochai. 2004. "Commons-Based Strategies and the Problems of Patents." *Science* 305(5687):1110–1111.

Bollier, David. 2004. "Why We Must Talk about the Information Commons." *Law Library Journal* 96(2):267–282. http://www.aallnet.org/products/2004 -17.pdf.

Boyle, James. 2003. "The Second Enclosure Movement and the Construction of the Public Domain." *Law and Contemporary Problems* 66(1–2):33–74. http://www.law.duke.edu/journals/66LCPBoyle.

Braman, Sandra. 1989. "Defining Information: An Approach for Policymakers." In D. M. Lamberton, ed., *The Economics of Communication and Information.* Brookfield, VT: Edward Elgar.

Brin, David. 1995. "The Internet as a Commons." *Information Technology and Libraries* 14(4):240–242.

Bromley, Daniel W. 1986. "Closing Comments at the Conference on Common Property Resource Management." In National Research Council, *Proceedings of the Conference on Common Property Resource Management,* 591–596. Washington, DC: National Academy Press.

Bromley, Daniel W., David Feeny, Margaret McKean, Pauline Peters, Jere Gilles, Ronald Oakerson, C. Ford Runge, and James Thomson, eds. 1992. *Making the Commons Work: Theory, Practice, and Policy.* San Francisco, CA: ICS Press.

Ciriacy-Wantrup, Siegfried V., and Richard C. Bishop. 1975. " 'Common Property' as a Concept in Natural Resource Policy." *Natural Resources Journal* 15/4 (October): 713–727.

Cohen, Julie E. 1998. "Lochner in Cyberspace: The New Economic Orthodoxy of 'Rights Management'." *Michigan Law Review* 97(2):462–563.

The Comprehensive Bibliography of the Commons. 2005. Compiled by C. Hess. Indiana University: Digital Library of the Commons.

Cunningham, R. L. 1967. "Ethics and Game Theory: The Prisoner's Dilemma." In G. Tullock, ed., *Papers on Non-Market Decision Making II.* Charlottesville, VA: Thomas Jefferson Center for Political Economy, University of Virginia.

Davenport, Thomas H., and Laurence Prusak. 1998. *Working Knowledge: How Organizations Manage What They Know.* Boston: Harvard Business School Press.

David, Paul A. 2000. *The Digital Technology Boomerang: New Intellectual Property Rights Threaten Global "Open Science."* Stanford, CA: Department of Economics, Stanford University. http://www-econ.stanford.edu/faculty/workp/swp00016.pdf.

Dietz, Thomas, Elinor Ostrom, and Paul C. Stern. 2003. "The Struggle to Govern the Commons." *Science* 302(5652):1907–1912. http://www.sciencemag.org/cgi/reprint/302/5652/1907.pdf.

Feeny, David, Fikret Berkes, Bonnie J. McCay, and James M. Acheson. 1990. "The Tragedy of the Commons: Twenty-Two Years Later." *Human Ecology* 18(1):1–19.

Gupta, Alok, Boris Jukic, Monoj Parameswaran, Dale O. Stahl, and Andrew B. Whinston. 1997. "Streamlining the Digital Economy: How to Avert a Tragedy of the Commons." *IEEE Internet Computing* 1(6):38–46.

Hanna, Susan S., Carl Folke, and Karl-Gören Mäler, eds. 1996. *Rights to Nature: Ecological, Economic, Cultural, and Political Principles of Institutions for the Environment*. Washington, DC: Island Press.

Hardin, Garrett. 1968. "The Tragedy of the Commons." *Science* 162:1243–1248.

Heller, Michael A. 1998. "The Tragedy of the Anticommons: Property in the Transition from Marx to Markets." *Harvard Law Review* 111(3):622–688.

Heller, Michael A., and Rebecca S. Eisenberg. 1998. "Can Patents Deter Innovation? The Anticommons in Biomedical Research." *Science* 280(5364): 698–701.

Hess, Charlotte. 1995. "The Virtual CPR: The Internet as a Local and Global Common Pool Resource." Presented at "Reinventing the Commons," the Fifth Annual Conference of the International Association for the Study of Common Property, Bodø, Norway, May 24–28, 1995.

Hess, Charlotte. 2000. "Is There Anything New under the Sun? A Discussion and Survey of Studies on New Commons and the Internet." Presented at the Eighth Conference of the International Association for the Study of Common Property, Bloomington, Indiana, May 31–June 4, 2000. http://dlc.dlib .indiana.edu/archive/00000512/.

Hess, Charlotte. 2003. "Why the IASCP Mission Statement Should Be Changed." *Common Property Resource Digest* 67:1–3. http://www.indiana.edu/~iascp/ E-CPR/cpr67.pdf.

Hess, Charlotte, and Elinor Ostrom 2003. "Ideas, Artifacts, and Facilities: Information as a Common-Pool Resource." *Law and Contemporary Problems* 66(1–2):111–146. http://www.law.duke.edu/journals/66LCPHess.

Huberman, Bernardo A., and Rajan M. Lukose. 1997. "Social Dilemmas and Internet Congestion." *Science* 277(5325):535–537.

Kollock, Peter, and Marc Smith. 1996. "Managing the Virtual Commons: Cooperation and Conflict in Computer Communities." In S. Herring, ed. *Computer-Mediated Communication: Linguistic, Social, and Cross-Cultural Perspectives*. Amsterdam: John Benjamins.

Kranich, Nancy. 2004. *The Information Commons: A Public Policy Report*. The Free Expression Policy Project, Brennan Center for Justice at NYU School of Law, New York. http://www.fepproject.org/policyreports/infocommons .contentsexsum.html.

Lange, David. 2003. "Reimagining the Public Domain." *Law and Contemporary Problems* 66(1–2):463–483.

Lessig, Lawrence. 1999. "Code and the Commons (Draft 2)." Keynote Address presented at a conference on Media Convergence, Fordham Law School, New York, February 9, 1999. http://www.lessig.org/content/articles/works/ Fordham.pdf.

Lessig, Lawrence. 2001. *The Future of Ideas: The Fate of the Commons in a Connected World*. New York: Random House.

Low, Bobbi S., Elinor Ostrom, Robert Costanza, and James Wilson. 2001. "Human-Ecosystems Interactions: A Basic Dynamic Integrated Model." In *Institutions, Ecosystems, and Sustainability*, ed. Robert Costanza, Bobbi S. Low, Elinor Ostrom, and James Wilson, 33–57. New York: Lewis Publishers.

Machlup, Fritz. 1983. "Semantic Quirks in Studies of Information." In F. Machlup and U. Mansfield, eds., *The Study of Information: Interdisciplinary Message*. New York: Wiley.

McGinnis, Michael D., ed. 1999. *Polycentricity and Local Public Economies: Readings from the Workshop in Political Theory and Policy Analysis*. Ann Arbor, MI: University of Michigan Press.

Meinzen-Dick, Ruth, Monica Di Gregorio, and Nancy McCarthy. 2004. *Methods for Studying Collective Action in Rural Development*. CAPRi Working Paper, no. 33. International Food Policy Research Institute, 2033 K Street, N.W., Washington, DC 20006. http://www.capri.cgiar.org/pdf/capriwp33.pdf.

Michelman, Frank. 1982. "Ethics, Economics, and the Law of Property." *Nomos* 24(3):3–40.

Musgrave, Richard A. 1959. *The Theory of Public Finance: A Study in Public Economy*. New York: McGraw-Hill.

Oakerson, Ronald J. 1993. "Reciprocity: A Bottom-Up View of Political Development." In V. Ostrom, D. Feeny, and H. Picht, eds., *Rethinking Institutional Analysis and Development: Issues, Alternatives, and Choices*. San Francisco: ICS Press.

Olson, Mancur. 1965. *The Logic of Collective Action: Public Goods and the Theory of Groups*. New York: Schocken Books.

Ostrom, Elinor. 1990. *Governing the Commons: The Evolution of Institutions for Collective Action*. New York: Cambridge University Press.

Ostrom, Elinor. 1998. "Foreword." In Susan Buck, *The Global Commons: An Introduction*. Washington, DC: Island Press.

Ostrom, Elinor. 2000. "Private and Common Property Rights." In B. Bouckaert and G. De Geest, eds., *Encyclopedia of Law and Economics, Vol. II: Civil Law and Economics*, 332–379. Cheltenham, UK: Edward Elgar.

Ostrom, Elinor. 2005. *Understanding Institutional Diversity*. Princeton, NJ: Princeton University Press.

Ostrom, Elinor, Joanna Burger, Christopher B. Field, Richard B. Norgaard, and David Policansky. 1999. "Revisiting the Commons: Local Lessons, Global Challenges." *Science* 284(5412):278–282.

Ostrom, Vincent, and Elinor Ostrom. 1977. "Public Goods and Public Choices." In E. S. Savas, ed., *Alternatives for Delivering Public Services: Toward Improved Performance*, 7–49. Boulder, CO: Westview Press.

Pinkerton, Evelyn, ed. 1989. *Co-Operative Management of Local Fisheries: New Directions for Improved Management and Community Development*. Vancouver: University of British Colombia Press.

Polanyi, Michael. 1958. *Personal Knowledge: Towards a Post-Critical Philosophy*. Chicago: University of Chicago Press.

Putnam, Robert D. 2000. *Bowling Alone: The Collapse and Revival of American Community*. New York: Simon and Schuster.

Reese, R. Anthony. 1995. "Reflections on the Intellectual Commons: Two Perspectives on Copyright Duration and Reversion." *Stanford Law Review* 47(4):707–747.

Reichman, Jerome H., and Jonathan A. Franklin. 1999. "Privately Legislated Intellectual Property Rights: Reconciling Freedom of Contract with Public Good Uses of Information." *University of Pennsylvania Law Review* 147(4):875–970.

Rheingold, Howard. 1993. *The Virtual Community: Homesteading on the Electric Frontier*. New York: Addison-Wesley.

Samuelson, Paul A. 1954. "The Pure Theory of Public Expenditure." *Review of Economics and Statistics* 36:387–389.

Sandler, Todd. 1992. *Collective Action: Theory and Applications*. Ann Arbor: University of Michigan Press.

Shiva, Vandana. 2002. "The Enclosure and Recovery of the Biological and Intellectual Commons." In D. K. Marothia, ed., *Institutionalizing Common Pool Resources*. New Delhi: Concept.

Wagner, Richard E. 2005. "Self-Governance, Polycentrism, and Federalism: Recurring Themes in Vincent Ostrom's Scholarly Oeuvre." *Journal of Economic Behavior and Organization* 57(2):173–188.

2

The Growth of the Commons Paradigm

David Bollier

In introducing his then-novel economic theories, John Maynard Keynes was not concerned about the merits of his new ideas. What worried him was the dead hand of the past. "The ideas which are here expressed so laboriously are extremely simple and should be obvious," he wrote. "The difficulty lies, not in the new ideas, but in escaping from the old ones, which ramify, for those brought up as most of us have been, into every corner of our minds."[1]

So it is in talking about the commons. The commons is not such a difficult frame of analysis in itself. It is, in fact, a rather simple and obvious concept. But because our culture is so steeped in a standard economic narrative about "how things work," the idea of the commons often seems exotic. American political culture is a dedicated champion of the "free market," after all. It celebrates the heroic individual, the self-made man, not the community. Perhaps because the Cold War was directed against communism and its cousin, socialism, Americans tend to regard collective-management regimes as morally problematic and destructive of freedom, at least in the abstract.

In the face of this cultural heritage, it can be a formidable challenge to explain that the commons is more pervasive than we may realize, and that it can be a highly effective way to create economic and social wealth. That is precisely what this book seeks to demonstrate and explain. A commons model is at work in the social systems for scholarly communication, in the work of research libraries as they gather and share knowledge, and in the behavior of scientific communities as they generate and disseminate their research. A commons model is at work in the new EconPort, which manages a large economics literature for its user community, and in the Conservation Commons, which is building a "global public domain" for literature about the environment and conservation.

Applying "the commons" to such intellectual and intangible endeavors may strike some people as odd, given the history of the term. The commons is traditionally associated with plots of land—and the supposed tragedy that results from its overexploitation by free riders. But as Hess and Ostrom make clear in chapter 1, there are significant differences between natural-resource commons like land, which are depletable and "rivalrous" (many people wish to use a resource to the exclusion of others), and commons that manage nondepletable, nonrivalrous resources such as information and creative works.

What makes the term *commons* useful, nonetheless, is its ability to help us identify problems that affect both types of commons (e.g., congestion, overharvesting, pollution, inequities, other degradation) and to propose effective alternatives (e.g., social rules, appropriate property rights, and management structures). To talk about the commons is to assume a more holistic vantage point for assessing how a resource may be best managed.

The commons has too many variations to be captured in a fixed, universal set of principles. Each commons has distinctive dynamics based on its participants, history, cultural values, the nature of the resource, and so forth. Still, there are some recurring themes evident in different commons. A key goal of this chapter is to showcase the many different sorts of commons operating in American life today and to illustrate how, despite significant differences, they embody certain general principles.

Recognizing the similarities is not difficult. In fact, a quiet revolution is going on right now as a growing number of activists, thinkers, and practitioners adopt a commons vocabulary to describe and explain their respective fields. Librarians, scholars, scientists, environmentalists, software programmers, Internet users, biotech researchers, fisheries scholars, and many others share a dissatisfaction with the standard market narrative. They are skeptical that strict property rights and market exchange are the only way to manage a resource well, particularly in the context of the Internet, where it is supremely inexpensive and easy to copy and share information.

In addition, more and more people are expressing alarm at the market's tendency to regard everything as a commodity for sale.[2] Genetic information is now routinely patented, freshwater supplies are being bought by multinational companies, and entire towns have been offered for sale on eBay. Because market theory postulates that "wealth" is created when private property rights and prices are assigned to resources, it often has trouble respecting the actual value of *inalienable* resources. Economists tend to regard market activity and growth as inherently good, when in fact it is often a force for eroding valuable nonmarket resources such as family time, social life, and ecosystems.

In this climate, the language of the commons serves a valuable purpose. It provides a coherent alternative model for bringing economic, social, and ethical concerns into greater alignment. It is able to talk about the inalienability of certain resources and the value of protecting community interests. The commons fills a theoretical void by explaining how significant value can be created and sustained outside of the market system. The commons paradigm does not look primarily to a system of property, contracts, and markets, but to social norms and rules, and to legal mechanisms that enable people to share ownership and control of resources. The matrix for evaluating the public good is not a narrow economic index like gross domestic product or a company's bottom line, but instead looks to a richer, more qualitative and humanistic set of criteria that are not easily measured, such as moral legitimacy, social consensus and equity, transparency in decision making, and ecological sustainability, among other concerns.

The spread of the commons discourse in recent years has had a double effect: it has helped *identify* new commons and, in providing a new public discourse, it has helped *develop* these commons by enabling people to see them as commons.

In this sense, the commons is a new (i.e., newly recognized) cultural form that is unfolding in front of us. The discourse of the commons is at once descriptive, constitutive, and expressive. It is descriptive because it identifies models of community governance that would otherwise go unexamined. It is constitutive because, by giving us a new language, it helps us to build new communities based on principles of the commons. And it is expressive because the language of the commons is a way for people to assert a personal connection to a set of resources and a social solidarity with each other.

The growth of the commons discourse, then, is one way that people are striving to develop more culturally satisfying "mental maps" for our time. Even though digital technologies have dramatically changed our economy and culture, our mental maps still tend to depict the landscape of the pre-Internet print era. For example, creative works and information used to be fixed in physical containers (paper, vinyl, film), which implied a whole set of social practices and market relationships that are now being challenged by digital networks. Many people see the commons as a useful template for making sense of the new social and market dynamics driving so much creativity and knowledge creation.

The commons is also invoked to assert certain political claims. To talk about the airwaves, the Internet, wilderness areas, and scientific literature as commons is to say, in effect, that these resources belong to the American people (or to distinct communities of interest) and that they therefore ought to have the legal authority to control those resources. To talk about the commons is to say that citizens (or user communities) are the primary stakeholders, over and above investors, and that these community interests are not necessarily for sale.

The growth of commons discourse is fundamentally a cultural phenomenon that bears many resemblances to the modern environmental movement. Duke law professor James Boyle has compared our current confusion in talking about digital culture to the 1950s, when American society had no shared, overarching narrative for understanding that synthetic chemicals, dwindling bird populations, and polluted waterways might be conceptually related. Few people had yet made *intellectual connections* among these isolated phenomena.[3] No analysis had yet been formulated or published that could explain how disparate and even adversarial constituencies such as birdwatchers and hunters might actually have common political interests.

The signal achievement of Rachel Carson, Aldo Leopold, and other early environmentalists, argues Boyle, was to popularize a compelling critique that forged a new public understanding of the brewing ecological disaster. In a very real sense, the rise of environmentalism as a political and cultural movement was made possible by a new language. This new language allowed us to see diverse abuses of nature in a more unified way. It canonized them in the public mind as "the environment." Over time, this cultural platform gave rise to a diversified social movement that extends from Greenpeace's civil disobedience to the Environmental Defense Fund's centrist, market-oriented advocacy to the Audubon Society's focus on conservation.

The "information commons" may yet play a similar role in our time. It can help us name and mentally organize a set of novel, seemingly disconnected phenomena that are not yet understood as related to each other or to the health of our democratic polity.

Unlike toxic chemicals in the environment, however, abuses of the information commons do not generally result in death and injury. This places a greater burden on language to expose the dangers now facing creative expression, information flows, and the experimental "white spaces" in our culture. As a discourse, the commons can help us begin to articulate these concerns and provide a public vernacular for talking about the politics of creativity and knowledge.

Articulating the case for the commons may not be enough to convince skeptics, of course. This was Keynes's insight. Truly understanding the commons requires that we first escape from the prevailing (prejudicial) categories of thought. We must be willing to grapple anew with on-the-ground realities and "connect the dots" among diverse, specific examples. In that spirit, the following pages provide a brisk survey of the more prominent commons being established by various disciplines and communities.

The Commons as a New Language

The scholarly literature on the commons has been developing steadily since the early 1990s, particularly since the publication of Elinor Ostrom's landmark 1990 book, *Governing the Commons*.[4] Much of this work has been stimulated through such academic centers as the Workshop in Political Theory and Policy Analysis at Indiana University, with its outstanding library on the commons, as well as the Digital Library on the Commons and its archives of the International Association for the Study of Common Property (IASCP).

In recent years, diverse citizen groups and professional constituencies have shown their own keen interest in the commons. Scholars, practitioners in various fields, public policy experts, and activists have begun new conversations about the commons, which in turn has quickened interest in the subject and popularized the commons discourse.

Environmentalists and conservationists fighting a relentless expansion of market activity have been among the most enthusiastic "early adopters" of commons language. Books such as *The Global Commons: An Introduction* by Susan J. Buck,[5] *Whose Common Future? Reclaiming the Commons* by *The Ecologist* magazine,[6] and *Who Owns the Sky? Our Common Assets and the Future of Capitalism* by Peter Barnes[7] have helped popularize the idea that certain shared natural resources should be regarded as commons and managed accordingly. The atmosphere, oceans, fisheries, groundwater and other freshwater supplies, wilderness and local open spaces, and beaches are all increasingly regarded as commons—resources that everyone has a moral if not legal interest in, and that should be managed for the benefit of all.

Environmentalists' embrace of the commons has been matched by a renewed interest in debunking Garrett Hardin's "tragedy of the commons" parable.[8] Hardin's powerful metaphor—that a commons that was not governed by individual property rights was likely to result in the overexploitation and ruin of the resource—has been an analysis that property-rights conservatives have used to fight government management of public resources. A large literature now shows, however, that with the proper institutional design and social norms, a socially managed commons can be entirely sustainable over long periods of time. A "tragedy" is not inevitable at all.

A number of factions in the environmental movement now look to the commons as a philosophical framework to contextualize and support their advocacy.[9] For example, environmentalists fighting the "Wise Use" and property-rights movements, especially in the west, have referenced the commons as a framework for helping to fight the private exploitation and abuse of public lands. They argue that forests, minerals, grasslands, and water on public lands belong to the American people, and should not be surrendered to private economic interests. Carl Pope, the president of the Sierra Club, has written about the commons of nature, and Public Citizen talks about the global commons of water in its campaign to thwart privatization of drinking-water systems.

Advocates of the public trust doctrine also call on the commons for philosophical support for their work. This doctrine declares that certain resources are inherently public in nature, and may not be owned by either private individuals or the government. The doctrine, which goes back to Roman law, holds that government is a trustee of the people's interests, not the owner of the public's property, and so it cannot sell or give away that property to private interests. In practice, the public trust doctrine is a legal tool for preserving public access to rivers, beaches, and other publicly owned natural resources. It is a bulwark against market enclosures of the environmental commons.

Champions of the "precautionary principle" in environmental law have also situated their work within the commons framework.[10] The precautionary principle holds that any proponents of new risks have a duty to take anticipatory action to prevent harm; it is neither ethical nor cost-effective to pay compensation for harm, after the fact, as many corporations prefer.

What unites these different invocations of the commons is their appeal to a fundamental social ethic that is morally binding on everyone. They are asserting the importance of ethical norms that may or may not yet be recognized in law. In the American polity, the will of the people *precedes* and *informs* the law. The sentiment of "we the people" is the pre-eminent source of moral authority and power, separate and apart from the interests of the market and the state. While the law is supreme, it is not synonymous with the will of the people, which is always struggling to express and codify itself.

Thus the commons is always a third force in political life, always struggling to express its interests over and against those of the market and the state. By the reckoning of commoners, individuals or companies who flout our society's moral consensus are essentially free riders trying to avoid accountability to accepted social norms. When the tobacco industry suppressed information about the dangers of smoking in order to protect its market revenues, for example, it was violating a social ethic that had not yet been fully recognized by law. When the automobile industry tries to require that "acceptable" levels of safety design be determined by cost-benefit analysis, it is trying to preempt the public's ethical expectations that foreseeable design hazards be abated.

As these examples suggest, the commons is often engaged with the market and state in struggles over fundamental rules of social governance. Many of these struggles involve issues of *alienability*—what resources should the state allow to be treated as private property? Should the law allow companies to control portions of the human genome? Should pharmaceutical companies be allowed to own the antibiotic capacities of proteins in human tears or genetic information about specific diseases?

Market discourse asserts that it is perfectly appropriate for the law to grant private property rights in such "living" matter. Proponents of the commons argue that such inherited elements of nature—seedlines, genetic information, wildlife, animal species, the atmosphere—are the common heritage of humankind. Ethically, such things belong to everyone (to the extent they should be controlled by humans at all), and should therefore be regarded as commons.

To be sure, property rights and market systems, properly constructed, can be useful approaches to conservation and pollution abatement. But they are no substitute for a commons discourse. That is because the language of markets and private property tends to see exchange value and price, not the thing-in-itself. The worldview embedded in economic discourse treats natural resources as essentially fungible, and scarcities as remediable through higher prices. Economics tends to regard nature as an objective resource to be exploited and governed by laws of supply and demand, not as an animate, beloved force that humans should perhaps interact with according to other criteria.

So however useful market-based policies may be in some arenas, the market system as a whole is not likely to conserve nature of its own accord. As essayist Wendell Berry has explained, "We know enough of our own history by now to be aware that people exploit what they have merely concluded to be of value, but they defend what they love. To defend what we love we need a particularizing language, for we love what we particularly know."[11] The commons is one way to assert a "particularlizing language" declaring that certain natural resources are "not for sale."

Varieties of Information Commons

If most natural commons are finite and depletable (forests can be clear-cut, groundwater can be drained), the commons featured in this book are quite different. The commons of science, academia, and scholarly communications are chiefly social and informational. They tend to involve nonrival goods that many people can use and share without depleting the resource.

Indeed, many information commons exemplify what some commentators have called "the cornucopia of the commons," in which more value is created as more people use the resource and join the social community.[12] The operative principle is "the more, the merrier." The value of a telephone network, a scientific literature, or an open-source software program actually *increases* as more people come to participate in the enterprise—a phenomenon that economists refer to as "network effects."

As the Internet and various digital technologies have become pervasive in American life, enabling robust new forms of social communication and collaboration, the cornucopia of the commons has become a widespread phenomenon. We are migrating from a print culture of scarce supplies of fixed, canonical works to a digital culture of constantly evolving works that can be reproduced and distributed easily at virtually no cost. Our mass-media system of centralized production and one-to-many distribution is being eclipsed by a multimedia network of decentralized production and many-to-many distribution.

One major effect of this epochal shift is the creation of new online social structures that themselves have sweeping economic and techno-logical consequences. Perhaps the most notable expression of this fact is open-source software, a powerful new genre of nonproprietary software created by open communities of programmers. The most famous example of open-source software is GNU Linux, a computer operating system that has become a major rival of proprietary software.[13] The commons-based production system that builds and refines hundreds of open-source programs is so powerful that major high-tech companies are building competitive strategies around open technical platforms. IBM and Sun Microsystems have gone so far as to make dozens of their soft-ware patents available on an open-source basis as a strategic way to spur technological innovation in given areas. They also are supporting a new legal defense project, the Software Freedom Law Center, to protect open-source software from lawsuits that would shut it down.

Not surprisingly, such radical changes in the economic and social premises of knowledge production and dissemination have created severe new tensions with copyright and trademark law, which originated, after all, in a more static technological and economic context. The radical effi-ciencies of "peer production" (open-source software, collaborative web-sites, peer-to-peer knowledge sharing, and so on) are challenging some foundational assumptions about free-market theory, at least as they apply to the networked, digital environment.[14] What was formerly taken for granted or minimized in free-market theory—the role of social and civic factors in economic production—is becoming a powerful variable in its own right.

The relevance of the commons paradigm, therefore, is only likely to grow as more and more commerce, academic research, and ordinary social life migrate to Internet platforms. Venture capitalists are already recognizing that some of the richest opportunities for innovation lie in leveraging the social dynamics of networked environments. Hence the current boom in "social networking" software and new schemes for organizing and retrieving information through socially based "folk-sonomies" (folk taxonomies) and "metatagging".[15] The high-tech world has never been more interested in social norms and collaborative structures as the basis for technology design. This means, in effect, that the governance design of online commons is a matter of increasing practical concern.

Far from being just an obsession of techies, a new network of "participatory media" is being embraced by the general public. Here, too, the commons paradigm can help elucidate what is going on. Web logs, or blogs, were one of the first major expressions of participatory media, but now a variety of follow-on innovations are sprouting up to empower direct, individual communications. These innovations include "syndication feeds" of blog posts, "podcasting" syndication of music and talk, and "grassroots journalism" websites. They include new web platforms for sharing photographs (Flickr), creative works of all types (Ourmedia.org), breaking news events (Publicnews.com), and favorite web bookmarks (del.icio.us). Wikipedia, an online encyclopedia open to anyone who wishes to contribute, is now one of the most popular sites on the web, with 5.3 million unique visitors a month. It has amassed more than one million entries and inspired wikipedias in more than five dozen languages.

As high-tech innovations have fostered the growth of online communities—while, conversely, companies have sought to lock up more content through encryption and broader copyright protection—many besieged scientific, academic, and creative communities have started to see the value of the commons model. From libraries to biotech researchers to musicians, many groups are coming to recognize the value of their own peer-based production and understandably wish to fortify and protect it.

In one sense, this is simply a rediscovery of the social foundations that have always supported science, academic research, and creativity. The scientific research community has long honored the sharing of knowledge and resources, open dialogue, and sanctions against fraudulent research. For years, academia has flourished with the same ethic of sharing and openness among the members of a self-governing community. The creativity of jazz, the blues, and hip-hop have always been rooted in musical communities and intergenerational traditions that encouraged borrowing, emulation, and the referencing of works by other artists.

But in another sense, awareness of the commons in these fields is being provoked by alarming new incursions by the market.[16] Customers are rebelling against the high prices companies are charging for scholarly journals, music CDs, and online databases. They are objecting to "digital rights management" schemes that lock up content, limit the fair-use rights of users, and shrink the public domain. They are balking at the lengthening terms of copyright protection and attempts to override the "first-sale doctrine" (which permits purchasers to rent or lend DVDs, books, and other products). People are objecting to "shrink-wrap" and "click-through" licenses on software and websites, respectively, that diminish their consumer protections and legal rights.

In response to such developments, many academic disciplines, universities, professional fields, creative sectors, and user communities are eager to assert more sovereignty over the ways their work is developed and distributed. Developing one's own information commons to bypass the market system is both technically attractive and financially feasible.[17] Many disciplines, for example, have adopted "open-access" principles for scholarly publishing as a way to ensure the widest access and distribution of their literature.[18] The National Institutes of Health has sought to make all medical research that it funds available under open-access rules within a year after publication in a commercial journal. (Commercial journal publishers in 2005 succeeded in weakening the rule by making it discretionary.) Individual universities are creating "institutional repositories" for the permanent archiving of preprints, dissertations, research data, and so forth.

In music, film, and the visual arts, millions of creators internationally have used one of six main Creative Commons licenses to signal the general public that their works can be shared with others for noncommercial purposes.[19] It is often hard for creators to use another artist's work because of difficulties in locating the rights holder and negotiating a license. The Creative Commons licenses facilitate the easier sharing and distribution of works that might otherwise be impossible. The licenses—and a number of ambitious online hosting services such as YouTube.com, a site for the sharing of "grassroots media"—are greatly reinvigorating the flow of information and creativity.

The Future of the Commons

The great virtue of the commons as a school of thought is its ability to talk about the social organization of life that has some large measure of creative autonomy from the market or the state. The commons reclaims the sovereignty of this cultural activity. It names it as a separate economy that works in tandem with the market, performing its own significant work (and often the most important work). The commons is not a manifesto, an ideology, or a buzzword, but rather a flexible template for talking about the rich productivity of social communities and the market enclosures that threaten them.

The breadth of interest in the commons is reaching new levels, which suggests that it is serving some very practical needs in culturally attractive ways. It enables a new set of values to be articulated in public policy discussions. It offers useful tools and a vocabulary that help various constituencies reassert control over their community resources. It helps name the phenomenon of market enclosure and identify legal and institutional mechanisms for protecting shared resources.

While champions of the commons often differentiate the dynamics of the commons from those of the market, I do not believe that the commons and the market are adversaries. What is usually being sought is a more equitable balance between the two. Markets and commons are synergistic. They interpenetrate each other and perform complementary tasks. Businesses can flourish only if there is a commons (think roadways, sidewalks, and communication channels) that allows private property to be balanced against public needs. Privatize the commons and you begin to stifle commerce, competition, and innovation as well as the means to address social and civic needs. To defend the commons is to recognize that human societies have collective needs and identities that the market cannot fulfill by itself.

The rediscovery of the commons in so many diverse fields is a heartening development. It suggests the beginnings of a new movement to make property law and markets more compatible with a larger set of ethical, environmental, and democratic values. At a more basic level, interest in the commons is leading to some practical new models for managing resources effectively and equitably.

I believe the future of the commons will depend a great deal on a dialectic conversation between practitioners who are inventing new legal and institutional mechanisms to protect the commons, and scholars and thinkers who are developing the intellectual tools to foster better understanding, strategic innovation, and public education. If the past decade is any indication, this dialogue is likely to produce many salutary results.

Notes

1. John Maynard Keynes, *The General Theory of Employment, Interest and Money* (1936; reprint edition, Prometheus Books, 1997), Preface, p. viii.

2. See, for example, James Ridgeway, *It's All for Sale: The Control of Global Resources* (Durham, NC: Duke University Press, 2004).

3. James Boyle, "A Politics of Intellectual Property: Environmentalism for the Net?", *Duke Law Journal* 47(1997):87–116.

4. Elinor Ostrom, *Governing the Commons: The Evolution of Institutions for Collective Action* (Cambridge: Cambridge University Press, 1990).

5. Susan J. Buck, *The Global Commons: An Introduction* (Washington, DC: Island Press, 1998).

6. *The Ecologist* magazine, *Whose Common Future? Reclaiming the Commons* (Philadelphia: New Society Publishers, 1993).

7. Peter Barnes, *Who Owns the Sky? Our Common Assets and the Future of Capitalism* (Washington, DC: Island Press, 2001).

8. Garrett Hardin, "The Tragedy of the Commons," *Science* 162 (December 13, 1968):1243–1248.

9. These groups include the Georgetown Environmental Law and Policy Institute, the Public Trust Alliance, and Riverkeepers, among others.

10. The Science and Environmental Health Network is the leading champion of the precautionary principle. In cooperation with the Tomales Bay Institute and the Johnson Foundation, it held a conference on "The Commons, the Public Trust and the Precautionary Principle" on May 13–16, 2004.

11. Wendell Berry, *Life Is a Miracle: An Essay Against Modern Superstition* (New York: Perseus Books, 2000), 40.

12. See, for example, Carol M. Rose, "The Comedy of the Commons: Custom, Commerce and Inherently Public Property," chapter 5 in *Property and Persuasion: Essays on the History, Theory, and Rhetoric of Ownership* (Boulder, CO: Westview Press, 1994).

13. Steven Weber, *The Success of Open Source Software* (Cambridge, MA: Harvard University Press, 2003).

14. See, for instance, Yochai Benkler, "Coase's Penguin, or Linux and the Nature of the Firm," *Yale Law Journal* 112(2002):369–446, available at http://www.benkler.org/CoasesPenguin.html; and "Sharing Nicely: On Shareable Goods and the Emerging of Sharing as a Modality of Economic Production, *Yale Law Journal* 114(2004):273–358, available at http://benkler.org/SharingNicely.html.

15. Metatagging and social software were major themes at Esther Dyson's PC Forum in 2005, and a topic of intense discussion on blogs run by social networking experts such as Howard Rheingold (www.smartmobs.com), Clay Shirky (www.shirky.com), and Corante's Many 2 Many (http://www.corante.com/many).

16. See, for example, Jennifer Washburn, *University Inc.: The Corporate Corruption of Higher Education* (New York: Basic Books, 2005); Seth Shulman, *Trouble on the"Endless Frontier": Science, Invention, and the Erosion of the Technological Commons* (Washington, DC: New America Foundation and Public Knowledge, 2002); David Bollier, *Brand Name Bullies: The Quest to Own and Control Culture* (New York: Wiley, 2005).

17. See, for instance, *The Common Property Resource Digest*, March 2005 (issue 72), available at http://www.indiana.edu/~iascp/e-cpr.html; David Bollier and Tim Watts, *Saving the Information Commons: A New Public Interest Agenda in Digital Media* (Washington, DC: New America Foundation and Public Knowledge, 2002).

18. An authoritative source for developments in this area is Open Access News, edited by Peter Suber, at http://www.earlham.edu/~peters/fos/fosblog.html.

19. More on the Creative Commons licenses can be found at http://www.creativecommons.org.

3

A Framework for Analyzing the Knowledge Commons

Elinor Ostrom and Charlotte Hess

Who has not heard of the six blind men of Indostan encircled around an elephant?[1] The six—a political scientist, a librarian, an economist, a law professor, a computer scientist, and an anthropologist—discover, based on their own investigations, that the object before them is a wall, a spear, a snake, a tree, a fan, and a rope. The story fits well with the question that propelled this chapter: How can an interdisciplinary group of scholars best analyze a highly complex, rapidly evolving, elephantine resource such as *knowledge*? Trying to get one's hands around knowledge as a *shared resource* is even more challenging when we factor in the economic, legal, technological, political, social, and psychological components—each complex in its own right—that make up this global commons.

Studying Institutions

In this chapter we adapt a framework that has been used for over three decades as the main theoretical structure by many commons scholars from multiple disciplines. The Institutional Analysis and Development (IAD) framework is a diagnostic tool that can be used to investigate any broad subject where humans repeatedly interact within rules and norms that guide their choice of strategies and behaviors. Most importantly, it can lead one out of the path dependency of existing patterns of practice when their accompanying ways of thinking have not yielded solutions (Oakerson 1978, 15).

The framework can be used to analyze static situations crafted by existing rules and relating to an unchanging physical world and relevant community. The framework can also be used to analyze dynamic situations where individuals develop new norms, new rules, and new physical technologies. Studying these developmental processes is more challenging than studies of fixed structures, but is very important for an understanding of the knowledge commons given the fast rate of change related to the physical world, the rules that are crafted to cope with new situations, and the enlarged community of producers and users.

We define institutions as formal and informal rules that are understood and used by a community. Institutions, as we use the term here, are not automatically what is written in formal rules. They are the rules that establish the working "do's and don'ts" for the individuals in the situation that a scholar wishes to analyze and explain.

The IAD framework has been developed to facilitate the development of a comparative method of institutional analysis. Those who engage in institutional analysis seek to understand one of the most fundamental political and social questions: How do fallible humans come together, create communities and organizations, and make decisions and rules in order to sustain a resource or achieve a desired outcome? The framework is an analytical scaffolding that contains a universal set of intellectual building blocks. As a *framework* (and not a static *model* such as the tragedy of the commons or prisoner's dilemma, discussed in chapter 1), the methodology is fluid and dynamic. In one way, it is a checklist of "those independent variables that a researcher should keep in plain sight to explain individual and group behavior" (Gibson 2005, 229). But the framework also structures the checklist into a "causal schema while allowing great flexibility in the determination of exactly what factors should be included" (p. 229). Its design allows for detailed analysis of specific resources and situations, while being general enough to apply to multiple types of inquiries (Oakerson 1992, 42).

Because the IAD obviates the need to invent a new framework for different research questions related to the study of human decision making in repetitive situations, it has been successfully applied in a wide variety of research projects. Examples of its application for diverse types of research questions are to

• Understand the role of institutions in influencing resource use in poor societies (Agrawal 1999)

• Make comparative studies on international higher education policies (Richardson 2004)

• Study how institutions influence behavior and outcomes in urban areas (Ostrom and Ostrom 1965)

• Examine the evolution of banking reform in the U.S. (Polski 2003)

• Better understand the role of information in the governance of forest resources (Andersson and Hoskins 2004)

• Model operational decision making in public organization (Heikkila and Isett 2004)

• Analyze governance and Aboriginal participation in forest management in Canada (Smith 2001)

• Investigate the property rights and communal arrangements in urban apartment communities in Seoul (Choe 1993)

• Analyze the various action situations involved in the open-source software commons, the Free/Libre and Open Source Software (FOSS) (see Schweik, chapter 10, this volume)

The IAD is particularly appropriate for analyses of various types of commons and common-pool resources. It has helped researchers see, for example, the need to factor in more than the trees when studying a forest. To understand why one forest is becoming deforested and another is thriving, researchers need to take into account not just the condition of the soil, the biodiversity of the flora, and the density of the tree growth. Equally important is the understanding of the user communities, the management systems, the various property rights involved, and the multiple levels of the rules-in-use (Gibson, McKean, and Ostrom 2000; Moran and Ostrom 2005). It would also lead researchers to take into consideration questions of multiple uses, conflict, equity, livelihood security, modes of production, and sustainability (see Berkes 1989, 11–13; National Research Council 2002).

This framework seems well suited for analysis of resources where new technologies are developing at an extremely rapid pace. New information technologies have redefined knowledge communities; have juggled the traditional world of information users and information providers; have made obsolete many of the existing norms, rules, and laws; and have led to unpredicted outcomes. Institutional change is occurring at every level of the knowledge commons.

Designing institutions to enhance the production and use of any kind of commons, whether natural or human-made, is a challenge. Effective design requires successful collective action and self-governing behaviors; trust and reciprocity; and the continual design and/or evolution of appropriate rules. We have learned that successful commons governance requires an active community and evolving rules that are well understood and enforced (Dietz, Ostrom, and Stern 2003). When a resource is large and complex, users may lack a common understanding of resource dynamics, and they frequently have substantially diverse interests; thus, the costs of sustaining large and diverse resources are much higher than when governing small and relatively homogeneous resources (Ostrom et al. 1999).

In the IAD framework, we posit three very broad clusters of variables that are basic underlying factors affecting institutional design and the patterns of interaction occurring within action arenas. The variables may also be considered at different scales of operation. Figure 3.1 delineates the local-regional-global scales. It is a suggestion of the "nestedness" of enterprises. Equally valid would be department-school-university or city-state-national-international arenas. The important point is that most of the variables within the clusters will change at different scales.

There are three ways to enter the framework when studying a question: one can start in the middle with the action arena, at the right-hand side with the outcomes, or at the left-hand side with the underlying factors (the physical/material characteristics, the attributes of the relevant community, and the rules-in-use at several levels). Entering the

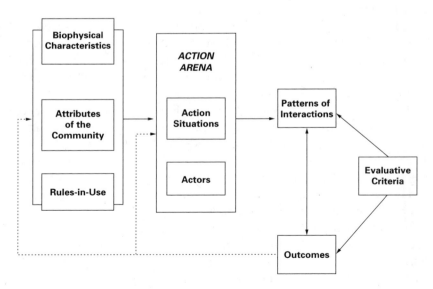

Figure 3.1
Institutional Analysis and Development framework

analysis with the physical/technical and institutional characteristics is most appropriate when one is trying to understand the nature of the resource being shared, by looking at the physical, biological, and technical constraints and capacities of the resource, as well as the boundaries, size, communities of users and producers, and the relevant rules-in-use. The action arena consists of the action situation and the participants (individuals or groups) involved. The action arena, often at the heart of the analysis, is particularly useful in analyzing specific problems or dilemmas in processes of institutional change. Within knowledge commons, it is an appropriate place to start when trying to think through the challenges of creating a new form of commons such as a new digital repository within an organization. Beginning with the outcomes makes sense with questions such as why and how information is being enclosed. Why do authors not voluntarily contribute to a repository? We will begin by discussing the left-hand side of the framework.

Resource Characteristics

For short-term analyses, the attributes of the physical and material world, of the community producing and using a resource, and of the rules-in-use affecting the decisions of participants are the *exogenous* factors in the analysis. Figure 3.2 highlights the left side of the framework illustrating these characteristics. At the time of analysis, one identifies the specific physical and institutional factors on the left-hand side of the framework. These factors then remain fixed throughout the analysis.[2] In this book, regardless of the type or aspect of knowledge commons discussed, the exogenous physical characteristics are those of *distributed digital information.*

Biophysical-Technical Characteristics

"Gallia est divisa in partes tres . . ."

When Julius Caesar began his *Commentaries on the Gallic Wars* around 58 BC, he understood the importance of starting with the physical lay of the land in order to situate the conflict. Likewise, de Tocqueville opens the first volume of his *Democracy in America* with a geographic description: "The Exterior Form of North America." The physical attributes of a resource always play an essential role in shaping the community and

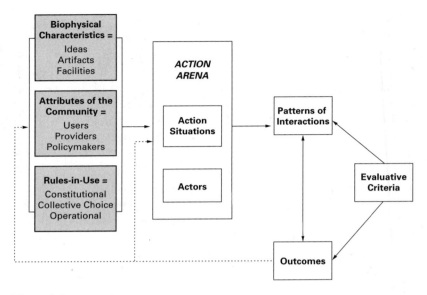

Figure 3.2
Biophysical, community, and institutional characteristics within the IAD

the decisions, rules, and policies. The physical nature and available technology determine the limitations and possibilities of a particular commons. These characteristics comprise such things as size, location, boundaries, capacity, and abundance of the resource. The technology determines the ability to harvest or appropriate the resource units.

Most of the "commons" characteristics of knowledge and information have developed from the effects of new technologies—that is, the physical nature of the resource. Before the digital era, types of knowledge commons were limited to libraries and archives. Only when vast amounts of knowledge began to be digitally distributed (after the development of the World Wide Web in 1992) did it take on more and more characteristics of commons and commons dilemmas. Examples of the vast amount of changed characteristics (from paper to information technologies) include

• More and more "standard" information born digital

• More and more digital information distributed through the Internet

• Improved search engines, databases, as well as word processors, HTML, and other software

- Synchronous exchange of information possible
- Access to digital information through personal computers

The physical attributes of digital technologies may be well understood by technologists and librarians. They may not be so apparent, however, to policymakers, administrators, and others who may be affecting the rules. As we will discuss, these physical changes have led to a complex web of rule changes as well as to new user and producer communities.

The intense and sometimes sudden effect of new technologies can occur with all types of resources. With many natural resources, the physical characteristics can remain constant until the introduction of new technologies (one need only think of the impact of chainsaws on forest ecology or gigantic trawlers on fishery populations). New technologies can introduce the likelihood of overharvesting, congestion, rivalry, and possibly even depletion—all severe commons dilemmas.

When investigating the physical conditions of a traditional natural-resource commons, scholars have found it helpful to distinguish between the *resource system* and *resource units*. In a fishery, the resource system (the facility) is the fishing grounds (Schlager 1994). The resource units are the fish. In groundwater, the groundwater basin is the resource system, while the water quantities or amounts withdrawn are the resource units (Blomquist 1992). The complex nature of knowledge as a commons requires a threefold distinction because it is made up of both nonhuman and human materials: *facilities, artifacts*, and *ideas* (Hess and Ostrom 2003).

Facilities store artifacts and make them available. Traditional facilities have been libraries and archives containing books, journals, papers, and other knowledge artifacts. These facilities had physical limits. The physical-network infrastructure includes the optical fiber, copper-wire switches, routers, host computers, and end-user workstations (Bernbom 2000). It also includes the amount of bandwidth, free-space optics, and wireless systems. The new technologies that have made electronic, distributed information possible are also a part of the evolving physical conditions of the knowledge commons. Many digital facilities today make it possible for digital information to be nonrivalrous—at least over time.

Artifacts are discreet, observable, namable representations of ideas, such as articles, research notes, books, databases, maps, computer files, and web pages. To use the term from copyright law, they are the *expressions* of the ideas. Here, too, whereas traditional knowledge artifacts (e.g., books and journals) are rivalrous, digital artifacts can often be used concurrently by multiple users. Artifacts are the physical resource or *flow units* of a facility. In a knowledge commons they are the expressions of the ideas presented in myriad formats, from the traditional paper, binding, microfilm, video, and so on to state-of-the-art computer graphics, text files, holograms, MIDI files, videos, searchable databases, and so forth.

Ideas are coherent thoughts, mental images, creative visions, and innovative information. Ideas are the intangible content and the *nonphysical flow units* contained in artifacts. There are certain idea types such as mathematical formulas, scientific principles, grammar, names, words, numbers, and facts that are not "capturable" by copyright and are considered to be in the public domain (Samuelson 2003b, 151). But ideas in digital form do not have the same protections as they did in the predigital world (Samuelson 2003b, 164). The most notable characteristic of an idea is that it is a pure public good and, therefore, nonrivalrous. One person's use of it does not subtract from another's.

In Donald Waters's exploration of preservation dilemmas in chapter 6, the physical characteristics of the resource—the decentralized, ever-changing nature of digital objects—are the heart of a social dilemma. Preservation is much trickier in the digital world. All of the instances of enclosure discussed by Kranich in chapter 4 have been brought on by the changed structure of the physicality of information. Suber underscores this connection in chapter 7 when he points out that nonrivalry in the open access [OA] commons is produced by the nature of the digital resource, not because it is OA per se.

Attributes of the Community
In contrast to the situation with a fishery or groundwater basin, it is much more difficult to grasp who the entire community is that is contributing to, using, and managing a knowledge commons. We can start by assessing who the information users, information providers, and information managers or policymakers are. The *users* are those appropriating digital information at any point in time. The *providers* are large diverse groups: those making the content available as well as those making the software, hardware, and infrastructure available. The *policymakers* may be a voluntary and self-governing community of insiders, such as a library committee, or those leading the Open Archives Initiative,[3] the contributors to the FOSS movement discussed in chapter 10,

or the participants of the World Summit on the Information Society (WSIS).[4] The provider and decision-making or policymaking communities are usually *nested*—that is, different groups functioning at various levels within this locally provided, globally appropriated commons (see the rules-in-use section below).

The community may be involved with various aspects of governance, regulation, enforcement, education, or other activities. Whether the values of a community are shared or divided, substantially affects the strategies adopted within action arenas and the resulting patterns of interactions. For example, the university community—even when divided by discipline—used to be fairly unified in its primary quest for the creation and production of new knowledge. In an earlier and slower world, the community using any of the components of the knowledge commons usually shared common values related to the creation of new knowledge, teaching students the knowledge they would need in order to be productive members of a community, a society, and an economy, and providing general information necessary for the sustenance of a democratic society. If these values erode or change dramatically, the resulting physical conditions and action arenas are also strongly affected. In fact, conflicting values now exist in the academy, which has close ties to corporate sponsorship and where the processes of education are increasingly commodified (Argyres and Liebeskind 1998; Vaidhyanathan 2002; Bollier 2002a). Thus the values of the community have become more complex and fragmented.

Traditional commons analysis has demonstrated that small, homogeneous groups are more likely to be able to sustain a commons (Cardenas 2003; National Research Council 2002). If a community of providers and decision makers are unified as to the purpose and goals of the information resource or knowledge commons at hand, then the community can be said to be *homogeneous*. Homogeneity can be quite important in the ultimate robustness of a commons. One of the surprising developments of global digital commons, such as the open-source movement, is the high degree of cooperation and coordination achieved by apparently disparate individuals, many of whom never have face-to-face contact.

Defining a digital knowledge community would be particularly fruitful in analyzing a complex commons since certain members or groups of members may not be easily recognizable, with all the different types and levels of users, providers, and policymakers. In Levine's chapter (chapter

9), the community is the central focus of the discussion. In his associational commons, the community is itself the resource. This is also the case with the open-access commons that Suber and others discuss in this book. These types of resources are similar to traditional village commons except that the shared space is virtual and/or intellectual rather than physical.

Rules-in-Use

Rules are shared normative understandings about what a participant in a position must, must not, or may do in a particular action situation, backed by at least a minimal sanctioning ability for noncompliance (Crawford and Ostrom 2005). When these normative instructions are merely written in administrative procedures, legislation, or a contract and not known by the participants or enforced by them or others, they are considered rules-in-form. Rules-in-use are generally known and enforced and generate opportunities and constraints for those interacting. These rules can be analyzed at three levels: operational, collective choice, and constitutional.

Multiple Levels of Rule Making   At the *operational* level, individuals are interacting with each other and the relevant physical/material world, making day-to-day decisions. For an organization's digital repository,[5] operational rules would affect who may submit what, as well as how to submit. The second level is the *collective-choice* (or policy) level of analysis where individuals interact to make the rules of an operational level. For a library, most collective-choice rules relate to the responsibilities of the library administration for making policy decisions. The *constitutional* level of analysis includes the rules that define who must, may, or must not participate in making collective choices. For a university library, the constitutional rules would exist in the general charter for the university and the broad division of responsibility within the university.

Rules matter at every level in that they "rule in" some behaviors and "rule out" others. When one wants to understand why some patterns of interactions and outcomes occur rather than others, one looks at the rules-in-use at these multiple levels for a key part of the explanation. Rules, however, rarely so constrain behavior that they are the sole structure factor affecting who participates, what their incentives are, what interactions ensue, and what outcomes are obtained.[6]

Too often, in environments with rapid technological change, the current rules-in-use are out of sync with the capabilities of the technologies. New rules or laws can be made based on lack of adequate information, awareness, or understanding of the true nature of the issues. Often the rules are hard to "see," as with protocols, standards, and computer code. Even more challenging is the occurrence of "technological inversion," where the capabilities of technology contradict traditional missions, values, or even constitutional rights.

Pre-1998 copyright law made clear exceptions in "fair use" for educational purposes. It is not clear whether the decision makers who passed the 1998 Digital Millennium Copyright Act (DMCA) were uninformed or blinded as to the wide ramifications of this possibly inadvertent rule change. With the DMCA, licensed software that restricts the number of copies that can be used does not contain the flexibility to make exceptions for fair use. This is an example of usage constrained by the resource's physical nature as well a newer rule (DMCA) contradicting an earlier rule (fair use). Circumventing the software, even for the sake of fair use, is against the law. During the DMCA hearings, none of the congressional witnesses expressed the opinion that the fair-use exemption should be eliminated. Nevertheless, the DMCA has paved the way for increasing digital-rights management (DRM).[7] Legal and library scholars are beginning to examine the enforcement of the "new rules" of DRM as a type of private governance (Samuelson 2003a; Madison 2000, 2003; Mendelson 2003). This situation calls for a few general comments on the way rule changes take place.

In an era of rapid change, participants will move from operational situations into collective-choice situations—sometimes without self-conscious awareness that they have switched arenas. While members of the technology team for a local digital repository are engaged in discussing the ongoing customization of the software, for example, a member of a team may casually reflect that one of the ways they have been doing things in the past was not working very well. The staff member may say—"Why don't we change our routine and do X next time rather than Y?" Sometimes X is simply a jointly agreed-on strategy within a given set of rules. But other times, X is a new rule that may be adopted by the team without ever self-consciously recognizing that they have just made a new rule for themselves! Thus, most governance systems that have a strong link to an operational-level situation move dynamically over time across levels, as changes in the physical environment and in the community produce outcomes that participants find less desirable than other outcomes they perceive to be feasible with a change from the Y to X way of operating.

Intellectual Property Rights as Rules   Intellectual property rights are national and international formal rules as well as informal rules-in-use (see Ghosh, chapter 8, this volume). Most authors and researchers are acquainted with the elementary rights and duties of copyright and patents, although both have become complex and surrounded by controversy within the digital arena. New information technologies allow the capture of information far beyond what the original drafters of this legislation ever imagined (Litman 2001; Samuelson 2003b). To provide an alternative to the brittle confines of copyright law, a group of legal scholars developed the Creative Commons in 2002. This service uses "private rights to create public goods . . . a single goal unites Creative Commons' current and future projects: to build a layer of reasonable, flexible copyright in the face of increasingly restrictive default rules."[8] This collective-action initiative is a case of changing operational rules in order to adapt to evolving technologies and new forms of restrictions. Millions of individual and corporate authors, musicians, and artists worldwide have already begun to use this licensing system.

In general, property rights define actions that individuals may take in relation to other individuals regarding some "thing." If one individual has a right, someone else has a commensurate duty to observe that right. Drawing on the earlier classification of Schlager and Ostrom 1992, we identify seven major types of property rights that are most relevant to use in regard to the digital knowledge commons.[9] These are access, contribution, extraction, removal, management/participation, exclusion, and alienation.

Access	The right to enter a defined physical area and enjoy non-subtractive benefits
Contribution	The right to contribute to the content
Extraction	The right to obtain resource units or products of a resource system
Removal	The right to remove one's artifacts from the resource
Management/ Participation	The right to regulate internal use patterns and transform the resource by making improvements

| Exclusion | The right to determine who will have access, contribution, extraction, and removal rights and how those rights may be transferred |
| Alienation | The right to sell or lease extraction, management/participation, and exclusion rights |

The rights outlined above may be useful in rule setting for an organization's digital repository. Understanding that property rights—whether intellectual or real—are bundles of rights is extremely important. There are many forests, for instance, that are government property but where a community has the right to manage, harvest, and sell the forest products but does not have the right to sell the land. It was this bundling of rights that the Creative Commons developers adapted with their six core licenses.[10] The understanding of the "bundle of rights" within property rights is steadily growing because of the increased online visibility of the Self-Archiving Initiative and the Creative Commons. Many authors, however, are still not aware that they can retain the copyright while making their works available through open access (Harnad 2001; Hess 2005).

For the purpose of analysis, it is important to remember that all knowledge and all technologies are human artifacts, with agreements and rules, and strongly tied to the rules of language itself.[11] Thus, knowledge has an important cultural component as well as intellectual, economic, and political functions. As such, it is a "flow resource" that must be passed from one individual to another to have any public value. The rules connected with knowledge, epistemic communities, and information technologies must continually be adapted as those technologies and communities change and grow. Rules need to be flexible and adaptable in order to create effective institutional design and ensure resource sustainability.[12]

The Action Arena

Action arenas (see figure 3.3) consist of participants making decisions within a situation affected by the physical, community, and institutional characteristics that will then result in varying patterns of interactions and outcomes (Ostrom 2005, chapter 2).

Action arenas can occur throughout all levels of rule and decision making, including the operational-choice, collective-choice, and

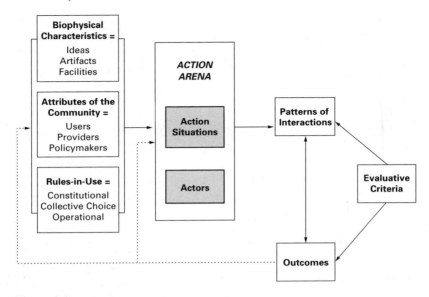

Figure 3.3
Action arena in the IAD

constitutional-choice levels discussed above. They can also occur at the local, regional, or global levels. Importantly, the action arena is at the heart of any analysis involving *institutional change*.

In our discussion we will apply the IAD framework specifically to the diverse arenas involved in developing digital repositories for research materials. The relevant actions could thus be trying to get faculty and departments to voluntarily submit their artifacts to the university repository, agreeing on the format and metadata standards for an international online global archive such as the microbiological commons, or deciding on the policies of who can access which collections held in the facility, as well as many others.

Action Situation: Building a Digital Repository

The action situation focuses on how people cooperate or do not cooperate with each other in various circumstances. The analysis needs to identify the specific participants and the roles they play within the situation. It will look at what actions have been taken, can be taken, or will be taken and how these actions affect outcomes. How much control does each participant have and how much information do they have about the situation? Are all the actors equally informed? Are decisions being made to address short-term dilemmas, or are long-term solutions being sought? Are varying types of outcomes possible? What are the costs and benefits?

In the example of building a university digital repository, the levels of actions and decisions will be polycentric—that is, there will be decentralized, alternative areas of authority and rule and decision making. Say the intended action is to build a digital repository and populate it with faculty research products—both published and unpublished. There will be actions and decisions made by library committees and subcommittees and by the library administration. At the same time, there will be actions taken by faculty groups and committees, and multiple actions and decisions made by computer technology committees and groups.

In analyzing situations, one is particularly concerned with understanding the *incentives* facing diverse participants. With an institutional repository, many incentives exist for faculty to want to submit their research. Most immediate is the high visibility, usage, and citation impact that free, online articles receive. It has been estimated that the citation rate of an article cited in other journals increases dramatically when the cited article is freely accessible online (Harnad and Brody 2004; Brody et al. 2004).[13] This *visibility/impact incentive* pertains to organizations as well as to individual authors (Savenije 2004; Crow 2002). Well-populated and widely used university repositories, for instance, can reflect a university's quality and can "demonstrate the scientific, societal, and economic relevance of its research activities, thus increasing the institution's visibility, status, and public value" (Crow 2002). Higher citation counts also lead to more research funding for the author and organization as well as to career/salary benefits for the author (Smith and Eysenck 2002; Harnad et al. 2003).

Valuable scholarly and scientific information that can be harvested through its metadata will greatly facilitate the global knowledge exchange and further the timeworn tradition of open science. It is no surprise, therefore, that even greater incentives exist in developing countries for the construction of digital repositories. Online accessibility gives voice, visibility, and impact to authors of important research who are often passed over in the western scientific journals.[14] At the same time, open access gives developing-country researchers greater access to the global scientific literature (Kirsop 2004), thereby informing and strengthening their research.[15]

The initial planning process requires strong leadership, great amounts of energy, and time *from individuals* or a small group. The impetus for MIT's DSpace repository software development (http://dspace.org/index.html) grew from discussions between the director of the libraries and faculty members.[16] The director then became the driving force behind the initiative. Kansas University's provost, David Shulenburger, encourages librarians to be those committed individuals, educating their university presidents and chief academic officers, as well as the faculty, about the current trends in scholarly publishing and the potential for open access. Most important, faculty need to "get the message."[17] Many already have, of course. For example, one of the strongest voices in the international self-archiving and institutional repository movement is Stevan Harnad, a professor of cognitive science at Southampton University.

For the incentives to be effective, the participating community—the faculty and researchers—need to be educated about them. Harnad (2003a) writes that "it is becoming apparent that our main challenge is not creating university repositories, but creating policies and incentives for filling them."[18] Many faculty are not yet familiar with the capabilities of global cross-archive metadata harvesting.[19] Since experience is already showing that creating a university repository and encouraging faculty to fill it is not enough, it may be that some kind of formal requirement would be the best method of filling such repositories (Swan and Needham 2005, 34). It may take much longer than hoped to build successful repositories where faculty participate routinely and willingly. The requirements for such institutional change may be much more complex than we imagine, while social capital and trust are built, and while the process of participating is simplified. Faculty from different disciplines will take varying amounts of time to assimilate the new and gravitate from the old ways of publishing.

A major impetus that may move many institutions from reluctance to action is the growing support for the Berlin Declaration.[20] The 2003 Declaration encouraged support for the principles of open access.[21] The 2005 Berlin 3 meeting in Southampton, UK, moved the initiative from one of passive support to actual implementation of the principles by recommending that institutions should (1) *require* that their researchers self-archive all of their published articles and (2) *encourage and support* publishing in OA journals as much as possible. Several institutions have adopted policies that now require self-archiving of non-OA journal articles and encourage and support publishing in suitable OA journals where possible. The University of Southampton has been the overwhelming leader in the open-archives movement. Its School of Electronics and Computer Science developed a very clear, systematic, and relentless mission in the mid-1990s to promote self-archiving. It prevailed in creating Cogprints in 1997, Eprints Open Source Software in 2000, Citebase in 2001, the Archive Registry, the Policy Registry, and the Journal Policy Directory, and it provided the model policy for both the Berlin Declaration and the UK Recommendation.[22] And, indeed, it may be universities like Southampton that will ultimately lead the way for the rest of the world. Referring to the slow rise of repositories and the difficulties of compliance in the United States, Indiana University Professor and Dean Blaise Cronin (2005) suggests that it may take the success of repositories from smaller countries with centralized educational systems, where policies are uniform and participation is required, to demonstrate the overwhelming value of a successful, well-populated repository.

The University of Kansas was the first U.S. university to sign the Registry of Institutional OA Self-Archiving Policies implementing the Berlin Declaration. Its endorsement was drafted by the university faculty senate and was backed by the university provost, who is an enthusiastic supporter of open access. The endorsement is not a requirement, but the provost and council have strongly urged faculty to deposit their publications in the university's repository.[23] But one year after the endorsement, the university's IR, KU ScholarWorks[24] has only around 650 records, which indicates a low compliance rate. Other institutions with new OA requirement policies are Minho University in Portugal, twelve Dutch universities, and the Max Planck Society with its seventy-eight institutes. Over time, it will become more evident which action strategies are most effective for implementing and populating repositories.

In this book, Kranich, Levine, Schweik, and Lougee all discuss action arenas within different knowledge commons. The measure of success will be how people behave in response to those actions and how those responses determine the outcomes.

Patterns of Interaction

The exogenous characteristics, the incentives, the actions, and the other actors all contribute to the patterns of interactions. In a commons, how the actors interact strongly affects the success or failure of the resource.

As figure 3.4 illustrates, the patterns of interaction are intricately linked to the action situations.

Developing a university repository is a commons activity. It requires multiple layers of collective action and coordination. It also requires a common language and shared information and expertise. One can free ride on that production process by not depositing materials that need to be in the repository. But the free riding can only occur with those members of the local knowledge commons—the faculty and researchers—who are expected to contribute to the repository.

Various aspects of free riding and misuse have to do with noncompliance with the rules related to the development of a university repository. A perverse outcome on the use side of the public-good aspect of a university repository is *underuse*. While scholars who have focused primarily on natural-resource commons will be amused to encounter a problem of underuse, it is an inefficient use of resources to make a major investment in a university repository when it is not used and the knowledge in it is not made available to those who need it. Others outside that community who browse, search, read, download, or print out documents in the repository are *not* free riding. In fact, they enhance the quality of the resource by using it.

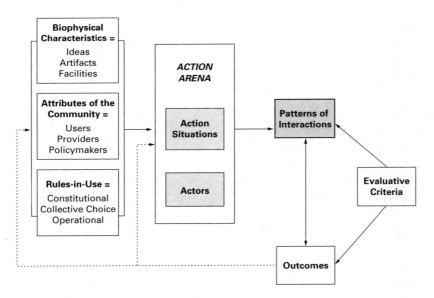

Figure 3.4
Patterns of interactions following the action situation

Patterns of interaction can be strongly conflictual especially when there is hyperchange in the community of users and in their values and goals. In addition to conflict, interactions may be simply unfocused and unthinking—a part of a growing "culture of carelessness" (Baron 2000) where quick-fix solutions take the place of collaborative analytical processes. In the university community, patterns of interaction may be influenced by hierarchies, lack of respect, and distrust that often accompanies the "tribalism" of disciplines (Becher and Trowler 2001; see Thorin 2003, 13, who discusses the "complexity embedded in the disciplines"). It is important that the participants gain sufficient information about the structure of the situation, the opportunities they and other participants face, and the costs of diverse actions. With adequate information they may develop increasing trust so that the situation can lead to productive outcomes.

We have focused so far on university or organizational repositories. Our own experience lies in the construction of an epistemic repository—the Digital Library of the Commons (DLC).[25] As of July 2006, there are 1,202 full-text papers, dissertations, and published articles in the repository. Epistemic repositories could be obstacles to institutional or university repositories. Work on the DLC began in 2000 when there were few repositories at all. The DLC encourages submissions by colleagues in developing countries where repositories are not yet established.[26] And it gives visibility to a widely interdisciplinary area of study that is often not recognized by local departments and universities as an important area of research. As we discussed, there are many incentives but participation is lagging. We have made numerous attempts to educate the community through demonstrations, presentations, and articles (see Hess 2005). Most of the documents contained in the repository have been submitted by the DLC staff and conference chairs after receiving author permissions through local, regional, and international conferences. This is a viable strategy to get authors to participate, with librarians, information technologies, and researchers working collaboratively in the provision of new knowledge.

Outcomes

In the environmental commons research, the analytical process often begins with the outcomes (see figure 3.5), especially negative outcomes, such as "why is there continual drought in the African Sahel?" or "why are the cod fisheries close to depletion?" Analysis can also be motivated

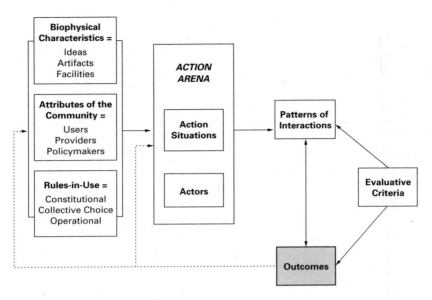

Figure 3.5
Outcomes in the IAD

by confusing and conflicting outcomes, such as "why is one forest depleted while another ten miles away is thriving?" Sometimes the outcomes in the knowledge commons seem crystal clear, as with the disappearance of footnote or citation URLs that Waters discusses in chapter 6 or the loss of important information through mandatory filters that Kranich talks about in chapter 4.

Most of the outcomes that have been written about in the newly emerging knowledge-commons literature are either types of enclosures of information that used to be open or the creation of new digital commons that provide better access to information.[27] Writers tend to point to outcomes that they like or dislike, but few have gone into in-depth analysis. Thus far we (all of us!) have mainly been at the "look what is happening!" stage. In the midst of the relentless hyperchange, it can seem like a full-time job just keeping up with what is happening in the realm of digital knowledge commons.

Within the broad spectrum of the knowledge commons, there are a myriad number of competing outcomes—some of which are considered negative, while others are seen as positive (see table 3.1). The conflicting outcomes reflect a highly complex resource where new technologies

Table 3.1
Potential positive or negative outcomes in various knowledge commons

Negative outcomes	Positive outcomes
Proprietary scientific databases (enclosure)	Open-access research libraries (access)
Digital divide and information inequity (inequity)	Global use, provision, and production (equity)
Lack of standards across collections (degradation)	Standards and interoperability of digital information (diversity and rich commons)
Conflict and lack of cooperation	Cooperation and reciprocity (social capital)
Lack of quality control (pollution)	Quality control of content (richness)
Overpatenting and anticommons (enclosure)	Open science (enhanced access/ communication)
Noncompliance (weak resource)	Compliance and participation (well-populated repositories)
Withdrawal of information (instability, degradation, depletion)	Preservation of information (access)
Spam (pollution)	Scholarly blogs (enhanced quality of information and communication)

have increased capabilities to "harvest" information as a commodity. There are now multiple uses by expanded communities for the same resource—not just scholarship, but entrepreneurship, competition, and financial gain. Because the outcomes are often the result of a number of desparate actions, it is helpful to keep an interdisciplinary frame of mind. The *desired* outcome may be the dissemination and preservation of the scholarly record, but contributing factors in the outcome formula are new computer technologies, financial constraints, university corporatization, declining numbers of tenured faculty, lack of information, and new intellectual property rights legislation.

Seeing outcomes in their context and as a progression of events may better help us see solutions. At the Workshop on Scholarly Communication as a Commons (the forerunner of this book, described in the preface), Clifford Lynch pointed out that it is difficult to know how we are doing in this uncharted territory of globally distributed information. Indeed, it is possible that the outcomes, such as underpopulated digital repositories, are the results of an old path. One might even surmise from using the IAD framework that if the physical characteristics have substantially changed, it is reasonable that the institutional characteristics, the actions, and the patterns of behaviors will have to change—to *adapt*—in order to have successful and sustainable outcomes.

It is possible that successful outcomes in the knowledge commons may be most apparent in the developing world. It is too soon to know. At a pan-African information communication conference in 2004,[28] many African participants were planning actions that would lead to further-reaching outcomes than their western/northern counterparts. They wanted to use university open-access repositories to communicate with indigenous communities, to inform government officials and policymakers of best practices and lessons learned from scientific research, and, ultimately as a way to help alleviate poverty and build sustainable economic development!

Evaluative Criteria

The evaluative criteria (see figure 3.6) allow us to assess outcomes that are being achieved as well as the likely set of outcomes that could be achieved under alternative actions or institutional arrangements. Evaluative criteria are applied to both the outcomes and the interactions among participants that lead to outcomes. While there are many potential evaluative criteria, some of the most frequently used criteria are (1) increasing scientific knowledge, (2) sustainability and preservation, (3) participation standards, (4) economic efficiency, (5) equity through fiscal equivalence, and (6) redistributional equity.

Increasing Scientific Knowledge
One of the core evaluations made of scientific research is whether it leads to an increase in the knowledge that has been recorded and made available to other scholars, students, and the public at large. The progress of scientific knowledge can be assessed based on the amount of high-quality information available; the quality and usefulness of the common pool; the local and global use of the information; and the percentage of free, open-access information versus closed, proprietary information. One can also evaluate the markup language, metadata, and format standards that facilitate or restrain interoperability. One of the hotly debated questions at this time is about the sustainability of the integrity of the scholarly

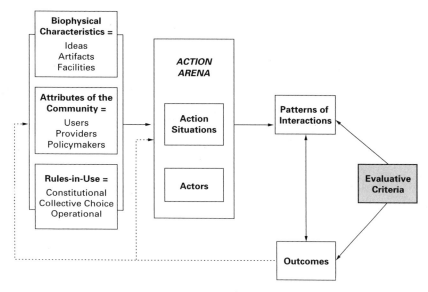

Figure 3.6
Evaluative criteria

record with the advance of institutional repositories, especially if it results in the demise of academic presses (Anscombe 2005).

Sustainability and Preservation
Sustainable systems are those that meet the current needs of many individuals involved in producing, deciding, and using a commons (e.g., students, faculty, researchers, librarians, administrators, citizens, public officials) without compromising the ability of future generations to also meet their needs. Unfortunately, because change is part of the human and physical condition, resources can never be sustained "once and for always." Sustainability is an ongoing process that requires monitoring and frequent reevaluation. Thus, when evaluating the sustainability of a system, one needs to examine the processes involving interactions among participants and whether they increase the physical, social, and human capital involved or slowly erode that capital. In regard to ecological systems, sustainability has usually meant the maintenance of the capacity of an ecological system to support social and economic systems over time (Berkes, Colding, and Folke 2003, 2). When applied to a knowledge commons, one is asking whether these systems can survive over time

as well as supporting ecological, social, and economic systems through increased access to relevant information. Are the preservation strategies economically feasible? Such strategic plans will need to factor in changing actors and participants, adaptive software systems, and constantly evolving rules. Efforts to sustain the knowledge commons will entail a continual process of juggling the requirements of sudden and demanding new technologies with the steadfastness of long-term commitments. Perhaps the successful plan for sustainability is in the balance.

Participation Standards

As we have pointed out, participation—that is, submission of research artifacts to an institution's repository—is essential to the quality of the whole. It is clear that the incentives and rules must change for authors to participate actively in the open and public provision of knowledge. The challenges for institutional change for a successful digital repository are daunting. Scholars are not used to thinking of themselves as archivists. Yet the self-archiving aspect of a repository requires just that. It may be that participation is successful when the amount of information in a repository has reached a critical mass, so that the norm will be to get one's documents into the system as soon as possible after production or publication. Librarians and technologists can help the system reach a critical mass by scanning and archiving retrospective documents of value. This is what MIT's DSpace repository did recently when the libraries digitized over 10,000 theses and dissertations and put them into the system. In a sense, they participated as information providers by being "proxy submitters."

Economic Efficiency

Economic efficiency is determined by the magnitude of the change in the flow of net benefits or costs associated with an allocation or reallocation of resources. The concept of efficiency plays a central role in studies estimating the benefits and costs or rates of return to investments, which are often used to determine the economic feasibility or desirability of public policies. When considering alternative institutional arrangements, therefore, it is crucial to consider how revisions in the rules affecting participants will alter behavior and, hence, the allocation of resources. Many studies have already shown the economic efficiency of open-access publishing, but finding the appropriate rules for sharing the new costs of this form of publication is still under development.

Achieving economic efficiency in path-dependent libraries is a delicate task. In most academic libraries, the "digital library programs" are separate from the traditional departments in the library, such as the subject areas, acquisitions, and cataloging. This made sense ten or fifteen years ago, but today almost all information resources are "born digital." How to integrate and make these two library systems efficient is a major concern.

Equity through Fiscal Equivalence

There are two principal means to assess equity: (1) on the basis of the equality between individuals' contributions to an effort and the benefits they derive and (2) on the basis of differential abilities to pay. The concept of equity that underlies an exchange economy holds that those who benefit from a service should bear the burden of financing that service. Perceptions of fiscal equivalence or a lack thereof can affect the willingness of individuals to contribute toward the development and maintenance of resource systems.

One of the perplexing issues related to the publication of journals in the digital age is how to "tap" the beneficiaries of the provision of a journal to pay for the cost of publication, including managing the flow of documents, choosing referees, refereeing, editing, and publication itself. The costs used to be borne by a mixture of academic disciplinary associations drawing on their membership fees, subscriptions by members of disciplines and by libraries, by universities who benefited from the prestige of having a well-respected journal housed at their university, by publishing houses, and by advertisers in the journal. As more journals are going online and not relying on publishers, a substantial proportion of the costs is being shifted to the authors of accepted articles. Trying to work out an equitable assignment of the costs to the various beneficiaries is a challenging process, given that there are few ways of determining the relative size of the benefit flow.

Redistributional Equity

Policies that redistribute resources to poorer individuals are of considerable importance. Thus, although efficiency would dictate that scarce resources be used where they produce the greatest net benefit, equity goals may temper this objective, resulting in the provision of facilities that benefit particularly needy groups. This is an example of a type of digital divide that is becoming more frequent. International scientific collaboration is steadily increasing, but the information divide between the haves and have-nots is also increasing. Should universities from developed countries take a more active role in providing access services with partners in developing countries?[29] On the other hand, redistributional objectives tend to conflict with the goal of achieving fiscal equivalence, and tough decisions are required in order to prioritize equity needs. Should an online journal charge authors from developing countries a lower "publication" fee in order to enhance redistributional objectives? But then who pays for the increased efforts to provide information to scholars in developing countries?

Requirements of Adaptive Governance in a Complex System

Researchers who have focused on the governance[30] of natural resources have struggled with the question of why some self-governing systems have survived for many years (some as long as 1,000 years), while others collapse within a few years, or even after a long and successful era. There is no simple answer. One of the core problems that has been documented is that rapid change in the environment and in the community is always a major challenge for any governance system. Over time, scholars have come to a general level of agreement that there are several requirements that somehow need to be met for a governance system to be adaptive and robust over time. These are: providing information, dealing with conflict, inducing rule compliance, providing infrastructure, and being prepared for change (see Dietz, Ostrom, and Stern 2003). A wide diversity of specific ways of meeting these requirements have been observed. Let us briefly discuss each of these requirements.

Providing Information

All effective governance systems at multiple levels depend on good, trustworthy information about stocks, flows, and processes within the entities being governed, as well as about the relevant external environment. This information must be matched with the level of aggregation that individuals are using to make decisions. All too often, large flows of data are aggregated. Decisions are, however, frequently made by much smaller units where there is substantial variance from the average reported in the aggregated data. Information must also be fit with decision makers' needs in terms of timing, content, and form of presentation. Informational systems that simultaneously meet high scientific standards and serve ongoing needs of decision makers and users are particularly useful. Information must not overload the capacity of users to assimilate it. Finding ways to measure and monitor the outcomes generated for a university repository that has substantial impact outside the university is an informational challenge for any governance system.

Dealing with Conflict

Sharp differences in power and in values across interested parties make conflict inherent in all choices of any importance. Conflict resolution can be as important a motive in designing institutions as is the concern with building and maintaining a resource itself. People bring varying perspectives, interests, and fundamental philosophies to problems of the scholarly commons. Conflicts among perspectives and views, if they do not escalate to the point of dysfunction, can spark new understandings and better ways of accomplishing outcomes. The core problem is designing conflict-resolution mechanisms that enable participants to air differences and to achieve resolutions that they consider legitimate, fair, and scientifically sound.

Inducing Rule Compliance

As we have learned, effective governance also requires that whatever rules are adopted are generally followed, with reasonable standards for tolerating small variations that always occur due to errors, forgetfulness, and urgent problems. It is generally most effective to impose modest sanctions on first offenders, and gradually increase the severity of sanctions for those who do not learn from their first or second encounter (Ostrom 1990). The challenge in designing a new governance system is how to use informal strategies for achieving compliance at the beginning that rely on participants' commitment to a new enterprise, the rules they have designed, and subtle social sanctions. When a more formal system is developed, those who are the monitors and those who impose sanctions must be seen as effective and legitimate by participants, or rule evasion will overwhelm the governance system.

Providing Infrastructure

Infrastructure includes physical and institutional structures and technology. Thus, the infrastructure affects how a commons can be utilized, the extent to which waste can be reduced in resource use, and the degree to which the physical conditions of a resource and the behavior of users can be effectively monitored. Indeed, the ability to choose institutional arrangements depends in part on infrastructure—largely in regard to ways of storing and communicating information. Infrastructure also affects the links between local commons and regional and global systems.

Being Prepared for Change

Institutions must be designed to allow for adaptation because some current understanding is likely to be wrong, the required scale of organization can shift, and biophysical and social systems change. Fixed rules are likely to fail because they place too much confidence in the current state of knowledge, while systems that guard against the low-probability, high-consequence possibilities and allow for change may be suboptimal in the short run but prove wiser in the long run. This is a principal lesson of adaptive management research.

Conclusion

The purpose of this chapter has been to clearly guide readers through the various components of the IAD framework. It has been a tested tool for analyzing traditional commons dilemmas, for understanding inexplicable outcomes, and for facilitating new institutional design. We expect that the framework will evolve to better fit with the unique attributes of the production and use of a knowledge commons. Over time, it will be possible to extract design principles for robust, long-enduring knowledge commons. After more efforts succeed and others fail, we will be able to better understand what makes various knowledge commons work and how we can better work toward robust and sustainable resources.

Notes

1. Referring to the poem of John Godfrey Sax (1816–1887), "The Blind Men and the Elephant": "It was six men of Indostan/To learning much inclined/ Who went to see the Elephant/(Though all of them were blind). . . ." http://www .wordfocus.com/word-act-blindmen.html.

2. For longer-term analyses, feedback from the outcomes of interactions tends to change these "temporarily" exogenous variables. And, when one is analyzing a rapidly evolving system with changes occurring at multiple levels relatively rapidly, these feedback loops are very important.

3. See http://www.openarchives.org/community/index.html and http://www.openarchives.org/organization/index.html.

4. See http://www.itu.int/wsis/documents/doc_multi.asp?lang=en&id=2266| 2267.

5. Usually referred to as an "institutional repository." We will refer to this kind of organizational archive as a "digital repository" to avoid confusion with our discussion of "institutions" and "institutional analysis."

6. For more on rules, see Commons [1924] 1968; Bromley 1989; Agrawal 1994; Crawford and Ostrom 2005.

7. See http://www.eff.org/IP/DRM/fair_use_and_drm.php and http://www.eff.org/IP/DMCA/20030102_dmca_unintended_consequences.html. Also see Julie Cohen, "Call It the Digital Millennium *Censorship* Act: Unfair Use," *The New Republic Online*, May 23, 2000, http://www.law.georgetown.edu/faculty/jec/unfairuse.html.

8. See http://creativecommons.org/.

9. In Schlager and Ostrom 1992, the term used for *extraction* is *withdrawal*.

10. "Offering your work under a Creative Commons license does not mean giving up your copyright. It means offering some of your rights to any member of the public but only on certain conditions." http://creativecommons.org/about/licenses.

11. Vincent Ostrom has repeatedly emphasized the artifactual nature of knowledge and institutions:

Every development—street sweeping, production of fertilizers, irrigation works, the development of new seed stocks—has a component to it that is concerned with how the activities of people are organized in relation to one another. (V. Ostrom 1969, 2)

12. There are numerous works on the nature and application of rules by commons scholars. See Agrawal 1994; Poteete and Welch 2004; Ostrom 2005; Young 1996; and search "rules" at http://dlc.dlib.indiana.edu/cpr/index.php.

13. See http://opcit.eprints.org/oacitation-biblio.html for a comprehensive list of visibility/usage/impact studies.

14. A 1995 survey revealed that the main index of scientific journals, the *Science Citation Index*, indexes 3,300 journals of the 70,000 that are published worldwide. Less than 2 percent of the journals are from developing countries (with 80 percent of the world's population). The author writes that the "near invisibility of less developed nations may reflect the economics and biases of science publishing as much as the actual quality of Third World Research" (Gibbs 1995, 92). We could find no evidence that these numbers have improved over the last ten years.

15. While rates of cited references vary among disciplines, multiple studies have demonstrated the overwhelming advantage for authors in the natural sciences who make their research artifacts freely available online by self-archiving their

non-OA journal articles on the web. Citation counts are compared for articles within the same issue of the same non-OA journal that are or are not made OA by their authors through self-archiving (Lawrence 2001; Harnad and Brody 2004a; Brody et al. 2004; Hitchcock et al. 2003; Murali et al. 2004). Some other impact studies show that citation rates for OA journals actually have fairly similar patterns to non-OA journals, but that the citations of OA journal articles appear earlier than for hardcopy articles (Testa and McVeigh 2004; Pringle 2004). See The Open Citation Project at http://opcit.eprints.org/oacitation-biblio .html for a comprehensive, frequently updated bibliography of open-access visibility studies.

16. See "MIT's DSpace Experience: A Case Study," http://www.dspace.org/ implement/case-study.pdf.

17. "Key to any success was defining the problem confronting us. It is not 'the library problem' or 'the Provost's problem,' but 'the scholarly communication problem'" (Shulenburger 1999).

18. One well-known study found that 49 percent of faculty have self-archived at least one article in some way, but out of the 51 percent who have not, 71 percent were unaware of the option (Swan and Brown 2005). Even more significant was the finding that 81 percent stated that they would comply willingly with self-archiving *if their institutions required them to,* 14 percent more would comply reluctantly, and only 5 percent said they would not comply (Swan and Brown 2005). Ninety-two percent of journals have already given authors a green light to self-archive, but authors are self-archiving only 15 percent of their articles.

19. OAIster harvests data from 6,073,500 records from 572 institutions. See http://oaister.umdl.umich.edu/o/oaister/.

20. See http://www.zim.mpg.de/openaccess-berlin/berlindeclaration.html.

21. OA means "immediate, permanent, free online access to the full text of all refereed research journal articles" (Harnad 2005).

22. http://www.ecs.soton.ac.uk/~harnad/Temp/UKSTC.htm.

23. The endorsement is online at http://www.provost.ku.edu/policy/scholarly _information/scholarly_resolution.htm.

24. https://kuscholarworks.ku.edu/dspace/.

25. At http://dlc.dlib.indiana.edu. The DLC went online in 2001.

26. The DLC staff will digitize hardcopy texts and images, convert them to PDF files, assign the metadata, and submit them for those who do not want to go to the trouble or who do not have the digital capability.

27. Examples of knowledge commons that have been analyzed are *congestion and overuse* on the Internet caused, for instance, by peak demand and not enough bandwidth (Gupta, Stahl, and Whinston 1995; Hess 1995; Huberman and Lukose 1997; Bernbom 2000); *free riding* (Adar and Huberman 2000); *conflict* (Carnevale and Probst 1997); *deception* (Grazioli 2004); *withdrawal* (such as the removal of presidential papers from the public domain pursuant to Executive

Order #13233) (Evans and Bogus 2004); *enclosure* (Boyle 2003); *inequity and the digital divide* (Greco and Floridi 2004); and other forms of degradation. Others have focused on positive interactions and outcomes, such as *cooperation* (Weber 2004; Kollock and Smith 1995); *institution building* (Dinwoodie 2004); *collective action* (Rheingold 2002; Mele 2003); and *self-organization* (Noonan 1998).

28. See F. F. Tusubira, and N. K. Mulira, eds. *Universities: Taking a Leading Role in ICT-Enabled Human Development* (Kampala, Uganda: Makerere University, 2005).

29. This is the notion of "common but differentiated responsibilities" frequently applied in international law and promoted in the World Summit on Sustainable Development, Johannesburg, August 2002. See http://www.cisdl.org/pdf/brief_common.pdf.

30. Governance has to do with humans trying to find ways of making decisions that reduce the level of unwanted outcomes and increase the level of desirable outcomes (Ostrom 1998).

References

Adar, Eytan, and Bernardo A. Huberman 2000. "Free Riding on Gnutella." *First Monday* 5(10). http://www.firstmonday.org/issues/issue5_10/adar/index.html.

Agrawal, Arun. 1994. "Rules, Rule Making, and Rule Breaking: Examining the Fit between Rule Systems and Resource Use." In E. Ostrom, R. Gardner, and J. M. Walker, eds., *Rules, Games, and Common-Pool Resources*. Ann Arbor: University of Michigan Press.

Agrawal, Arun. 1999. *Greener Pastures: Politics, Markets, and Community among a Migrant Pastoral People*. Durham; NC: Duke University Press.

Altarelli, Guido. 2005. "Continuing CERN Action on Open Access." CERN Scientific Information Policy Board. http://doc.cern.ch/archive/electronic/cern/preprints/open/open-2005-006.pdf.

Andersson, Krister P., and Marilyn W. Hoskins. 2004. "Information Use and Abuse in the Local Governance of Common-Pool Forest Resources." *Forests, Trees and Livelihoods* 14:295–312.

Anscombe, Nadya. 2005. "Repositories: Archive Programmes Gain Momentum." *Research Information* 19 (October/November). http://www.researchinformation.info/rioctnov05repositories.html.

Argyres, N. S., and J. P. Liebeskind 1998. "Privatizing the Intellectual Commons: Universities and the Commercialization of Biotechnology." *Journal of Economic Behavior and Organization* 35(4):427–454.

Baron, Cheryll A. 2000. "High Tech's Missionaries of Sloppiness." *Salon.com* (December 6). http://dir.salon.com/tech/feature/2000/12/06/bad_computers/index.html.

Baron, Robert A. 2002. "Reconstructing the Public Domain: Metaphor as Polemic in the Intellectual Property Wars." Presented at the VRA-ARLIS NINCH Copyright Town Meeting "The Changing Research and Collections Environment: The Information Commons Today," St. Louis, Missouri, March 23, 2002. http://www.studiolo.org/IP/VRA-TM-StLouis-PublicDomain.htm#Ch004.

Barrett, D. 1998. *The Paradox Process.* New York: AMACOM.

Becher, Tony, and Paul Trowler. 2001. *Academic Tribes and Territories: Intellectual Enquiry and the Culture of Disciplines.* 2nd ed. Philadelphia: Open University Press. http://mcgraw-hill.co.uk/openup/chapters/0335206271.pdf.

Benkler, Yochai. 1998. "The Commons as a Neglected Factor of Information Policy," Remarks at the Telecommunications Policy Research Conference, September 1998. http://www.law.nyu.edu/benklery/commons.pdf.

Benkler, Yochai. 2003. "The Political Economy of the Commons." *Upgrade: The European Journal for the Informatics Professional* 4/3 (June): 6–10. http://www.upgrade-cepis.org/issues/2003/3/up4-3Benkler.pdf.

Benkler, Yochai. 2004. "Commons-Based Strategies and the Problems of Patents." *Science* 305(5687):1110–1111.

Berkes, Fikret, ed. 1989. *Common Property Resources: Ecology and Community-Based Sustainable Development.* London: Belhaven.

Berkes, Fikret, Johan Colding, and Carl Folke. 2003. *Navigating Social-Ecological Systems: Building Resilience for Complexity and Change.* New York: Cambridge University Press.

Bernbom, Gerald. 2000. "Analyzing the Internet as a Common Pool Resource: The Problem of Network Congestion." Presented at the Eighth Conference of the International Association for the Study of Common Property, Bloomington, Indiana, May 31–June 4, 2000. http://dlc.dlib.indiana.edu/documents/dir0/00/00/02/18/index.html.

Blomquist, William. 1992. *Dividing the Waters: Governing Groundwater in Southern California.* San Francisco: Institute for Contemporary Studies Press.

Bollier, David. 2002a. "The Enclosure of the Academic Commons." *Academe* 88(5):18–22. http://www.aaup.org/publications/Academe/2002/02so/02sobol.htm.

Bollier, David. 2002b. *Silent Theft: The Private Plunder of Our Common Wealth.* New York: Routledge.

Boyle, James. 2002. "Fencing Off Ideas: Enclosure and the Disappearance of the Public Domain." *Daedalus* 131(2):13–25.

Boyle, James. 2003. "The Second Enclosure Movement and the Construction of the Public Domain." *Law and Contemporary Problems* 66/1–2 (winter/spring): 33–75. http://www.law.duke.edu/journals/66LCPBoyle.

Brody, T., H. Stamerjohanns, S. Harnad, Y. Gingras, and C. Oppenheim. 2004. "The Effect of Open Access on Citation Impact." Poster presentation at National Policies on Open Access (OA) Provision for University Research Output: An

International Meeting, Southampton, February 19, 2004. http://opcit.eprints.org/feb19oa/brody-impact.pdf.

Bromley, Daniel W. 1989. *Economic Interests and Institutions: The Conceptual Foundations of Public Policy.* New York: Blackwell.

Brown, John Seely, and Paul Duguid. 2000. *The Social Life of Information.* Boston: Harvard University Press.

Bush, Vannevar. 1945. *Science, the Endless Frontier: A Report to the President.* Washington, DC: U.S. Government Printing Office. http://www.nsf.gov/od/lpa/nsf50/vbush1945.htm.

Cardenas, Juan-Camilo. 2003. "Real Wealth and Experimental Cooperation: Experiments in the Field Lab." *Journal of Development Economics* 70(2): 263–289.

Carnevale, Peter J., and Tahira M. Probst. 1997. "Conflict on the Internet." In S. Kiesler, ed., *Culture of the Internet.* Mahwah, NJ: Erlbaum.

Choe, Jaesong. 1993. "The Organization of Urban Common-Property Institutions: The Case of Apartment Communities in Seoul." (PhD dissertation, Indiana University).

Commons, John H. [1924] 1968. *Legal Foundations of Capitalism.* Madison: University of Wisconsin Press.

Computer Science and Telecommunications Board, National Research Council. 2000. *The Digital Dilemma: Intellectual Property in the Information Age.* Washington, DC: National Academy Press.

Costanza, Robert, Bobbi S. Low, Elinor Ostrom, and James Wilson, eds. 2001. *Institutions, Ecosystems, and Sustainability.* Washington, DC: Lewis.

Crawford, Sue E. S., and Elinor Ostrom. 2005. "A Grammar of Institutions." In Elinor Ostrom, ed., *Understanding Institutional Diversity*, 137–174. Princeton, NJ: Princeton University Press. Originally published in *American Political Science Review* 89/3 (1995): 582–600.

Cronin, Blaise. 2005 "On Libraries and the Digital Environment." Presentation given at the Indiana University Herman B. Wells Library, Bloomington Campus. http://video.indiana.edu:8080/ramgen/vic/blaise_cronin_20051201.rm?start=00:09:30.

Crow, Raymond. 2002. "The Case for Institutional Repositories: A SPARC Position Paper." Washington, DC: Scholarly Publishing & Academic Resources Coalition, July 2002. http://www.arl.org/sparc/IR/ir.html.

Dalrymple, Dana. 2003. "Scientific Knowledge as a Global Public Good: Contributions to Innovation and the Economy." In J. M. Esanu and P. F. Uhlir, eds., *The Role of Scientific and Technical Data and Information in the Public Domain: Proceedings of a Symposium.* Washington, DC: National Academies Press. http://www.nap.edu/books/030908850X/html.

Davenport, Thomas H., and Laurence Prusak. 1998. *Working Knowledge: How Organizations Manage What They Know.* Boston: Harvard University Press.

David, Paul A. 2000. "A Tragedy of the Public Knowledge 'Commons'? Global Science, Intellectual Property, and the Digital Technology Boomerang." Stanford, CA: Stanford Institute for Economic Policy Research, Stanford University. SIEPR Discussion Paper, no. 0002. http://ideas.repec.org/p/wpa/wuwpdc/0502010.html.

Davis, Philip M. 2003. "Tragedy of the Commons Revisited: Librarians, Publishers, Faculty, and the Demise of a Public Resource." *Portal* 3/4 (October): 547–562. http://people.cornell.edu/pages/pmd8/3.4davis.pdf.

Dietz, Tom, Elinor Ostrom, and Paul C. Stern. 2003. "The Struggle to Govern the Commons." *Science* 302 (December 12):1907–1912.

Dinwoodie, Graeme B. 2004. "Private Ordering and the Creation of International Copyright Norms: The Role of Public Structuring." *Journal of Institutional and Theoretical Economics* 160(1):161–180.

Duderstadt, James J., ed. 2001. *Issues for Science and Engineering Researchers in the Digital Age.* Washington, DC: National Academy Press. http://www.nap.edu/html/issues_digital/notice.html.

Duderstadt, James J., Daniel E. Atkins, and Douglas Van Houweling. 2002. *Higher Education in the Digital Age: Technology Issues and Strategies for American Colleges and Universities.* Westport, CT: Praeger.

Evans, R. Sean, and Brad Bogus. 2004. "Federal Government Information Access in the Wake of 9/11." http://jan.ucc.nau.edu/~rse/FederalAccess.htm.

Ewing, John. 2003. "Copyright and Authors." *First Monday* 8/10 (October). http://www.firstmonday.dk/issues/issue8_10/ewing/.

Futrelle, Joe. "Emerging Tools for Building Integrated Scientific Data Resources." National Center for Supercomputing Applications. http://www.ncsa.uiuc.edu/People/futrelle/ppt/NIH0106.ppt.

Gibbs, W. Wayt. 1995. "Lost Science in the Third World." *Scientific American* (August): 92–99.

Gibson, Clark C. 2005. "In Pursuit of Better Policy Outcomes." *Journal of Economic Behavior & Organization* 57(2):227–230.

Gibson, Clark, Margaret McKean, and Elinor Ostrom. 2000. *People and Forests: Communities, Institutions, and Governance.* Cambridge, MA: MIT Press.

Ginsparg, Paul. 2000. "Creating a Global Knowledge Network." *BioMed Central.* http://www.biomedcentral.com/meetings/2000/foi/editorials/ginsparg.

Golich, Vicki L. 1991. "A Multilateral Negotiations Challenge: International Management of the Communications Commons." *Journal of Applied Behavioral Science* 27(2):228–250.

Grazioli, Stefano. 2004. "Where Did They Go Wrong? An Analysis of the Failure of Knowledgeable Internet Consumers to Detect Deception over the Internet." *Group Decision and Negotiation* 13(2):149–172.

Greco, Gian Maria, and Luciano Floridi. 2004. "The Tragedy of the Digital Commons." *Ethics and Information Technology* 6(2):73–81.

Guédon, Jean-Claude. 2001. *In Oldenburg's Long Shadow: Librarians, Research Scientists, Publishers, and the Control of Scientific Publishing.* Washington, DC: Association of Research Libraries. http://www.arl.org/arl/proceedings/138/guedon.html.

Gupta, Alok, Dale O. Stahl, and Andrew B. Whinston 1995. "The Internet: A Future Tragedy of the Commons." Presented at the Conference on Interoperability and the Economics of Information Infrastructure, Rosslyn, Virginia, July 6–7, 1995. http://cism.mccombs.utexas.edu/alok/wash_pap/wash_pap.html.

Harboe-Ree, Cathrine, Michele Sabto, and Andrew Treloar. 2003. "The Library as Digitorium: New Modes of Information Creation, Distribution and Access." http://eprint.monash.edu.au/archive/00000018/.

Hardin, Garrett. 1968. "The Tragedy of the Commons" *Science* 162:1243–1248.

Harnad, Stevan. 2001. "The Self-Archiving Initiative: Freeing the Refereed Research Literature Online." *Nature* 410 (April 26):1024–1025. http://www.ecs.soton.ac.uk/~harnad/Tp/nature4.htm.

Harnad, Stevan. 2003a. "Publish or Perish: Self-Archive to Flourish." In the American Scientist Open Access Forum. http://www.ecs.soton.ac.uk/~harnad/Hypermail/Amsci/2838.html.

Harnad, Stevan. 2003b. "For Whom the Gate Tolls? How and Why to Free the Refereed Research Literature Online through Author/Institution Self-Archiving, Now." http://www.ecs.soton.ac.uk/~harnad/Tp/resolution.htm#1.4.

Harnad, Stevan. 2005. "The Implementation of the Berlin Declaration on Open Access." *D-Lib Magazine* 11(3). http://www.dlib.org/dlib/march05/harnad/03harnad.html.

Harnad, Stevan, and Tim Brody. 2004. "Comparing the Impact of Open Access (OA) vs. Non-OA Articles in the Same Journals." *D-Lib Magazine* 10(6). http://www.dlib.org/dlib/june04/harnad/06harnad.html.

Harnad, Stevan, Les Carr, Tim Brody, and Charles Oppenheim. 2003. "Mandated Online RAE CVs Linked to University Eprint Archives." *Ariadne*, issue 35. http://www.ariadne.ac.uk/issue35/harnad/.

Heikkila, Tanya, and Kimberley R. Isett. 2004. "Modeling Operational Decision Making in Public Organizations: An Integration of Two Institutional Theories." *American Review of Public Administration* 34(1):3–19.

Heller, Michael A. 1998. "The Tragedy of the Anticommons: Property in the Transition from Marx to Markets." *Harvard Law Review* 111(3):622–688.

Hess, Charlotte. 1995. "The Virtual CPR: The Internet as a Local and Global Common Pool Resource." Presented at "Reinventing the Commons," the Fifth Annual Conference of the International Association for the Study of Common Property, Bodø, Norway, May 24–28, 1995.

Hess, Charlotte. 2005. "A Resource Guide for Authors: Open Access, Copyright, and the Digital Commons." *Common Property Resource Digest* 72 (March): 1–8. http://www.indiana.edu/~iascp/E-CPR/cpr72.pdf.

Hess, Charlotte, and Elinor Ostrom. 2003. "Ideas, Artifacts, and Facilities: Information as a Common-Pool Resource." *Law and Contemporary Problems* 66(1–2):111–146. http://www.law.duke.edu/journals/66LCPHess.

Hitchcock, Steve, Tim Brody, C. Gutteridge, Les Carr, and Stevan Harnad 2003. "The Impact of OAI-Based Search on Access to Research Journal Papers." *Serials* 16(3):255–260. http://opcit.eprints.org/serials-short/serials11.html.

Holman, JoAnne. 1997. "An Information Commons: Protection for Free Expression in the New Information Environment." Doctoral dissertation, Indiana University.

Huberman, Bernardo A., and Rajan M. Lukose. 1997. "Social Dilemmas and Internet Congestion." *Science* 277 (July 25): 535–537.

Ianella, Renato. 2001. "Digital Rights Management (DRM) Architectures." *D-Lib Magazine* 7(6). http://www.dlib.org/dlib/june01/iannella/06iannella.html.

Imperial, Mark, and Tracy Yandle 2005. "Taking Institutions Seriously: Using the IAD Framework to Analyze Fisheries Policy." *Society and Natural Resources* 18(6):493–509.

Kahle, Brewster, Rock Prelinger, and Mary E. Jackson. 2001. "Public Access to Digital Material." *D-Lib Magazine* 7(4). http://www.dlib.org/dlib/october01/kahle/10kahle.html.

Kirsop, Barbara. 2004. "Impact of OA on Science in Developing Countries (including a report on the recent World Summit on the Information Society (WSIS) meeting)" (Presentation slides). Presented at "National Policies on Open Access (OA) Provision for University Research Output: An International Meeting," University of Southampton, Southampton, UK, February 19, 2004. http://opcit.eprints.org/feb19oa/kirsop-dc.ppt.

Kollock, Peter, and Marc Smith. 1995. "Managing the Virtual Commons: Cooperation and Conflict in Computer Communities." In Susan Herring, ed., *Computer-Mediated Communication*. Amsterdam: John Benjamins.

Kranich, Nancy. 2003. "Libraries: The Information Commons of Civil Society." In D. Schuler, ed., *Shaping the Network Society*. Cambridge, MA: MIT Press. http://dlc.dlib.indiana.edu/documents/dir0/00/00/09/75/index.html.

Lawrence, Steve. 2001. "Online or Invisible." *Nature* 411(6837):521. http://www.neci.nec.com/~lawrence/papers/online-nature01/.

Lee, Edward. 2003. "The Public's Domain: The Evolution of Legal Restraints on the Government's Power to Control Public Access through Secrecy or Intellectual Property." *Hastings Law Journal* 55:94–209.

Lessig, Lawrence. 1999. "Code and the Commons." Keynote Address at the Conference on Media Convergence, Fordham University Law School, February 9, 1999. http://cyber.law.harvard.edu/works/lessig/fordham.pdf.

Lessig, Lawrence. 2003. "The Creative Commons." *Florida Law Review* 55(3):763–778.

Levin, Simon. 1999. *Fragile Dominion: Complexity and the Commons*. Reading, MA: Perseus Books.

Libecap, Gary D. 1989. *Contracting for Property Rights*. New York: Cambridge University Press.

Litman, Jessica. 2001. *Digital Copyright: Protecting Intellectual Property on the Internet*. Amherst, NY: Prometheus Books.

Lougee, Wendy Pradt. 2002. *Diffuse Libraries: Emergent Roles for the Research Library in the Digital Age*. Perspectives on the Evolving Library. Washington, DC: Council on Library and Information Resources. http://www.clir.org/pubs/reports/pub108/contents.html.

Lutzker, Arnold. 1999. "What the DMCA and the Copyright Term Extension Act Mean to the Library Community: Primer." http://www.ala.org/washoff/primer.html.

Lynch, Clifford. 2003. "Institutional Repositories: Essential Infrastructure for Scholarship in the Digital Age." *ARL Bimonthly Report* 226. http://www.arl.org/newsltr/226/ir.html.

Madison, Michael J. 2000. "Complexity and Copyright in Contradiction." *Cardozo Arts and Entertainment Law Journal* 18:125–174.

Madison, Michael J. 2003. "Reconstructing the Software License." *Loyola University Chicago Law Journal* 35 (fall): 275–340.

McCord, Alan. 2003. "Institutional Repositories: Enhancing Teaching, Learning, and Research." EDUCAUSE Evolving Technologies Committee. http://www.educause.edu/ir/library/pdf/DEC0303.pdf.

Mele, Christopher. 2003. "Cyberspace and Disadvantaged Communities: The Internet as a Tool for Collective Action." In M. A. Smith and P. Kollock, eds., *Communities in Cyberspace*. New York: Routledge.

Mendelson, Laura L. 2003. "Privatizing Knowledge: The Demise of Fair Use and the Public University." *Albany Law Journal of Science and Technology* 13: 593–612.

Merges, Robert P. 1996. "Property Rights Theory and the Commons: The Case of Scientific Research." *Social Philosophy and Policy* 13(2):145–167.

Moran, Emilio, and Elinor Ostrom, eds. 2005. *Seeing the Forest and the Trees: Human-Environment Interactions in Forest Ecosystems*. Cambridge, MA: MIT Press.

Murali, N. S., H. R. Murali, P. Auethavekiat, P. J. Erwin, J. N. Mandrekar, N. J. Manek, and A. K. Ghosh. 2004. "Impact of FUTON and NAA Bias on Visibility of Research." *Mayo Clinic Proceedings*, 79/8 (August): 1001–1006. http://www.mayoclinicproceedings.com/inside.asp?AID=611&UID.

National Research Council. 2002. *The Drama of the Commons*. Committee on the Human Dimensions of Global Change, ed. Elinor Ostrom, Tom Dietz, Nives

Dolšak, Paul Stern, Susan Stonich, and Elke Weber. Washington, DC: National Academy Press. http://www.nap.edu/catalog/10287.html.

Noonan, Douglas S. 1998. "Internet Decentralization, Feedback, and Self-Organization." In J. A. Baden and D. S. Noonan, eds., *Managing the Commons*. Bloomington: Indiana University Press.

Oakerson, Ronald J. 1978. "The Erosion of Public Highways: A Policy Analysis of the Eastern Kentucky Coal-Haul Road Problem." Doctoral dissertation, Department of Political Science, Indiana University. http://dlc.dlib.indiana.edu/documents/dir0/00/00/07/33/index.html.

Oakerson, Ronald J. 1992. "Analyzing the Commons: A Framework." In D. Bromley et al., eds., *Making the Commons Work: Theory, Practice, and Policy.* San Francisco: ICS Press.

Oakerson, Ronald J. 1993. "Reciprocity: A Bottom-Up View of Political Development." In V. Ostrom, D. Feeny, and H. Picht, eds., *Rethinking Institutional Analysis and Development: Issues, Alternatives, and Choices.* San Francisco: ICS Press.

Oakerson, Ronald J., and S. Tjip Walker. 1995. "Analyzing Policy Reform and Reforming Policy Analysis: An Institutionalist Approach." In D. Brinkerhoff, ed., *Policy Analysis Concepts and Methods: An Institutional and Implementation Focus.* Greenwich, CT: JAI Press.

Odlyzko, Andrew. 2002. "The Rapid Evolution of Scholarly Communication." *Learned Publishing* 15/1 (January): 7–19. http://www.catchword.com/alpsp/09531513/v15n1/contp1-1.htm.

Open Citation Project. 2005. "The Effect of Open Access and Downloads ('Hits') on Citation Impact: A Bibliography of Studies." http://opcit.eprints.org/oacitation-biblio.html#harnad-brody04a.

Ostrom, Elinor. 1985. "Formulating the Elements of Institutional Analysis." Workshop in Political Theory and Policy Analysis, Indiana University, Bloomington. Working Paper, no. W85-15. http://dlc.dlib.indiana.edu/archive/00000738/.

Ostrom, Elinor. 1990. *Governing the Commons: The Evolution of Institutions for Collective Action.* New York: Cambridge University Press.

Ostrom, Elinor. 1998. "A Behavioral Approach to the Rational Choice Theory of Collective Action." *American Political Science Review* 92(1):1–22.

Ostrom, Elinor. 2005. *Understanding Institutional Diversity.* Princeton, NJ: Princeton University Press.

Ostrom, Elinor, Joanna Burger, Christopher Field, Richard B. Norgaard, and David Policansky. 1999. "Revisiting the Commons: Local Lessons, Global Challenges." *Science* 284(5412):278–282. http://www.sciencemag.org/cgi/content/full/284/5412/278.

Ostrom, Elinor, Roy Gardner, and James M. Walker, eds. 1994. *Rules, Games, and Common-Pool Resources.* Ann Arbor: University of Michigan Press.

Ostrom, Elinor, Larry Schroeder, and Susan Wynne. 1993. *Institutional Incentives and Sustainable Development: Infrastructure Politics in Perspective.* Boulder, CO: Westview Press.

Ostrom, Vincent. 1969. "Organization." Workshop in Political Theory and Policy Analysis, Indiana University, Bloomington. Working Paper, no. W69-2. http://dlc.dlib.Indiana.edu/documents/dir0/00/00/09/45/index.html.

Ostrom, Vincent. 1973. *The Intellectual Crisis in American Public Administration.* Tuscaloosa: University of Alabama Press.

Ostrom, Vincent. 1983. "Configurations of Relationships in Human Societies." Workshop in Political Theory and Policy Analysis, Indiana University, Bloomington. Working Paper, no. W83-21. http://dlc.dlib.indiana.edu/archive/00000115/.

Ostrom, Vincent. 1997. *The Meaning of Democracy and the Vulnerability of Democracies: A Response to Tocqueville's Challenge.* Ann Arbor: University of Michigan Press.

Ostrom, Vincent, and Elinor Ostrom. 1965. "A Behavioral Approach to the Study of Intergovernmental Relations." *The Annals of the American Academy of Political and Social Science* 359:137–146.

Polski, Margaret M. 2003. *The Invisible Hands of U.S. Commercial Banking Reform: Private Action and Public Guarantees.* Boston: Kluwer Academic.

Polski, Margaret M., and Elinor Ostrom. 1998. "An Institutional Framework for Policy Analysis and Design." Workshop in Political Theory and Policy Analysis, Indiana University, Bloomington. Working Paper, no. W98-27.

Poteete, Amy R., and David Welch 2004. "Institutional Development in the Face of Complexity: Developing Rules for Managing Forest Resources." *Human Ecology* 32(3):279–311.

Pringle, J. 2004. Do Open Access Journals Have Impact? *Nature* (Web Focus). http://www.nature.com/nature/focus/accessdebate/19.html.

Putnam, Robert D. 2000. *Bowling Alone: The Collapse and Revival of American Community.* New York: Simon and Schuster.

Reese, R. Anthony. 1995. "Reflections on the Intellectual Commons: Two Perspectives on Copyright Duration and Reversion." *Stanford Law Review* 47(4):707–747.

Rheingold, Howard. 2002. *Smart Mobs, The Next Social Revolution: Transforming Cultures and Communities in the Age of Instant Access.* Cambridge, MA: Basic Books.

Richardson, Richard C. 2004. *A Conceptual Framework for Comparative Studies of Higher Education Policy.* New York: Alliance for International Higher Education Policy Studies (AIHEPS). www.nyu.edu/iesp/aiheps/drafts/092004Draft.pdf.

Samuelson, Pamela. 2003a. "Digital Rights Management {and, or, vs.} the Law." *Communications of the ACM* 46/4 (April): 41–55.

Samuelson, Pamela. 2003b. "Mapping the Digital Public Domain: Threats and Opportunities." *Law and Contemporary Problems* 66(1–2):147–171. http://www.law.duke.edu/journals/66LCPSamuelson.

Savenije, Bas. 2004. "The SPARC Initiative: A Catalyst for Change." Presented at the "The Digital Library and e-Publishing for Science, Technology and Medicine," TICER, Geneva, June 15, 2004. http://www.library.uu.nl/staff/savenije/publicaties/ticer2004.htm.

Schlager, Edella. 1994. "Fishers' Institutional Responses to Common-Pool Resource Dilemmas." In E. Ostrom, R. Gardner, and J. Walker, eds. *Rules, Games, and Common-Pool Resources.* Ann Arbor: University of Michigan Press.

Schlager, Edella, and Elinor Ostrom. 1992. "Property Rights Regimes and Natural Resources: A Conceptual Analysis." *Land Economics* 68(3):249–262.

Sexton, John. 2003. "The Role of Faculty in the Commons Enterprise University." Presented on the Occasion of the First Meeting of the Trustees Council on the Future of New York University, June 12, 2003. http://www.nyu.edu/president/faculty.enterprise/faculty-enterprise.pdf.

Shiva, Vandana. 1997. *Biopiracy: The Plunder of Nature and Knowledge.* Boston: South End Press.

Shulenburger, David E. 1999. "Moving with Dispatch to Resolve the Scholarly Communication Crisis: From Here to NEAR." *ARL Newsletter,* issue 202 (February). http://www.arl.org/arl/proceedings/133/shulenburger.html.

Shulenburger, David E. 2001. "Principles for a New System of Publishing for Science." In *Proceedings of the Second UCSU/UNESCO International Conference on Electronic Publishing in Science, Paris, February 20–23, 2001.* http://eos.wdcb.rssi.ru/eps2/eps02019/eps02019.pdf.

Smith, A. T., and M. Eysenck. 2002. *The Correlation between RAE Ratings and Citation Counts in Psychology.* Technical Report, Psychology, University of London, Royal Holloway. http://cogprints.org/2749/.

Smith, P. 2001. "Indigenous Peoples and Forest Management in Canada." In T. J. Rolfe, ed., *The Nature and Culture of Forests: Implications of Diversity for Sustainability, Trade and Certification.* Vancouver: Institute for European Studies, University of British Columbia.

Suber, Peter. 2002. "Open Access to the Scientific Journal Literature." *Journal of Biology* 1/1 (June): 3. http://www.earlham.edu/~peters/writing/jbiol.htm.

Swan, Alma, and Sheridan Brown. 2005. "Open Access Self-Archiving: An Author Study." Key Perspectives. http://eprints.ecs.soton.ac.uk/10999/.

Swan, Alma, and Paul Needham. 2005. "Developing a Model for E-prints and Open Access Journal Content in UK Further and Higher Education." *Learned Publishing* 18(1). http://cogprints.org/4120/.

Tabb, Winston. 2004. "Academic Libraries: New Directions, New Partners." Presented at the Seventh International Bielefeld Conference, "Thinking beyond

Digital Libraries: Designing the Information Strategy for the Next Decade," Bielefeld, Germany, February 4, 2004. http://conference.ub.uni-bielefeld.de/proceedings/tabb.pdf.

Testa, J., and M. E. McVeigh. 2004. "The Impact of Open Access Journals: A Citation Study from Thomson ISI." http://www.isinet.com/media/presentrep/acropdf/impact-oa-journals.pdf.

Thorin, Suzanne. 2003. "Global Changes in Scholarly Communication." Presented at e-Workshops on Scholarly Communication in the Digital Era, Feng Chia University, Taichung, Taiwan, August 11–24, 2003. http://www.arl.org/scomm/disciplines/Thorin.pdf.

Turner, Roy M. 1993. "The Tragedy of the Commons and Distributed AI Systems." Presented at the Twelfth International Workshop on Distributed Artificial Intelligence. University of New Hampshire Computer Science Department Technical Report, no. 93-01.

Vaidhyanathan, Siva. 2002. "The Content-Provider Paradox: Universities in the Information Ecosystem." *Academe* 88(5):34–37.

Waters, Donald. 2002. "Good Archives Make Good Scholars: Reflections on Recent Steps Toward the Archiving of Digital Information." Council on Library and Information Resources (CLIR). http://www.clir.org/pubs/reports/pub107/contents.html.

Weber, Steven. 2004. *The Success of Open Source.* Cambridge, MA: Harvard University Press.

Young, Oran R. 1996. "Rights, Rules, and Resources in International Society." In S. S. Hanna, C. Folke, and K.-G. Maler, eds., *Rights to Nature: Ecological, Economic, Cultural, and Political Principles of Institutions for the Environment.* Washington, DC: Island Press.

II

Protecting the Knowledge Commons

4

Countering Enclosure: Reclaiming the Knowledge Commons

Nancy Kranich

For centuries, scholars, students, and the general public have relied on libraries to serve as their knowledge commons—a commons where they could share ideas and "promote the Progress of Science and useful Arts."[1] For scholarship to flourish, researchers have always needed free and open access to ideas. In today's digital age, this means access to knowledge and information online. In the early days of the Internet, new technologies promised exactly that—abundant open access to an infinite array of resources available anywhere, anytime. By the dawn of the twenty-first century, new technologies transformed the way students learn, faculty members teach, scholars inquire, and librarians deliver research resources. But the same technologies that enable unfettered access also enclose these commonly shared resources, thereby restricting information choices and the free flow of ideas. As a result, many of the scholarly resources formerly available through libraries are now enclosed, unavailable from the commons where they were openly shared in the past.

Librarians, scholars, civil libertarians, and others favoring open access to information and ideas have struggled against enclosure. Despite impressive efforts, they have faced an uphill battle to influence outcomes in Congress, the courts, and beyond. Now, however, they are coming together around the emerging notion of the *knowledge commons*, which offers a new model for stimulating innovation, fostering creativity, and building a movement that envisions information as a shared resource. The knowledge commons offers a way not only of responding to the challenge posed by enclosure, but also of building a fundamental institution for twenty-first century democracy.

In this chapter, I examine the numerous forces enclosing the knowledge commons and threatening the sustainability of scholarly communication. I describe strategies deployed to counter enclosure, many of which are undertaken through the collective action of librarians and scholars working together worldwide. I then consider alternative models for delivering research resources that expand access and participation, as well as the role of research libraries in these efforts. I also discuss the challenges to achieving these new operational modes. In addition, I propose some designs for governance structures, financial models, and advocacy efforts that will help transform the academy into a twenty-first century institution that organizes, safeguards, preserves, and promotes the knowledge assets of the scholarly community. Finally, I suggest research that is needed to advance theory and practice related to the development of sustainable knowledge commons in the digital age.

Enclosing the Scholarly Commons

During the last quarter of the twentieth century, traditional means for acquiring and distributing information began to be transformed. With increased availability of digital content and high-speed telecommunications, industries raced to dominate the burgeoning information marketplace. While news about media monopolies, telecommunications deregulation, and the dot-com boom played in prime time, a less visible transformation was changing dissemination modes for scholarly information. Government information was privatized and classified, journal publishers merged, and copyright laws were modified in response to corporate pressure and shifts in policy discourse, the rise of a global economy, adoption of new technologies, and the ease of copying computer files. As a result, even though more people than ever have access to computers and the Internet, much valuable information is being withdrawn, lost, privatized, or restricted from the public, who used to be able to rely on this same information. In effect, this "walled garden" or "enclosure" online creates an increasing threat to democratic principles of informed citizens and academic principles of building on the shoulders of giants. Looks are deceiving: while it appears that we have more, we actually have less and less.

Instead of fulfilling the promises of the information age, large portions of online content have come under government-imposed restrictions or corporate controls like technological protection measures, licensing, and other digital-rights management techniques, all of which impede access to information and limit its use. As a result, much online content is now restricted, wrapped, and packaged—treated as secret or private rather than public or common property. Like medieval times when enclosure of agricultural pasturelands occurred both piecemeal and by general legislative action, no single decision or act is causing today's enclosure of the commons of the mind.[2] Some of the enclosures of the knowledge commons have been rapid, others gradual; many brought on by digitization and electronic distribution; others brought on by economic exigencies. No matter what the reason, a cumulative series of public- and private-sector policies have resulted in less access to the knowledge essential to "promote the Progress of Science and useful Arts."

The story of enclosure of the knowledge commons began unfolding after World War II. In the mid-twentieth century, the government contracted with the defense industry to use computers to develop databases that could manage information efficiently and effectively. One of these companies, Lockheed, launched the "Dialog" system, which indexed educational and medical information along with defense-related data.[3] But after a decade of federal start-up support, the information industry that emerged in the 1960s began urging the government to curtail or eliminate its publication programs, and warned of the dangers of a government monopoly over information. As Paul Zurkowski, the director of the newly formed Information Industry Association (IIA), put it, "Just as surely as the Berlin Wall stands today, in the absence of a concerted industry-wide effort, user choice in information one day soon will be replaced by 'free information' from one source."[4]

Over the next decade, the Reagan administration eliminated scores of government-produced publications, contracting out federal library and information programs (which resulted in the closing of many important federal research libraries), and placing "maximum feasible reliance" on the private sector to disseminate government information.[5] The privatization platform advocated by the IIA and fostered by the Reagan administration was the backdrop for many of the battles to come over ownership and control of information.[6] With the subsequent development of networks, the World Wide Web, and digitized content, government publications in electronic format became big business. But many of those still produced by the government are no longer included in standard catalogs, distributed through the depository library program, or archived or preserved for permanent public access.

In the 1980s, at the same time that government publications were becoming privatized, many scholarly societies inadvertently facilitated enclosure of the commons when they turned over their journal publishing to private firms as a way to contain membership fees and generate income. Prices of scholarly journals soon soared, and publishing conglomerates restricted or enclosed access through expensive licenses that often required bundled or aggregated purchase of titles. Unfortunately, once journal prices outpaced library budgets, the short-term financial gains for the societies were quickly offset by serious losses in terms of access to research results. Initially, price increases were offset by resource-sharing networks that facilitated rapid delivery through interlibrary loan. Later, though, these counterbalancing arrangements were undermined by restrictive licensing agreements.

By the early 1990s, mergers of academic journal publishers left only a few international conglomerates in control, straining already tight higher education budgets by charging as much as $20,000 for subscriptions to journals like *Nuclear Physics, Brain Research*, and *Tetrahedron Letters*, while returning profits as high as 40 percent.[7] According to a study by Bergstrom and Bergstrom, these commercial press charges differed remarkably from the prices charged by nonprofits, typically differing by six times the average per-page price for journals published in the same field.[8] Dependence on the private sector for scholarly journals essentially compels universities to finance research, give it away to for-profit publishers for free, and then buy it back at astronomical prices. Because of the extraordinary increases in journal costs—220 percent since 1986 (compared to an increase in the consumer price index of 64 percent)[9]—research libraries have had no recourse but to cut many of their journal subscriptions. At the same time, the stress on budgets has resulted in far fewer purchases of books, particularly titles of marginal interest or those published oversees, and has strained the revenues of university presses that traditionally relied heavily on libraries for sales.[10]

In addition to steep price increases for some publications, publishers and information aggregators began requiring consumers and libraries to sign restrictive licensing agreements if they were to acquire or use digital materials—both copyrighted and public domain—that are compiled into databases such as *Lexis/Nexis* and *Science Direct*. Some licenses are simply imposed on consumers when they open shrink-wrapped packages or download software from the Internet. Others signed by libraries require complex negotiations prior to electronic purchases, and often force libraries to buy bundled suites of items—many of low interest—if they are to receive titles in greater demand. In addition, these contracts centralize control over the flow of information and eliminate many user protections guaranteed under copyright laws, such as fair-use rights to view, reproduce, and quote limited amounts of copyrighted materials.[11] In addition, licensing contracts prevent libraries from loaning materials to outsiders or archiving and preserving them for posterity. Moreover, because these licensed databases are leased rather than owned, the library has nothing to offer users if it discontinues its subscription, even after it has paid annual fees for many years.[12] When budget cuts come, says Siva Vaidhyanthan, "The library has no trace of what it bought: no record, no archive. It's lost entirely."[13]

At the same time that libraries and scholars are pressed to sustain the production and preservation of knowledge, they are facing the imposition of new "technological protection measures" such as "digital-rights management" techniques that prevent individuals from lawful lending and sharing of creative works, or making "fair use" of them through commentary, parody, scholarship, or news reports. Congress has exacerbated this problem by passing such laws as the 1998 Digital Millennium Copyright Act (DMCA), which imposes criminal penalties for circumventing encryption and other technological protection measures, or even distributing circumvention tools,[14] and the Sonny Bono Copyright Term Extension Act (CTEA), which extends the already lengthy duration of copyright for twenty years, thereby freezing the public domain where works are freely available to distribute, copy, and share.[15] Another DRM tool is the "broadcast flag," a digital mark that signals conditions allowing or disallowing TV programs to be copied. In November 2003, the FCC mandated that all digital television (DTV) equipment recognize and obey a broadcast flag, an approach struck down by the D.C. Circuit Court in May 2005, but revived for consideration by Congress.[16]

Recently, the courts have reinforced these congressional actions that further enclose the public domain and limit the public's rights to use information. In *Eldred v. Ashcroft* in 2003, the Supreme Court rejected a constitutional challenge to the Sonny Bono law, in a decision that seems to give Congress the power to extend the copyright term at will into the future.[17] In 2000, the lower courts shut down the music file-sharing service Napster. Less centralized systems like Grokster and KaZaA took Napster's place, but they too have been sued for "contributory" copyright infringement. In 2003, the recording industry began filing lawsuits against hundreds of people accused of downloading copyright-protected music, even though many were practicing lawful file sharing. The continuing efforts of the companies that make up the "copyright industry" to shut down file-sharing services, prosecute individuals for alleged copyright violations, and otherwise lock up or enclose information have resulted in a highly contested policy terrain for information and culture, and chilled lawful exchange of information.[18]

Perhaps the most hotly contested technological measure used to control information access is the Internet filter. Initially designed for home use, filters are now required for use in schools and public libraries if they are to receive federal grant support under the Children's Internet Protection Act, upheld by the Supreme Court in June 2003. Unfortunately, filters do more harm than good, blocking the use of thousands of legal and useful resources for adults while many banned images remain available. Although Congress mandated filters in order to limit the exposure of minors to child-pornography images or other material considered harmful to minors on the Internet, it requires that public libraries install this restrictive software on all computers, including those used by adults and staff. Even though colleges and universities are not directly affected by this law, many of the affected public libraries, such as those in New York and Boston, serve scholars as well as the general public.[19]

Another type of enclosure was resurrected following the terrorist attacks on September 11, 2001, when the government put in place a series of measures to secure the nation by locking down "sensitive" information. These measures, similar to many imposed during the cold war,[20] greatly expand government secrecy at almost every level, restricting access to critical health and safety information and removing sensitive but unclassified information from websites and scientific journals. Most visible of these measures is the Patriot Act, passed with a variety of controversial surveillance measures just forty five days after the attacks. Among the most contested provisions are the sections that open up confidential library and bookstore records to law enforcement review, chilling free expression and eroding the civil liberties of innocent Americans.[21] Even before this law passed, Attorney General John Ashcroft tried to restrict open access to government information when he sent a memo to government agencies urging them to refuse Freedom of Information Act requests whenever possible, reversing previous policy that denied the release of information only if it would result in foreseeable harm.[22] The government is also withholding more information through the classification process. The U.S. Information Security Oversight Office reported a record 15.6 documents classified in 2004, an increase of 10 percent over 2003 and 50 percent since 2001. Furthermore, the pace of declassification has slowed to a crawl, from a high of 204 million pages in 1997 to just 28 million pages in 2004.[23] Not only are agencies withholding more information because of a perceived national security risk, they are also labeling public data as "sensitive but unclassified," further restricting access. In March 2002, White House Chief of Staff Andrew Card ordered a reexamination of public documents posted on the Internet, resulting in the removal of thousands of items that might aid terrorists.[24] But the terror-related categories used by the government to "take down" sensitive sites are considered so vague by the American Library Association and others that virtually any type of information conceivably related to terrorism can now be withheld from public scrutiny.[25] About the same time but apparently unrelated to national security, President George W. Bush issued Executive Order 13233 preventing public access to presidential records, formerly ordered for release (under the Presidential Records Act of 1987) twelve years after a president leaves office.[26]

Beyond government-produced documents, the Bush administration has reached into the private research arena to restrict public access to sensitive information. In 2003, officials struck a pact with the editors of peer-reviewed scientific journals that relies on the voluntary withdrawal of articles and rejection of future submissions that could compromise national security.[27] Since then, targeted articles have vanished from electronic versions of scientific journals. All of these post-9/11 limitations on public access have prompted policymakers from across the political spectrum, including the chair of the 9/11 Commission, to raise alarms that the government is placing unnecessary restrictions on everyday information essential to ensuring public health and safety.[28] While restrictions are necessary to protect against real threats, scholars, civil libertarians, and librarians caution that a presumption of secrecy rather than disclosure chills the openness necessary to accelerate the progress of technical knowledge and enhance the nation's understanding of potential threats.[29] Such overzealous restrictions on public access to information result in unnecessary enclosure of public data—enclosure that thwarts innovation and creativity by scholars and researchers eager to solve global problems.

Finally, a discussion about the enclosure of information must not overlook differential access to the Internet and other communications tools that exclude many from the benefits of the digital age.[30] No matter whose data is used to describe the "digital divide" between rich and poor, between black and white, between urban and rural, between English- and Spanish-speaking, between old and young, between immigrants and Native Americans, this gap between those with high levels of access and those without persists not only within American communities, but also among colleges and universities. As Larry Irving, former administrator of the National Telecommunications and Information Administration (NTIA), points out, a big issue for colleges is differential levels of technology infrastructure and information resources.[31] He contends that students who attend elite, well-equipped schools often come with greater exposure to and experience with sophisticated information tools, giving them a big head start. In contrast, those at historically black colleges and universities, Hispanic-serving institutions, or the tribal schools are likely to experience older technology, worse infrastructures, and fewer electronic subscriptions than others, paralleling their limited precollege experiences that put them further behind in preparation for the workforce. Even those not falling behind in their ownership or access to computers and telecommunications networks often lack the skills necessary to utilize these resources effectively.[32] Far too many students, faculty, and other citizens are unable to identify, evaluate, and apply information and communicate it efficiently, effectively, and responsibly—essential skills if they are to learn, advance knowledge, and flourish in the workplace as well as carry out the day-to-day activities of citizens in a developed, democratic society.[33]

In the face of these enclosures, librarians along with their colleagues in the scholarly community have struggled to protect access to critical research resources, balance the rights of users and creators, preserve the public domain, and protect public access for all in the digital age. Although they have fought hard to stop enclosure, they face an uphill battle to influence outcomes in a society that emphasizes individual ownership over sharing of resources. In effect, those striving to promote open access remain trapped in political limbo between two opposing solutions—either privatization or government intervention—in order to solve the problem of Hardin's "tragedy of the commons."[34] As Hess and Ostrom point out in their introduction to this book, one of Hardin's mistakes is that he failed to recognize other possibilities such as management by groups under suitable conditions. Rather than getting caught between these battling camps, the scholarly community can change the terms of the discourse about who owns its knowledge by adopting a different paradigm for creating, managing, and preserving knowledge in the digital age.

Reclaiming the Knowledge Commons

Digital age information-sharing initiatives, or *knowledge commons,* allow scholars to reclaim their intellectual assets and fulfill critical roles—the advancement of knowledge, innovation, and creativity through democratic participation in the free and open creation and exchange of ideas. Understanding knowledge as a commons offers a way not only of countering the challenges of access posed by enclosure, but of building a fundamental institution for twenty-first century democracy. Such an institution facilitates not only expression "as diverse as human thought,"[35] but also "peer production"—that is, decentralized production and distribution of information that bypasses the centralized control of more traditional publishing. As the legal scholar Yochai Benkler writes, peer production is "a process by which many individuals, whose actions are coordinated neither by managers nor by price signals in the market, contribute to a joint effort that effectively produces a unit of information or culture."[36] The result is commons-based production of knowledge that, while not challenging individual authorship, fundamentally alters the current system in which commercial producers and passive consumers are the primary players.[37] In effect, peer production allows everyone to be a creator, thereby privileging "more idiosyncratic, unpredictable, and democratic genres of expression."[38]

The notion of knowledge commons also provides expanded opportunities to present a new narrative needed to persuade policymakers and the public of the promises and opportunities of an approach that is neither private nor government—one that employs collective action to ensure equitable access, free expression, and fair use in the digital age. The metaphor of the commons provides a language to explain how the extraordinary public assets invested in the nation's information infrastructure can deliver democratic opportunities for the participation of all citizens. As Bollier explains in this book and elsewhere, focusing on the commons helps people recognize that public participation and freedom of expression are at stake in the battle to control the flow of information and ideas. The commons elevates individuals to a role above mere consumers in the marketplace, shifting the focus to their rights, needs, and responsibilities as citizens.[39]

Countering Enclosure of the Knowledge Commons

No longer able to cope with enclosure of the knowledge commons, scholars, librarians, academic leaders, computer and information scientists, nonprofit publishers, and professional societies have joined forces to reclaim control of their research and scholarship. By creating more competition in, and alternative modes of, publishing, the scholarly community has launched well-managed, self-governed knowledge commons that allow the creators of this content to take back their information assets while promising sustainability and an alternative to the private market or government.[40] The emergence of knowledge commons offers a new model for sharing information, stimulating innovation, fostering creativity, and building a unified movement that envisions the sharing of information with each member of a community.

Working together, librarians and scholars are undertaking novel collaborative efforts among communities with common interests. These new paradigms for creating and disseminating scholarly communication embody many of the characteristics of common property resources or commons. They take advantage of the networked environment to build real and virtual information communities, and they benefit from network externalities, meaning the greater the participation, the more valuable the resource. Cost to these communities is often free or low, ensuring equitable, democratic participation and encouraging interactive discourse and exchange among members. Participants contribute new creations after they gain and benefit from access. Such reciprocity enhances both the human and social capital of these sustainable common goods. Their governance is shared, with rules and norms defined and accepted by constituents. While not every example fully embodies all aspects of commons, they all represent exciting new approaches to populating the marketplace of ideas.

New scholarly communication paradigms, or knowledge commons, have the potential to transform the roles of scholars as well as librarians as they advance teaching, learning, and research in the digital age. As scholars reclaim control over their intellectual assets, their role changes, in the words of Hess and Ostrom, "from passive *appropriator* of information to active *provider* of information by contributing directly into the common pool." Hess and Ostrom also point out that scholars worldwide are capable of "not only sustaining the resource (the intellectual public domain) but building equity of information access and provision, and creating more efficient methods of dissemination through informal, shared protocols, standards, and rules."[41]

According to Peter Levine, what is appealing about such efforts is that they are not controlled by bureaucrats, experts, or profit-seeking companies and they encourage more diverse uses and participation. At the same time, however, they are vulnerable if they fail to adopt appropriate governance structures, rules, and management techniques in order to defend themselves against rival alternatives, influence democratic discourse, and avoid the anarchy that can result in the tragedy of the commons as described by Hardin.[42] That is one of the many reasons why the sponsorship and collaboration of institutions like libraries and universities remain so vital to protecting, promoting, sustaining, and preserving newly emerging knowledge commons.

Open Access to Scholarly Journals

Today, scholarly communities are actively creating new and exciting approaches to managing and disseminating their collective knowledge resources. Foremost among them is the Scholarly Publishing and Academic Resources Coalition (SPARC), founded in 1998 as an alliance of research libraries, universities, and organizations. SPARC, with 300 member institutions in North America, Europe, Asia, and Australia, was formed as a constructive response to market dysfunctions in the scholarly communication system. SPARC helps incubate alternatives to high-priced journals and digital aggregated databases, publicize key issues and initiatives, and raise awareness among the scholarly community about new publishing possibilities.[43] Beyond projects undertaken by SPARC, a number of professional societies in the United States are adopting their own new paradigms for sharing research results. A good example is the American Anthropological Association's (AAA) AnthroSource and AnthroCommons portal, which offers members online access to a vast array of resources in anthropology. In 1999, a group of research librarians urged the Association to develop a portal as a way to control journal costs as well as retain ownership and control of content based on the values and working habits of its members. By 2005, the AAA was making content available through its scholars' portal, designed by and for anthropologists in collaboration with the University of California Press with a grant of $756,000 from the Andrew W. Mellon Foundation. A steering committee is assessing the work habits of members and articulating how to distinguish AnthroSource as a "tool of immense value" for anthropologists.[44]

Another approach to solving enclosure problems with scholarly publishing is open access (OA), which promises to make scholars' ideas more readily available, reduce costs, and slow the commercialization of online scholarly literature. In this book and elsewhere, Peter Suber, publisher of SPARC's *Open Access Newsletter,* illustrates how adopting new standards and structures will not only reduce costs, but also overcome barriers to access such as restrictive copyright laws, licenses, and DRM.[45] To encourage open access, the Soros Foundation's Open Society Institute created the Budapest Open Access Initiative, which provides leadership, software, technical standards, and funding.[46] For scholars, free availability of open-access publications over the Internet has dramatically increased their frequency of citation, ensuring greater impact and faster scientific progress, particularly beyond the borders of North America and Europe.[47]

Among the nearly 2,000 open-access journals now distributed are titles as diverse as *Cell Biology Education, Journal of Arabic and Islamic Studies,* and *The New England Journal of Political Science.*[48] Many of these online open-access journals began publication with funds from foundations, learned societies, and other nonprofits, and with assistance from SPARC and the Open Society Institute. Because the crisis in scholarly publishing hit science early and hard, the scientific community has led the way in designing new modes to exchange research and data. In 1999, BioMed Central became the first scientific publisher to institute an alternative model that offers open-access online journals that are fully peer-reviewed. It recovers costs through author charges, some advertising, and institutional support from universities and foundations.[49] Three years after the introduction of BioMed Central, the Public Library of Science (PLoS), conceived by Nobel Laureate Harold Varmus with his colleagues Michael Eisen and Pat Brown, and funded by a $9 million grant from the Gordon and Betty Moore Foundation, was founded as a nonprofit scientific publishing initiative. Its first open-access journal, *PLoS BIOLOGY,* launched in October 2003, was so popular that it received more than 500,000 hits in a matter of hours, bringing the server down temporarily.[50] Another scientific open-access initiative, BioOne, offers an innovative partnership between scientific societies, academe, and the commercial sector with financial support from close to 900 libraries.[51] In recognition of the value of open access to advance science, expand and speed public access, and preserve research findings, the National Institutes of Health (NIH) now supports a full-text archive of grantees' manuscripts accepted for publication based on research supported with NIH funding, available through the National Library of Medicine's PubMed Central.[52]

Digital Repositories
In October 1999, the library community helped launch the Open Archives Initiative (OAI) in order to provide low-barrier, free access to publicly accessible articles in electronic journals through digital repositories. OAI utilizes new technologies, along with standardized descriptive cataloging (or metadata) to facilitate the efficient dissemination of these scholarly papers.[53] Using the OAI tool, a number of universities, disciplines, and individuals now share scholarship, take a more active and collaborative role in modernizing scholarly publishing, and provide an unprecedented alternative to the limited access dictated by ever-more restrictive copyright legislation, licensing agreements, and technological protection measures utilized by many scholarly journals.[54]

Best known of the new institutional digital repositories is MIT Library's *DSpace*, launched in November 2002 with a $1.8 million grant from Hewlett-Packard as an open-source software platform that enables the capture and description of digital articles, distribution over the web through a search-and-retrieval system, and long-term preservation.[55] Aimed at making MIT faculty members' scholarship more widely available, this project has encouraged the development of a federation of similar systems at many of the world's leading research institutions, such as Érudit at the University of Montreal, eScholarship, sponsored by the University of California's Digital Library, and the Institutional Repository of Utrecht University (DISPUTE).[56] According to Clifford Lynch, executive director of the Coalition for Networked Information, institutional repositories emerged "as a new strategy that allows universities to apply serious, systematic leverage to accelerate changes taking place in scholarship and scholarly communication." This strategy moves universities "beyond their historic relatively passive role of supporting established publishers," and enables them to explore "more transformative new uses of the digital medium."[57]

Like universities, academic disciplines have also created a rich array of digital repositories. The first, the Los Alamos ArXiv.org, begun in 1991 by physicist Paul Ginsparg, provides low-cost access to scientific research papers in physics and related fields before peer review and subsequent publication in journals. This open-access, electronic archive and distribution server, now maintained by the Cornell University Libraries, receives as many as 300,000 queries per day, and includes more than 350,000 papers.[58] By 2003, papers located on the ArXiv.org e-print service were cited about twice as often as astrophysics papers that were not, according to a report presented at the American Astronomical Society (AAS) Publications Board in November 2003.[59] Following the success of ArXiv.org, numerous other disciplines have created repositories, such as EconWPA, the Oxford Text Archive, the PhilSci Archive, the Networked Digital Library of Theses and Dissertations, the Conservation Commons, and the Digital Library of the Commons.[60]

Individual authors are also distributing their own scholarly papers through personal websites or independent repositories. By retaining rights to archival copies of their publications, scholars become part of an international information community that increases access and benefits for everyone. According to Stevan Harnad and other researchers at the RoMEO project at the University of Loughborough in England, 55 percent of journals now officially authorize self-archiving, and most others will permit it on request, demonstrating the dedication of many scholarly publications to promoting rather than blocking research impact. The more that research is read, used, cited, and applied, the greater the impact. As with many forms of information, rewards are reaped from increased reading and use, not from sales.[61]

Digital Libraries
Over the past two decades, librarians have transcended the boundaries of their traditional buildings by delivering their collections of research materials remotely. To assist scholars and transform the academy into a twenty-first century digital enterprise, they have developed digital libraries by converting works to machine-readable form from their own collections, purchasing and linking to electronic resources, establishing standards and best practices for describing and preserving electronic materials, and teaching the skills users need to utilize these new tools. Today, faculty and students can use their library's research materials

anytime and anyplace, and they can receive expert assistance with the click of a mouse.

Daniel Greenstein and Suzanne Thorin describe the decade-long evolution of digital libraries, explaining that much of the early work was grant-funded and experimental, focusing on the development of best practices and standards, as well as on demonstrations showcasing particular collections and services online. Toward the end of the 1990s, these efforts began focusing on users and their preferences and needs. Today, individual institutions have sought partnerships to participate in more collaborative development of digital collections, to create closer ties to the communities most interested in these collections, and to integrate these programs into mainstream library services.[62] Authors and publishers have challenged some of these collaborative partnerships, like Google Print,[63] on the basis of copyright infringement. Amazon, Random House, and Microsoft intend to get around copyright challenges by offering full text access on a "pay-per-view" basis.[64] A different model under development by the Open Content Alliance (OCA), which was established by the Internet Archive with a long list of international library, cultural, technology, and business partners, is structured to provide universal electronic access (through Yahoo) to public-domain or otherwise open-access collections from multiple research institutions for use by scholars, teachers, students, and the public.[65]

Another collaborative digital library effort, the Distributed Open Digital Library (DODL), was begun solely by research libraries in order to provide universal electronic access to public-domain humanities and social science collections from multiple research institutions for use by scholars, teachers, students, and the public.[66] A similar effort in the United Kingdom will extend beyond universities to include some twenty public-sector and other organizations that will form a Common Information Environment Group to serve the information needs of a wider audience of learners.[67] For science, the National Science Foundation (NSF) has worked across the private and nonprofit sectors to develop a collaborative national science digital library (NSDL) of high-quality content and services needed by major communities of learners.[68] One other noteworthy collaborative effort is the Digital Promise Project, proposed to create the Digital Opportunity Investment Trust (DO IT) with proceeds from the auction of the public spectrum, which would fund public- and private-sector partnerships to digitize high-quality content from the archives of our nation's universities, libraries, and museums.[69] All of these private and nonprofit initiatives aim to open up research collections to a broader audience of users.

Community-Based Preservation Efforts

Traditionally, libraries preserved the materials they purchased from publishers in accord with their condition and the needs of users. While they alerted each other about various conservation efforts, they undertook most of their work locally. With licensed online electronic materials, however, they have no local copy to preserve. Their licensed (leased) subscriptions reside with publishers, presenting unusual challenges for permanent public access. In this book, Donald Waters explores key roles and responsibilities that "community-based" stakeholders might assume when preserving digital common-pool resources.[70] He describes two fledgling projects, both funded by the Mellon Foundation, that create trusted third-party agents to store and archive publishers' content. One, called Portico, sets up a new organization to preserve publishers' electronic source files. The other, developed at Stanford University and called LOCKSS for Lots Of Copies Keeps Stuff Safe, relies on the collective action of libraries (eighty so far) working with publishers (more than fifty) to share responsibility for copying and storing journal content, using a common infrastructure for systematic capturing of files. LOCKSS has spawned a variety of related projects, ranging from government-document preservation to archiving of 9/11 websites, which depend on member libraries to take responsibility for preserving copies of titles—with the publisher's permission. Member libraries agree to preserve the titles chosen by other libraries as well, thereby ensuring a sufficient number of copies for safety and spreading the workload among participants.[71] These prototype systems provide opportunities for the library community to work collectively to archive and preserve valuable resources. But to sustain the effort, libraries will need to manage and coordinate their participation carefully as well as develop a viable, sustainable long-term financial plan.

Learning and Information Communities

On campuses around the country, integrated digital learning centers are creating an environment where traditional boundaries blur and many constituent activities flow across old unit divisions. Libraries have established these centers in conjunction with academic colleagues who run information technology services as well as teaching and learning facilities. Some of these spaces are called information commons, where disparate information resources are brought together by librarians and information technology staff. Others are referred to as learning commons, where students come together around shared learning tasks. What distinguishes these centers from the more traditional computer labs located in many university libraries and academic computer facilities is that they aim not to encourage the mastery of information, but to facilitate collaborative learning using all forms of media.[72] The challenge, according to Scott Bennett, is to ensure that these learning commons are "conceptually 'owned' by learners, rather than by librarians or teachers."[73]

Noteworthy are such commons located at the University of Arizona, where the library, the University Teaching Center, and the Center for Computing and Information Technology developed a dramatic shared facility in partnership with other units on campus.[74] A similar collaboration between the Indiana University Libraries and University Information Technology Services offers a "technology and information center" with more than 250 individual and group workstations, reference services and resources, technology consultants, and a multimedia production laboratory. Since opening in September 2003, the library's commons has become a major hub of campus life, raising overall use of the library by 20 percent; the overwhelming success of the facility prompted the adding of 250 more workstations in early 2005.[75] Another example of a learning commons is one designed for first-year students at Indiana University–Purdue University at Indianapolis (IUPUI). These students are enrolling in special seminars or learning communities, led by a collaborative of librarians, faculty, staff, and administrators, who teach critical thinking skills that will enhance their learning experiences.[76] While all of these commons are popular, evaluators have yet to assess their impact and how they will be sustained, governed, and financed over the long term.

Opposing Enclosure

As far back as the 1920s, librarians opposed federal attempts to prohibit importation of materials deemed subversive or obscene. Ever since, the American Library Association (ALA) has provided librarians opportunities to voice their collective concerns about the future of library and information policy in the United States. That voice is heard through federal and state legislative action, promotion of intellectual freedom, and advocacy. Sometimes, the ALA speaks out to protest actions by the federal government to stifle free expression, such as the Patriot Act's chilling effects on library users and communities. Other times, the ALA takes legal action, such as suing to overturn the Communication Decency Act (CDA), the Children's Internet Protection Act, and the FCC's attempt to mandate the broadcast flag. While the librarians do not always prevail, members' communications have influenced outcomes like the modification of the so-called library-records provision of the Patriot Act and the unanimous decisions striking down portions of the CDA and the broadcast flag. The ALA is among several library associations that maintain Washington offices; Association staff and members work tirelessly to protect free expression and promote the free flow of ideas in the digital age. Almost always, these lobbying efforts are collective, involving coalitions and alliances across a broad spectrum of educational, public interest, and other organizations. One such group, the Information Access Alliance, made up of six library groups including the ALA and the Association of Research Libraries (ARL), was formed to promote a new standard for antitrust review of mergers among scholarly and legal publishers.[77] These six library groups have also formed coalitions with others like education, scientific, and civil liberties organizations to influence issues such as access to government information, copyright and fair use, funding, filtering, and antiterrorism legislation. Much of this work to shape policy relies on influencing the court of public opinion as well as educating stakeholders about what is at stake in the battles to protect public access. The recently launched public relations effort called "Create Change," sponsored by ALA's Association of College and Research Libraries (ACRL), the Association of Research Libraries (ARL), and SPARC goes a long way toward telling the story about the crisis in scholarly communication to a wider audience.[78] Also helpful are toolkits like the one ACRL produced on scholarly communication to educate, inform, and support advocacy efforts that work toward changing the scholarly communication system.[79]

Licensing Information Sharing

To encourage open exchange of ideas, authors and artists can take advantage of a set of flexible copyright licenses offered by the Creative Commons. Established in 2001 by Lawrence Lessig, James Boyle (a contributor to this volume), and other cyberlaw and computer experts, these licenses help creators dedicate their works to the public domain or license them as free for public use, with some rights reserved. With support from the Center for the Public Domain, the Creative Commons is now used by millions around the world, increasing the sum of raw source material online, cheaply and easily.[80]

The Role of Research Libraries

New methods for creating and disseminating scholarly information provide extraordinary opportunities to transform research libraries into twenty-first century institutions for collective action and to provide the type of sponsorship and collaboration needed to build and sustain knowledge commons that will thrive in a complex and competitive information marketplace. Actually, this transition began as far back as the mid-twentieth century. Clifford Lynch has cogently summarized the four stages of this transition, beginning in the 1950s with the automation of day-to-day library operations, followed by reference use of computerized databases in the late 1970s, then direct patron access to the Internet in the 1990s, and finally purchase of commercial databases and conversion of collections to digital formats.[81] By automating and then networking their operations, librarians built bridges that connected collections and reference services directly to faculty and students needing context, connectivity, content, and capability to navigate the bewildering sea of information flooding their desktops.

Today, rather than simply supporting the teaching and research of members of the academy, librarians are serving as partners in a common enterprise that relies on their expertise and guidance. Twenty-first century librarians are working together with information/learning communities to enhance the production, availability, and preservation of knowledge; collaborating beyond their facilities to create active, resource-based learning models that encourage critical thinking; and fostering the creation of information communities, both within and outside the library.[82] Along with colleagues throughout the university, librarians foster not just access, but also the creation, exchange, and preservation of ideas among diffuse communities of scholars. Through this transition, libraries are evolving into "institutions of collective action," or commons, in order to ensure the long-term, productive use of scholarly assets.[83]

In this book and in her report titled *Diffuse Libraries*, Wendy Pradt Lougee analyzes the changing role of research libraries in the digital age. As digital efforts have evolved from projects to programs, Lougee contends that research libraries are becoming less hierarchical, relinquishing control to more democratic modes of governance and participation. This changing relationship between libraries, content creators, publishers, and consumers as information becomes more distributed and access more open, has resulted in "a shift from publication as product to publication as process."[84] As information distribution becomes more diffused, libraries become more involved in the process of scholarly communication and in building information communities. This transformation into more engaged, collaborative institutions will transform libraries as creators and not just sustainers of knowledge commons.

No longer are research libraries confined to a specific place or schedule; their resources and staff are now diffused throughout the campus and beyond. In these new roles, libraries must be flatter, more agile organizations that can respond to the changing needs of their institutions. They must organize services around content rather than function-based activities and build teams that combine various types of specialties like subject, cataloging, instruction, and reference expertise that can work directly with user communities. But to succeed with this transition, libraries must reconsider not only their structures, but also the scope and boundaries of their responsibilities.

To engage in the process of scholarly communication, research libraries are embarking on collaborative ventures in new territories that need flexible rules and boundaries, carefully negotiated among a variety of stakeholders, some seeking guidance from the library, and others competing with the library for control. New activities like learning commons and digital repositories raise questions of jurisdiction and priorities. What role will faculty and other academic colleagues play? How will rules be negotiated? Who will determine the scope and effectiveness of their activities? What kinds of reciprocity will be required for sustaining these activities? How will they build the trust of their new colleagues? And what kinds of communication channels will they need to establish and maintain? Ultimately, how will libraries synthesize these disparate collaborative projects into a more integrated, coherent information creation and delivery system?

Transforming Research Libraries into Twenty-First Century Knowledge Commons

Over the centuries, libraries and librarians have played an important role as caretakers of the cultural record and custodians of knowledge commons by applying their extensive experience in managing and disseminating information as well as their principled positions on intellectual freedom, equitable access, diversity, and democratic participation to forge policies and practices that serve the common good. To reclaim and expand that role in an era of enclosure, librarians must conceptualize and articulate the role of libraries as commons—as collective-action institutions that not only protect ideas, but also facilitate their creation, sharing, preservation, and sustainability. Their challenge is to educate scholars, the public, and policymakers about the benefits of open access while they continue to fight against enclosure. And they must engage the larger community of information users and providers in their quest to constitute, develop, and sustain structures designed as alternatives to the prevailing digital marketplace. As James Boyle has suggested in this book, librarians will need to rethink their systems and services as open rather than closed, designed with and for a broad array of potential users, not just those in their immediate communities. Moreover, librarians will need to determine if they will serve as leaders or followers in the chaotic digital world.

What can librarians do to reclaim their pivotal role in building and sustaining knowledge commons? First, librarians must act collectively to solve the multitude of problems facing scholarly communication. They cannot work alone or in a vacuum. They need to extend their networks beyond libraries, including the full spectrum of information creators and users of information resources. Second, they must explore new ways of sharing information by participating in initiatives like open access, digital repositories, and community-based preservation, and by involving stakeholders in the design, creation, and management of these tools. Third, they must shape legislation and participate in policy discourse, promoting the value and benefits of open access and conveying the perils of enclosure. Fourth, they must create their own learning communities to stay abreast of new developments and communicate their implications to the public. To facilitate dialogue and participation, they can utilize innovative collaboration tools like web logs (blogs) and RSS feeds to share ideas and customize information dissemination to colleagues and users.

Governing the Knowledge Commons

As control over the creation, dissemination, and preservation of scholarship becomes more democratic and shared, what governance structures are necessary? Following the framework outlined by Ostrom and Hess in this book and elsewhere, self-governance of these newly emerging commons will require definition of boundaries (which tend to be "fuzzy"), design and enforcement of rules, extension of reciprocity, building of trust and social capital, and delineation of communication channels.[85] With research resources diffused throughout the campus and beyond, their broad scope requires stewardship well beyond the boundaries of the edifices or structures that defined them in the past. The ideas and artifacts resulting from collaborative creation and dissemination of knowledge will need rules that are carefully negotiated by a variety of stakeholders, some relying on facilities like libraries, archives, and scholarly societies for guidance, while others carve out new structures for control.

Collective-action organizations like open-access publishers, digital repositories, and digital libraries must develop democratic governance structures if they are to avoid the tragedy of the commons. This means that they must raise difficult questions like: What is our jurisdiction and what are our priorities? What role will faculty and other academic colleagues play? How will our rules be negotiated? Who will determine the scope and effectiveness of our activities? What kinds of reciprocity will be required for sustaining our activities? How will we build the trust of our new colleagues? And what kinds of channels will we need to establish and maintain communication and facilitate action?

Never before has collaboration been so essential to the successful introduction, development, and widespread utilization of scholarly resources. In the past, librarians and scholars cooperated on many levels. But collaboration means something far more demanding than the cooperative endeavors relied on in the past. It means the development of a common new mission and goals, new organizational structures, more comprehensive planning, additional levels of communication, new kinds of authority structures with dispersed leadership, and shared and mutual control. To transform into more open collaborative organizations, knowledge commons will need new organizational frameworks, with serious commitments by administrators and their parent organizations. In addition, they must broker new relationships, entrepreneurial activities, and communication structures. While these new relationships sound promising, they often face pitfalls, such as conflicting institutional priorities and competition for scarce funding. Furthermore, some universities may not be prepared to retool so as to contribute efficiently and effectively to the development of knowledge commons. Indeed, without a strong commitment to these new paradigms, universities are unlikely to preserve their existing libraries as commons, let alone advance new knowledge commons in order to enhance teaching and learning.

Financing the Knowledge Commons

Developing, sustaining, and governing knowledge commons will also require significant investment in infrastructure and content to pay for start-up and ongoing costs. While scholars may gain more free or low-cost access under these new arrangements, someone must pay to sustain these resources. Moving from an unsustainable subscription-based structure will shift long-standing financial and social relationships. As highlighted throughout this chapter, many emerging knowledge commons are supported by foundations and other grant-making agencies; benefactors like the Mellon Foundation and the Open Society Institute are unlikely to sustain commons indefinitely. At some point, these efforts will need to generate revenues that replace the subscriptions and grants that either previously covered or now cover costs.

In the case of open-access publishing, for example, the burden of production expenses is shifting from purchasers to creators. Such transitions require capital for starters, and then new streams of revenue for sustainability. Rather than charge subscriptions, open-access publishers collect author and/or membership fees. One such publisher, BioMed Central (BMC), began by offering journals to libraries on a flat-fee basis. Now BMC is asking institutions to pay membership renewals based on the estimated number of articles that faculty are likely to generate.[86] Understandably, participating institutions are outraged by this unannounced steep rise in fees. Yet the flat-fee model paid previously removes authors from any sensitivity to the costs of sustaining publications.[87] Given resistance to rising costs, new financial models may fail to solve all the problems they were designed to fix.

Indeed, these new publishing paradigms carry risks and costs for libraries, authors, and publishers alike, along with concerns that they might overlook the importance of peer review and drive commercial publishers out of business. Such institutions as Stanford, MIT, Harvard, Cornell, University of Connecticut, and North Carolina State University are balking at renewing multiyear Reed Elsevier licensing contracts and some are even discouraging faculty from submitting articles to their journals.[88] Commercial publishers like Reed Elsevier are beginning to feel the effects of these actions. Not only do they lose revenues from discontinued library subscriptions, but they also lose credibility with creditors. In the fall of 2003, a securities firm, BNP Paribas, judged the company to "underperform" because its subscription-based access was weak "compared to the newer and more successful article fee-based open-access system."[89]

Beyond coping with rising subscription costs for both open-access and commercial publications, institutions worry about finding additional funds to finance the transition from subscription to a production business model. Low-cost journals and digital archives may be welcome, but they are becoming available at a moment when research libraries face serious budget constraints that limit their ability to pay for long-standing commitments, let alone new ventures. At the same time, universities need to redirect resources if they are to become publishers as well as consumers of their faculty's scholarship, authors need incentives and rewards if they are to migrate toward new publishing ventures that may demand high publication fees, and professional societies and other publishers need new revenue streams that compensate for the loss of commercial revenues. In short, new publishing ventures on or among campuses that involve libraries, academic presses, technology centers, and scholars will need sound business plans and not just grant funds to succeed. And this probably means, as the Committee on Institutional Cooperation (CIC) has recommended, that many of these new efforts to improve scholarly communication must build on interinstitutional relationships already underway.[90]

Advocating for Knowledge Commons

Libraries, universities, professional societies, and scholarly publishers can no longer rely on the old adage: "Build it and they will come." Instead, they must devote scarce resources to projects chosen through careful consideration of user needs. To assess these needs, they must rely on focus groups, surveys, and other evaluation techniques to provide feedback for strategic planning. In addition, they must apply sophisticated packaging, advertising, and promotion techniques to encourage greater awareness of the valuable resources they are working hard to create and sustain on behalf of scholars. After all, competing with Google will remain a big challenge even with the most appealing initiatives.

More importantly, they must tell a compelling story about the value of a new scheme for managing their intellectual assets. Rather than relying solely on an uphill battle to counter enclosure, they must also offer a fresh approach to constructing a fundamental institution for the digital age. This means that they must use language that explains how the extraordinary assets invested in advancing knowledge can reap more benefits for scholarship and society. Legal scholar Carol Rose believes that property arrangements are basically what "people have quite consciously talked themselves into." She stresses that "narratives, stories, and rhetorical devices may be essential in persuading people of that common good."[91] For scholarly communication, a new narrative is needed to persuade librarians, academics, policymakers, and the public of the promises and opportunities of more open access in the digital age. The proponents of new paradigms must capture people's imagination and demonstrate how knowledge commons will transform educational institutions so they can meet the needs of twenty-first century democracy.

To meet the challenge of access to information in the digital age, proponents of knowledge commons need to band together to amplify their voices and extend their reach. Their individual efforts are impressive, but now they must mobilize to create a movement comparable to the environmentalism established in the last two decades of the twentieth century. Boyle considers information an "ecosystem." As such, he recommends creating coalitions of people currently engaged in individual struggles that have little or no sense of the larger context.[92] He is joined by a growing list of practitioners, including librarians, scholars, and self-publishers who recognize the need to identify and mobilize a broad array of individuals, information communities, and organizations concerned with the production and distribution of knowledge and ideas—people often inexperienced at working in concert to promote common concerns and collective action. The people whose voices need amplification range from authors, journalists, artists, musicians, scientists, and scholars to independent and academic publishers, lawyers, librarians, public interest groups, readers, listeners, viewers, and other users of information.

Building powerful coalitions and partnerships will require extensive organizing and fundraising. To stop enclosure of the knowledge commons as well as promote public access, those committed to sharing information must first find each other and then look far beyond the normal sources for allies. They must find common threads to tie various constituents together and to recognize that allies on some issues may become enemies on others—for example, publishers and librarians, who coalesce in support of First Amendment causes but approach copyright and fair use very differently. Before carving out new territory for producing and sharing intellectual assets, they must engage many within the academy who still remain unaware of the crisis and their role in solving it.

Champions of collective action must also articulate the positive economic value of the commons. Good examples and best practices abound, demonstrating that commons are a viable, effective alternative to creating and delivering information resources. Unless these models are documented and shared widely, however, stories will not resonate with policymakers, the media, and the general public.

If knowledge commons are to defend themselves against rival alternatives as suggested by Levine, the scholarly community will need to continue to navigate through the highly contested information policy arena of copyright, distance education, next-generation Internet, and intellectual freedom issues. On campus, librarians and others must educate administrators, faculty, and students about their rights and responsibilities, and they must advise legal staff about the dangers of enclosure presented by restrictive license agreements, challenges to fair use, and other policies that affect both creators and users of resources. All must work together to articulate what is at stake and shape policy on campus, at the federal level, and beyond.

Research Opportunities

New models for creating and distributing information are proliferating. What is needed now is a survey documenting the impact and diffusion of these efforts so we can get an overview of the success and extent of adoption nationally. The scholarly community also needs a better sense of how these efforts are making a difference and why they are important to the future of the academic enterprise. As knowledge commons evolve, we need to learn how to avoid the tragedy of the commons by studying viable governance, management, and financial structures. We need to conduct case studies of mature projects like arXiv.org so we can learn best practices, apply them to other projects, and inform the discourse about commons. Likewise, we need to monitor and evaluate the impact of such endeavors as open-access publishing and digital repositories. Do these efforts improve access and lower costs? Will scholars participate in them? Will tenure committees consider such publications worthy? We need to gain insight into the characteristics of both successful and failing efforts, and determine how good projects can survive and thrive over the long term. Moreover, we need to explore whether open public access actually contributes to the "Progress of Science and useful Arts," to reiterate the phrase from the copyright clause in the U.S. Constitution. Finally, we need to construct narratives that tell stories that we have learned about open access to information and the negative effects of enclosure.

Conclusion

New technologies offer unprecedented possibilities for human creativity, global communication, and access to information. Yet digital technology also invites new forms of information enclosure. In the last decade, information providers have deployed new methods of control that undermine the public's traditional rights to use, share, and reproduce information and ideas. These technologies, combined with dramatic consolidation in the media industry and new laws that increase control over intellectual products, threaten to undermine the political discourse, scientific inquiry, free speech, and creativity needed for a healthy democracy.

At stake in today's debates about the future of information access is not only the availability and affordability of information, but also the very basis on which citizens' and scholars' information needs are met. The new information infrastructure must preserve traditional commons institutions like schools and universities, libraries, nonprofits, and government organizations, as well as buoy the development of more contemporary information communities committed to promoting and fulfilling the future resource-sharing needs of scholars, creators, students, and citizens. To counter enclosure of the commons, librarians, scholars, and other public interest advocates have sought alternative ways to expand access to the wealth of resources over the Internet, and have begun to build online communities, or "knowledge commons," for producing and sharing scholarship, information, creative works, and democratic discussion.

If everyone is to be ensured free and open access to information, proponents of commons must change the terms of the debate by focusing on what is needed, not just on what is unacceptable. They must articulate why knowledge commons advance scholarship, civil society, and democratic participation. They must inform themselves about a broad array of complex issues and the various perspectives held by players on all sides. Moreover, they must undertake research that demonstrates the contributions of open public access to the advancement of knowledge, map public opinion, and compile narratives about the positive effects of open access to information and the negative impact of enclosure.

Finally, it is important to recognize that building information commons does not mean a total rejection of the for-profit media industry. As Frederick Emrich, the editor of the info-commons.org website, points out: "Commercial uses of information serve a vital role in ensuring that new ideas are produced. So long as commercial uses of information are balanced with effective public access to information, there is good reason to see the information commons and information commerce as mutually beneficial aspects of one system of managing ideas."[93] In the twenty-first century, no single model for creating and distributing information is likely to emerge. But knowledge commons will provide useful alternatives that ensure a meaningful role for users and creators alike.

Designers of knowledge commons are making significant strides in demonstrating and promoting new paradigms for information access. Having proven the concept, they must bring these disparate projects together to construct a fundamental new research institution for the digital age. Collaborative partnerships are broadening the reach of these efforts while showcasing the value of each endeavor. Although the challenges are great, the potential for success keeps growing. With so many new projects unfolding, the scholarly community is well positioned to reclaim their intellectual assets by nurturing and sustaining technologically sophisticated knowledge commons. Otherwise, many scholars, students, and others will be left behind in the information age.

Notes

1. U.S. Copyright Clause, U.S. Constitution, Article 1, Section 8, Clause A.

2. See J. A. Yelling, *Common Field and Enclosure in England 1450–1850* (Hamden, CT: Archon Books, 1977); Michael Turner, *Enclosures in Britain 1750–1830* (London: Macmillan, 1984); Harriett Bradley, *The Enclosures in England: An Economic Reconstruction* (New York: Columbia University Press, 1918).

3. Roger Summit, "Reflections on the Beginnings of Dialog: The Birth of Online Information Access," *Dialog Corporation History* (June 2002), http://support .dialog.com/publications/chronolog/200206/1020628.shtml; see also Christine Borgman, *From Gutenberg to the Global Information Infrastructure: Access to Information in the Networked World* (Cambridge, MA: MIT Press, 2000).

4. Quoted in John N. Berry III, "Free Information and the IIA," *Library Journal* 100/8 (April 15, 1975): 795.

5. The privatization policy was promulgated by the Office of Management and Budget through its Circular A-130, "The Management of Federal Information Resources," 50 *Federal Register* 52730–52751 (December 24, 1985). When the policy was revised in 1993, it eliminated the phrase "maximum feasible reliance on the private sector" (Office of Management and Budget, "The Management of Federal Information Resources, Circular A-130 Revised," 58 *Federal Register* 36070–36086 (July 2, 1993).

6. Peter Hernon and Charles McClure, *Federal Information Policies in the 1980s: Conflicts and Issues* (Norwood, NJ: Ablex, 1987). See also Charles McClure, Peter Hernon, and Harold Reylea, eds., *United States Government Information Policies: Views and Perspectives* (Norwood, NJ: Ablex, 1989); Toby McIntosh, *Federal Information in the Electronic Age: Policy Issues for the 1990s* (Washington, DC: Bureau of National Affairs, 1990).

7. Scott J. Turner, "Library Sees Red over Rising Journal Prices: Dangling Red Tags Are Marking Periodicals That Have One-Year Subscription Rates of $1,000 or Higher," *George Street Journal* 24 (March 10–16, 2000), http:// www.brown.edu/Administration/George_Street_Journal/vol24/24GSJ19c.html; Lee Van Orsdel and Kathleen Born, "Big Chill on the Big Deal?", *Library Journal,* 128/7 (April 15, 2003): 51–56, http://www.libraryjournal.com/ index.asp?layout=article&articleid=CA289187&publication=libraryjournal.

8. Carl T. Bergstrom and Theodore C. Bergstrom, "The Costs and Benefits of Library Site Licenses to Academic Journals," *Proceedings of the National Academy of Sciences (PNAS)* 101/3 (January 20, 2004): 897.

9. Association of College and Research Libraries, Association of Research Libraries, SPARC, *Create Change: New Systems of Scholarly Communication* (Washington, DC: Association of Research Libraries, October 2003), http://www.arl.org/create/resources/CreateChange2003.pdf.

10. For more details about the impact of these developments, see Brian Hawkins and Patricia Battin, *The Mirage of Continuity: Reconfiguring Academic Information Resources for the 21st Century* (Washington, DC: Council on Library and Information Resources and the Association of American Universities, 1998); Suzanne Thorin, "Global Changes in Scholarly Communication," paper presented at e-Workshops on Scholarly Communication in the Digital Era, Feng Chia University, Taichung, Taiwan, August 11–24, 2003, http://www.arl.org/ scomm/Thorin.pdf; Information Access Alliance, *Publisher Mergers Threaten Access to Scientific, Medical, and Research Information* (Washington, DC: Information Access Alliance, 2003), http://www.arl.org/scomm/mergers/background _info.pdf.

11. Ann Okerson, "The LIBLICENSE Project and How it Grows," *D-Lib Magazine*, 5/9 (September 1999), http://www.dlib.org/dlib/september99/okerson/09okerson.html; Yale University Libraries and the Council on Library Resources, *Liblicense*, website for resources about library licenses, http://www.library.yale.edu/~llicense/index.shtml; AFFECT: Americans for Fair Electronic Commerce Transactions, "Why We Oppose UCITA," http://www.affect.ucita.com/why.html.

12. Brian Kahin, "Scholarly Communication in the Networked Environment: Issues of Principle, Policy, and Practice," in Robin P. Peek and Gregory B. Newby, *Scholarly Publishing: The Electronic Frontier* (Cambridge, MA: MIT Press, 1996), 277–298.

13. Siva Vaidhyanathan, *The Anarchist in the Library* (New York: Basic Books, 2004), 120.

14. Digital Millennium Copyright Act, 12 U.S. Code §1201.

15. Sonny Bono Copyright Term Extension Act, 17 U.S. Code §§301–304. The public domain consists of works whose copyrights have expired as well as works that, like government resources, were never covered by copyright.

16. "Report and Order and Further Notice of Proposed Rulemaking," *In the Matter of: Digital Broadcast Content Protection*, MB Docket 02-230, November 4, 2003, http://hraunfoss.fcc.gov/edocs_public/attachmatch/FCC-03-273A1.pdf. In March 2004, the American Library Association and Public Knowledge filed suit challenging the FCC's authority to issue these regulations. See *American Library Association v. FCC*, No. 04-1037 (D.C. Cir., filed March 3, 2004). The U.S. Appeals Court for the D.C. Circuit ruled that the Federal Communications Commission had exceeded its authority in establishing the so-called broadcast flag, D.C. Cir., May 6, 2005. See also Center for Democracy and Technology, *Implications of the Broadcast Flag: A Public Interest Primer (version 2.0)* (Washington, DC: Center for Democracy and Technology, December 2003), http://www.cdt.org/copyright/031216broadcastflag.pdf; Public Knowledge, *Broadcast Flag*, http://www.publicknowledge.org/issues/current-issues/issue-broadcast-flag/.

17. *Eldred v. Ashcroft*, 123 S.Ct. 769 (2003), http://www.supremecourtus.gov/opinions/02pdf/01-618.pdf. Documents filed in the case are available at http://eldred.cc/; for additional background, see Marjorie Heins, *"The Progress of Science and Useful Arts": Why Copyright Today Threatens Intellectual Freedom* (New York: Free Expression Policy Project, 2003), 15–23; American Library Association, *Eldred v. Ashcroft* website, http://www.ala.org/Template.cfm?Section=copyrightcases&Template=/ContentManagement/ContentDisplay.cfm&ContentID=20264; Open Law, *Eldred v. Ashcroft* website, http://cyber.law.harvard.edu/openlaw/eldredvashcroft/; "Eldred v. Ashcroft," *Wikipedia*, http://en.wikipedia.org/wiki/Eldred_v._Reno.

18. *A & M Records v. Napster*, 239 F.3d 1004 (9th Cir. 2001); *Metro-Goldwyn-Mayer Studios v. Grokster*, U.S. Supreme Court, No. 04-480, *Syllabus and Opinion of the Court, June 27, 2005*. For an overview of these cases and attempts

to stop file-sharing, see Heins, "*The Progress of Science and Useful Arts*," 35–41.

19. For more information about filters and CIPA, see U.S. Supreme Court, *United States et al. v. American Library Association, et al., No. 02-361, Syllabus and Opinion of the Court*, 2003, http://www.supremecourtus.gov/opinions/02pdf/02-361.pdf; National Research Council, *Tools and Strategies for Protecting Kids from Pornography and Their Applicability to Other Inappropriate Internet Content* (Washington, DC: National Research Council, 2001), http://books.nap.edu/html/youth_internet/; U.S. Children's Online Protection Act Commission, *Final Report of the COPA Commission Presented to Congress, October 20, 2000* (Washington, DC: Government Printing Office, 2000), http://www.copacommission.org/report/; U.S. District Court for Eastern Pennsylvania, *American Library Association v. the United States et al. No. 01-1303: Opinion of the Court*, Philadelphia, May 31, 2002, http://www.ala.org/ala/washoff/WOissues/civilliberties/cipaweb/legalhistory/internet.pdf; American Library Association, "CIPA," website, http://www.ala.org/cipa.

20. Nancy Kranich, "Government Information: Less Is Dangerous," *Thought and Action: The NEA Higher Education Journal* 4 (spring 1988): 37–48.

21. Nancy Kranich, *The Impact of the USA PATRIOT Act on Free Expression* (New York: Free Expression Policy Project, May 2003), http://www.fepproject.org/commentaries/patriotact.html; "Update" (August 27, 2003), http://www.fepproject.org/commentaries/patriotactupdate.html.

22. National Security Archive, *The Ashcroft Memo: "Drastic" Change or "More Thunder Than Lightning"*? (Washington, DC: National Security Archive, 2003), http://www.gwu.edu/%7Ensarchiv/NSAEBB/NSAEBB84/index.html.

23. Information Security Oversight Office, *Report to the President, 2004*, U.S. National Archives and Records Administration, Information Oversight Office, 2005, http://www.archives.gov/isoo/reports/2004-annual-report.html#10.

24. Andrew Card, "Memorandum for Heads of Departments and Agencies: Action to Safeguard Information Regarding Weapons of Mass Destruction and Other Sensitive Documents Related to Homeland Security," (Washington, DC: U.S. Office of the President, March 21, 2002), http://www.usdoj.gov/oip/foiapost/2002foiapost10.htm.

25. American Library Association, Washington Office, *Sensitive Homeland Security Information* (Washington, DC: American Library Association, 2003), http://www.ala.org/Template.cfm?Section=governmentinfo&Template=/ContentManagement/ContentDisplay.cfm&ContentID=80795#shsi.

26. American Library Association, Washington Office, "Executive Order 13233, November 1, 2001, Further Implementation of the Presidential Records Act," http://www.ala.org/ala/washoff/WOissues/governmentinfo/laadmin.htm#exec.

27. "Statement on Scientific Publication and Security—January 2003," *Science* 299/5610 (February 21, 2003): 1149.

28. Scott Shane, "Since 2001, Sharp Increase in the Number of Documents Classified by the Government," *New York Times* (July 3, 2005): 1, 14.

29. American Association of University Professors, Academic Freedom and National Security in a Time of Crisis, "Report of an AAUP Special Committee," *Academe: Bulletin of the American Association of University Professors* 89/6 (November–December 2003), http://www.aaup.org/statements/REPORTS/Post9-11.pdf; National Research Council (NRC), Committee on Research Standards and Practices to Prevent the Destructive Application of Biotechnology, *Biotechnology Research in an Age of Terrorism* (Washington, DC: National Academies Press, 2004); John Podesta, "Need to Know: Governing in Secrecy," in Richard C. Leone and Greg Anrig Jr., *The War on Our Freedoms: Civil Liberties in the Age of Terrorism* (New York: Century Foundation, 2003).

30. Susannah Fox, *Digital Divisions: There Are Clear Differences among Those with Broadband Connections, Dial-Up Connections, and No Connections At All to the Internet* (Washington, DC: Pew Internet and American Life Project, October 5, 2005), http://www.pewinternet.org/pdfs/PIP_Digital_Divisions_Oct_5_2005.pdf; Robert W. Fairlie, *Are We Really a Nation Online? Ethnic and Racial Disparities in Access to Technology and Their Consequences* (Washington, DC: Leadership Conference on Civil Rights Education Fund, September 20, 2005), http://www.civilrights.org/issues/communication/digitaldivide.pdf.

31. Jeffrey Young, "Technology Gap among Colleges Perpetuates 'Digital Divide' in Society, Expert Warns: Logging in with Larry Irving," *Chronicle of Higher Education* (June 4, 2002), http://chronicle.com/free/2002/06/2002060402t.htm.

32. Eszter Hargittai, "Second-Level Digital Divide: Differences in People's Online Skills," *First Monday,* 7/4 (April 2002), http://firstmonday.org/issues/issue7_4/hargittai/index.html.

33. Nancy Kranich, "Literacy in the Digital Age," in Susan Kretchmer, ed., *Navigating the Network Society: The Challenges and Opportunities of the Digital Age* (Thousand Oaks, CA: Sage, 2006).

34. Garrett Hardin, "The Tragedy of the Commons," *Science* 162 (December 1968): 1243–1248.

35. *Reno v. American Civil Liberties Union,* 521 U.S. 842, 870 (1997) (quoting in part from the lower-court decision).

36. Yochai Benkler, "Freedom in the Commons: Towards a Political Economy of Information," *Duke Law Journal* 55/6 (April 2003): 1245–1276 (quote on 1256), http://www.law.duke.edu/shell/cite.pl?52+Duke+L.+J.+1245.

37. Yochai Benkler, "From Consumers to Users: Shifting the Deeper Structures of Regulation toward Sustainable Commons and User Access," *Federal Communications Law Journal* 52/3 (2000): 579, http://www.law.indiana.edu/fclj/pubs/v52/no3/benkler1.pdf.

38. David Bollier, "Artists, Technology and the Ownership of Creative Content," Center for the Creative Community, November 2003, p. 98, http://www.culturalcommons.org/comment-print.cfm?ID=10.

39. See David Bollier, chapter 2, this volume; David Bollier, "The Missing Language of the Digital Age: The Commons," *The Common Property Resource Digest* 65 (June 2003): 1–4; David Bollier, *Public Assets, Private Profits: Reclaiming the American Commons in an Age of Market Enclosure* (Washington, DC: New America Foundation, 2001), http://www.newamerica.net/ Download_Docs/pdfs/Pub_File_650_1.pdf; David Bollier and Tim Watts, *Saving the Information Commons: A New Public Interest Agenda in Digital Media* (Washington, DC: New America Foundation and Public Knowledge, 2002), http://www.newamerica.net/Download_Docs/pdfs/Pub_File_866_1.pdf; David Bollier, *Silent Theft: The Private Plunder of Our Common Wealth* (New York: Routledge, 2002).

40. Thorin (see note 10); Richard E. Abel and Lyman W. Newlin, eds., *Scholarly Publishing: Books, Journals, Publishers, and Libraries in the Twentieth Century* (Indianapolis, IN: Wiley, 2002).

41. Charlotte Hess and Elinor Ostrom, "Ideas, Artifacts, and Facilities: Information as a Common-Pool Resource," *Law & Contemporary Problems* 66/1–2 (winter/spring 2003): 144–145, http://www.law.duke.edu/journals/66LCPHess.

42. Peter Levine, "Building the Electronic Commons," *The Good Society* 11/3 (2002): 5–8, http://www.peterlevine.ws/goodsociety.pdf.

43. For more information, see SPARC, http://www.arl.org/sparc/core/index.asp ?page=a0.

44. American Anthropological Association, *AnthroSource: Enriching Scholarship and Building Global Communities,* http:///www.aaanet.org/anthrosource/ index.htm. See also "Open-Access Policy Statements by Learned Societies and Professional Associations," http://www.earlham.edu/~peters/fos/lists.htm. For more information about these issues, see the Association of Learned and Professional Society Publishers, website, http://www.alpsp.org/default.htm; the *Free Online Scholarship Newsletter* and blog, http://www.earlham.edu/~peters/fos/.

45. Peter Suber, "Removing the Barriers to Research: An Introduction to Open Access for Librarians," *College & Research Libraries News* 64/2 (February 2003): 92–94, 113, http://www.earlham.edu/~peters/writing/acrl.htm; Gerry McKiernan, "Open Access and Retrieval: Liberating the Scholarly Literature," in David Fowler, ed., *E-Serials Collection Management: Transitions, Trends, and Technicalities* (New York: Haworth Information Press, 2004), 197–220, http://www.public.iastate.edu/~gerrymck/Open.pdf; Association of Research Libraries, "What Is Open Access," Washington, DC, http://www.arl.org/scomm/ open_access/framing.html#openaccess; David Prosser, "On the Transition of Journals to Open Access," *ARL Bimonthly Report*, no. 227 (April 2003): 1–3, http://www.arl.org/newsltr/227/openaccess.html; Walt Crawford, "A Scholarly Access Perspective," *Cites & Insights: Crawford at Large*, 3/13 (November 2003), http://cites.boisestate.edu/civ3i13.pdf; Paula Hane, "The Latest Developments in Open Access, E-Books and More," *Information Today*, 21/1 (January 2, 2004), http://www.infotoday.com/IT/jan04/hane1.shtml. For a timeline of the open-access movement, see Peter Suber, "Timeline of the Free Online

Scholarship Movement," http://www.earlham.edu/~peters/fos/timeline.htm. See also *SPARC Open Access Newsletter* (Washington, DC: SPARC), http://www.earlham.edu/~peters/fos/; Peter Suber, *Open Access News Blog,* http://www.earlham.edu/~peters/fos/fosblog.html.

46. For more information including a Guide to Business Planning, see Budapest Open Access Initiative, http://www.soros.org/openaccess/.

47. Steve Lawrence, "Online or Invisible?", *Nature* 411/6837 (2001): 521.

48. Lund University Libraries, *Directory of Open Access Journals* (Lund, Sweden: Lund University Libraries), http://www.doaj.org.

49. For more information about BioMedCentral, see http://www.biomedcentral .com.

50. Public Library of Science, http://www.plos.org/. For background information about PLoS, see Kurt Kleiner, "Free Online Journal Gives Sneak Preview," *New Scientist.com* 18/18 (August 19, 2003), http://www.newscientist.com/news/news.jsp?id=ns99994071; Marydee Ojala, "Intro to Open Access: The Public Library of Science," EContent: Digital Content Strategies and Resources (October 2003), http://www.econtentmag.com/?ArticleID=5552.

51. For more information about BioOne, see SPARC, *BioOne,* http://www.arl .org/sparc/core/index.asp?page=d3.

52. National Institutes of Health, Public Access, http://publicaccess.nih.gov/.

53. For more information, see Open Archives Initiative, website, http://www .openarchives.org/.

54. This effort was boosted by articulation of the characteristics and responsibilities for large-scale, heterogeneous collections, which helped digital repositories provide the reliable, long-term access to resources. See Research Libraries Group and OCLC, *Trusted Digital Repositories: Attributes and Responsibilities* (Mountain View, CA: Research Libraries Group, May 2002), http://www.rlg.org/longterm/repositories.pdf; see also Hess and Ostrom, "Ideas, Artifacts, and Facilities," 139–141.

55. DSpace Federation, http://www.dspace.org.

56. See University of Montreal, *Erudit,* www.erudit.org; California Digital Library, *eScholarship,* http://repositories.cdlib.org/escholarship/; Institutional Repository of Utrecht University, http://dispute.library.uu.nl/.

57. Ann Wolford, "The Role of the Research University in Strengthening the Intellectual Commons: The OpenCourseWare and DSpace Initiatives at MIT," in National Academy of Sciences, Board on International Scientific Organizations (BISO), *The Role of Scientific and Technical Data and Information in the Public Domain: Proceedings of a Symposium* (Washington, DC: National Academy Press, 2003), 187–190, http://books.nap.edu/books/030908850X/html/187.html#pagetop; Clifford A. Lynch, "Institutional Repositories: Essential Infrastructure for Scholarship in the Digital Age," *portal: Libraries and the Academy,* 3/2 (April 2003): 327, http://muse.jhu.edu/journals/portal

_libraries_and_the_academy/v003/3.2lynch.html. See also Vivien Marx, "In DSpace, Ideas Are Forever," *New York Times* (August 3, 2003): 4A, 8. The MIT DSpace digital repository is available at http://www.dspace.org/. MIT has also created OpenCourseWare, a collaborative courseware exchange, http://ocw.mit .edu/.

58. See Los Alamos e-Print Archive, http://www.arxiv.org/. Site use is reported at http://arxiv.org/show_weekdays_graph; site submissions are reported at http://arxiv.org/show_monthly_submissions. See also Paul Ginsparg, "Can Peer Review Be Better Focused?", http://arxiv.org/blurb/pg02pr.html.

59. "Summary of presentation by Greg Schwartz at the November 3–4 meeting of the American Astronomical Society (AAS) Publications Board," PAMnet posting, November 13, http://listserv.nd.edu/cgi-bin/wa?A2=ind0311&L= pamnet&D=1&O=D&P=1632.

60. For more information about these repositories, see EconWPA, http://econwpa.wustl.edu/; Oxford Text Archive, http://ota.ahds.ac.uk/; PhilSci-Archive, http://philsci-archive.pitt.edu/; NELLCO Legal Scholarship Repository, http://lsr.nellco.org; Networked Digital Library of Theses and Dissertations, http://www.ndltd.org/; IUCN—World Conservation Union, Conservation Commons, http://www.conservationcommons.org, the Digital Library of the Commons, http://dlc.dlib.indiana.edu/.

61. Stevan Harnad, "Self-Archive Unto Others," *University Affairs: Canada's Magazine on Higher Education and Academic Jobs* (December 2003), http://www.universityaffairs.ca/issues/2003/dec/opinion.html; Stevan Harnad, "Maximizing University Research Impact through Self-Archiving," University of Quebec at Montreal, http://www.ecs.soton.ac.uk/~harnad/Temp/che.htm; Hess and Ostrom, "Ideas, Artifacts, and Facilities," 143. See also Project RoMEO (Rights MEtadata for Open Archiving) at the University of Loughborough, http://www.lboro.ac.uk/departments/ls/disresearch/romeo/; EPrints.org—Self-Archiving and Open Archives, http://www.eprints.org/.

62. Daniel Greenstein and Suzanne E. Thorin, *The Digital Library: A Biography* (Washington, DC: Digital Library Federation, December 2002), http://www.clir.org/pubs/reports/pub109/contents.html.

63. John Markoff and Edward Wyatt, "Google Is Adding Major Libraries to Its Database," *New York Times* (December 14, 2004): A1; Scott Carlson and Jeffrey R. Young, "Google Will Digitize and Search Millions of Books from 5 Leading Research Libraries," *Chronicle of Higher Education* (December 14, 2004).

64. "Google Makes Its First Public Domain Books Available Online," *American Libraries Online* (November 4, 2005), http://www.ala.org/al_onlineTemplate .cfm?Section=American_Libraries&template=/ContentManagement/Content Display.cfm&ContentID=108705.

65. Open Access Alliance, http://www.opencontentalliance.org/; "The Open Content Alliance," *SPARC Open Access Newsletter*, no. 91 (November 2, 2005), http://www.earlham.edu/~peters/fos/newsletter/11-02-05.htm.

66. "New Digital Initiatives Have Import for All Higher Education," *CLIRing-house*, no. 19 (November–December 2003), http://www.clir.org/pubs/clirinhouse/house19.html.

67. Philip Pothen, "Building a Common Information Environment," *CILIP Library/Information Update* (December 2003), http://www.cilip.org.uk/publications/updatemagazine/archive/archive2003/december/update0312d.htm

68. National Science Foundation, "The National Science Digital Library: About NSDL," http://nsdl.org/about/index.php; Lee Zia, "The NSF National Science, Technology, Engineering, and Mathematics Education Digital Library (NSDL) Program: New Projects and a Progress Report," *D-Lib Magazine* 7/11 (November 2001), http://www.dlib.org/dlib/november01/zia/11zia.html.

69. See http://www.digitalpromise.org. See also Thomas Kalil, *Designing a Digital Opportunity Investment Trust: An Information Commons for e-Learning* (Washington, DC: New America Foundation, June 2002), http://www.newamerica.net/index.cfm?sec=programs&pg=article&pubID=848&T2=Article. A bill to support this effort, "The Digital Opportunity (HR2512) Trust Act," was introduced in the House of Reprentatives on May 19, 2005.

70. Donald Waters, chapter 6, this volume.

71. LOCKSS [website]. http://lockss.stanford.edu/.

72. For more background on learning communities, see John Seely Brown and Paul Duguid, "Universities in the Digital Age," in Brian L. Hawkins and Patricia Battin, *The Mirage of Continuity: Reconfiguring Academic Information Resources for the 21st Century* (Washington, DC: Council on Library and Information Resources and Association of American Universities, 1998), 39–60; Peter Lyman, "Designing Libraries to Be Learning Communities: Towards an Ecology of Places for Learning," in Sally Criddle, Lorcan Dempsey, and Richard Heseltine, eds., *Information Landscapes for a Learning Society: Networking and the Future of Libraries* (London: Library Association Publishing, 1999); Joan Lippincott, "Developing Collaborative Relationships; Librarians, Students, and Faculty Creating Learning Communities," *College and Research Libraries News* 63/3 (March 2002): 190–192.

73. Scott Bennett, *Libraries Designed for Learning* (Washington, DC: Council on Library and Information Resources, November 2003), 43–44, http://www.clir.org/pubs/reports/pub122/pub122web.pdf.

74. Donald Beagle, "Extending the Information Commons: From Instructional Testbed to Internet2," *Journal of Academic Librarianship* 28/5 (September 2002): 287–296; Donald Beagle, "Conceptualizing an Information Commons: New Service Model in Academic Libraries," *Journal of Academic Librarianship* 25/2 (March 1999): 82–89. For a list and links to academic library commons, see Laurie A. MacWhinnie, "The Information Commons: The Academic Library of The Future," *portal: Libraries and the Academy* 3/2 (2003): 241–257.

75. "At Indiana U., Information Commons Stats Show Library's Importance," *Library Journal Academic Newswire* (December 9, 2003); "Let's Build Two! At

Indiana U., Success of First Info Commons Leads to a Second," *Library Journal Academic Newswire: The Publishing Report* (September 16, 2004).

76. Donald G. Frank, Sarah Beasley, and Susan Kroll, "Opportunities for Collaborative Excellence: What Learning Communities Offer," *College & Research Libraries News* 62/10 (November 2001): 1008–1011. See also "IUPUI First Year Seminars," http://www.universitycollege.iupui.edu/frameindex.asp?LostChild=http://www.universitycollege.iupui.edu/LC/.

77. The Information Access Alliance website, http://www.informationaccess.org/.

78. Association of College and Research Libraries, Association of Research Libraries, SPARC, *Create Change: New Systems of Scholarly Communication* (Washington, DC: Association of Research Libraries, October 2003), http://www.arl.org/create/resources/CreateChange2003.pdf.

79. Association for College and Research Libraries, *Scholarly Communication Toolkit* (Chicago: American Library Association, 2005), http://www.ala.org/ala/acrl/acrlissues/scholarlycomm/scholarlycommunicationtoolkit/toolkit.htm.

80. For background information and licensing forms, see Creative Commons, website, http://creativecommons.org/. See also Glenn Otis Brown, "Academic Digital Rights: A Walk on the Creative Commons," *Syllabus* (April 1, 2003), http://www.syllabus.com/article.asp?id=7475; Richard Poynder, "Reclaiming the Digital Commons: Investigative Report," *Information Today* 20/6 (June 2003): 33–35.

81. Clifford Lynch, "From Automation to Transformation: Forty Years of Libraries and Information Technology in Higher Education," *Educom Review* (January–February 2000): 60–68.

82. For greater elaboration on these roles, see, for example, Carla J. Stoffle, "Choosing Our Futures," *College and Research Libraries* (May 1996): 213–231; Nancy Kranich, "Libraries in the Digital Age: Enhancing Teaching and Learning," in James Ohler, ed., *Future Courses: Technological Trends That Will Change Education* (Bloomington, IN: Technos Press, 2001): 97–110.

83. Elinor Ostrom, *Governing the Commons: The Evolution of Institutions for Collective Action*, New York: Cambridge University Press, 1990.

84. Wendy Pradt Lougee, *Diffuse Libraries: Emergent Roles for the Research Library in the Digital Age* (Washington, DC: Council on Library and Information Resources, August 2002), 4, http://www.clir.org/pubs/reports/pub108/evolution.html.

85. Ostrom and Hess, chapter 3, this volume; Hess and Ostrom, 2003.

86. "Evolution in Open Access: Biomed Central Alters Its Membership Model," *Library Journal Academic Newswire* (February 17, 2004).

87. "A Failure to Communicate? Librarians Taken Aback by Biomed Central Change," *Library Journal Academic Newswire* (February 17, 2004).

88. See, for example, University of Connecticut Faculty Senate, *Report and Resolution on the Crisis in Scholarly Communication* (February 9, 2004), http://

senate.uconn.edu/Report.20040209.Budget.scholarlycommunications.htm.   See also Christopher A. Reed, "Just Say No to Exploitative Publishers of Science Journals," *Chronicle of Higher Education* (February 20, 2004), and "One Year at a Time: MIT Declines Multi-Year Deals with Elsevier, Wiley," *Library Journal Academic Newswire* (February 10, 2004).

89. "Reed Elsevier Initiated with 'Underperform,'" *BNP Paribas* (October 13, 2003): 1.

90. Committee on Institutional Cooperation (CIC), *Report of the CIC Summit on Scholarly Communication in the Humanities and Social Sciences* (Chicago: Committee on Institutional Cooperation December 2, 2003), http://www.cic .uiuc.edu/groups/CIC/archive/Report/ScholarlyCommSummitReport_Feb04.pdf.

91. Carol M. Rose, *Property and Persuasion: Essays on the History, Theory, and Rhetoric of Ownership* (Boulder, CO: Westview Press, 1994), 6.

92. James Boyle, "A Politics of Intellectual Property: Environmentalism for the Net?", 1997, http://www.law.duke.edu/boylesite/intprop.htm.

93. Frederick Emrich, *Welcome to Info-Commons.org* (Washington, DC: American Library Association, June 2002), http://info-commons.org/arch/1/ editor.html.

5

Mertonianism Unbound? Imagining Free, Decentralized Access to Most Cultural and Scientific Material

James Boyle

I have written far too many pages on intellectual property, the public domain, and the commons.[1] I care deeply about the future of scholarly communications, particularly in the sciences. Designing an architecture for freer and more usefully accessible scholarly work is a fascinating task, and I agree with many of the contributors to this book that the literature on the commons has a number of insights to offer.[2] So I was pleased to be given the task of writing about the commons and the public domain in scholarly communications. This enthusiastic prologue notwithstanding, I am going to stray from that task—one that is performed ably by others in this collection—and instead suggest that we need to think still more broadly about our subject matter. My topic is Mertonianism *beyond* the world of scholarly communications.

Mertonianism, of course, is a term borrowed from the sociology of science, generally used to describe a process of free, open inquiry, without crippling secrecy norms or strong property claims, strongly reliant on the process of peer-reviewed publication and citation to drive hypotheses closer to an underlying objective reality.[3] Access to and citation of the peer-reviewed literature is crucial to the scientific project as Merton describes it, indeed it is one of its principal methods of error correction. It is for that reason that I chose the term for my title. I am using it loosely and provocatively to suggest an inquiry that at first might seem to run partly at odds to Merton's project. My goal is to ask what impact more open access to cultural and scientific materials, both scholarly and nonscholarly, by individuals and groups *outside* the academy might have on scholarship, culture, and even—though this is more speculative and unlikely—on science. Merton described science as a relatively autonomous process in which specialists used the sociological disciplinary mechanisms of peer review and citation reputation to winnow results. He would have cared deeply about restrictions on access to the scholarly literature or the underlying data if those restrictions were applied to *scientists*. The issue of access by the public was simply not one that presented itself. But it is that question that I wish to raise, for culture, the humanities, and the sciences as well.

One implication of the commons literature is that in attempting to construct a "comedic" commons,[4] one must think very carefully about its boundaries—the limits on who may use it and for what types of use. The tendency of my argument here is that, in the scholarly communications commons, the boundaries ought to be very wide indeed. In fact, the design principle I argue for here is that wherever possible neither use, nor the ability to participate in the fine-tuning of the system, should be restricted to professional scholars.

"You Can Have My Library of Congress When . . ."

I was searching the Library of Congress catalog one night, tracking down a seventy-year-old book about politics and markets, when my son came in to watch me. He was about eight years old at the time, but already a child of the Internet age. He asked what I was doing, and I explained that I was printing out the details of the book so that I could try to find it in my own university's library. "Why don't you read it online?", he said, reaching over my shoulder and double-clicking on the title, frowning when that merely led to another information page. "How do you get to read the actual book?"

I smiled at the assumption that all the works of literature were not merely in the Library of Congress, but actually on the Net, available to anyone with an Internet connection anywhere in the world—so that you could not merely search for, but read or print, some large slice of the Library's holdings. Imagine what that would be like. Imagine the little underlined blue hyperlink from each title—to my son it made perfect sense. The book's title was in the catalog and when you clicked the link, surely you would get to read it. That is what happened in his experience when one clicked a link. Why not here? It was an old book, after all, no longer in print. Imagine being able to read the books, hear the music, watch the films—or at least the ones that the Library thought it worthwhile to digitize. Of course, that is ridiculous. It took Google's recent attempts to do so to fire the popular imagination, but also to reveal the massive legal pitfalls involved.

I tried to explain this. I showed him that there were some works that could be seen online. I took him to the photograph library, meaning to show him the wealth of amazing historical photographs, but instead finding myself brooding over the lengthy listing of legal restrictions on the images, the explanation that reproduction of protected items may require the written permission of the copyright owners and that in many cases, only indistinct and tiny thumbnail images display to those searching outside the Library of Congress "because of potential rights considerations." The same was true of the scratchy folk songs from the twenties, or the early film holdings. The material was in the library, of course, remarkable collections in some cases, carefully preserved and digitized at public expense—and some tiny fraction of it available online. (There is a fascinating set of Edison's early films, for example.) Most of the material available online came from so long ago that the copyright could not possibly still be in force. But since copyright lasts for seventy years after the death of the author (or ninety-five years if it was a corporate "work for hire"), that could be a very, very long time indeed. Long enough, in fact, to keep off limits almost the whole history of moving pictures, the entire history of recorded music. Long enough to lock up almost all of twentieth-century culture.

But isn't that what copyright is supposed to be doing? To be granting the right to restrict access, so as to allow authors to charge for the privilege of granting it? Yes indeed. And this is a very good idea. Yet the goal was to give the minimum monopoly necessary to provide an incentive, and after that to let the work fall into the public domain, where all of us can use it, transform it, adapt it, build on it, republish it as we wish. For most works, the answer is that the owners expect to make all the money they are going to recoup from the work with five or ten years of exclusive rights. The rest of the term is of very little use to them except as a kind of lottery ticket in case the work proves to be a one-in-a-million perennial favorite. The one-in-a-million lottery winner will benefit, of course, if his ticket comes up. And if the ticket is "free," who would not take it? But the ticket is not free to the public, who pay higher prices for the works still being commercially exploited and, frequently, the price of complete unavailability for the works that are not.

Think of the one-in-a-million perennial favorite—Harry Potter, say. Long after J. K. Rowling is dust we will all be forbidden to make derivative works, to publish cheap editions or large-type versions, or simply to reproduce it for pleasure. I am a great admirer of Ms. Rowling's work, but my guess is that little extra incentive was provided by the thought that her copyright will endure seventy rather than merely fifty years after her death. Some large costs are being imposed here, for a small benefit. And the costs fall even more heavily on the other 999,999 works, works that are available nowhere but in some moldering library stacks. To put it another way, if copyright owners had to purchase each additional five years of term, the same way we buy warranties on our appliances, or insurance policies, the economically rational ones would mainly settle for a fairly short period.

Of course, some works are still being exploited commercially long after their publication date. Obviously the owners of these works would not want them freely available online. This seems reasonable enough, though even with those works the copyright should expire eventually. But remember, in the Library of Congress's vast wonderful pudding of songs and pictures and films and books and magazines and newspapers, there is maybe half a raisin's worth of works that anyone is making any money from, and the vast majority of those come from the last ten years. If one goes back twenty years, maybe a raisin fleck's worth. Fifty years? A slight raisinous aroma. We restrict access to the whole pudding, in order to give the owners of the raisin sliver their due. But this pudding is almost all of twentieth-century culture—and we are restricting access to it, when almost all of it could be available.

If you do not know much about copyright, you might think that I am exaggerating. After all, if no one has any financial interest in the works or we do not even know who owns the copyright, surely the library would be free to put those works online? Doesn't "no harm, no foul" apply in the world of copyright? In a word, no. Copyright is what lawyers call a "strict liability system." This means that it is generally not a legal excuse to say that you did not believe you were violating copyright, or that you did so by accident, or in the belief that no one would care and that your actions benefited the public. Innocence and mistake do not absolve you, though they might reduce the penalties imposed. Since it is so difficult to know exactly who owns the copyright (or copyrights) on the work, many libraries simply will not reproduce the material or make it available online, until they can be sure the copyright has expired—which may mean waiting for over a century. They cannot afford to take the risk. As for the cases where the copyright owners are identifiable, they would treat any digitizing of their work as a great new financial opportunity, though they themselves are doing nothing to distribute it, or sell it, or make it available, and have not for years.

What is wrong with this picture? Copyright has done its job and encouraged the creation, and the initial distribution, of the work. But now it acts as a fence, keeping us out, and restricting access to the work to those who have the time and resources to trudge through the stacks of the nation's archives. In some cases, as with film, it may simply make the work completely unavailable.

So far I have been talking as though copyright was the only reason the material is not freely available online. But of course this is not true. Digitizing costs money (though less money every year), and there is a lot of rubbish out there, stuff no one would ever want to make available digitally (though it must be noted that one man's rubbish is another man's delight). But that still leaves vast amounts of material that we would want, and be willing to pay to have digitized. Remember also that if the material were legally free, then anyone could get in the act of digitizing it and putting it up.

If you are shaking your head as you read this, saying it would never work, look at the Internet and think about where the information came from the last time you did a search. Was it an official and prestigious institution? A university or a museum or a government? Sometimes those are our sources of information, of course. But don't you find the majority of the information you need by wandering off into a strange click-trail of sites, amateur and professional, commercial and non, hobbyist and entrepreneur, all self-organized by internal referrals and search engine algorithms?

The most satisfying kinds of proofs are existence proofs. Could a mammal lay eggs? The platypus provides an existence proof. The Internet is an existence proof of the remarkable information-processing power of a decentralized network of hobbyists and amateurs and universities and businesses and volunteer groups and professionals and retired experts and who knows what else. It is a network that produces useful information and services. It frequently does so for at no cost to the user beyond the telecommunications access charge and it does so without anyone guiding it. Imagine that energy, that decentralized and idiosyncratically dispersed pattern of interest, turned loose not only on the cultural artifacts of the twentieth century, but on the universe of scholarly literature. Think of the people who would work on Buster Keaton, or the literary classics of the 1930s, or the films of the Second World War, or footage on the daily lives of African Americans during segregation, or the music of the Great Depression, or theremin recordings, or the best of vaudeville. But think also of those who are fascinated by Civil War history, or the analysis of the works of Dickens, or the latest paper on global warming, or Tay-Sachs disease. Where are the boundaries of the academy now? This is a more radical vision than making journals freely available online to scholars. Imagine your Internet search in such a world. Imagine that Library of Congress. A character in one of Bruce Sterling's novels utters the immortal line: "Man, you'll get my Library of Congress when you pry my cold dead fingers off it."[5]

Now, anyone who cannot sell to scholars the desirability of freer access to scholarly and cultural materials could not sell fire extinguishers to the burning. But in your willingness to agree with me that this would be a fine thing, you may miss my point. Two further stories may suffice to make it. The first I owe particularly to the work of Jessica Litman[6] and Yochai Benkler. The second comes from my experiences working on digital archive projects.

A Global Network for Open-Source Fact-Checking . . .

If I had come to you in 1994 and told you that in the space of ten years, a decentralized global network consisting of a *lot* of volunteers and hobbyists and ideologues and a *few* scholars and government or commercially supported information sources could equal and sometimes outperform standard reference works or reference librarians in the provision of accurate factual information, you would have laughed. Your incredulity would surely have deepened if I had added that this global network would have no external filters, and that almost anyone with an Internet connection would be able "publish" whatever they wanted, be it accounts of Area 51, the Yeti, and the true authorship of William Shakespeare, or painstaking analyses of Scottish history, how to raise saluki dogs, and the internal struggles in the American Communist Party. There is no "editor," no formal "peer-review" system, and the very identity of the writers and publishers is frequently in doubt. Worse still, many inhabitants of this strange new space will wilfully and joyfully spread the wildest of rumors and speculations as facts, without going through the careful source checking or argument weighing that scholars are supposed to engage in. Your first reaction to this flight of fancy (and the correct first impression of the World Wide Web as of its inception) was that this would thus be a *uniquely* and *entirely* unreliable source of information. This seems to be the very opposite of Mertonian science—it lacks the boundaries, requirement of professional credentials, and disciplinary constraints like those of peer review. And yet . . . when your child last had a research question from school did you go to Google, or the *Encyclopaedia Britannica*?[7]

Think of the standard account of the property regime necessary to generate a public good such as an encyclopedia or other comprehensive reference work. Strong property rights would be necessary for at least three reasons—each of them related to the tragedy of the commons. First, without the guarantee of a future legally protected monopoly called copyright, one could not attract the investment necessary to engage scores or hundreds of researchers to produce a work that could easily be copied by the first free rider to come along. Second, without the ability to control the resource provided by a legal right to exclude content, quality could not be maintained: the encyclopedia can reject the articles on Area 51 and the Yeti. Single-entity control, backed by property rights, allows for semiotic as well as agricultural stewardship. Third, without control over the name of the resource, such as that provided by trademark, there would be inadequate incentives to generate a quality product, and inefficient signaling to consumers. Why would a publisher invest in the production of a high-quality product if its name could be used by anyone? Why would consumers trust the name as a signal of quality if they could not be sure this was the real *Encyclopaedia Britannica*? Names as well as pastures can be overgrazed. In other words, without single-entity control and strong property rights, we will not get the generation of useful and reliable reference information. And yet, as I said before, when was the last time you turned to an encyclopedia rather than to the web? How many of the things you have found on the web *could* have been found in a standard reference work? When it comes to the generation and retrieval of useful factual information, the web is an existence proof of the viability of commons-based production, validation, and distribution. In fact, as Jessica Litman points out, one reason for the success of the system is the *absence* rather than the presence of property rights in factual data—facts cannot be copyrighted:

This information system is vital and dynamic because information sharing is almost frictionless. Material is passed along at low cost with few practical or legal barriers. Jeff Dalehite, webmaster of <scratchdj.com>, is free to post the details of the early history of the phonograph without seeking the consent of his sources. Dalehite's site tells us that Thomas Edison invented the cylinder phonograph in the 1870s and patented it in 1878. Dalehite recounts the details of the commercial standards competition between Edison's phonograph and the disk gramophone introduced to the U.S. market in 1901 by the Victor Talking

Machine Company. He attributes none of his sources; he need not even know whether the information he has abstracted was original to the references he used or derived by them from some other source. Technical writer Samuel Berliner III has posted a site honoring famous people throughout history named Berliner. His site reports that the disk gramophone was invented by Emile Berliner in 1887. Berliner needs no permission from Frederick W. Nile, the author of a 1926 biography of Emile Berliner, nor the National Inventors Hall of Fame, who have posted a short profile of Berliner, from whom he initially learned that information. Neither Dalehite nor Berliner has secured a license from Tommy Cichanowski for any facts they might have learned by studying *Tommy's History of Western Technology*, nor have they sought the blessing of the periodical *Electronic Design*,[8] whose February 1976 issue commemorating the U.S. bicentennial furnished many of the dates that Cichanowski reports. If one were unable to post facts without determining who controlled them and obtaining a license to pass those facts on, this online information space would not exist.[9]

Take a step back for a moment. The original work on the tragedy of the commons *overestimated* the applicability of the tragic-commons paradigm, and *underestimated* the extent to which we could have a well-managed commons governed by a variety of formal and informal norms. Elinor Ostrom and her colleagues taught us this, and a variety of intellectual property theorists have shown the applicability of their work to the world of the intellectual commons. Certainly, the world of scholarly communications is a promising place for this application. But if we confine our analysis to the world of scholarly communications *as currently constituted*, are we guilty of a similar error to the original tragedians? Are we underestimating the power of a lay audience, given free access to cultural materials and factual data as well as scholarly work, to add richness and depth to the world of scholarship in the same way that they have in the world of the provision of factual information? Are we underestimating the power of an enlarged audience to enrich our scholarship as well as merely reading it?

Obviously, one would want to be very careful not to overstate the potential here. In the context of factual data, search engine algorithms have managed to provide a strange kind of layperson's peer review so that we can get usable quality out of contributions of distinctly varied worth. So-called water-hole ranking relies on the assessments of other users about the relevance of a particular page; how many people link to this page on this topic? And what do other users think about the pages that provide the links? Just as markets have provided relatively good signals about the likelihood of factual events, some of them requiring considerable scientific knowledge to predict, so Google-type algorithms generally provide an aggregated sense of the collective judgment. Even if the page rank accurately reflects the collective judgment, of course, that does not mean the collective judgment is correct. Yet search engines will give us a snapshot of a debate if issues are controversial and, with surprising frequency, give prominence to dissenting views, particularly if those seem backed by expertise and recourse to data. The result is a rough winnowing process that often allows us to free-ride on the judgment of those who have expertise on the issue. Like markets (or peer review?), the system can be distorted by intentional gaming, fads, cascades of enthusiasm, and undeserved reputational advantages. Nevertheless, the results are clearly useful.

An important qualification is in order here. Most educated readers apply their own additional filters to the material retrieved by search engines. They look at several results to see if answers converge rather than merely relying on just one (and search further if they do not). They give different levels of credibility to work depending on its origin, its authors, and their credentials. They assess its presentation (everything from grammar and syntax to the look and feel of the page, and the pages it links to). They may cross-check with a recognized authority that itself was produced through more conventional means, such as a dictionary or a book of quotations. These "filters" are often applied unconsciously, but they dramatically increase the accuracy of the results. The decentralized search engine of the web requires an entirely different level of skepticism, and acquired sophistication about indicators of credibility, than does a static encyclopedia. Thus one cannot simply assume that the web, plus distributed creation and reference, plus search engine algorithms, are enough to produce a reliable information-retrieval system. Social capital, in the form of educated skepticism, is also vital. Yet the process does not stop here. Collectively created reference tools such as Wikipedia formalize the process of decentralized research. Those with a particular interest in one subject put up their own entries on it, only to have them commented on, edited, and subject to a strange form of lay peer review. The process is often anarchic and contentious, but the results are remarkably impressive. To paraphrase a credo of open-source software, "With enough eyeballs, and an interested community, many errors will be caught."

Thus let me return to my central questions. Are we underestimating the power of a lay audience, given free access to cultural materials and factual data as well as scholarly work, to add to the world of scholarship and knowledge generation in the same way that they have in the world of the provision of factual information?

My analogy might seem inapposite. Yes, decentralized systems are surprisingly good at generating factual reference material that can be winnowed through the processes I describe. But here our subject is scholarly communication, and surely there are differences between scholarship and simple factual reference? I completely agree. Let me stress the point: *the need for specialized expertise, sensitivity to source material, historical knowledge, and professional analytical tools means that most scholarly work will not be affected, or usefully supplemented by some imagined distributed process of lay volunteerism.* Indeed, just on the level of *reading*, most scholarship would not even be of interest to a lay audience. And yet with huge numbers of potential global readers, very low costs, and the possibility of decentralized methods of assessment that mimic peer review, the possibilities of productive exchange are surely above zero. Are they sufficiently far above zero to be worthwhile? After all, any enlargement of literacy, any broadening of the franchise, any new influx of opinion will bring with it a lot of noise as well as signal. Can current and future filtering methods, ranging from credibility assessment to peer review and search engine algorithms, manage to separate signal from noise? The answer is, I think, that we do not know. But our failure to predict the Net's role as a useful information source coupled with our experience with the tendency of individuals to underestimate the potential of "the well-run commons" should impose on us a double dose of humility before we write off the potential of such contributions altogether.

In one sense, the question I describe here is fundamental to the division between the progressive and the populist impulses in American politics. The progressive notes the dangers of collective irrationality, of lack of understanding, of availability cascades that violently skew perceptions of risk and benefit. He puts faith in the expertise of technocratic specialists working for the public interest, but isolated from public pressure and hubbub. The populist, by contrast, is skeptical of claims that restrict knowledge, decision making, or power to an elite group. He sees the experts as being subject to their own versions of narrowness and prejudice, their own cascades. Most sensible people acknowledge that each of these perspectives on the world has important truths to offer. The question is where the balance is to be drawn. Despite the tendency of some of my arguments so far, my goal is not to wave the banner for a populist movement in scholarship. Instead, it is to argue that we do not *know* the benefits and costs that wider access to cultural and scholarly material could bring. What's more, we have at least one reason not to reject the notion out of hand. At every stage of the development of mass literacy, it has seemed reasonable to doubt that anything productive could come out of widening the circle of participants—whether in biblical exegesis, in reading the law in English rather than in "Law French,"[10] in exercising popular sovereignty in the move toward mass democracy, or in the changes to politics wrought by easy Internet access to public documents. Is there a lesson there?

Having thus chastened both our expectations and our tendency to discount the possibility altogether, in the remainder of this chapter I will consider how a larger universe of readers might be interested in scholarly literature and how scholarship might even occasionally benefit from the process.

Beyond the Specialist Archive? Users as Designers

I was recently at a meeting of academics, digital librarians, and technologists, talking about the construction of usable specialized digital archives. The librarians and technologists told of constructing beautiful systems, with twenty four different metadata fields and incredibly powerful search capabilities. They also explained the "dirty little secret" of many of these archives: no one uses them. The response from the group was a thoughtful one—academics from within the discipline should be included in the design process, so that the system fits their patterns of work and conceptual categories, rather than being imposed based on some alien categorical scheme. Who could disagree? Nevertheless, I was struck by the similarity of the scene to a whole series of moments in the history of technology: moments where the experts dramatically misunderstood the likely patterns of use of a technology. The telephone was, famously, initially imagined as a one-to-many communication device, useful for weather reports distributed from a central source and the like. It found such use only in Albania.[11] AT&T predicted that cell phones would be used by a maximum of 900,000 people in the United States by the year 2000.[12] The FCC's prediction was lower (would that they had been correct!). Who predicted that IM would be a killer app, or imagined that e-mail would replace the phone call in much of corporate culture? Indeed, to go back to my earlier example, who predicted the explosion of the web, or the extent to which people would rush to share knowledge, impressions, opinions—generally at some inconvenience to themselves and without monetary incentives to do so? Who predicted that free and open source software written and assembled largely by volunteers would outperform proprietary software in mission-critical applications and would be endorsed by parts of the national security apparatus?

The point is, if the history of technology teaches us anything, it teaches us that we are extremely bad at predicting ex ante the uses of technology. This fact has an overlooked, but absolutely vital design corollary: wherever possible, design the system to run with open content, on open protocols, to be potentially available to the largest possible number of users, and to accept the widest possible range of experimental modifications from users who can themselves determine the development of the technology.[13] Then sit back and wait to see what emerges. It may be that your predictions of how the technology will be used, *and even your predictions about the potential user group*, will be completely wrong. All other things being equal, the more open the system is to change from multiple sources, the more open the content is to users beyond your initial target group, and the more the system can actually accept experimental changes from multiple external sources, the quicker you are likely to find the best use of the technology. Precisely because of the limits of foresight, making the entire archive available on the web, so that anyone can develop a search engine, or simply use Google, may well be better than building a wildly sophisticated specialist system designed by experts and used by no one. It is not an accident that some of the greatest recent successes in new technologies—the web itself and the technologies it enables—present exactly this model of development. In other words, having end users in the design stage is definitely a step forward from having technologists or librarians dream up an archival scheme from scratch. But even end users may misunderstand their own patterns of use, fail to anticipate important functions, or generally be unable to replicate the successes of a more open process of cybernetic adjustment.

Can one succeed with a closed model? Of course. We all use highly specialized databases that, for copyright or other reasons, are closed to the outside world. For lawyers, Westlaw is an example. When I want to know what the Second Circuit thinks about the copyright doctrine of "merger" I do not want an open archive, or a loose search engine. I want a very particular search restricted to a very particular set of materials, using a fairly precise and fiddly Boolean search engine that capitalizes on esoteric knowledge and employs technical jargon. The system, driven by the competitive urge to be more attractive than Lexis and relying on feedback from countless users, offers a well-designed and extremely useful service. Market pressure can make proprietary systems highly responsive to emerging user needs and desires. Open-source platforms searching open content offer an attractive model, but hardly the only model. In any world I can imagine there will be a vibrant, and profitable, specialized set of "closed" information ecologies that rely on technology and proprietary rights to exclude all but high-valuation users, and offer sophisticated tools of little interest to the majority. Nevertheless, I would stick with my default design principle: wherever possible, design the system to run on open protocols, make the content available to the largest possible number of users, and accept the widest possible range of experimental modifications and additions from users who can themselves determine the development of the technology. There are two simple reasons for adopting this as the default rule. First, the traditions of the academy, of scholarship, and of Mertonianism itself dictate that openness in both content and structure should be our baseline, deviations from which require justification. Second, where one is uncertain whether a closed or open architecture is better, start with the one from which it is easier to develop alternatives if you have chosen wrongly. And shifts from open to closed are made with fuller information held by more parties (by definition) than the reverse.

With Enough Brains . . . , Is All Content Interesting?

My argument depends in part on the virtues of a larger-than-expected audience, and on the serendipitous uses that unrestricted access and open, malleable protocols for searching can allow to develop. Is this assumption realistic? Open-source software developers tell us that with enough eyeballs all bugs are shallow.[14] With enough brains is all content interesting? Is there a lay audience for scholarly work, and the cultural and scientific materials on which it is based? Not always, of course. But this bolsters my argument rather than undermining it. The point is that we cannot predict confidently where and when there is a broad audience for scholarly work, or archival material, still less where and when non-scholars can actually contribute usefully to the field. And this again argues that openness to the public—rather than merely to a scholarly audience—ought to be a general design principle. Take the world of medical research. This seems like the paradigmatic example of esoteric material in which laypeople have little interest and less knowledge. Yet the Internet has meant a dramatic surge in laypeople using the scholarly literature to research their or a family member's illness, to help frame questions to doctors, to look at the results of new studies, and the like. The NIH has actually redesigned Medline to make it more accessible to laypeople.[15]

Sometimes, of course, this means that medically untrained people misdiagnose their illnesses, pester their doctors with fanciful interpretations of irrelevant studies, or refuse vaccines based on unproven charges of their effects. These are real costs, yet the consensus seems to be that the benefits are even greater—improving health knowledge, helping to catch misdiagnoses, encouraging people to seek medical care more quickly when it is appropriate, assisting in the formation of patient groups, and sometimes even catalyzing patient-led attempts to encourage development of new therapies.[16] The pre–Digital Reformation model in which a priestly intermediary always stood between the scholarly text and the laity no longer seems so inevitable. In fact, this tendency is frequently cited as a reason to encourage open access to scholarly journals. In the words of the Budapest Open Access Initiative,

An old tradition and a new technology have converged to make possible an unprecedented public good. The old tradition is the willingness of scientists and scholars to publish the fruits of their research in scholarly journals without payment, for the sake of inquiry and knowledge. The new technology is the internet. The public good they make possible is the world-wide electronic distribution of the peer-reviewed journal literature and completely free and unrestricted access to it by all scientists, scholars, teachers, students, and other curious minds. Removing access barriers to this literature will accelerate research, enrich education, share the learning of the rich with the poor and the poor with the rich, make this literature as useful as it can be, and lay the foundation for uniting humanity in a common intellectual conversation and quest for knowledge.[17]

Recently, this desire has even prompted a worthily intentioned but misguided attempt to require that all articles based on government-funded research be published without copyright restrictions, *precisely so that citizens can have unrestricted access to the scholarly literature*:

Scientific research paid for by the U.S. government would be required to be given free to the public, under a bill introduced in Congress last week. Representative Martin Olav Sabo, a Minnesota Democrat, said he introduced the Public Access to Science Act (PASA) of 2003 because U.S. residents shouldn't have to pay twice—once with tax dollars and a second time with subscription fees to scientific journals—for research that improves their health or saves their lives. "It is wrong when a breast cancer patient cannot access federally funded research data paid for by her hard-earned taxes," Sabo said in a statement. "It is wrong when the family whose child has a rare disease must pay again for research data their tax dollars already paid for. Common sense dictates we provide the most cutting-edge research to all who may benefit from it—especially when they've already paid for it with their tax dollars, and my legislation will do just that."[18]

Most, but not all, of the use by laypeople of this literature is "consumptive" in the non–Jane Austen sense of the word. Citizens seek information to solve practical problems, to instruct themselves and family members. Instructional aid has always been an important and worthy goal of scholarly literature. It is also worth noting, though, that whether it is Sharon Terry, the PXE patient group advocate, or the dedicated environmental activist researching groundwater contamination near his home, there are a growing number of cases in which motivated groups of laypeople actually help shift policy and even occasionally redirect research. Nonscholars can make productive as well as consumptive uses of our work.

So much for medical scholarship. That is an area where people have a real functional need, and where smart search engines can take us an admittedly small, but important step along the road that separates the citizen from the specialist. Does this kind of interest—and the associated importance of making sure that both primary sources and secondary literature are available to the widest audience possible—exist beyond the medical realm? I would say that the answer is clearly yes, both in terms of access to scholarly literature and in terms of access to archival materials. We have examples in genealogical research, astronomy, Civil War history, and environmental science, with more examples popping up every day. More saliently perhaps, in those (sadly few) places where copyrights have actually expired on texts, movies, music, pictures—we have an explosion of efforts by laypeople to comment, annotate, digitize, and in short make usefully available the works of the past. Project Gutenberg is only the most salient example.

What does the web teach us? It is not merely that "with enough brains all content is interesting." To paraphrase some earlier work on distributed creativity,[19]

1. If one has a global network, with very low barriers to entry and participation, and

2. If the type of creation involved is in some sense "modular" or built by accretion, and

3. If there is a random distribution of interests in particular topics (ornithology, literary history, open-source software, etc.), and

4. If there is a random distribution of incentive structures (greed, pride, altruism, desire to display virtuosity, hope of attracting interest, etc.), then

5. On any given topic, one will find a lot of motivated people with useful skills.

The web has already taught us these lessons in the context of factual research. It may be that they have some application to the design principles for the "commons" of scholarly communications.

Conclusion

The literature on the commons has much to teach us about intellectual production. It teaches us that the "tragedy of the commons" is only part of the picture; that there are comedic, well-run commons. It teaches us that the commons is not the same as the public domain;[20] successful commons are frequently characterized by a variety of restraints—even if these are informal or collective, rather than coming from the regime of private ownership. It even gives us generalizable tools that can help us to match types of resources with types of commons regimes. The web confirms those lessons. As I pointed out earlier, standard intellectual property theory would posit that to get high-quality factual reference works, we need strong property rights and single-entity control for at least three independent reasons related to the tragedy of the commons: the need for exclusive control over reproduction in order to produce the incentives necessary for large-scale investment in writers and fact-checkers, the need for control over content and editing in order to ensure quality, and the need for control over the name or symbol of the resource itself as a signal to readers and an inducement to invest in quality in the first place. In this case, though, the standard story was wrong, or at least incomplete. The fact that the Net has actually become a high-quality factual resource through a distributed process run largely by volunteers, with no central organizing body, is nothing short of fascinating. Indeed, it is precisely the comparative *absence* of intellectual property rights to exclude from facts and references that has been the key to the cooperative enterprise. There are provocative similarities between the possible future of digital scholarship and the remarkable successes of systems that harness lay volunteers in order to produce high quality out of individual contributions whose quality varies widely.

When coupled with our inability to predict accurately the best uses of new technologies, and the remarkable successes of free and open-source style development in which users are also designers, the Net's success as a reference work offers a persuasive analogical argument for a particular design principle in the construction of the scholarly commons: wherever possible, design the system to run with open content, to run on open protocols, to be potentially available to the largest possible number of users, and to accept the widest possible range of experimental modifications from users who can themselves determine the development of the technology. Then sit back and wait to see what emerges. We might be as surprised as we were when the Net stopped symbolizing inaccuracy and became a default reference source.

The second implication of my argument here is even simpler. In practice, the scholarly readers of this book have access to at least some version of the online Library of Congress that my son imagined. The wonders of interlibrary loan and subscription services can provide us with access to the resources of the world's libraries, though we cannot "click to get the out-of-print book" in the way a more rational copyright system would permit.[21] When many of us—I exempt librarians from this statement—think of a world in which one could "click to get the book," we do so with regret but little passion. Partly, that is because we think of the issue as simply one of consumptive access—it would be nice for nonscholars to have a greater ability to read, see, or hear the works of the past. The literature on the commons, and the past history of the Net as a factual resource, give us another reason to cherish this idea—a productive, even a scholarly one. Working in an arena where facts are largely free from intellectual property rights, the Net has assembled a wonderful cybernetically organized reference work. What might it do to the 97 percent of the culture of the twentieth century that is not being commercially exploited if that culture was available for everyone to annotate, remix, compare, compile, revise, create new editions, link together in archives, or make multimedia reference works?

The second part of my argument went beyond popular access to the cultural material of the twentieth century. I suggested that the scholarly-communication commons should be designed under the default assumption that, where possible, one would seek to ensure that both the repositories and participation in the design of repositories were available to the broadest number of people. What if dramatically more scholarly material on everything from medicine to literature were freely available and easily searchable? What if specialized scholarly archives lived side by side with archives whose design reflected participation by both scholarly and lay users—"Democratizing Innovation," in Von Hippel's terms?[22] What, in other words, if we imagined a world of potential colleagues rather than a universe of passive consumers? But that is a very large scholarly commons indeed.

Notes

This work is also made available on the author's website, http://james-boyle.com, under the terms of a Creative Commons Attribution, Non-Commercial, No-Derivs License; see http://creativecommons.org/licenses/by-nc-nd/2.5/. It draws on sections of a manuscript in progress called "The Public Domain: An Environmentalism for Information."

1. See, for example, James Boyle, *Shamans, Software, and Spleens: Law and the Construction of the Information Society* (Cambridge, MA: Harvard University Press, 1996); "The Second Enclosure Movement and the Construction of the Public Domain," *Law and Contemporary Problems* 66(1–2):33–74. http://www.law.duke.edu/journals/66LCPBoyle "A Manifesto on WIPO and the Future of Intellectual Property," *Duke Law and Technology Review* 9(2004):1–12.

2. Charlotte Hess and Elinor Ostrom, "Ideas, Artifacts, and Facilities: Information as a Common-Pool Resource," *Law and Contemporary Problems* 66(1–2):111–146. http://www.law.duke.edu/journals/66LCPHess

3. Merton's own views are, in fact, much more subtle than this abbreviated account suggests. See Robert K. Merton, *On Social Structure and Science* (Chicago: University of Chicago Press, 1996).

4. The phrase is Carol Rose's—used to describe cases where, contrary to the suggestion of Hardin's tragedy of the commons, resources are actually *more* efficiently used and managed collectively rather than under individual ownership. See Carol Rose, "The Comedy of the Commons: Custom, Commerce, and Inherently Public Property," *University of Chicago Law Review* 53:3(1986):711–781.

5. Bruce Sterling, *Heavy Weather* (New York: Bantam, 1996) 73.

6. In particular, I owe a considerable debt to Jessica Litman's wonderful "Sharing and Stealing" (Working paper, Wayne State University Law School,

http://www.law.wayne.edu/litman/papers/sharing&stealing;pdf.)   See   also Yochai Benkler, *Coase's Penguin or Linux and the Nature of the Firm*, http://www.benkler.org/CoasesPenguin.PDF; James Boyle, "The Second Enclosure Movement."

7. Jeffrey Selingo, "When a Search Engine Isn't Enough, Call a Librarian," *New York Times* (February 5, 2004), G1 (noting that professional librarians rely heavily on search engines). I admit that the data on comparative accuracy is hard to pin down—particularly because scholars apply a set of unconscious filters to the information provided by the search engine, filters that themselves are not so easily replicated. For some older discussions, see Joseph Zumwalt and Robert Pasicznyuk, "The Internet and Reference Services: A Real-World Test of Internet Utility," *Reference & User Services Quarterly* 38:2(1998):165–172; Joseph Janes and Charles McClure, "The Web as a Reference Tool: Comparisons with Traditional Sources," *Public Libraries* 38:1(January–February 1999):30–39, 165–172; Tschera Harkness Connell and Jennifer Tipple, "Testing the Accuracy of Information on the World Wide Web Using the Alta Vista Search Engine," *Reference & User Services Quarterly* 38:4(summer 1999):360–368.

8. See   http://www.hbci.com/~wenonah/history/index.html   and   http://www.elecdesign.com/.

9. Litman, "Sharing and Stealing".

10. "Law French" was an increasingly corrupt variety of Norman French used in the English common law. Its users believed that its arcane terminology gave greater precision while, to outsiders, it appeared merely another way to make the legal system incomprehensible to the laity. See http://en.wikipedia.org/wiki/Law_French and *Oxford English Dictionary*, 2nd ed. (Oxford: Oxford University Press, 1989).

11. *Ithiel de Sola Pool, Forecasting the Telephone: A Retrospective Technology Assessment* (Norwood, NJ: ABLEX, 1983).

12. The true number was closer to 10,000,000; http://knowledge.wharton.upenn.edu/121901_ss7.html some estimates there are now closer to 1 billion cell phones worldwide.

13. Eric Von Hippel is the undisputed master of the literature on user-based innovation. See his *Democratizing Innovation* (Cambridge, MA: MIT Press, 2005), available in full online at http://web.mit.edu/evhippel/www/democ.htm. Allowing users to participate, formally or informally, in the shaping of repositories obviously runs into a nontrivial design problem because of the "negative network externalities" that can result. What is a negative network externality? Think of the Tower of Babel: the original model of a system in which all users design their own protocols. However, the open-source software community, Wikipedia, and our own experience in scholarly disciplines show us that a variety of formal and informal norms can help to manage a process of commons-based production, without letting it collapse into a Babel of incompatible efforts. And to return to the linguistic example, languages themselves manage just fine without a single property owner, or authoritative Académie Française vetting all possible

linguistic innovations—a fact that both commons theorists and Hayekian market enthusiasts noticed long ago.

14. See Eric S. Raymond, *The Cathedral and the Bazaar: Musings on Linux and Open Source by an Accidental Revolutionary* (Cambridge, MA: O'Reilly 1999). "Bugs" are problems with software. Raymond is saying that with enough people reviewing the code, as allowed by open source, all problems will be "shallow"—that is to say, easy to fix.

15. See Elana Varon, "Medline Plus: Online Medical Info for Ordinary People," http://edition.cnn.com/TECH/computing/9901/18/medline.idg/. "Although the National Library of Medicine has always provided information to the public, its resources, including online databases, were designed for medical professionals. Now the agency has developed a World Wide Web site, Medline Plus, that aims to deliver the latest medical research and health information to lay people. The Medline Plus site collects information on common diseases and conditions and offers dozens of reference tools used by medical librarians. It is a work in progress, NLM director Dr. Donald Lindberg said. 'We have known for many years that it's very, very desirable to provide biomedical information to the public, but we've not done it directly,' he said. Among the reasons the agency is trying to provide such information now are that it is easier to disseminate information through the Internet, and there is growing public demand for health information."

Medline Plus can be found at http://www.nlm.nih.gov/medlineplus/. See also http://www.ncbi.nlm.nih.gov/PubMed/, a site that offers the following resources: "PubMed, a service of the National Library of Medicine, includes over 14 million citations for biomedical articles back to the 1950's. These citations are from MEDLINE and additional life science journals. PubMed includes links to many sites providing full text articles and other related resources."

16. Sharon Terry, a mother of children with PXE, was named one of the coinventors on the patent over the PXE gene. See "Eliot Marshall, Patient Advocate Named Co-Inventor on Patent for the PXE Disease Gene," *Science* 305/5688 (August 27, 2004): 1226. Terry has spoken frequently on the ways access to medical literature is vital for patient groups and advocates. See *In the Public Interest: Open Access and Public Policy*, 2005 ACRL/SPARC Forum (2005), http://www.arl.org/sparc/meetings/ala05mw/2005MW%20Forum%20_report. pdf.

17. From the Budapest Open Access Initiative website, http://www.soros.org/openaccess/.

18. Grant Gross, "Bill Seeks Free Access to Federally Funded Research." *BIO-IT World* (July 1, 2003), http://www.bio-itworld.com/news/070103_report2813 .html. I support the overall goal of wider and freer access, but the tool chosen is a blunt and unfortunate one.

19. See Boyle, *The Second Enclosure Movement*; Benkler, *Coase's Penguin*.

20. James Boyle, "The Opposite of Property," *Law and Contemporary Problems* 66(1–2):1–32.

21. This applies only to reading, however. Other uses of texts—republishing, annotating, using substantial excerpts in a course book—may still be suffocatingly difficult because of long copyright terms as well as the prevalence of orphan works. And even gaining access to old films and music is often hard even for professional scholars. See "Duke Center for the Study of the Public Domain: Comments to the Copyright Office on Orphan Works," http://www.law.duke .edu/cspd/pdf/cspdproposal.pdf.

22. See Von Hippel, *Democratizing Innovation.*

6

Preserving the Knowledge Commons

Donald J. Waters

In 1997, Anthony Grafton, the distinguished Princeton historian, published a remarkable history of the footnote. He argued that the footnote is an intellectual tool that is "the humanist's rough equivalent of the scientist's report on data." It offers "the empirical support for stories told and arguments presented." However, footnotes work their magic as part of a scholarly reference structure if and only if the underlying works—the referents—have been reliably preserved and are available to be tested and verified for their ability to support new advances in knowledge.

Many readers will no doubt remember their own experiences of awe and wonder when they learned how to interpret a footnote and so began to understand the mechanics of scholarly reference. According to Grafton, however, "no one has described the way that footnotes educate better than Harry Belafonte, who recently told the story of his early reading of W. E. B. DuBois." As a young West Indian sailor, Belafonte learned to read critically when he figured out how the footnote opened a world of learning. "I discovered," Belafonte said, "that at the end of some sentences there was a number and if you looked at the foot of the page the reference was to what it was all about—what source DuBois gleaned his information from." However, Belafonte did not find the task of learning from references to be easy at first and was stymied by the methods that DuBois used to cite his references. Trying to track them down, he says that he went to a library in Chicago with a long list of books. "The librarian said, 'that's too many, young man. You're going to have to cut it down.' I said, 'I can make it very easy. Just give me everything you got by Ibid.' She said, 'There's no such writer.' I called her a racist. I said, 'Are you trying to keep me in darkness?' And I walked out of there angry."

Of course, footnotes are not the only or, in a variety of research and educational contexts, even the best method of reference, and, as the Belafonte story indicates, there can be many obstacles in tracking a reference path. However, as Grafton concludes in his study, the footnote is a critical part of the scholarly apparatus because it is such a clear and efficient mechanism to link one piece of scholarship with what its author has identified as the key reference points for the work. It serves as a guarantee, Grafton says, "that statements about the past derive from identifiable sources. And that is the only ground we have to trust [those statements]" (Grafton 1997, vii, 233–235).

In other words, when scholars use systems of reference to link one work to another, they establish and exercise underlying fabrics of trust. These fabrics serve to tie researchers to other researchers, teachers to students, and creators to users over time and place into durable and productive scholarly communities. The linked works represent the common pools of knowledge—the knowledge commons—over which members of these communities labor to produce new knowledge. The links work, the trust endures, and the commons nourishes the intellectual life only when the reader is able to check the reference at the other end, and that checking depends on a reliable, ongoing system of preserving the knowledge commons.

The Changing Nature of Preservation in Systems of Scholarly Communication

Grafton's account of the development of the footnote provides a useful glimpse into the process and apparatus of scholarly reference, and more generally, into the complex systems of scholarly communication by which research and other scholarly products are, by formal and informal means, "created, evaluated for quality, disseminated to the scholarly community and preserved for future use" (Association of College and Research Libraries 2003). Currently, these systems are under considerable stress and are changing rapidly as scholars incorporate digital technologies into their research and methods of dissemination, and as they use and generate information in digital as well as other formats. The contributions to this book together represent an attempt to understand and evaluate the stress and change in terms of the political economy of public goods, and related concepts of the commons, common-pool resources, and collective action. The knowledge commons described elsewhere in the book all are subject to the intricate challenges of preservation, and some of my colleagues have highlighted some of the key issues. Ostrom and Hess have carefully situated the preservation challenges within a broad analytical framework. Kranich draws attention to the effects on preservation of political and economic enclosure; Ghosh shows the constraints of intellectual property regimes; and others underscore the need for preservation as they describe, for example, how the development of knowledge commons gives rise to new opportunities for library service (Lougee) and disseminating scholarly publications (Suber). Here, in this chapter, full attention is devoted to the topic of preservation. This is the process of ensuring that the knowledge commons endures—that scholarly materials are available for citation and, if cited, are available for consultation and further study.

Academic libraries have traditionally taken responsibility for preserving the scholarly record in printed form by buying books and journals from publishers for their local researchers, teachers, and students. They store these works at specific locations in protective environments, fix bindings and pages when necessary, and microfilm or digitize those volumes in danger of deterioration. Today, increasing numbers of scholars are contributing articles to electronic journals, taking part in projects to publish electronic books, and building new kinds of resources that take advantage of digital capacities to link and aggregate materials and to simulate and visualize complex relationships. They also support their scholarship with citations to these and a wide range of other digital materials as well as to more traditional sources (see Lynch 2003b). Such electronic scholarship is as important for the cultural record and the building of knowledge as printed publications have been, and is therefore as important to preserve. But libraries generally do not buy electronic journals and books. They license them, and provide access to digital resources based on servers elsewhere and outside of their direct control. Given such a profound change in the pattern of distribution and ownership, the research library is being transformed from a steward to an active collaborator with scholars and students in the production and use of scholarly information resources (Lougee, chapter 11, this volume). So who is taking responsibility for preserving these materials?

Although the case is persuasive for why digital preservation is a necessary and vital component of the system of scholarly communications, an impressive array of factors and incentives—including the fundamental shift from buying to licensing—leads otherwise well-intentioned actors in different directions (see, for example, Waters and Garrett 1996 and Library of Congress 2002; but also Morris 2000; Waters 2002; Jones 2003; Lavoie 2003, 2004; Honey 2005). Meanwhile, digital materials are proving to be fragile and fleeting, with potentially serious consequences for the knowledge commons. Brewster Kahle, who founded the Internet Archive to preserve portions of the web, estimates that a web object now has an average life expectancy of 100 days (Weiss 2003). Mortality is also high for web-based scholarly literature. A study published in *Science* in October 2003 found that more than 30 percent of the articles in selected high-impact medical and scientific journals contained one or more Internet references, but "the percentage of inactive Internet references increased from 3.8% at 3 months to 10% at 15 months and to 13% at 27 months after publication" (Dellavalle et al. 2003, 787). A similar study conducted in 2001 found that the percentage of inactive Internet references increased from 23 percent at two years to 53 percent at seven years after publication (Lawrence et al. 2001; see also Ho 2005). With additional effort, many of the works cited in the inactive references could still be found, but at different locations and without evidence of provenance or proof that the contents had not been altered. The results of these studies cast doubt on the wisdom of citing online references at all—a practice nonetheless followed in this chapter—and clearly indicate that the digital ecology of the knowledge commons is highly unstable, and its preservation is far from assured. Reviewing one of the recent studies on the high mortality rate of scholarly citations to online references, Anthony Grafton commented that "I'm looking at a world in which documentation and verification melt into air" (Carlson 2005).

In this chapter, I focus specifically on the problem of preserving electronic scholarly journals (e-journals). To provide a framework for analyzing the problem and possible solutions, I first define it as a problem of preserving a commons, and then explore key roles and organizational models in the preservation process. I conclude by identifying key features of what might emerge as community-based preservation efforts.

E-Journal Preservation as a Commons Problem

In the fall of 2000, the Andrew W. Mellon Foundation invited seven of the nation's leading universities, along with publishers that they each selected, to participate in a preservation planning process (Cantara 2003; see also Waters 2002). Together, the participants would develop and share detailed understandings of the requirements for setting up and implementing trustworthy archives for the preservation of electronic journals, create technology to facilitate the archiving process, and organize the implementation and operation of electronic journal archives. Although they demonstrated in many ways the technical feasibility of preserving electronic journals, most of these seven planning projects stalled when they ran smack into some of the classic problems of the political economy of public goods: What are the incentives for individuals and institutions to participate in the provision and maintenance of a good when others cannot be readily excluded from enjoying the benefit? What are the organizational options? What are sustainable funding plans?

Commons—or more specifically common-pool resources—are a kind of modified public good. They share with public goods the feature that it is difficult to exclude beneficiaries, but differ in that use may reduce the availability of the resource to others (Ostrom et al. 1999, 278). Knowledge in the abstract, such as the theory of relativity, is strictly speaking a public good, because it is difficult to exclude people from benefiting from the theory and use of the theory does not diminish its availability to others. Knowledge in the form of specific works, such as articles in electronic journals, resembles a public good because it is also difficult to exclude beneficiaries who can readily copy, discuss, or otherwise disseminate the material. Copyright protection is meant to provide incentives to those who might be deterred by the threat of copying from contributing in the form of publications to the common pool of knowledge. However, once a scholarly work is available in the form of a published electronic artifact, the artifact can, like other kinds of common-pool resources, be used up and, as linked references in e-journals, may simply disappear.

To have its beneficial effects, a published work needs to be available to the broadest possible audience both in the present and over time. However, access is not equivalent to preservation. The free or open access of common-pool resources may encourage use by many today, but it does not necessarily encourage any specific individual or institution to preserve them for future use. Insuring against the loss of electronically published works is a common-pool resource problem that requires special attention.

To explore the nature of the problem further, let us examine the idea that the preservation, or "archiving," of electronic journals and other forms of electronic publications is in fact insurance against loss. Is preservation really like insurance, in the sense of fire or life insurance? Would a business approach based on an insurance model induce people to take on responsibility for archiving? If you have fire insurance and your house burns down, you are protected. If you have life insurance and you die, your heirs benefit. There is an economy in these kinds of insurance that induces you to buy. If you fail to buy, you are simply out of luck; you are excluded from the benefits. Unfortunately, the insurance model for preserving electronic journals is imperfect, because insurance against the loss of information does not necessarily enforce the exclusion principle.

A special property of archiving is that if one invests in preserving a body of electronic journals and the works are eventually lost to others who did not take out the insurance policy, the others are not excluded from the benefits, because the knowledge in the works still survives. Because free riding is so easy, there is little economic incentive to take on the problem of digital preservation. Potential investors conclude: "It would be better for me if someone else paid to solve the archiving problem." As we have seen, one of the defining features of a common-pool resource is that it is difficult and costly to exclude beneficiaries.

Given the huge free-riding problem associated with the maintenance of the knowledge commons, what are the alternatives? Reflecting in part on the free-riding problem, Garrett Hardin in "The Tragedy of the Commons" (1968) despaired of solutions, and offered little hope that selfish individuals would cooperate in preserving their commons. Hardin followed Thomas Hobbes, who lamented the state of nature, a commons in which people pursue their own self-interest and lead lives that are "solitary, poore, nasty, brutish, and short" ([1651] 1934, 65). Focused on preserving digital information in 1996, the Task Force on Archiving of Digital Information echoed both Hobbes and Hardin in writing that "rapid changes in the means of recording information, in formats for storage, in operating systems, and in application technologies threaten to make the life of information in the digital age 'nasty, brutish, and short'" (Waters and Garrett 1996, 2).

One of Hardin's solutions to the tragedy of the commons was, like Hobbes's, to rely on the leviathan—the coercive power of the government. Governments, in fact, have funded many of the early efforts to create digital archives (Beagrie 2003; Library of Congress 2002). Hardin's other solution was to encourage privatization, trusting in the power of the market to optimize behavior and preserve the commons.

Efforts such as Brewster Kahle's Internet Archive demonstrate the kinds of contributions that private investment could make.

Certainly, both the government and private interests have roles to play in preserving the knowledge commons, but substantial experimental and field research in the political economy of public goods has also shown Hardin's pessimism about the prospects of maintaining common-pool resources goods to be unwarranted. Case after case demonstrates that groups of people with a common interest in a shared resource will devise and agree on community-based mechanisms for controlling and financing the preservation of the resource (Ostrom 1990; Dietz et al. 2002; Dietz, Ostrom, and Stern 2003). However, understanding the potential interaction of government, private, and community interests in the systematic preservation of a digital knowledge commons requires a close analysis of potential roles, responsibilities, and models of organization.

Preservation Roles, Responsibilities, and Models of Organization

According to Brian Lavoie (2003), there are essentially three roles at play in the archiving equation. Lavoie uses slightly different labels, but I would refer to them as Producer, Consumer, and Archive. The producer is the individual or set of individuals who generates an information object and is initially responsible for the bundle of ownership rights associated with the object. The consumer is the individual or set of individuals that comprises the public (or publics) interested in the long-term preservation of an object. I use the word *consumer* deliberately to indicate the potentially complex relationship in which the producer may be selling, licensing, or otherwise supplying services to the consumer based on the very same object that the consumer wants to be preserved. And, as I would define it, the archive is responsible for exercising the rights and duties of preserving the cultural, historical, or scholarly record.

As Lavoie observes, these three roles could logically be combined in five different ways, representing distinct organizational models (see figure 6.1). The real world, of course, is a lot messier than these simple representations suggest, but there is a heuristic value in considering these abstractions because they help us identify some of the key issues. I am departing from Lavoie's analysis here to suggest that two of the models, which I have labeled Models A and B, represent forms of organizational archives.

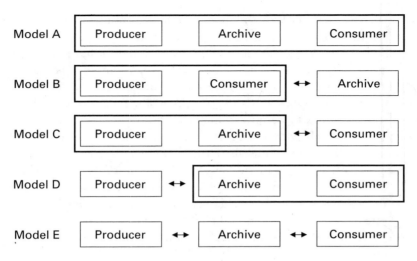

Figure 6.1
Organizational models

Organizational Archives

The key defining quality of both models is that the producer of the information objects and the consumer of the preservation service belong to the same organization. The organization in effect has a compelling interest and incentive to preserve the objects that it produces. The difference between the two models is that in the one case—Model A—the archive is housed within the boundaries of the organization, while in the other case—Model B—the archive is outsourced to some third-party provider.

The roles and responsibilities in these models are easy to define and understand and, within academic organizations, they are an increasingly important component of the scholarly-communication infrastructure (Lynch 2003a). Because the organization controls its own finances and structure, it controls the demand for archiving, the allocation of roles and responsibilities, and the wherewithal to enable actors within the organization to carry out their responsibilities. Note, however, that if the institution is a complex one, in which roles are highly differentiated and specialized, and if we take a perspective from within the organization, it may well be that to many of the internal actors the model would appear indistinguishable from Model E, in which the producer, consumer, and archive each belong to different organizations.

Note also that one of the heuristic values of modeling roles and responsibilities in this schematic way is that it allows us to distinguish at least two senses in which the phrase "institutional repository" is used, often ambiguously, in current discourse. On the one hand, the phrase refers in a strict sense to the case of an organization managing its own records. The organization is its own customer for purposes of archiving, and is not concerned with a broader public. DSpace is an open-source software platform developed at MIT for "institutional repositories" in this sense. It was designed and deployed in its early implementation to address the internal needs of MIT, with departments and groups within the organization contracting with the library to create an archive as an internal record of digital products that they have generated (Barton and Walker 2003).

On the other hand, a good deal of the discussion about "institutional repositories" follows the argument developed in a recent position paper of the Scholarly Publishing and Academic Resources Coalition (SPARC), and suggests that repositories like DSpace could do much more, including holding copies of published papers produced by faculty, and thereby appealing to a demand for preservation from a customer base that extends well beyond the bounds of the archiving organization (Crow 2002; see also Heery and Anderson 2005). Although such a vision is surely worth pursuing, there is little evidence that it would be feasible to implement it in the short term. Moreover, in terms of the formal models outlined here, the SPARC view is not strictly speaking an organizational archives; instead, when universities embrace such a vision, the relevant actors share roles and responsibilities more like those in Model C, which I would call producer archives.

Producer Archives

Model C represents cases in which the producer and the archive are aligned organizationally to preserve a portion of the cultural record for a broad consumer base. Besides the SPARC vision of colleges and universities creating archives of the publications that their faculty authors produce, other examples of producer archives would be publisher archives and so-called author self-archives. Is preservation in the mission of such producers and are they credible archives?

Universities as the producers of knowledge have traditionally relegated collecting and preserving the scholarly literature to their libraries. Libraries, in turn, have taken it as their mission to embrace collections that are broadly useful as resources for research and teaching within the institution, rather than to focus on archiving the published output of their faculty. Shifting the preservation mission of academic institutions is not inconceivable but, as Clifford Lynch (2003b) has pointed out, it would likely require significant, and potentially costly, cultural, policy, and technical changes that could distract from the larger academic mission of encouraging innovation and the expansion of knowledge, and may require federating technologies that either do not exist or are currently too immature to be useful.

For their part, publishers, including many scholarly societies, understand the general social benefits of preservation, and certainly have a strong interest in preserving the own content—either themselves or through a third party—for as long as their databases are commercially viable. Moreover, scholarly publishers also have an incentive to contribute to preservation activity in the interests of their authors, who want their works to endure, be cited, and serve as building blocks for knowledge. However, journal publishers generally do not regard long-term preservation as falling within the scope of their mission and responsibility. The long-term viability of any producer archives that they create is therefore subject to doubt, and the primary concern is whether their electronic publications are produced in a preservable format that could endure outside the cocoon of the publisher's proprietary system. One necessary ingredient in a proof of preservability is the transfer of data out of their native home into external archives, and as long as publishers refuse or are unable to make such transfers, this proof cannot be made.

Another concern about producer archives is more subtle, and perhaps more pernicious in its implications for the future of the knowledge commons in electronic form. In part, because electronic publications are generally maintained online, rather than being physically transferred as paper publications are in a sale, publishers appear to be more vulnerable to legal demands, editorial second-guessing, and other activities that result in the removal of materials from the publishers' archive. In 2003, following an article titled "Elsevier's Vanishing Act" in the *Chronicle of Higher Education* (Foster 2003), a correspondent on the LIBLICENSEL Mailing List documented more than thirty-five instances in which Elsevier removed articles from its Science Direct. Reasons for retraction included previous publication of the article in another publication, scientific misconduct, disputes over copyright, and perceptions of offensive content (Lapelerie 2003). In relation to the overall size of Elsevier's database, the number of vanishing articles was, of course, relatively small, but Elsevier is not the only journal publisher that has been subject to such pressures. The overall consequence of removal is that it produces a "Swiss cheese" effect in the scholarly record and casts doubt on the ability of publishers in general to preserve the integrity of the commons, at least on their own.

The LibLicense discussion about publisher-removed articles then prompted James O'Donnell (2003), the provost of Georgetown University, to observe that the "vanishing-act" discussion "is disturbing, because it is the tip of the iceberg, I think: If for fairly transient reasons, publishers will pull articles, when might not publishers prove unreliable for other reasons?" He went on then to highlight how the failure to account for reliable preservation is one of the most poorly examined open spaces under the head of steam known as "author self-archiving." O'Donnell wrote:

But the question that follows on this discussion for me is this: If we were to ask that not publishers but authors be the guarantors of permanence, self-publishing or publishing in institutional repositories where the author retains control over the copyright and disposition of his/her material—what protection do we then have to assure us that articles will remain archived, unchanged, in perpetuity? Are there articles I have written that I wouldn't mind disappearing? Actually, yes. Are there pieces of articles that I would quietly change if I could? Well, interesting thought, sure.

Consumer Archives

Let me now turn briefly to Model D, which represents what I would suggest is a consumer archive. In the digital realm, as with other forms of information, the passions and interests of what Edward Tenner has called "freelance selectors and preservers" will almost surely result in valuable collections of record (2002, 66; see also Beagrie 2005). Just as publishers undoubtedly have a role in digital archiving, so too will individual consumers. However, just as there is reason to question the commitment of producers to the long-term task of preservation, so too are consumer archives subject to similar, and perhaps even greater, concern, and provision must be made to ensure the eventual transfer of archived materials to archives capable of providing long-term care.

Community-Based Archives

This brings me to the last and perhaps most interesting and complex organizational model, Model E. In this case, each of the three significant roles is played by independent actors. Ideally, a network of competent digital archives will emerge that would be responsible for preserving electronic journals and other digital materials of cultural and scholarly significance. Indeed, if the model being developed by the Library of Congress (2002) eventually succeeds, the archival function itself may depend on a complex and distributed division of labor among parties with various responsibilities for selection and custodianship, security, and repositories. But the key organizational feature of this model for the preservation of electronic journals is that members of the scholarly community, including producers (especially publishers), consumers as represented by scholars and their academic institutions, and libraries would find ways jointly to solve this pressing problem.

The Mellon Foundation also expects to play a supporting role as part of the community, especially given its long-standing philanthropic interest in the preservation of the cultural record as a condition of excellence in higher education. However, it is looking, as it does in nearly all cases of support, for ways to promote a self-sustaining, businesslike activity. It cannot in this, or in any other initiative, support long-term operating costs without compromising its mission. As a result, the foundation seeks to foster the development of communities of mutual interest around preservation, help legitimize archiving solutions reached within these communities, and otherwise stimulate the necessary support from within the scholarly community. The premise of the Mellon e-journal planning projects, which I mentioned above, was that concern about the lack of solutions could be addressed only by hard-nosed discussions among stakeholders about what kinds of division of labor and rights allocations are practical, economical, and trustworthy, and from those planning projects two fledgling community-based preservation services were born.

One is Portico, a new organization that is affiliated with Ithaka and JSTOR and is being designed to preserve the source files used to publish electronic journals (Fenton 2005). Since its inception in late 2002, Portico has developed a business relationship with ten publishers. It has developed mechanisms for transferring data from these publishers, and has designed and constructed a prototype repository. It has verified through a detailed study that a shift from print to electronic journals would generate huge savings in nonsubscription processing and storage costs within libraries (Schonfeld et al. 2004), and it is now negotiating with publishers and libraries to finalize its pricing and service model.

The other initiative is based at Stanford University and is developing an archiving system called LOCKSS, for Lots Of Copies Keeps Stuff Safe (Reich and Rosenthal 2001). In the LOCKSS system, a low-cost web crawler under the control of a participating library is used for systematically capturing presentation files—web-based materials that publishers use to present journal content to readers. Publishers allow the files to be copied and stored in web caches that are widely distributed on local campuses but highly protected. A critical feature of LOCKSS is that it is designed to prevent failure within the archived system by creating redundancy and removing single points of failure (Rosenthal et al. 2005). The caches communicate with each other through a secure protocol, checking each other to see whether files are damaged or lost and repairing any damage that occurs. Caching institutions have the right to display requested files to those who are licensed to access them if the publisher's site is unavailable and to provide the local licensed community the ability to search the aggregated files collected in the institutional cache. Much work remains, but Stanford has attracted more than 80 libraries and more than 50 publishers to test the system, and expects LOCKSS to be preserving 100 electronic journal titles from eight to ten publishing platforms when a full production system is released. Like Portico, however, LOCKSS has yet to generate the revenue needed from the community to sustain the enterprise.

Properties of Community-Based Efforts to Preserve the Knowledge Commons

Trusted third-party agents in the archival role, whether it is a repository organization such as Portico or a distributed caching system as in the case of LOCKSS, promise greatly to benefit the knowledge commons. Trusted third parties whose primary mission is preservation can help overcome the multiple weaknesses of producer archives. They offer a mechanism for producers to transfer their content and help prove that it is preservable, and such a transfer would also mitigate the dangers to the scholarly and cultural record associated with the "vanishing act." In addition, as common infrastructure for preserving the scholarly and cultural record over time, trusted third-party archives can create economies of scale for both producer and consumer archives, thus generating the public good of preservation while, at the same time, producing systemwide savings in implementation. However, of the five general types of organizations discussed above, trusted third-party archives such as Portico and LOCKSS pose a unique set of problems because the roles and responsibilities, which are embedded in different organizations, must be turned to a common preservation mission, and this kind of coordination across organizations is difficult to achieve. Agreement is needed, for example, on the definition of what materials need to be preserved. Although there may be little disagreement that scholarly journals need to be preserved, it is not always easy in other domains to predict what sources future readers will need. In fact, the acts of coordination among the parties by which they set up a trusted archive are, in themselves, acts of community building by which the parties define what needs to be preserved, and establish and cement their mutual interest in preserving the knowledge commons.

In formal economic terms, the coordination problem that must be addressed in creating community-based preservation archives is a problem, from the perspective of the archive, of creating a two-sided market (Rochet and Tirole 2003; Evans 2003; Wright 2003). In a traditional market, a producer creates and sells a product that consumers demand. A journal publisher, for example, produces a journal of articles for readers and libraries. In a two-sided market, two different groups need the services of an intermediary in creating a new product. The specific services provided with the product are different on each side and the task of the intermediary is to create a business model that strikes a balance and manages to get both sides on board because the market flourishes only if the number of participants on both sides is large and growing.

A typical example of an intermediary in a two-sided market is a credit card company, which must create a business model that both induces businesses to accept a credit card and provides incentives for customers to use it. Working both sides of the market is necessary because businesses will not accept the card if too few customers want to use it, and customers will not use it if not enough businesses accept it. Visa and MasterCard charge businesses a transaction fee and create huge demand by giving cards away with no up-front fees. They then charge customers high interest on unpaid balances. By contrast, American Express balances the two sides by charging businesses and then also in levying up-front fees on customers and expecting full payment on credit balances. The two-sided problem in the case of community-based archives is similar because they must find a model that gets both publishers and readers on board. Readers and particularly libraries would not want to participate in the archives unless a large number of journals are being preserved, and publishers would be reluctant to contribute their journals unless library and reader demand for preservation through the archives is real.

The two-sided market problem that faces community-based archives is compounded because the product—preservation—that they are trying to create for the community is a public good. As we have seen, it is difficult to exclude members of the community from the benefits of preservation. The possibility of free riding thus makes it difficult for the community-based archives to induce participation. However, even though exclusion is difficult, it is not impossible.

What preservation ensures is future access to the preserved work, and one community-based solution to the free-riding problem is to create a voluntary association, or club, of participants that derive mutual benefit from membership, and to treat preservation as a club good in which key benefits, including the benefit of ensured future access, are limited to the participants. As Richard Cornes and Todd Sandler argue, clubs provide an important "nongovernmental alternative to the provision of public goods" (1996, 393; see also Buchanan 1965). Portico and LOCKSS have in fact organized clubs as a means of providing their community-based preservation solutions. The experience of these initiatives in developing clubs and club goods, and particularly clubs in a two-sided market, suggests the need for further attention to at least three specific features: the definition of the club as an archive, specific legal protections that may be needed for such archives, and the access restrictions that provide the basis of exclusion and sustainable business models.

Definition of Archives

The first feature I would highlight is that *the role of archives must be narrowly defined in terms of the rights and duties needed to preserve the historical, cultural, or scholarly record*. Others are better qualified than I to comment on whether the various recent revisions to the copyright law are constitutional or how well they balance private interest and the public good. There is little evidence, though, that activities aimed at preserving digital materials are sufficiently distinguished in debates about intellectual property, and so the implications of new law or court review for preservation receive scant attention and little protection in what are otherwise sweeping and potentially far-reaching changes. Part of the problem is that, as a community, we have not been very rigorous in defining the archival role with respect to digital information.

Over the last decade, the semantics of the word *archives* have grown increasingly complex. The narrow, traditional definition of an archives as a repository with a long-term responsibility for preserving the cultural record has been extended in such uses as the "Open Archives Initiative," "scholar self-archives," and "computer archives," to refer simply to collections of interest or even more simply to ordinary daily backup systems. These loosely defined senses are often used interchangeably or in association with the more rigorous definitions, and so tend to generate more confusion than clarity.

Here, for example, is a fairly common definition of the mission of a digital archive, which appeared in a recent report of a Mellon-funded project: "To ensure the long-term survival and broad availability of digital information." I will return shortly to the highly problematic assertion about access in the phrase "broad availability," but even the term "long-term survival" is overly broad because everything cannot be saved and the archival function, in a strict definition, is specifically associated with the highly particular and selective function of identifying and preserving historical, cultural, or scholarly records. Preservation is a daunting task in any case. When the definition of archives is not restricted to this highly focused objective it is hard for policymakers, such as members of Congress, judges, and especially the clerks who do their research for them, to see the distinct value of the task and take it seriously enough to consider its implications when making decisions that may affect the scholarly community's ability to manage and preserve its cultural record.

Legal Protection
A second feature that I would highlight is that *electronic journal archives, strictly defined, may need legal protection from the negative effects of liability and other tort actions against publishers.* If transfer of an e-journal from a producer to an archive is proof of preservability, then it behooves the archives to institute the transfer as soon after formal publication as possible to ensure against producer actions that might change or remove material. However, even if a hand-off were immediate, a license or other form of contract between the producer and the archive may govern the transfer, and may not protect the archive from requests to withdraw material in the same way that the sale and physical transfer of a printed publication would (Ayre and Muir 2004). In other words,

the interactions among contract, tort actions, business decisions, and copyright may leave long-term archives exposed in the digital environment in ways that they are specifically protected in other media, at least in U.S. copyright law.

Given this definition of the problem, the Mellon Foundation recently commissioned a comparative study that is looking carefully at the interaction of contract, tort, and copyright law in the United States and a few other countries. If this study proves that there is a deeper structural problem, it may be necessary to create or employ appropriate legal and policy constructs, analogous to those that accompany the sale of a paper copy of a journal with an offending article that would shield qualified archives from demands to change or withdraw material from online view. Thus, for example, if a publisher has deposited a copy of an electronic journal in a trusted third-party archive and one of the articles later has to be retracted because it involves significant errors or plagiarism, the archive would be allowed to keep a copy. The archive might need to restrict access, but could still make it available to researchers who need to take account of the historical role of the retracted article as part of the record of scholarly discovery.

Such remedies for the "disappearing-act" problem might be part of a broader articulation of "safe-harbor" principles about intellectual property rights that could form the basis of digital archiving agreements among interested parties. In building JSTOR and ARTstor as archival resources, the Mellon Foundation has found that content owners are much more comfortable with agreements that limit uses of intellectual property to not-for-profit educational purposes than they are with agreements that leave open the possibility of creating competing commercial profit-making access to the property. Lawrence Lessig (2001, 249–261) has also argued for the utility of the distinction between not-for-profit educational uses and other kinds of uses of intellectual property. Because educational use is certainly consistent with the Constitutional mandate for intellectual property law in the United States to promote "the Progress of Science and useful Arts," perhaps it is time to build a safe-harbor framework for digital archiving on just such a distinction.

Access Rights and Restrictions in a Sustainable Business Model

The third and final feature that I would highlight in this discussion is *the need for an adequate and sustainable business model based on access rights and restrictions.* To create community-based archives organized as clubs of publishers and consumers, key questions still need immediate and imaginative attention: What access rights and privileges would archives have to have in order to induce libraries and other consumers to support the archives? How should third-party archives separate their market from that of publishers in order to motivate publishers to participate and contribute content? What is the right balance of exclusive benefits and restrictions that would create an economy for digital archiving—a set of services for which publishers and consumers are willing to pay to sustain the archives and preserve the scholarly and cultural record?

Over and over again in conversations with publishers, scholars, librarians, and academic administrators, we have found that one special privilege that would likely induce investment in digital archiving would be for the archive to bundle specific and limited forms of access services with its larger and primary responsibility for preservation (see Honey 2005). Although there is disagreement over the types of access services that would be desirable and permissible, the key phrase here is "specific and limited." User access in some form is needed in any case for an archive to certify that its content is viable, but "broad availability," to use the phrase that I quoted earlier from the proposed mission statement of prospective digital archives, goes too far. Indeed, extended and complicated forms of access not only add to the costs of archiving, they also make publishers very nervous that the archives will in effect compete for their core business. We desperately need models of archival access that serve the public good; we do not need models that, in effect, set up archives as competitors to publishers, because publishers will find it very difficult to support them.

Secondary, noncompeting uses might include aggregating for not-for-profit educational use a broad range of journals in the archive—a number of publications larger than any single publisher could amass—for data mining and reflecting the search results to individual publishers' sites. Another kind of limited, secondary use might be based on direct user access to the content, again for not-for-profit educational use, with "moving walls" of the kind pioneered in JSTOR. Still other possibilities exist for even further development. Files aggregated across publishers in the archives could provide abstract and indexing publishers with a single source of texts, both saving them from going to each and every publisher for the texts to index and enabling them to use computational linguistic and other modern techniques to improve their products. Source files might also be "born archival" at the publisher and deposited in the archive, from which they might then serve as the masters for the derivative published files that the publisher creates for its different markets. These latter two possibilities are not likely to emerge immediately, mainly because they would require intense negotiation among the interested parties, but they are suggestive of how a thoughtful, entrepreneurial, community-based approach to archiving might add incremental improvements that would actually lead to more dramatic transformations of the system of scholarly communications.

Much work still needs to be done to sort out what the right access models might be so that they attract the necessary ongoing flow of revenue to sustain the archives. But just as "broad availability" may be going too far on one side, care needs to be taken on the other side in defining the conditions or "triggers" under which access might be provided to so-called dark or restricted archives. Finding the right balance is essential to moving forward in this complicated arena.

Conclusion

In a recent work titled *The Ethics of Memory*, Avishai Margalit (2002, 54) observes that "shared memory in a modern society travels from person to person through institutions, such as archives, and through communal mnemonic devices, such as monuments and street signs." He might have added schools and universities to his list of institutions, and footnotes to his list of mnemonic devices. The task of sustaining these institutions and devices for memory is not an easy one, and is a burden that falls on us all collectively. "We are," Margalit writes, "collectively responsible to see to it that someone looks after the ill. But we are not obligated as individuals to do it ourselves, as long as there are enough people who will do it" (p. 58; see also Appiah 2003). In other words, a division of labor is needed for preserving the knowledge commons that is analogous to the complex division of labor that secures health care for the sick. None of us alone is responsible for that support, but we do, in concert with others, have a responsibility to make sure that incentives are in place so that at least some preserve the commons on which future scholarship and education so clearly depend. This chapter has tried to suggest how we might together construct those necessary incentives.

References

Appiah, Kwame Anthony. 2003. "You Must Remember This." *New York Review of Books* 50/4 (March 13): 35–37.

Association of College and Research Libraries, Scholarly Communications Committee. 2003 "Principles and Strategies for the Reform of Scholarly Communication." http://www.ala.org/ala/acrl/acrlpubs/whitepapers/principlesstrategies.htm.

Ayre, Catherine, and Adrienne Muir. 2004. "The Right to Preserve: The Rights Issues of Digital Preservation." *D-Lib Magazine* 10(3). http://www.dlib.org/dlib/march04/ayre/03ayre.html.

Barton, Mary R., and Julie Harford Walker. 2003. "Building a Business Plan for DSpace, MIT Libraries' Digital Institutional Repository." *Journal of Digital Information* 4(2). http://jodi.ecs.soton.ac.uk/Articles/v04/i02/Barton/.

Beagrie, Neil. 2003. *National Digital Preservation Initiatives: An Overview of Developments in Australia, France, the Netherlands, and the United Kingdom and of Related International Activity*. Washington, DC: Council on Library and Information Resources and the Library of Congress. http://www.clir.org/pubs/reports/pub116/pub116.pdf.

Beagrie, Neil. 2005. "Plenty of Room at the Bottom? Personal Digital Libraries and Collections." *D-Lib Magazine* 11(6). http://www.dlib.org/dlib/june05/beagrie/06beagrie.html.

Buchanan, James M. 1965. "An Economic Theory of Clubs." *Economica*, New Series, 32(125):1–14.

Cantara, Linda, ed. 2003. *Archiving Electronic Journals: Research Funded by the Andrew W. Mellon Foundation*. Washington, DC: Digital Library Federation, Council on Library and Information Resources. http://www.diglib.org/preserve/ejp.htm.

Carlson, Scott. 2005. "Scholars Note 'Decay' of Citations to Online References." *Chronicle of Higher Education* 51(28):A30.

Cornes, Richard, and Todd Sandler. 1996. *The Theory of Externalities, Public Goods, and Club Goods*. 2nd ed. Cambridge: Cambridge University Press.

Crow, Raym. 2002. *The Case for Institutional Repositories: A SPARC Position Paper*. Release 1.0. Washington, DC: Scholarly Publishing and Academic Resources Coalition. http://www.arl.org/sparc/IR/IR_Final_Release_102.pdf.

Dellavalle, Robert, Eric Hester, Lauren Heilig, Amanda Drake, Jeff Kuntzman, Marla Graber, and Lisa Schilling. 2003. "Going, Going, Gone: Lost Internet References." *Science* 302 (October 31): 787–788.

Dietz, Thomas, Nives Dolšak, Elinor Ostrom, and Paul Stern. 2002. "The Drama of the Commons." In Elinor Ostrom, Thomas Dietz, Nives Dolsak, Paul Stern, Susan Stonich, and Elke Weber, eds., *The Drama of the Commons*, 3–35. Washington, DC: National Academy Press.

Dietz, Thomas, Elinor Ostrom, and Paul Stern. 2003. "The Struggle to Govern the Commons." *Science* 302 (December 12): 1907–1912.

Evans, David S. 2003. "The Antitrust Economics of Two-Sided Markets." *Yale Journal of Regulation* 20(2):325–381.

Fenton, Eileen. 2005. "Overview of Portico: An Electronic Archiving Service." Conference of European Librarians, Luxembourg, September 30, 2005. http://www.portico.org/about/Portico.Overview.CENL.pdf.

Foster, Andrea L. 2003. "Elsevier's Vanishing Act." *Chronicle of Higher Education* 49(18):A27.

Grafton, Anthony. 1997. *The Footnote: A Curious History*. Cambridge, MA: Harvard University Press.

Hardin, Garrett. 1968. "The Tragedy of the Commons." *Science* 162 (December 13): 1243–1248.

Heery, Rachel, and Sheila Anderson. 2005. *Digital Repositories Review*. A Report to Accompany the Joint Information Systems Committee Digital Repositories Programme Call in February 2005. http://www.jisc.ac.uk/uploaded _documents/digital-repositories-review-2005.pdf.

Ho, James. 2005. "Hyperlink Obsolescence in Scholarly Online Journals." *Journal of Computer-Mediated Communication* 10(3), article 15. http://jcmc .indiana.edu/vol10/issue3/ho.html.

Hobbes, Thomas. [1651] 1934. *Leviathan*. London: J. M. Dent & Sons.

Honey, Sadie L. 2005. "Preservation of Electronic Scholarly Publishing: An Analysis of Three Approaches." *Portal* 5:59–75.

Jones, Maggie. 2003. *Archiving E-Journals Consultancy: Final Report*. Report Commissioned by the Joint Information Systems Committee (JISC). http://www.jisc.ac.uk/uploaded_documents/ejournalsfinal.pdf.

Lapelerie, François. 2003. "Re: Vanishing Act." E-mail to liblicense-l@yale.edu, January 23. http://www.library.yale.edu/~llicense/ListArchives/0301/msg00092 .html.

Lavoie, Brian F. 2003. "The Incentives to Preserve Digital Materials: Roles, Scenarios, and Economic Decision-Making." White paper published electronically by OCLC Research. http://www.oclc.org/research/projects/digipres/ incentives-dp.pdf.

Lavoie, Brian F. 2004. "Of Mice and Memory: Economically Sustainable Preservation for the Twenty-first Century." *Access in the Future Tense*, 45–54. Washington, DC: Council on Library and Information Resources. http://www.clir.org/ pubs/abstract/pub126abst.html.

Lawrence, Steve, David Pennock, Gay William Flake, Robert Krovetz, Frans Coetzee, Eric Glover, Finn Årup Nielsen, Andries Kruger, and C. Lee Giles. 2001. "Persistence of Web References in Scientific Research." *IEEE Computer* 34(2):26–31.

Lessig, Lawrence. 2001. *The Future of Ideas: The Fate of the Commons in a Connected World.* New York: Random House.

Library of Congress. 2002. *Preserving Our Digital Heritage: Plan for the National Digital Information and Infrastructure Preservation Program.* Washington, DC: Library of Congress. http://www.digitalpreservation.gov/repor/ndiipp_plan.pdf.

Lynch, Clifford. 2003a. "Institutional Repositories: Essential Infrastructure for Scholarship in the Digital Age." *ARL Bimonthly Report* 226 (February). http://www.arl.org/newsltr/226/ir.html.

Lynch, Clifford. 2003b. "Preserving Digital Information to Support Scholarship." In *The Internet & the University: Forum 2002.* Boulder, CO: EDUCAUSE. http://www.educause.edu/ir/library/pdf/ffpiu029.pdf.

Margalit, Avishai. 2002. *The Ethics of Memory.* Cambridge, MA: Harvard University Press.

Morris, Sally. 2000. "Archiving Electronic Publications: What Are the Problems and Who Should Solve Them?" *Serials Review* 26(3):65–68. http://www.alpsp.org/arcsm00.pdf.

O'Donnell, James. 2003. "Re: Vanishing Act." E-mail to liblicense-l@yale.edu, January 29. http://www.library.yale.edu/~llicense/ListArchives/0301/msg00118.html.

Ostrom, Elinor. 1990. *Governing the Commons: The Evolution of Institutions for Collective Action.* Cambridge: Cambridge University Press.

Ostrom, Elinor, Joanna Burger, Christopher Field, Richard Norgaard, and David Policansky. 1999. "Revisiting the Commons: Local Lessons, Global Challenges." *Science* 284 (April 9): 278–282.

Reich, Vicky, and David Rosenthal. 2001. "Lockss: A Permanent Publishing and Web Access System." *D-Lib Magazine* 7(6). http://www.dlib.org/dlib/june01/reich/06reich.html.

Rochet, Jean-Charles, and Jean Tirole. 2003. "Platform Competition in Two-Sided Markets." *Journal of the European Economic Association* 1(4):990–1029.

Rosenthal, David, Thomas Robertson, Tom Lipkis, Vicky Reich, and Seth Morabito. 2005. "Requirements for Digital Preservation Systems: A Bottom-Up Approach." *D-Lib Magazine* 11(11). http://www.dlib.org/dlib/november05/rosenthal/11rosenthal.html.

Schonfeld, Roger, Donald King, Ann Okerson, and Eileen Gifford Fenton. 2004. "Library Periodicals Expenses: Comparison of Non-Subscription Costs of Print and Electronic Formats on a Life-Cycle Basis." *D-Lib Magazine* 10(1). http://www.dlib.org/dlib/january04/schonfeld/01schonfeld.html.

Tenner, Edward. 2002. "Taking Bytes from Oblivion." *U.S. News & World Report* 132 (April 1): 66–67.

Waters, Donald J. 2002. "Good Archives Make Good Scholars: Reflections on Recent Steps toward the Archiving of Digital Information." In *The State of*

Digital Preservation: An International Perspective. Conference Proceedings, 78–95. Washington, DC: Council on Library and Information Resources. http://www.clir.org/pubs/abstract/pub107abst.html.

Waters, Donald J., and John Garrett, eds. 1996. *Preserving Digital Information: Report of the Task Force on Archiving of Digital Information.* Washington, DC, and Mountain View, CA: Commission on Preservation and Access and Research Libraries Group. http://www.rlg.org/ArchTF/.

Weiss, Rick. 2003. "On the Web, Research Work Proves Ephemeral: Electronic Archivists Are Playing Catch-Up in Trying to Keep Documents from Landing in History's Dustbin." *Washington Post* (November 24): A08.

Wright, Julian. 2003. *One-Sided Logic in Two-Sided Markets.* AEI-Brookings Joint Center Working Paper No. 03-10. http://ssrn.com/abstract=459362.

III

Building New Knowledge Commons

7

Creating an Intellectual Commons through Open Access

Peter Suber

What Is Open Access?

Open access (OA) is free online access. OA literature is not only free of charge to everyone with an Internet connection, but free of most copyright and licensing restrictions. OA literature is barrier-free literature produced by removing the price barriers and permission barriers that block access and limit usage of most conventionally published literature, whether in print or online.[1]

The physical prerequisites for OA are that a work be digital and reside on an Internet server. The legal prerequisite for OA is that a work be free of copyright and licensing restrictions (statutory and contractual restrictions) that would bar OA. There are two ways to eliminate these restrictions: put the work in the public domain or obtain the copyright holder's consent for all legitimate scholarly uses, such as reading, downloading, copying, sharing, storing, printing, searching, linking, and crawling. Consenting to these uses means waiving some rights granted by copyright law. But this is compatible with retaining other rights, such as the right to block the distribution of mangled or misattributed copies. Some OA authors also retain the right to block commercial reuse.[2]

Obviously there is some flexibility about which rights to waive and which to retain, and even some mild intramural dispute about which rights must be waived in order to create open access. The Budapest Open Access Initiative, which made "open access" the term of art for this kind of literature (February 2002), put it this way:[3]

There are many degrees and kinds of wider and easier access to this literature. By "open access" to this literature, we mean its free availability on the public internet, permitting any users to read, download, copy, distribute, print, search, or link to the full texts of these articles, crawl them for indexing, pass them as data to software, or use them for any other lawful purpose, without financial, legal, or technical barriers other than those inseparable from gaining access to the internet itself. The only constraint on reproduction and distribution, and the only role for copyright in this domain, should be to give authors control over the integrity of their work and the right to be properly acknowledged and cited.

The economic prerequisite for OA is to find the means to pay for the physical and legal prerequisites. If the work is not yet digital, then one cost is digitization. If the work is digital but not yet online, then another cost is putting it online. Sometimes this is the high cost of lobbying the recalcitrant, not the negligible cost of FTP'ing a file to a web server or moving a file from a closed online directory to an open one. Permission is sometimes the least expensive part of an OA project, and sometimes the most expensive. In any case, permission is only necessary, not sufficient, to create OA.

If the OA literature is to be peer reviewed, then the cost of peer review must be added to the tab. If the OA literature is to be enhanced in other ways, for example through copyediting, reference linking, or alert services, then their costs must be added as well. Most OA resources have limited funds and focus on essentials in order to keep their costs down. Different OA journals draw the line between essentials and inessentials at different places, based in part on their funding and in part on cultural differences among disciplines. (For example, science journals use copyediting because so many submissions come from nonnative speakers of the language, which is seldom a factor for humanities journals.) All agree, however, that peer review is essential for scientific and scholarly journal literature.

In short, OA literature is free of charge for readers and users, but not for producers. The producers require revenue or subsidies. OA owes its origin and part of its deep appeal to the fact that publishing to the Internet permits both wider dissemination and lower costs than any previous form of publishing. This revolutionary conjunction is too good to pass up. But even low costs must be recovered if OA is to be sustainable.

There are two major ways of delivering open access, and they differ in their costs and funding models:

1. OA *archives* or *repositories* do not perform peer review, but simply make their contents freely available to users around the world. They may contain unrefereed preprints, refereed postprints, or both. Archives may contain the research output of institutions, such as universities and laboratories, or disciplines, such as physics and economics. When archives

comply with the metadata harvesting protocol of the Open Archives Initiative,[4] then they are interoperable and users can find their contents without knowing which archives exist, where they are located, or what they contain. There are a dozen open-source software packages for building and maintaining OAI-compliant archives. The costs of an archive are negligible: some server space and a fraction of the time of a technician.

2. OA *journals* perform peer review and then make the approved contents freely available to the world. Their expenses consist of peer review, manuscript preparation, and server space. Of these, peer review is the most significant. But peer review is essentially editorial judgment and paper handling (or file handling). In most journals and most fields, the editors and referees who exercise editorial judgment donate their services, just like the authors. The cost of peer review, then, is limited to the costs of distributing the files to reviewers, tracking progress, nagging dawdlers, facilitating communication, and collecting data. But the costs of these essentially clerical chores are steadily decreasing as they are taken over by increasingly sophisticated software, including open-source software.[5]

If journals are to be OA, then they cannot cover their expenses by charging readers or their libraries. About half of them[6] charge a processing fee on every accepted article to be paid by the author or the author's employer, research funder, or government. If the processing fee for an article covers all the costs of vetting and publishing it, then the journal can provide free online access to the resulting full-text article without losing money. Most OA journals waive the fee in cases of economic hardship.

The up-front funding model charges the author's sponsor for outgoing papers, not the reader's sponsor for incoming papers. It charges for dissemination, not access. In this respect it resembles the funding model for broadcast television and radio. If advertisers can pay all the costs of production, then a TV studio can broadcast a show without charging viewers. In the case of TV and radio, the model works because advertisers are willing to pay to get their message across. In the case of scholarly research articles, the model works because authors are willing to relinquish royalties to get their message across and a growing number of institutions that employ researchers or fund research are willing to consider the cost of dissemination to be part of the cost of research.[7]

We can be confident that the funding model is sustainable because it works in an industry—broadcasting—where there are far greater expenses and no tradition of creators relinquishing revenue from their work. An even more secure ground for confidence is that the true costs of peer review, manuscript preparation, and OA dissemination are much lower than the price now paid for access to published journals.

But the up-front funding model is not the only one for OA journals. It works best in fields like biomedicine where most research is funded and where the major funders are already on the record as willing to pay these fees.[8] But in less prosperous fields, including the humanities, other models will be needed. One attractive model is for university libraries to publish OA journals. The *Philosophers' Imprint*, for example, is a peer-reviewed journal published by the University of Michigan.[9] Its motto is, "Edited by philosophers, published by librarians." Because the philosophers and librarians are already on the university payroll, the journal need not charge processing fees. The point is that there is not just one way to cover the expenses of a peer-reviewed OA journal, and we have a long way to go before we can say that we have exhausted our cleverness and imagination.

Royalty-Free and Royalty-Producing Content

There is already OA to some music and movies, novels and news, sitcoms and software. One day there may be much more. But these genres of content all earn royalties for their creators, which makes it very difficult to get the needed permissions for OA. Either OA will deprive the content owners of revenue or they fear it will. There is some evidence that OA need not interfere with revenue in these ways, and in some circumstances can even enhance it. But these are reasons for copyright holders to reconsider, not reasons to disregard their decisions. So far, most of them decide against OA.[10]

The focus of the OA movement is on a special category of content that does *not* earn royalties for its creators: peer-reviewed research articles and their preprints. Ever since the first scientific journals were founded in 1665 in London and Paris, journals have not paid authors for articles.[11]

What incentive do authors have to publish without payment? If there were royalty-paying journals, then authors would very likely steer their work toward them. So part of the answer is that royalty-free journals are the only game in town.[12] But if that were the whole story, then over time many journals would have begun to pay authors, in order to attract the best submissions, especially today when the profits of commercial journal publishers approach 40 percent. Moreover, if the absence of alternatives were the whole story, authors might forgo royalties with resignation and write journal articles as a job obligation, like committee meetings. But this is not what we see when we look.

The more important part of the answer, then, is that authors want their work to be noticed, read, taken up, built upon, applied, used, and cited. They also want the journal's time stamp in order to establish priority over other scientists working on the same problem. If they work at a university, this way of advancing knowledge will also advance their careers. These intangible rewards (made nearly tangible in tenure and promotion) compensate scholars for relinquishing royalties on their journal articles. It explains why they are not merely willing, but eager, to submit their articles to journals that do not pay for them, and even to journals with the temerity to ask for ownership or copyright as well.

We could say that royalty-free literature is *donated* literature. Authors of journal articles donate them to journals. If this term is simpler and more direct, we can use it, provided we understand that relinquishing income from journal articles is not the same as relinquishing intellectual property rights. Authors of journal articles typically do both, but with the new generation of OA journals, authors tend to retain copyright, or at least key rights, while continuing to relinquish income.

Author donation is closely connected to academic freedom. Scholars can *afford* to donate their journal articles because they are paid salaries by universities. Their salaries free them from the market, so they can write journal articles without considering what would "sell" or what would appeal to the widest audience. This frees them to be controversial, or to defend unpopular ideas, a key component of academic freedom. It also frees them to be microspecialized, or to defend ideas of interest to only a few people in the world. The same insulation frees some scholars to be obscure, and it frees others, who did not quite get the point, to be faddish and market-driven. But because the same insulation from the market makes two important freedoms possible—open access and academic freedom—we have good reason to resist any development that would remove this insulation and make scholars' income—through salaries or royalties—depend on the popularity of their ideas.[13]

The fact that scholarly journal articles are royalty-free means that scholars can consent to OA without fear of losing revenue. That is important, and decisively distinguishes them from musicians and movie makers. The readiness of scholars to relinquish royalties is an important part of the economic basis of OA. Their resulting willingness to consent to OA is the crux of the legal basis of OA.

The royalty-free character of journal articles also means that scholars do not need the temporary monopoly of copyright in order to give them an incentive to write or to stimulate their productivity, a role for copyright often claimed for authors of royalty-producing genres. Scholars have royalty-independent incentives for writing journal articles, and hence do not lose their incentives when they waive or transfer most of the rights that accrue to them under copyright law.[14]

The royalty-free nature of journal articles also explains why scholars would not be hurt if copyright law were dramatically reformed to restore balance between copyright holders and users. Or, to see this from the other end of the stick, publishers who pretend to speak for authors in defending the current imbalance in copyright law speak for authors of royalty-producing literature. Authors of royalty-free literature have very different interests.

Scholars have an interest in disseminating their work to all who can make use of it. They want the widest possible audience. That is the best way to be noticed, read, used, and cited. For royalty-free literature, enlarging the sphere of fair use serves the author's interests; for royalty-producing literature, it invades the author's interests. Having relinquished royalties, authors of royalty-free literature have no need to protect a revenue stream, so they have everything to gain by consenting to OA and nothing to lose.[15]

In short, authors of scholarly journal articles write for impact, not for money. An even stronger way to put this point is that conventional journals that limit access to paying customers *harm* the interests of scholarly authors and are only attractive when they offer some compensation in prestige. Prestige often wins the day for scholars pursuing tenure or promotion. But when OA journals have been around long enough to earn prestige in proportion to their quality, this last attraction of conventional journals will disappear.[16]

Royalty-free literature is rare. It is so rare that we should pause for a moment to appreciate just how anomalous or peculiar it is in our landscape of intellectual property. Most content is priced for users. Even most content that is free for users—like broadcast TV—produces royalties for its creators. To be royalty-free, the creators must relinquish any demand for payment, even if they do not relinquish intellectual property rights. If we describe this category for intelligent people without first providing an example, we should not be surprised if they think the category is empty, or filled only with ephemera that lack market value. But the category includes the primary literature of science—peer-reviewed research articles and their preprints—the primary texts of public law, such as statutes and judicial opinions. Despite their importance, however, these are professional bodies of literature barely known to people outside the professions, and their rarity causes ignorance and misunderstanding about their status. With the exception of gray literature like school homework assignments and interoffice memos, most people never encounter royalty-free literature.

In most countries, statutes and judicial opinions, like other government works, are in the public domain from birth, or are not copyrightable.[17] This makes copyrightable royalty-free literature even rarer than royalty-free literature as such. At the same time, it makes clear that scientific and scholarly research articles are easily the most significant examples of the type.

The rarity of royalty-free literature causes a couple of problems for those trying to create an intellectual commons through OA. One is that copyright rules are written to protect authors and publishers of royalty-producing genres and to protect users with fair-use claims on royalty-producing genres. Even the law of the public domain is focused on the expiration of rights to royalty-producing genres. Legislators and lobbyists alike tend to be heedless of the need to treat royalty-free literature separately. The result is that when royalty-free literature is copyrighted, it is regulated as if it were royalty-producing, laying needlessly onerous duties on users to seek permission for anything beyond fair use. If royalty-free literature were the subject of separate, thoughtful legislative attention, it is likely that the rules of fair use, first sale, and copyright-term duration, would all differ from the standard rules for royalty-producing genres. In this sense, royalty-free literature is collateral damage in a war over royalties and the limits on royalties.[18]

Another problem is that the rarity of royalty-free literature increases the difficulty of changing policy, enlisting support, and disarming objections. In my experience, most nonacademics—including policymakers—do not realize that scholarly journals publish articles without buying them or paying the authors. So until corrected, most nonacademics are not inclined to support OA, thinking it calls on authors to make a sacrifice or that it depends on abolishing or violating copyright. When they are told that journal articles are royalty-free, some see the logic of OA immediately but just as many doubt that one is telling the truth.[19]

Not all academic research literature is royalty-free. Scholars write journal articles, which are royalty-free, but also books, which are royalty-producing. They also write software, which is sometimes one and sometimes the other. OA may enlarge the audience and increase the impact for all three kinds of content, but in the case of journals there is no offsetting loss of revenue and in the case of books and software there is or may be. So the very same researcher may consent to OA for articles but not for books. The important distinction, then, for setting priorities in promoting OA, is whether the content is royalty-free or royalty-producing, not whether it is scholarly or nonscholarly.

In the worldwide effort to create an intellectual commons through OA, we can distinguish three phases, in increasing order of difficulty:[20]

Phase 1   Provide OA to royalty-free literature and to all other content for which there is already permission. This includes public-domain content and content for which the copyright holder already consents to OA or would consent after a little education. This is the low-hanging fruit of OA. At least the legal hurdles have been cleared. There may still be technical and financial hurdles, such as digitizing print content and investing in robust delivery vehicles.

Phase 2   Provide OA to royalty-producing literature and to content for which copyright holders are not yet consenting to OA. Since OA to copyrighted content must be consensual, this will require persuasion. Copyright holders have a right to try to earn money from their content, and they have at least some grounds for believing that OA conflicts with any plan to earn money from their content. Hence, persuasion will often fail, which explains why this is higher-hanging fruit. I will say more later about the kinds of arguments that might persuade royalty-earning authors to provide OA to their work.[21]

Phase 3   Enlarge and protect the public domain by rolling back copyright-term extensions and ensuring that federal copyright law preempts state contract or licensing law. Make permission-seeking less often necessary by establishing the first-sale doctrine for digital content and restoring fair-use rights denied by copy-protection technologies. If Phase 2 persuades copyright holders to reevaluate their interests, then Phase 3 persuades legislators to revise copyright law. Successes at Phases 1 and 2 would make Phase 3 largely unnecessary, and vice versa. Phase 3 is higher-hanging fruit because revising copyright law in the right ways is very difficult and unlikely. As a remedy it is slow, incomplete, and uncertain. We cannot count on it and fortunately need not wait for it.

Open-Access Research Literature as an Intellectual Commons

Some kinds of commons depend essentially on the public domain. As we have seen, this is not true for OA research literature. The public domain is only one way to remove the permission barriers that would bar OA. Copyright-holder consent[22] is just as effective and more frequent in practice. When we take this path, then the OA commons is not only compatible with copyright, but depends essentially on decisions made by copyright holders.

Let's focus for a moment on OA created by copyright-holder consent, when the copyright holder retains at least some rights, such as the right to act against plagiarists or to block the distribution of misattributed copies. This kind of OA literature is still owned, and its owner reserves an important right. It is nevertheless a true intellectual commons because the copyright holder has removed enough permission barriers to create freedom for all the uses that matter for legitimate scholarship. For those uses, no further permission is needed.

Two Legal Foundations for Open Access

Public domain	Copyright-holder consent
No owner	Owner
No rights retained	Some rights retained
All rights either expired or waived	Some rights waived (permitting the uses needed for free and legitimate scholarship)
Not always voluntary (copyright expiration may be resisted; uncopyrightability may be resisted)	Always voluntary, though sometimes required in exchange for a job or research grant
No permission needed for scholarly uses	Permission already granted for scholarly uses

In June 2003, Martin Sabo (D-MN) introduced the Public Access to Science Act (HR 2613) in the U.S. House of Representatives. Its purpose was to take a large step toward providing OA to government-funded research, which constitutes most natural-science research in the United States. Its strategy was to deny copyright to all the results of government-funded research, and treat it like in-house government research. The bill was controversial and not even widely supported by friends of OA. One of the main reasons is that it chose to base OA on the public domain rather than on copyright-holder consent, needlessly alienating friends of copyright.[23]

But whether the legal foundation for OA lies in the public domain or copyright-holder consent, OA research literature is a commons precisely because it makes permission unnecessary for scholarly uses.

The OA research commons is enhanced by the fact that it is nonrivalrous (or nonsubtractive). It is not diminished or depleted by use, so that any number may use it without preempting or interfering with one another. This prevents the classical form of a tragedy of the commons in which opening a common resource for use by all diminishes it for all.[24]

Note, however, that the OA commons is nonrivalrous because it is digital, not because it is OA. Even proprietary digital information with price and permission barriers firmly in place is nonrivalrous. Users do not have unpaid access to it, but paying users do not diminish it by their use, no matter how many there are.

Certain Categories of Intellectual Property in Relation to OA

	Rivalrous	Nonrivalrous
Royalty-free	Not OA because rivalrous, hence nondigital	The easiest case for OA
Royalty-producing	Not OA because (1) rivalrous, nondigital, and (2) lacking copyright-holder consent	Rarely OA because rarely carries copyright-holder consent

The Same, with Examples

	Rivalrous	Nonrivalrous
Royalty-free	Research articles in print	Research articles online
Royalty-producing	Music on copy-protected CDs	Music in unprotected MP3 files

OA is not about research literature in general, because some research literature is rivalrous (print journals) and some of it is royalty-producing (books). And it is not about nonrivalrous content in general, because some nonrivalrous content is royalty-producing (digital music and movies) and most of the royalty-producing portion does not carry the copyright holder's consent for OA.

OA is about the much narrower category of content that is *both* non-rivalrous and royalty-free. When I stand back, I do not know what is more remarkable, that this narrow category is nonempty (and contains important literature) or that we have not long since succeeded in providing OA to the important literature in this category.

While the category to which OA applies seems very narrow, it can easily be generalized to the wider category of nonrivalrous content for which copyright holders can be *persuaded* to provide OA, either because there is no money at stake (royalty-free content), because they believe that the benefits of OA outweigh the money at stake, or because they believe that OA will actually increase net sales.[25]

We know that nonrivalrousness does not suffice to make a commons because this property is possessed even by priced, copyrighted, and copy-protected digital content, the exemplar of digital enclosure.

Strictly speaking, the property of being royalty-free does not suffice either; it merely increases the chances that the copyright holder will consent to OA. But it is a fair surrogate for copyright-holder consent, since creators of royalty-free property create it voluntarily, knowing they will not be paid for it. If they want it to reach an audience, then OA will give them an unusually wide audience at unusually low cost, without any loss of revenue. These conditions readily bring scholar consent.[26]

Copyright-holder consent suffices to make a commons, but it does not suffice to make an OA commons. This is simply because copyright-holder consent is just the legal precondition of OA, not OA itself. Works must be digitized and put online to be OA, and copyright-holder consent (or public-domain status) does not, unfortunately, suffice for that. Otherwise all public-domain books, for example, would already be OA.

Does the removal of permission barriers suffice to make a commons? If we say that it does, then it follows that there could be a commons even in print literature—for example, public-domain print literature and literature carrying the copyright holder's consent for free use. I see no problem saying this provided we distinguish the use of print literature, no matter how free, from OA, which takes advantage of the digital character and worldwide reach of the Internet. In this sense, OA was physically impossible in the age of print, but a textual commons in print was not. Indeed, Ben Franklin surely believed that his idea of a free lending library was the idea of an intellectual commons, even if it was based on the first-sale doctrine and fair-use rights rather than copyright-holder consent.[27]

By definition, OA literature excludes no one, or at least no one with an Internet connection. By contrast, non-OA electronic journals try very hard to exclude nonsubscribers from reading the articles, even if non-subscribers are welcome to browse the table of contents, abstracts, and other features. This exclusion costs the excluder money. One cost is digital-rights management or DRM, the software lock that opens for authorized users and blocks access to the unauthorized. A second cost is writing and enforcing the licensing agreement that binds subscribers. A third is subscription management: keeping track of who is authorized, and performing associated tasks such as soliciting, collecting, and renewing subscribers, and maintaining their current addresses or authentication data.

One reason why OA literature is less expensive to produce than conventional literature is that it dispenses with print and publishes directly to the Internet, usually from author submissions that are already in electronic form. But a second reason why OA literature is cheaper to produce is that it dispenses with DRM and subscription management—the whole infrastructure of payment and exclusion. The very feature, therefore, that makes OA literature a useful public good—its openness, or its freedom from price and permission barriers—is one reason why it is economically feasible. Public interest and business efficiency both support the OA commons, appealing to both altruists and bean counters.

It is often said that no one has an incentive to maintain or improve common property, or a commons, which can lead to its deterioration. This is not true of OA literature. One reason, surely, is that most OA literature is not in the public domain and still has owners. On the other hand, the original proposition falsely assumes that the only reason to maintain property is to protect a revenue stream or some other private interest like the right of exclusion. We know this is false because it cannot explain our strong incentives for protecting public goods like air and water. Like air and water, OA literature is valuable even if it generates no revenue stream. It is very likely that this value would be protected even if the literature were not privately owned.

A good example is the way OA journal publishers take steps to ensure the long-term preservation of their articles. Both BioMed Central and the Public Library of Science deposit every one of their published articles in an OA archive beyond their control, so that the articles will not only survive, but remain OA, in case the original publisher fails, is bought out, or changes its access policies.[28]

OA literature removes all price barriers. It removes enough permission barriers to support all the uses customary in legitimate scholarship (essentially every use except plagiarism and misrepresentation). It removes enough access barriers to deserve to be called an intellectual commons. However, it does not remove all access barriers.

Even after we have removed price and permission barriers, there will be four kinds of barriers left to overcome before we reach truly universal access.[29]

1. *Handicap access barriers.* Most websites are not yet as accessible to handicapped users as they could be.

2. *Language barriers.* Most online literature is in English, or just one language, and machine translation is very weak.

3. *Filtering and censorship barriers.* More and more schools, employers, and governments want to limit what you can see.

4. *Connectivity barriers.* The digital divide keeps billions of people, including millions of serious scholars, offline.

Tragedies of the OA Commons

In the OA commons, free use is preauthorized. It is an enhanced or tragedy-proof commons because it is nonrivalrous. The nonrivalrous character of OA literature insulates it from classical forms of the tragedy of commons, and explains why it is fundamentally unlike grazing land, Atlantic salmon, or Pennsylvania coal. But it is not proof against other tragedies. It is vulnerable, or at least apparently vulnerable, to several kinds of vicious circles.

Let's distinguish *tragic depletions* from what could be called *tragic stalemates*. A tragic depletion is the classic tragedy of the commons. The village green is overgrazed and depleted by unrestrained use. A tragic stalemate occurs when many separate individuals or organizations want to make the same decision but none wants to go first. Or, all want to follow a common plan or realize a common good, but none wants to take steps toward it before the others.

The result is not the destruction of a common good, but a paralysis that prevents otherwise motivated players from creating a common good. In a classic tragedy of depletion, individual users have an incentive to deplete, even to deplete what they agree is useful. In a tragic stalemate, individuals have an incentive to wait or delay, even to delay creating what they agree is useful. The first perversely kills what is already valuable, and the second perversely prevents something valuable from coming into being.

For example, all the merchants in a town might want a day of rest (say, on Sunday), but the first to close on Sundays will lose customers to those who do not. Before the Social Security Act was passed, many states wanted to raise taxes to provide a relief fund for the poor, but none wanted to go first, fearing that they would drive businesses out of state and attract indigents who would overburden the fund. These are cases in which early adopters fear that they will be exploited by freeloading late adopters or invite burdens that late adopters will be spared because of their lateness.

Here is a simple example. One study has shown that different players in the academy want open access, but administrators expect librarians to take the lead and librarians expect administrators to take the lead.[30] Perhaps that kind of stalemate can be broken by more effective communication. But here is a more complex example that cannot. If OA spreads, then it will provide mainstream or nonacademic search engines like Google and Yahoo with a larger and more useful body of content to index. As soon as they index it, they can expect to see more traffic and sell more advertising. For these reasons, it is in their interest to encourage OA and even help pay for it. There is growing evidence that they see it just this way—but none of them wants to go first. As soon as one of them pays to convert a fee-based resource to OA, then their rivals will index it at the same time. The late adopters will freeload on the early adopters and deprive them of the competitive advantage that alone might justify the investment.[31]

Stalemates or vicious circles are sometimes cited as objections to OA, but they are really just obstacles. They do not show that OA is undesirable or unattainable, merely that something desirable is more difficult to attain than we might first have thought.

Here are three vicious circles or stalemates that affect progress toward the OA commons in research literature.[32] (I am putting each of these in the strongest terms I can, which often overstate the case; I sketch the solutions or escape routes further below.)

1. If all or most journals were OA, then universities would save money. They would only have to pay for outgoing articles by their own faculty, not for incoming articles by faculty elsewhere. But paying for outgoing articles is a new expense. Overall, the OA system may cost less than the present subscription-based system, but universities may not have the money for the new system until the old system has withered away. In short, universities cannot afford OA for their outgoing articles until they have canceled enough conventional journals; but they cannot cancel enough conventional journals until OA spreads.

During an indefinite transition period, universities or other research sponsors will have to pay for both kinds of journals. This transition cost might deter or delay the emergence of a publishing model that is not only superior for all the purposes of scholarship, but also less expensive. Here the stalemate is not universities waiting for one another, but universities waiting for OA to bring them the savings that will enable them to pay for OA.

2. If some universities invest in the superior alternative and pay for outgoing articles, other universities can enjoy OA to those articles without reciprocating. Late adopters of OA can freeload on early adopters. Universities might think: "We won't make this investment, benefiting others, until enough others make it, benefiting us." Universities thinking this way end up waiting for one another, paralyzing them all.

3. Journals compete for excellent articles, and journal prestige is one of the major incentives attracting author submissions. But OA journals are generally new. Even if excellent from birth, they have not had time to acquire the prestige or impact factors of older journals, even inferior older journals. In short, new journals need prestige in order to attract excellent submissions, and need excellent submissions in order to generate prestige.

These three circles are not as vicious as they appear. Here is how to escape them.

1′. First, universities will not pay all or perhaps even most of the processing fees charged by OA journals. Many will be paid by foundations funding the research. Second, most OA journals do not charge processing fees at all. Third, many universities are not waiting for the success of OA in order to cancel expensive subscriptions. In 2004 and 2005, for example, major cancellations have taken place at major universities

(Harvard, Cornell, Duke, the University of California).[33] Fourth, universities can provide OA through archiving in digital repositories, at very little cost, long before they decide whether to provide OA through processing fees for OA journals. Finally, the transition to OA may be more expensive than a steady-state future in which OA journals predominate, but that does not mean it will be unaffordable. Universities, like other institutions, often invest money now to save money later.

2′. Freeloading late adopters enjoy OA to the literature produced by the early adopters. But early adopters are compensated for their early adoption even if others do not reciprocate. They have purchased OA to the research output of their faculty, increasing the visibility and impact of the work, the authors, and the institution. Universities would not have "publish or perish" policies if they had not already decided that this kind of visibility and impact was in their interest.

Moreover, late adopters are punished for their late adoption. They are missing a chance to provide heightened visibility and impact to their own research output, and they are slowing the general transition to OA, prolonging the time during which they must still pay for subscriptions.

If the freeloading late adopters are institutions that produce virtually no research literature, then they are not delaying the transition to OA and harm no one.[34]

By speaking about "freeloaders" (or "free riders") I do not want to give the impression that making free use of OA literature is freeloading in any objectionable sense. This free use is exactly what the OA providers intend and desire, just as the producers of broadcast TV welcome "freeloading" by viewers. Freeloading in the objectionable sense only occurs when someone enjoys free use who should be paying for it instead, or when free use depletes the public good. OA providers (journals and archives) only provide OA when they have some way of paying their expenses. Hence, users who enjoy the free access are not evading some obligation to pay. On the contrary, they are seizing an opportunity deliberately created by the author and helping the author's work to become known. And because OA literature is nonrivalrous, use does not deplete it.

3′. First, journal prestige is only one incentive for authors to submit their work. Circulation and impact are other incentives. OA journals have a wider circulation than any conventional journals, even the most prestigious and least expensive. Steve Lawrence was the first in a continuing series of scholars to produce evidence that by increasing audience or circulation, OA increases citation impact.[35] Second, OA journals can become as prestigious as any conventional journals, even if this takes time. Some jumpstart this process by recruiting eminent editors and members of the editorial board.[36] Finally, of course, we can bypass this problem entirely by converting a prestigious conventional journal to OA rather than launching a new OA journal and working to make it prestigious.[37]

These methods of breaking the vicious circles probably suffice. But whether they suffice or not, we should take note of an additional method. One solution to any tragic stalemate is an external force nudging all the stalled and stymied actors into action at the same time. For example, if all the merchants in a town really do want a day of rest, and are prevented only by the tragic stalemate, then they would support legislation to impose a day of rest on everyone. Not only does this break the stalemate, but it wins the consent and support of all the parties "coerced" by the statute.[38] Likewise, the stalemate in which the U.S. states feared to be the first to create a relief fund for the poor was one reason cited by Justice Cardozo for upholding the constitutionality of the Social Security Act, which compelled them all to act at once within a larger federal plan.[39]

There are several external forces that can nudge scholars into adopting the system they would prefer. One is for funding agencies to put an OA condition on their research grants, requiring grantees to provide OA to the results of their funded research, either through OA journals or OA archives.[40] Another is for governments to require OA to all the results of taxpayer-funded research.[41] A third is for universities to require their faculty to deposit their research output in the institution's OA repository.[42] In 2004, Alma Swan and Sheridan Brown found that 71 percent of authors would comply with an OA mandate from their funder or employer, and in 2005 they found that the figure had grown to 81 percent.[43]

There are two ways to reconcile these strategies with the bedrock principle that OA to copyrighted works must be consensual. First, as with sabbatarian legislation, if we can show that all the parties to be bound by the requirement are consenting, then the requirement is consensual in the relevant sense. Second, research grants and university positions already carry many conditions that we enforce against grantees and employees on a contract or consent theory: by agreeing to take the grant or the job, they agree to be bound by its conditions. An OA condition would be no different. I prefer the second method to the first, because it is less susceptible to self-deception by the policymaker, although there is no need to choose.

Finally, note that OA literature not only resists the classical tragedy of depletion, because it is digital and nonrivalrous,[44] but it also resists *enclosure*. Copyright holders who authorize OA by waiving certain rights could always deauthorize OA by reasserting those rights later if they wished, although I do not know of a single case in which this has happened. The author's decision to reassert her rights might be completely effective in law, if the legal status of the literature is ever tested in court. But the author has to reckon on the gap between law and compliance. At the time she decides to revoke her consent to OA, the OA edition of her work is online and contains some label or licensing language explaining that the copyright holder has consented to OA. Since OA literature may be copied and redistributed freely, chances are good that there are copies around the web, many of them unknown to the author.[45] If the author revokes her consent to OA, and removes the copies she knows about, chances are good that she will not have removed them all.

This makes the revocation of consent partially ineffective.[46] But above all, it gives an author a reason not even to try revocation. OA makes the enclosure of previously unenclosed content largely futile and, just as important, makes it *appear* largely futile. In this way, OA protects itself and intrinsically resists or deters enclosure.

The Primacy of Authors in Achieving an OA Commons

Of all the groups that want open access to scientific and scholarly research literature, only authors are in a position to deliver it.[47] There are three reasons why:

- Authors decide whether to submit their work to OA journals.
- Authors decide whether to deposit their work in OA archives.
- Authors decide whether to transfer copyright.

So even though readers, libraries, universities, foundations, and governments want OA for their own reasons, most of what they can do to promote OA takes the form of guiding, helping, or nudging authors. In this sense, authors have primacy in the campaign for OA, and the single largest obstacle to OA is author inertia or omission.

Once we recognize this, we will focus on four author-centric strategies for achieving OA:

1. Educate authors about OA
2. Help authors provide OA to their work
3. Remove disincentives for authors to provide OA to their work
4. Create incentives for authors to provide OA to their work

Let's consider these in order.

Educate Authors about OA

Author inertia or omission is not a sign of opposition. Usually it is a sign of ignorance or inattention.[48] Most scientists and scholars are too pre-occupied with their research to know what open access is—even today, after years of rising public recognition. This inattention harms OA, science, and the authors themselves, but it is hard to criticize directly. Researchers are good at what they do because they are absorbed in their projects and have extraordinary talents for focusing on their work and shutting out distractions. Here we are facing a side effect of this strength, not a simple weakness.

A March 2004 study showed that 82 percent of senior researchers (4,000 in 97 countries) knew "nothing" or just "a little" about OA. Even if the numbers are better for junior faculty, we clearly have a long way to go just to educate the scientists and scholars themselves.[49]

A February 2004 study, however, showed that when authors do learn about OA, they support it in overwhelming majorities.[50] This gives us hope that getting authors' attention will actually do some good—and in fact that the spread of the OA meme is unstoppable.

If you are a researcher, talk to your colleagues about OA. Talk to them on campus and at conferences. Talk to them in writing through the journals and newsletters that serve your field. Talk to your students, the authors of tomorrow.

If you have provided OA to your own work, talk to your colleagues about your experience. Firsthand testimonials from trusted colleagues are much more effective than policy arguments, even good policy arguments. They are also more effective with this audience than advice from librarians or university administrators, even good advice. The chief problem is getting the attention of busy colleagues and showing them that this matters for their research impact and career. Only researchers can do this for other researchers.

A surprising number of OA converts—I am one—did not go beyond understanding to enthusiasm until they provided OA to their own writings and saw for themselves the signs of rising impact. There is a discernible increase in e-mail from serious readers, inclusions in course syllabi, links from online indices, invitations to important conferences, and citations from other publications. When you experience this in your own case, it is anecdotal but compelling. When you hear it from a trusted colleague, it makes a difference.

If it is true that 5 to 10 percent of university faculty publish 80 percent of the articles,[51] then a slight widening of the current circle of researchers who already use OA can reach a critical mass of authors.

Many scholars are not at all ignorant of OA, but say they are just too busy to take the steps to provide it for their own research articles. I am sympathetic, but not very sympathetic. Scholars who have time to do research and write it up do not begrudge this time, because this is work they love. But if they get this far, then they always find time for follow-up steps that they do not love, such as submitting the articles to journals and responding to referee comments. Finally, they always seem to have time to bring their published articles to the attention of department chairs, deans, promotion and tenure committees, and colleagues in the field. Scholars find the time for the unloved steps in this process because they see the connection between them and career building.

Providing OA to our work is career building. The benefits to others are significant, but dwelling on them might have drawn attention away from the strong self-interest that authors have in OA. Get the attention of your colleagues and make this point. OA enlarges our audience and increases our impact. Anyone who takes half an hour to e-mail an updated bibliography to the department chair or to snail-mail offprints to colleagues on other campuses should take five minutes to deposit a new article in an open-access archive or repository.

Help Authors Provide OA to Their Work

Even when scholars see the connection between OA and research impact, they have to set priorities. It is not surprising that they give new research priority over enhancing the dissemination of old research, or that they give work with near deadlines priority over work with no deadlines. Here is where concrete help comes in.

Librarians can help faculty members deposit their work in an open-access, OAI-compliant archive, such as the university's OA repository. It does not matter whether authors need help because they are too busy, because they are intimidated by metadata, or because their past work is voluminous or predigital. Librarians can help them digitize and deposit it. In most cases, student library workers can help in the same way.

Universities can help by providing the funds to pay librarians or student workers to provide this kind of help. They can help by paying the processing fees charged by OA journals when funding agencies will not do so. They can help by offering workshops on how authors can retain the rights they need to authorize OA. They can help by suggesting model language for authors to use in copyright transfer agreements.

Remove Disincentives for Authors to Provide OA to Their Work

When Franz Ingelfinger was the editor of the *New England Journal of Medicine*, he adopted a policy not to accept any article that had previously been published or publicized elsewhere. As the policy spread to other journals, it became known as the Ingelfinger Rule. It seems to be in decline nowadays, but is hard to tell because many journals do not say explicitly on their websites whether or not they follow the rule. The rule deters authors from depositing their preprints in OA archives, and so does uncertainty about where the rule still applies. Researchers who proudly disregard the risk that their work will offend church and state flee from the risk that preprint archiving will disqualify their work for later publication in a peer-reviewed journal.

The best way for journals to remove this disincentive is to abandon or modify the Ingelfinger Rule and to say so publicly. Journals only have to modify the rule enough to let authors take advantage of online preprint exchanges. They can still refuse to consider submissions that have been formally published elsewhere. The second best way for journals to remove this disincentive is to make their policies clear and explicit on their websites. This will let authors make informed decisions about the risks. Authors in fields where the rule is rare, or who have no plans to submit their work to journals where it is still in force, will then have the confidence to provide OA to their preprints.

Promotion and tenure committees (P&T committees) create a disincentive for submitting work to OA journals when they only reward work published in a certain set of high-impact journals. The problem is that most OA journals are new and do not yet have impact factors.[52] When a committee makes impact factor a necessary condition for review, then it discriminates against new journals, even excellent new journals.

It discriminates not only against new journals trying out a new business and distribution model, but also against journals exploring a new research niche or methodology. The problem is not the committee's attempt to weed out the second rate. The problem is doing it badly, with a crude criterion, so that the committee also rules out much that is first rate.

Administrators who understand this problem can set policy for their P&T committees. Faculty who understand this problem can volunteer to serve on the committee.

Foundations that fund research are often as blinkered as P&T committees, even if the same foundations try to support OA through other policies. If they tend to award grants only to applicants who have published in the usual small set of high-impact journals, then they deter authors from publishing in OA journals, even while they show support by offering to pay the processing fees charged by OA journals.

Create Incentives for Authors to Provide OA to Their Work

Universities can create an incentive by requiring OA to all the research articles that faculty would like the P&T committee to consider. Because this can be done through OA archives, it is compatible with publishing the same articles in conventional, subscription-based journals. The policy need not limit the freedom of authors to publish in any journal that will accept their work.[53]

Funding agencies, public and private, can create an incentive for authors by requiring OA to the results of the funded research.[54] Authors would not oppose these steps. As noted,[55] Swan and Brown found that an overwhelming majority of authors would willingly comply with an OA mandate from funders or employers.

Finally, we could provide a significant incentive for authors if we could make OA journals as prestigious as conventional journals of the same quality. Unfortunately, it is easier to control a journal's actual excellence than its reputed excellence. One way to boost prestige is to recruit eminent scholars to serve on the editorial board, a method used effectively by *PLoS Biology* and BMC's *Journal of Biology*.[56] Another way is for eminent scholars who are beyond the reach of myopic P&T committees to submit new, excellent work to OA journals. This will help break the vicious circle by which new OA journals need excellent submissions to build prestige, and need prestige to attract excellent submissions.[57]

Contrasting Perspectives on the OA Commons

Anything as large and complicated as the OA commons will inspire analysis from different points of view.

One distinction apparent in the literature is between the standpoint of scholars and the standpoint of librarians. Scholars want OA because, as authors, they want to enlarge their audience and increase their impact, and as readers, they want free and ready access to the literature they need to keep up with their field. Librarians want OA because it will solve the serials pricing crisis, at least as far as OA extends, and it will solve a related "permission crisis" in which unbalanced copyright laws, non-negotiable licensing agreements, and software locks that often go beyond the terms of either one, prevent libraries and their patrons from making use of expensive electronic journals in the way that they could make use of print journals.[58] Scholars and librarians can join forces and work toward the same end, but they rarely cite the same arguments as reasons for doing so.

Another distinction in the literature is between First- and Third-World advocacy. Researchers and governments in developing countries tend to be strong supporters of OA.[59] It solves the problem of delivering access to institutions that have not been able to pay retail prices for it, and it solves the problem of making Third-World research available to the First World. By contrast, First-World analysis tends to focus on the inability of even affluent institutions to buy the access needed for contemporary research, and the need of publishing scholars to reach an audience larger than the audience of affluent subscribers. Again, First- and Third-World friends of OA can join forces and work toward the same end, but they often differ in their arguments.[60]

A third distinction in the literature is between appeals to self-interest and appeals to the public interest. All the stakeholders—scholars, universities, libraries, learned societies, journals, publishers, foundations, and governments—have some interest in the emergence of OA, although this interest is easier to see for some stakeholders than for others. Some, like the learned societies, have just about as much interest favoring OA as opposing it. Some, like the commercial publishers, have more interest opposing OA than favoring it, but this fact often blinds us to the side of their interest favoring OA.[61] Still, strong and honest arguments can be made to any stakeholder that it is in their interest to adopt OA or at least to experiment with it.

But a very different kind of advocacy focuses on normative arguments that disregard self-interest, much as appeals to duty disregard self-interest. Authors who relinquish royalties *deserve* to reach their audience without a profiteering intermediary standing in the way, collecting tolls. It is *unfair* to make taxpayers pay a second fee for access to taxpayer-funded research. Profit-seeking *should not* interfere with truth-seeking. Knowledge is not a commodity (just as facts are not copyrightable) and *ought* to be shared. Science *ought* to be controlled by institutions committed to the growth of knowledge, not by institutions committed to the enrichment of shareholders. Information *should* be free.

Finally, there is a distinction between two ways of thinking about free online access to research literature. University faculty already have free online access to the electronic journals to which their institutions subscribe. A few years ago, when faculty heard the arguments for OA, many would say, "Why is this an issue? I already have free online access."[62] (This objection is less common today.) Let's say that researchers have a *narrow interest* in free access if they only care about whether they have to pay for it out of their own pocket. If their employer buys it for them, they do not care whether the employer paid a high price for it, and they do not care whether researchers without wealthy employers are left in the cold. By contrast, let's say that researchers have a *wide interest* in free online access if they want it to be free for everyone with an Internet connection.[63]

Fewer and fewer faculty nowadays say that they have only the narrow interest in free access. But more and more often we hear the large commercial publishers asserting that faculty *should* have only the narrow interest.[64]

Commercial publishers can satisfy the narrow interest in free access, provided they keep their prices within reach of institutions (which they are failing to do). Why should faculty demand more? If the narrow interest covers their professional interest, and they are still not satisfied, are they not simply adding political idealism to their legitimate professional interests?

That is how Elsevier would like to frame the issue, but it does not work. First, we may concede that many OA arguments have a political or quasi-political edge. OA is not just about accelerating research and saving money; it is also about freedom from needless barriers, fairness to taxpayers, returning control of scholarship to scholars, de-enclosing a commons, and serving the underserved. But even if we disregarded these quasi-political goals and cared only about the professional needs of researchers, we would have to agree that the wider interest has the more enlightened view. Researchers want to see their institutions free up money from expensive journal subscriptions in order to spend it on other pressing needs, including the superior OA alternative, books the library could not afford while it paid for expensive journals, infrastructure, equipment, and staff.

Moreover, the narrow interest would only suffice to cover their professional interest if every library subscribed to every journal. But not even the wealthiest research library can make this claim, and the reason is the unbearable cost.[65] We must move beyond the narrow interest to the wider one if only to have a realistic chance of gaining access to all the research literature in our field. Finally, research advances more quickly and surely if more people are able to participate. If the lesson of open-source software is that "given enough eyeballs, all bugs are shallow" (Eric Raymond), then the analogous lesson of OA is that "given enough researchers in the loop, all research errors and omissions are shallow"— or, shallower than they would be when the pertinent literature is locked away behind price and permission barriers. To take advantage of this opportunity, we must enfranchise all who are connected—and connect all who are not.

A Word about Phase 2 Initiatives

Peer-reviewed research articles and their preprints are a Phase 1 problem. They are royalty-free literature. Author donation is already a fact of life, and thanks to it author consent to OA is readily forthcoming. We are far from having OA to this entire corpus, but progress is steady and gaining momentum.[66]

But books, for example, are a Phase 2 problem. They generate royalties, at least if sales permit. Authors often earn nothing from research monographs, but they rarely donate them or volunteer to relinquish the chance of royalties.

One argument that might persuade authors of research monographs to consent to OA is that their royalties are meager at best and the benefits of OA—enlarged audience and increased visibility and impact—are documented and significant. For research authors below the bestselling strata, the benefits of OA are worth paying for, and many will find them more valuable than the likely royalties. For monograph authors who understand the issues, OA can win against royalties in a cost-benefit analysis.

But monograph authors may not have to choose. There is evidence that OA is not only compatible with print sales and royalties, but increases them.

The National Academies Press publishes research monographs and has provided free online full-text for each of them since 1994. At the same time, it tries to sell its books in print editions. The free editions undoubtedly subtract some from the sales of the priced editions. But remarkably, they add more than they subtract.[67] The Ludwig von Mises Institute follows the same practice for its research monographs, with the same results,[68] and so does the Baen Free Library, for science fiction novels.[69]

At first this is counterintuitive and mysterious. Aren't these plans scuttled by freeloaders who read the free editions online and never buy the print editions? The answer is that very few people are willing to read whole books online or print whole books on their home printers. Most people use free online full-text books for sampling. When they are sure that a book matches their needs and interests, they will pay for a print edition.

Amazon is banking on this theory with its new service, Search Inside the Book,[70] which provides free full-text searching—but not free full-text reading—for a growing number of royalty-producing books. If free full-text searching supports sampling sufficiently well, then it will probably trigger the same net increase in sales seen by NAP and Baen, at least for the right kinds of books. The program may not work for reference works and cookbooks, which many readers consult only for snippets, but it could well increase net sales for research monographs and novels.

The NAP, Baen, and Amazon experience suggests a second argument that might persuade authors of research monographs to consent to OA: It will stimulate a net increase in sales.

Amazon used a variation on this argument to persuade a group of commercial publishers to put their full-text books into Amazon's index. If these publishers do not lose sales, or if they gain, then the tide will have turned. More publishers will want to participate. Participating publishers will want to participate with more books. More kinds of books will at least be tried—out-of-print books, low-selling books, specialized market books, beautifully illustrated books, and books for which impact is more important than revenue. Some publishers will undoubtedly go beyond the Amazon experiment to the original NAP and Baen model, and try free online full-text for reading, printing, and copying, not just for searching. An intellectual commons of many kinds of OA book literature is already under way, joining the intellectual commons of OA research articles.

One important result is that OA is not limited to royalty-free literature. OA still depends on the public domain or copyright-holder consent, but we are now seeing that copyright-holder consent is compatible with royalties. This enlarges the scope of OA from the small and anomalous category of royalty-free literature to the very large, mainstream category of royalty-producing literature. Not all royalty earners will walk through the open door, but as we see more of them experiment, and more of them report greater sales or benefits that outweigh sales, then we will see more follow suit.

Books will be the first Phase 2 success, and will succeed where music and movies failed. The reason is simply that free online access to a digital music file, or movie, is all that most users want. They can enjoy it exactly as intended, either online or downloaded to the right kind of player. The prospect of reading a whole book online, or printing a whole book on one's own printer, is the ergonomic hurdle that makes all the difference. Journal articles do not face this hurdle, but they do not need to in order to win copyright-holder consent to OA. They depend on the very different inducement that they are royalty-free and written for impact rather than income.[71]

One conclusion: an online, open-access intellectual commons in research literature is growing from many sources for many reasons. The incentives and economics differ from genre to genre, discipline to discipline, and decade to decade. But ever since texts have been stored in bits, which makes it possible to produce perfect copies at virtually no cost, and ever since the emergence of a global network of bit-switching machines, which makes it possible to share these copies with a worldwide audience at virtually no cost, the trajectory has always been up. There is no going back.

Notes

1. For more detail on the definition of "open access," and some of the discrepancies among the published definitions, see Peter Suber, "How Should We Define 'Open Access'?", *SPARC Open Access Newsletter* (August 2, 2004), http://

www.earlham.edu/~peters/fos/newsletter/08-04-03.htm#define. For an introduction designed for those new to the concept, see Peter Suber, *Open Access Overview*, http://www.earlham.edu/~peters/fos/overview.htm.

2. BioMed Central and the Public Library of Science, the two largest OA publishers, both use the Creative Commons Attribution license. See http://www.biomedcentral.com/info/about/copyright and http://www.plos.org/journals/license.html. I have used the same license for my newsletter on open access since July 2003, http://www.earlham.edu/~peters/fos/newsletter/archive.htm.

   Author rights can be enforced through copyright law, licensing contracts, or informal norms in the scholarly community. Creative Commons licenses are most common licenses used for OA works, though they are not the only ones. See http://creativecommons.org/. Many OA authors believe that informal mechanisms are as effective as formal licenses and more convenient for authors. The Bethesda Statement on Open Access Publishing (June 2003) asserted that "community standards, rather than copyright law, will continue to provide the mechanism for enforcement of proper attribution and responsible use of the published work, as they do now." See http://www.earlham.edu/~peters/fos/bethesda.htm.

3. Budapest Open Access Initiative, http://www.soros.org/openaccess/read.shtml.

4. Open Archives Initiative, http://www.openarchives.org/. Raym Crow, *A Guide to Institutional Repository Software*, Open Society Institute, version 2.0, January 2004 (a guide to the open-source software for building and maintaining OAI-compliant archives). http://www.soros.org/openaccess/software/.

5. Despite the fact that peer review consists of donated time and clerical tasks, the costs are greater than most authors would guess. A recent review of the literature put the figure at $400 per published article. One reason the figure is so high is that it covers the cost of reviewing rejected articles. See Fytton Rowland, "The Peer-Review Process," *Learned Publishing* 15/4 (October 2002): 247–258, http://miranda.ingentaselect.com/vl=4928683/cl=179/nw=1/rpsv/cgi-bin/linker?ini=alpsp&reqidx=/catchword/alpsp/09531513/v15n4/s2/p247. The cost of peer review will drop steadily as more and more of the necessary clerical tasks are automated by journal-management software.

6. Cara Kaufman and Alma Wills determined that the figure is 47 percent. See their report, *The Facts about Open Access*, ALPSP (October 11, 2005), http://www.alpsp.org/publications/FAOAcomplete.pdf.

7. I am not saying that scholarly journals, like broadcast TV programs, can support themselves through advertising, merely that they can support themselves through a similar up-front subsidy system that pays for dissemination so that the audience need not pay for access. I elaborate further on the comparison to the funding model for television and radio in "Where Does the Free Online Scholarship Movement Stand Today?", *Cortex* 38/2 (April 2002): 261–264, http://www.earlham.edu/~peters/writing/cortex.htm.

8. The largest private funder of medical research in the United States, the Howard Hughes Medical Institute, and the largest in Britain, the Wellcome Trust, have adopted this policy. In June 2003, they and other stakeholders issued the *Bethesda Statement on Open Access Publishing*, calling on others to follow suit. See http://www.earlham.edu/~peters/fos/bethesda.htm.

9. See http://www.philosophersimprint.org/.

10. See below for some reasons to think that some book authors could be persuaded, including evidence that free online full text might stimulate a net increase in sales.

11. For more on the history of scientific journals and their relationship to open access, see Jean-Claude Guédon, "In Oldenburg's Long Shadow: Librarians, Research Scientists, Publishers, and the Control of Scientific Publishing," *ARL Proceedings* (May 2001), http://www.arl.org/arl/proceedings/138/guedon.html.

12. But see my "Open Access When Authors Are Paid," *SPARC Open Access Newsletter* (December 2, 2004), http://www.earlham.edu/~peters/fos/newsletter/12-02-03.htm#payingauthors.

13. I discuss the connection between author donation and academic freedom in "The End for Free Online Content?", *Free Online Scholarship Newsletter* (June 8, 2001), http://www.earlham.edu/~peters/fos/newsletter/06-08-01.htm.

14. Strong copyright protections may be part of the incentive for authors of royalty-producing genres, but not for authors of scholarly journal articles. One reason, of course, is that journal articles are royalty-free. If scholars make no income from their articles, they need no monopoly on that income in order to goad their productivity. Another reason is that scholars tend to transfer the copyright in journal articles to journal publishers (even if they could often negotiate another arrangement). The copyright in journal articles therefore tends to protect publishers, not authors. See Sam Vaknin, "Copyright and Scholarship: Interview with Peter Suber, Part I," *United Press International* (February 19, 2002), http://www.upi.com/view.cfm?StoryID=15022002-015414-4119r.

15. A common misunderstanding among nonacademics, and even some academic publishers, is that OA appeals primarily to scholarly readers, not scholarly authors. But in fact, it originated with scholarly authors looking for ways to enlarge their audience, increase their impact, and make their work more visible, more discoverable, more retrievable, more accessible, and for all these reasons more useful than conventional publication allowed.

16. The oldest peer-reviewed, OA journals were launched in the late 1980s. See my *Timeline of the Open Access Movement*, http://www.earlham.edu/~peters/fos/timeline.htm. However, the most prestigious OA journals are much more recent. One reason prestige does not correlate with age here is that the OA movement had to incubate for a while before it was possible to recruit eminent scientists and scholars to OA journal editorial boards.

17. In the United States, this is mandated by 17 USC 105, http://www.title17.com/contentStatute/chpt01/sec105.html. Peter Veeck encountered a

disturbing exception in which a private organization held the copyright to a publicly enacted statute and wanted to use its copyright to block Veeck's OA version of the text. See my "When Public Laws Are in the Public Domain and When They Are Not," *Free Online Scholarship Newsletter* (June 25, 2001), http://www.earlham.edu/~peters/fos/newsletter/06-25-01.htm. Also see *Veeck v. Southern Building Code Congress*, 5th Cir., No. 99-40632, en banc decision, June 7, 2002, http://laws.findlaw.com/5th/9940632cv2.html.

18. On December 6, 2001, the French Académie des Sciences released a public statement calling on the European Commission not to apply copyright rules for royalty-producing content to scientific publications for which the authors seek no payment. See "Pétition sur la Directive européenne" (December 6, 2001), http://www.revues.org/calenda/nouvelle1580.html.

19. For example, see Francis Muguet's "Activity Report" (October 24, 2003) on negotiations to produce a meaningful endorsement of OA at the World Summit for the Information Society. The negotiations were thwarted again and again by the common misunderstanding that all literature is royalty-producing literature. See http://www.wsis-si.org/si-prepcom3-report.html.

20. I discuss the distinction between royalty-free and royalty-producing content, and the three phases of the OA movement, in "Not Napster for Science," *SPARC Open Access Newsletter* (October 2, 2003), http://www.earlham.edu/~peters/fos/newsletter/10-02-03.htm#notnapster.

21. See below.

22. When the author and copyright holder differ, then it is the copyright holder's consent that matters for purposes of OA. OA journals typically let authors retain copyright to their articles. But conventional or subscription-based journals (non-OA journals) typically ask authors to transfer copyright to the journal and authors typically agree to do so.

Hence, if we want OA to the preprint (the version of an article prior to peer review), then we ask the author. Authors who deposit their preprints in OA archives typically do so before submitting their work to journals and long before transferring copyright. But if we want OA to the postprint (the version of an article accepted by a journal's peer-review process, often after some revision), then we must usually ask the publisher. An increasing number of journals allow authors to deposit the postprint in an OA archive. See the database of publisher policies on copyright and OA archiving maintained by Project SHERPA, http://www.sherpa.ac.uk/romeo.php.

23. Martin O. Sabo, Public Access to Science Act (HR 2613), submitted to the U.S. House of Representatives on June 26, 2003. See http://thomas.loc.gov/cgi-bin/query/z?c108:H.R.2613: (the final colon is part of the URL). Also see my "Martin Sabo's Public Access to Science Act," *SPARC Open Access Newsletter* (July 4, 2003), http://www.earlham.edu/~peters/fos/newsletter/07-04-03.htm#sabo.

24. Here is an interesting exception. The Public Library of Science is a major open-access publisher. The launch of its first OA journal, *PLoS Biology*, on October 1, 2003, was long-awaited. Many major newspapers and science journals wrote stories in anticipation of it. In the first few hours after the launch, the journal website received over 500,000 visits and over 80,000 requests for a single article. The PLoS servers could not handle the traffic and crashed. See Paul Elias, "Free Online Journal Seeks Revolution in Science Publishing," *Associated Press* (October 16, 2003), http://www.signonsandiego.com/news/computing/20031016-1421-openaccessscience.html. Is this a negligible exception? Or should web traffic and server load count as diminution of a common, Internet resource? If so, then the Internet cannot support true nonrivalrous commons, except perhaps unpopular or well-funded ones. But even when server load diminishes use for others, Net-based digital commons are much more robust and less susceptible to tragic overuse than analog commons like grazing land. Moreover, the burden of overuse is temporary. When they slow down or crash, they can be restored to full service after insignificant delay.

25. See below.

26. I mean that being royalty-free is a fair surrogate for copyright-holder consent when we are estimating which bodies of literature will carry copyright-holder consent to OA. I do not mean that we can infer consent from the fact that a work is royalty-free. (Otherwise, we could always buy consent or its equivalent by ceasing to pay authors.) On the other hand, there are ways that authors who do consent can manifest their consent so that users need not ask them individually every time they want to go beyond fair use. See the Budapest Open Access Initiative FAQ, "Must Users Ask the Author (or Copyright Holder) for Consent Every Time They Wish to Make or Distribute a Copy?", http://www.earlham.edu/~peters/fos/boaifaq.htm#consentqueries.

27. Because OA depends on the digital character and worldwide reach of the Internet, it was physically impossible in the age of print. But how close could we come in the age of print, simply by removing permission barriers? The free lending library is one example. I learned the following example, very analogous to OA archiving, from Barbara McManus, an emerita classicist at the College of New Rochelle. J. A. K. Thomson, a classicist at King's College London, wrote the following in a letter to Gilbert Murray, a fellow classicist at Oxford, March 26, 1944 (p. 4). The original is in the MS. Gilbert Murray Box 174, Fols. 165–67, at the Bodleian Library, Oxford:

I am concerned at the amount of good work in scholarship which has no chance of being published—unless of course the Government should subsidise it. I am pessimistic about the immediate, though not the ultimate, prospect for the Classics. I think compulsory Latin will be abolished and when that happens the Classical Departments in other places than Oxford and Cambridge will dwindle to nothing. Even now it does not pay a publisher to put out a Latin, let alone a Greek, book, however excellent, and the University Presses cannot carry the burden unsupported. But would it be possible for the B.M. [British Museum] or

Oxford or Cambridge to invite really good scholars to deposit with them a typed or manuscript copy of some magnum opus on which they had spent long time and labour? It would then become available to other scholars, even if it could not be published.

28. Also see BMC's Open Access Charter, http://www.biomedcentral.com/info/about/charter. I outline several other steps taken by BMC in Lila Guterman and Peter Suber, "Colloquy on Open Access Publishing," *Chronicle of Higher Education* (January 29, 2004), http://chronicle.com/colloquylive/2004/01/openaccess/.

29. Peter Suber, "How Should We Define 'Open Access'?", *SPARC Open Access Newsletter* (August 2, 2004), http://www.earlham.edu/~peters/fos/newsletter/08-04-03.htm#define.

30. Randall Ward, David Michaelis, Robert Murdoch, Brian Roberts, and Julia Blixrud, "Widespread Academic Efforts Address the Scholarly Communication Crisis: The Results of a Survey of Academic Institutions," *College & Research Library News* (June 2003), http://www.ala.org/ala/acrl/acrlpubs/crlnews/backissues2003/june4/widespreadcademic.htm.

31. I first pointed this out in "Predictions for 2004," *SPARC Open Access Newsletter* (February 2, 2004) (prediction #3), http://www.earlham.edu/~peters/fos/newsletter/02-02-04.htm#predictions. Shortly afterward (March 2, 2004), Yahoo announced a program to index OA content in a more useful form than is publicly available to its rivals only in a less useful form. See the Yahoo press release, http://biz.yahoo.com/bw/040302/25391_1.html. In December 2004, Google announced its plan to digitize and index the full texts of millions of books from five major research libraries. See http://www.google.com/press/pressrel/print_library.html.

32. I talk about these and related obstacles, including other vicious circles, in "Why FOS Progress Has Been Slow," *Free Online Scholarship Newsletter* (May 15, 2002), http://www.earlham.edu/~peters/fos/newsletter/05-15-02.htm, and "Dissemination Fees, Access Fees, and the Double Payment Problem," *Free Online Scholarship Newsletter* (January 1, 2002), http://www.earlham.edu/~peters/fos/newsletter/01-01-02.htm.

33. See my catalog, *University Actions against High Journal Prices*, http://www.earlham.edu/~peters/fos/lists.htm#actions.

34. Occasionally one hears the objection that elite research universities, which produce more research articles per capita than lesser institutions, will bear the heaviest load in a future dominated by OA journals. The objection assumes that universities would pay the author-side fees whenever their faculty members published in an OA journal. Four quick responses: (1) Universities will not be the only payors. Foundations will pay at least as often. (2) Elite research institutions will *save* the most from the conversion, cancellation, or demise of conventional, subscription-based journals. (3) Fewer than half of all OA journals charge author-side fees. (4) Elite research universities currently pay more for journals than lesser institutions do, but they clearly regard this as the price of supporting

a higher level of research. Do they want to say that they only buy more journals than lesser institutions because they cannot persuade lesser institutions to share the cost with them?

35. Steve Lawrence, "Free Online Availability Substantially Increases a Paper's Impact," *Nature* (May 31, 2001), http://www.nature.com/nature/debates/ e-access/Articles/lawrence.html.

36. The Electronic Society for Social Science uses the phrase "instant reputation" for success in this endeavor. See Manfredi La Manna, "The Story of ELSSS: A New Model of Partnership between Academics and Librarians" (May 11, 2002), http://www.elsss.org.uk/documents/CURL_11_03_02.pdf. For example, the Public Library of Science acquired instant reputation or instant prestige when it recruited Vivian Siegel to be its new editor-in-chief. Siegel was formerly the Editor of *Cell*. Both PLoS and BioMed Central have recruited Nobel laureates to serve on the editorial boards of their OA journals.

37. A good example is *Nucleic Acids Research*, from Oxford University Press. NAR published for thirty-two years as a subscription-based journal and earned an ISI rating as one of the "hottest" journals of the decade in biology and biochemistry. After a period of OA experimentation, NAR decided in June 2004 to make a full conversion to OA, effective January 2005. See http://www3 .oup.co.uk/nar/special/14/default.html.

38. See John Stuart Mill, *On Liberty* (Indianapolis: Hackett [1859] 1982), 88:

Without doubt, abstinence on one day in the week, so far as the exigencies of life permit, from the usual daily occupation . . . is a highly beneficial custom. And inasmuch as this custom cannot be observed without a general consent to that effect among the industrious classes, therefore, in so far as some persons by working may impose the same necessity on others, it may be allowable and right that the law should guarantee to each, the observance by others of the custom, by suspending the greater operations of industry on a particular day.

39. *Steward Machine Co. v. Davis*, 301 U.S. 548, 588 (1937). See http:// laws.findlaw.com/us/301/548.html.

40. The Wellcome Trust adopted such a policy on October 1, 2005. The WT is the largest private funder of medical research in the UK, giving £400 million per year in research grants. See http://www.wellcome.ac.uk/doc_WTD002766.html. I proposed a policy along these lines in my *Model Open-Access Policy for Foundation Research Grants* (July 8, 2003), http://www.earlham.edu/~peters/ fos/foundations.htm.

41. In July 2004, the U.S. House Appropriations Committee asked the National Institutes of Health (NIH) to require free online access to articles arising from NIH-funded research. By the time the NIH actually adopted a policy, however, it had been weakened to a mere request. The NIH public-access policy took effect on May 2, 2005; see http://www.nih.gov/about/publicaccess/index.htm. For some of the procedural history, see my FAQ on the NIH policy, http://www .earlham.edu/~peters/fos/nihfaq.htm. Also in July 2004, the UK House of

Commons Science and Technology Committee recommended that the UK require open access to the results of all taxpayer-funded research. The government rejected the recommendation, but it was taken up by the independent Research Councils UK (RCUK), which actually disburse publicly funded research grants. For the House of Commons Science and Technology Committee recommendations, see http://www.publications.parliament.uk/pa/cm200304/cmselect/cmsctech/399/39902.htm. For the RCUK open-access policy, see http://www.rcuk.ac.uk/access/index.asp. I discuss the arguments for public access to publicly funded research in "The Taxpayer Argument for Open Access," *SPARC Open Access Newsletter* (September 4, 2003), http://www.earlham.edu/~peters/fos/newsletter/09-04-03.htm.

42. At the time of this writing, five universities mandate open access to their research output. For these and related university policies, see the *Institutional Self-Archiving Policy Registry*, http://www.eprints.org/openaccess/policysignup/. All universities that require OA do so through institutional repositories rather than OA journals. This preserves the freedom of faculty to publish in the journals of their choice. I support versions of all three of these external forces or nudges—by private foundations, public funding agencies, and universities. See *What You Can Do to Promote Open Access*, http://www.earlham.edu/~peters/fos/do.htm.

43. See Alma Swan and Sheridan Brown, "Authors and Open Access Publishing," *Learned Publishing* (July 2004); *Open Access Self-Archiving: An Author Study* (May 2005). For details, see http://eprints.ecs.soton.ac.uk/11003/ and http://cogprints.org/4385/.

44. I do not want to give the impression that all digital and nonrivalrous commons inherently resist tragedies of depletion. For example, I believe that spam triggers a tragic depletion in the usefulness of e-mail. If the worldwide network of e-mail users is a commons that we are all free to graze at will, then spammers are the overgrazers that are starting to spoil it for the rest. In the case of real grazing land, the overgrazers must be a significant fraction of the common users. But in the case of e-mail, spammers are a tiny minority. Moreover, they only succeed in ruining the e-mail experience for others because a tiny minority of their recipients buy their products. Insofar as spammers are to blame, the cause is greed. Insofar as their customers are to blame, the cause is credulity. The resulting tragedy of the e-mail commons does not deplete the content, but it does deplete the usefulness of the medium.

45. See my "The Many-Copy Problem and the Many-Copy Solution," *SPARC Open Access Newsletter* (January 2, 2004), http://www.earlham.edu/~peters/fos/newsletter/01-02-04.htm#manycopy.

46. Or, to be more precise: since OA to copyrighted content must be consensual, revoking consent to OA is fully effective in negating the status of OA. But it could be completely ineffective at introducing access barriers to that content.

47. Versions of this material have appeared earlier as "It's the Authors, Stupid!", in *SPARC Open Access Newsletter* (June 2, 2004), http://www.earlham.edu/

~peters/fos/newsletter/06-02-04.htm#authors, and as "The Primacy of Authors in Achieving Open Access," in *Nature* (June 10, 2004), http://www.nature.com/nature/focus/accessdebate/24.html.

48. When "presented with a list of reasons why they have not chosen to publish in an OA journal and asked to say which were important . . . the reason that scored highest (70%) was that authors were *not familiar enough with OA journals in their field*" (Alma Swan and Sheridan Brown, "Authors and Open Access Publishing," *Learned Publishing* (July 2004): 220, http://eprints.ecs.soton.ac.uk/11003/). "Of the authors who have not yet self-archived any articles, 71% remain unaware of the option" (Alma Swan and Sheridan Brown, *Open Access Self-Archiving: An Author Study* (May 2005), http://cogprints.org/4385/.

49. Ian Rowlands, Dave Nichols, and Paul Huntingdon, *Scholarly Communication in the Digital Environment: What Do Authors Want?*, CIBER (March 18, 2004), http://ciber.soi.city.ac.uk/ciber-pa-report.pdf.

50. Alma Swan and Sheridan Brown, *JISC/OSI Journal Authors Survey Report* (London: Key Perspectives Ltd., February 2004), http://www.jisc.ac.uk/uploaded_documents/JISCOAreport1.pdf.

51. I have heard this estimate from several sources but so far without documentation. I do not vouch for the numbers. But the true numbers will very likely be close to these.

52. However, some OA journals are old enough to have impact factors. A study by Thomson ISI showed that these were comparable to the impact factors of conventional journals. See James Testa and Marie E. McVeigh, "The Impact of Open Access Journals," Thomson ISI, April 15, 2004. Here is an excerpt from the study: "These journals all adhere to high publishing standards, are peer reviewed comparably to other journals in their respective fields, and are cited at a level that indicates they compete favorably with similar journals in their field. The chief difference between these and some other journals covered by ISI is that the entire content of the OA journals is available without cost to the user" (http://www.isinet.com/media/presentrep/acropdf/impact-oa-journals.pdf).

53. A common way to avoid copyright problems is to require deposit of the final version of the author's manuscript, incorporating all changes from the peer-review process, but not necessarily the copyedited or published version. Publishers who object to the proliferation of versions may deposit the published version in place of the author's final manuscript. Currently about 70 percent of surveyed journals permit authors to deposit the published version of their article in an OA repository. See the e-prints "Journal Policies—Summary Statistics So Far," http://romeo.eprints.org/stats.php. In addition, 100 percent of affected journals are cooperating with the NIH policy that asks NIH grantees to deposit the final version of the author's manuscript in PubMed Central, an OA archive. See my "Publisher Policies on NIH-Funded Authors," *SPARC Open Access Newsletter* (June 2, 2005), http://www.earlham.edu/~peters/fos/newsletter/06-02-05.htm#nih.

54. For more on funding agency OA mandates, see notes 40 and 41, above.

55. See note 43.

56. See note 36.

57. See the section "Tragedies of the OA Commons" for more discussion of this vicious circle.

58. I discuss the two standpoints, and elaborate on the library's standpoint, in "Removing the Barriers to Research: An Introduction to Open Access for Librarians," *College & Research Libraries News*, 64 (February 2003): 92–94, 113, http://www.earlham.edu/~peters/writing/acrl.htm.

59. See for example Bioline, http://www.bioline.org.br/; the Electronic Publishing Trust for Development, http://www.epublishingtrust.org/; the International Network for the Availability of Scientific Publications, http://www.inasp.info/; SciDev.Net, http://www.scidev.net/; SciELO, http://www.scielo.br/. Also see Peter Suber and Subbiah Arunachalam, "Open Access to Science in the Developing World," *World-Information City* (October 17, 2005), http://www.earlham.edu/~peters/writing/wsis2.htm.

For public statements calling for open access in developing countries, see the Declaration of San José (March 27, 1998), the Declaration on Science and the Use of Scientific Knowledge (July 1, 1999), the Declaration of Havana (April 27, 2001), the Beijing Declaration (October 19, 2003), the IAP Statement on Access to Scientific Information (December 4, 2003), the Valparaiso Declaration (January 15, 2004), the Declaration from Buenos Aires (August 28, 2004), the Library-Related Principles for the International Development Agenda of WIPO (January 26, 2005), and the Salvador Declaration (September 23, 2005), http://www.earlham.edu/~peters/fos/timeline.htm.

60. Many journal publishers donate electronic subscriptions to Third-World research institutions. See Ann Okerson's list of such programs, http://www.library.yale.edu/~llicense/develop.shtml. But this creates another reason why north and south friends of OA use different arguments in their analysis and advocacy. A major issue for developing countries is whether these donated subscriptions to toll-access journals are good enough, or whether researchers must press for true OA.

61. Here are three examples of publisher self-interest favoring OA: (1) Commercial publishers have raised subscription prices four times faster than inflation since 1986. It was inevitable that this could not continue forever. Starting in late 2003 and continuing through the present, more and more libraries are making the courageous but painful decision to cancel important journals rather than pay another price increase. On January 7, 2004, the University of California Academic Senate and all the library directors of the UC campuses said in a public letter, "The economics of scholarly journal publishing are incontrovertibly unsustainable." See http://libraries.universityofcalifornia.edu/news/facmemoscholcomm_010704.pdf. The letter was referring to conventional, subscription-based journals, not OA journals. It is now in the self-interest of commercial publishers to experiment with OA because they cannot continue business as usual. (2)

Publishers that have digitized the back run of a journal can make a trickle of income by selling access to it. But more and more journals will discover that providing OA to the back run will bring more net gain than the revenue. It will increase the visibility and impact of the journal, and its "brand," which any competent journal can translate into advantage in the competition for submissions, advertising, and subscriptions. (3) Learned societies and nonprofit organizations that publish journals often want to charge subscription fees and generate revenue, but they may have more to fear from the giant commercial publishers, whose "big deals" soak up disproportionate shares of library budgets, than they do from OA.

62. I heard this often myself. Bob Parks heard it often too and describes his observations in "The Faustian Grip of Academic Publishing," a preprint posted to WoPEc (Working Papers in Economics) (July 2001), http://econwpa .wustl.edu:8089/eps/mic/papers/0202/0202005.pdf. Parks: "The point is that readers do not necessarily want [free online journals], especially if they can have [priced journals] without giving up their office or phone or secretarial services. . . . Readers do care about free availability. But will they demand [free online journals] versus [priced journals]? Free availability to readers is no out-of-pocket costs." Parks is describing the view of others, not necessarily his own.

63. I discuss this distinction in more detail in "Elsevier CEO on the Public Library of Science," *Free Online Scholarship Newsletter*, February 6, 2002, http://www.earlham.edu/~peters/fos/newsletter/02-06-02.htm.

64. When Derk Haank was CEO of Reed Elsevier, he made this argument in an interview in *Information Today*. See Dick Kaser, "Ghost in a Bottle," *Information Today* (February 2002), http://www.infotoday.com/it/feb02/kaser.htm. It has been a favorite Elsevier argument ever since.

65. I discuss some measurements showing the journal gaps at leading U.S. research libraries in "What's the Ullage of Your Library?", *SPARC Open Access Newsletter* (January 2, 2004), http://www.earlham.edu/~peters/fos/ newsletter/01-02-04.htm#ullage.

66. See for example my account of the progress of OA last year, "Open Access in 2003," *SPARC Open Access Newsletter* (January 2, 2004), http://www .earlham.edu/~peters/fos/newsletter/01-02-04.htm.

67. See Michael Jenson, "Academic Press Gives Away Its Secrets," *Chronicle of Higher Education* (September 14, 2001), http://chronicle.com/prm/weekly/ v48/i03/03b02401.htm. Jensen is the director of Publishing Technologies at the NAP. Also see the National Academies Press website, http://www.nap.edu/, and browse the free full-text books.

68. Jeffrey Tucker, "Why We Put Books Online" (March 12, 2004), posting to the Ludwig von Mises Institute blog, http://www.mises.org/blog/archives/ why_we_put_books_online_001698.asp; later turned into an article, "Books, Online and Off," Ludwig von Mises Institute (March 22, 2004), http://www .mises.org/fullstory.asp?control=1473.

69. Baen Free Library, http://www.baen.com/library/. Also see Eric Flint's explanation of Baen's business model and success, "Prime Palaver #6" (April 15, 2002), http://www.baen.com/library/palaver6.htm.

70. See the Search Inside the Book home page, http://www.amazon.com/exec/obidos/tg/browse/-/10197021/002-8790426-8727260. Also see Amazon press release, http://phx.corporate-ir.net/phoenix.zhtml?c=97664&p=IROL-NewsText &t=Regular&id=462057& (October 23, 2003), and FAQ, http://www .amazon.com/exec/obidos/tg/browse/-/10197041/002-2808347-4161631.

8

How to Build a Commons: Is Intellectual Property Constrictive, Facilitating, or Irrelevant?

Shubha Ghosh

The term *intellectual property* elicits the question: Is the subject matter of patent and copyright law, as well as its close cousins, meaningfully described as "property"? That this question is compelling is indicated by the countless articles that adopt it as a key focus of inquiry.[1] But whatever the accepted meaning of property, whatever property's status as metaphor, and however interesting these topics are to discuss and debate, the question of whether intellectual property is actually property is a distraction. The more relevant question is what role the concept of intellectual property plays in building an information commons.

In this chapter, my primary goal is to refocus the primacy of property in the intellectual property debate by recognizing that intellectual property, whatever the term means, should best be understood as a means and not an end. My suggested focus, it is hoped, will provide a better understanding of intellectual property as a tool to build a commons. By recognizing intellectual property as a tool, we can better understand it as a legal category. Toward this goal, I frame this chapter around the problem of how to build a commons and the specific problem of whether intellectual property constricts or facilitates the creation of an information commons. Of course, it would be foolish to ignore the third possibility—that intellectual property is completely irrelevant for the building of the commons. Although most readers would find that possibility incredible, addressing the relevance of intellectual property is key to our understanding, not only of what intellectual property can be, but also of what we mean by the information commons.

My aim of challenging property talk in intellectual property discussion, however, begs another conceptual question: What is the information commons? The meaning of information commons is less contested than that of intellectual property. Although we may differ in the normative desirability of the information commons, we can all accept that what we mean by an information commons is an organization of the production and distribution of knowledge that ensures open access. Much of the normative debate over the desirability of the information commons and its structure reflects the controversy over how open that access should be (Lessig 2001, 76). For some, open access is synonymous with free access, mandating that all knowledge be available at no cost to the user. Practical considerations place limits on equating open with costless. While free information may be desirable for journalists, researchers, and consumers who seek understanding of products and services, free access for spammers, perpetrators of fraud, and other threats to privacy and security are hardly desirable. One limit to freedom of access would entail legal or technological restrictions that prevent the improper uses of information. Needless to say, the scope of these restrictions is contested, but whatever their shape, the implication is that open access cannot mean unfettered access. Even more controversial is the notion that open access cannot even mean access at no cost. Critics of open access contend that free information, in the sense of information distribution at a zero price to the user, is no information since the inability to charge would reduce the incentive to discover and disseminate information. According to this view, open access is a doomed exercise, the true tragedy of the commons. Defenders of open access would point out that market systems themselves are not costless and need to be compared with alternatives. Furthermore, defenders of open access would assert, competitive markets depend on some degree of openness of information to survive. For example, information about price, quantity, and quality has to be freely and openly available for perfectly competitive markets to function properly. In markets that deviate from the ideal of perfect price competition, such as certain types of markets structured as auctions, information regarding the quality and quantity of what is being auctioned needs to be accessible to the participants for the market institution to be trusted and to function effectively. Therefore, an institution as seemingly proprietary as a market depends on some degree of open access at its foundation. The information commons, with its frequent commitment to open access, raises deep questions of institutional design and organization that will be the focus of this chapter.

Brett Frischmann categorizes the issues I have raised as a problem of "commons management," which can be understood in terms of the various resources that constitute the commons (Frischmann 2005, 933–934; Lessig 2005, 1034–1035). Resources, according to Frischmann, are divided into ones that are rival and ones that are nonrival in consumption, borrowing a well-known category from public economics (pp. 959–970). Among the set of nonrival resources, Frischmann identifies certain resources, such as highways, the environment, and telephony, as inputs for the creation of other resources (pp. 974–978; Lessig 2005, 1037–1038). Inputs that tend to be nonrival resources are what he calls infrastructure, a resource that should not be made proprietary through legal restrictions, such as intellectual property. Frischmann's theory provides one way to build a commons and to define intellectual property rights based on the identification of certain resources as infrastructure that necessarily have to be jointly owned and managed through collective entities in order to ensure efficiency.

While I like the term *commons management*, I suggest an approach to commons construction that goes beyond the reliance on the traditional, and overused, category of nonrivalry. As I have discussed in previous work, whether we characterize a resource as nonrival rests largely on the property-rights structure used to protect the resource (Ghosh 2003, 401–420). Therefore, it is circular to base property rights on the categorization of a resource as nonrivalrous. Such a theory would entail "public goods all the way down" (with apologies to Bertrand Russell) (Hawking 1988, 1). My blueprint for building a commons is richer, with a focus on the behavioral underpinnings that make a commons necessary and on the institutional arrangements that facilitate a certain form of open access. The blueprint rests on three principles. First, I start with the behavioral principle that imitation is important for the production and dissemination of knowledge. This behavioral principle is important because it explains why patent and copyright are concerned with the problem of unauthorized copying. I show that control of copying is a crucial means to control how learning and knowledge dissemination occur. Second, human beings not only imitate each other, they also exchange ideas and commodities. While imitation rests on individuals attempting to be the same, exchange demands that individuals be different in order for exchange to be meaningful. Exchange is the principle that provides the basis for markets and other institutions in which human interactions can occur. Finally, imitation and exchange give rise to governance systems, both formal and informal, that make possible cultural production. For the rest of the chapter, I will show how my theory of commons construction and the corollary role of intellectual property rest on the three principles of imitation, exchange, and governance.

The organization of the chapter is as follows. The next section will address the arguments for how intellectual property can constrict, facilitate, and be irrelevant to the information commons. I argue that the case for each role of intellectual property rests on how one understands the relationship between formal laws and informal norms in shaping the commons. I conclude the next section by pointing out that our understanding of intellectual property should be subsidiary to our vision of the commons. In the third section, I turn to the three guiding principles for designing a commons: imitation, exchange, and governance. I explain these three principles and explore their implications for commons management. In the fourth section, I turn to two examples that demonstrate my blueprint for designing a commons: file sharing and experimental use in the pharmaceutical industry. I show how the guiding principles work to design each of these respective commons. The fifth section summarizes and concludes.

The Case for and against Intellectual Property

Intellectual property refers to a body of legal rights that comprise patents, copyrights, trademarks, and assorted doctrines such as trade secrets, right of publicity, and contract-based rights. This hodgepodge of legal rules and doctrines has two things in common. First, they each relate to some aspect of the association of the creative process with the manufacture of information. Second, they each give to the legally designated creator of information the right to exclude others from copying and distributing the information. Within this shared framework, the several bodies of intellectual property law differ in the type of information protected. Patents, for example, protect the products of inventive activities; copyright protects the products of expressive activities. Trademarks, on the other hand, protect business signifiers that are valuable to consumers for distinguishing the source of a product or service. Similarly, the law of trade secrets protects information that is valuable to the economic success of an enterprise, while the right of publicity protects personal attributes, such as a likeness or a voice from which economic value can be obtained. For the purposes of this chapter, I will focus on patents and copyrights. Within the U.S. legal system, patents and copyrights have a constitutional dimension through Article I, Section 8, Clause 8 of the U.S. Constitution, which expressly empowers Congress to enact patent and copyright laws. When emerging economies seek to copy U.S.-style intellectual property law, it is often patent and copyright that is being emulated.

In this section, I will discuss the relationship between intellectual property, as defined in the previous paragraph, and the information commons, as described in the introduction. The relationship is a controversial one, and opinion can be divided into three camps: those who view intellectual property as constrictive of the commons, those who view intellectual property as facilitating the commons, and those who view intellectual property as irrelevant to the commons. I will present the salient arguments for each of these three positions in order to clarify both the meaning of intellectual property and the task of constructing an information commons. The three positions differ not so much in their conclusions, but in their views on the relationship among formal law, informal norms and customs, and salient institutions and practices in the information commons. Those who argue that intellectual property is hostile to the creation of the commons, for example, emphasize the role of formal law in limiting access to information. By contrast, the position that intellectual property facilitates the commons is grounded in the importance of the market for creating a particular vision of the commons. Finally, those who argue that intellectual property is irrelevant point to informal norms and customs as creating the necessary foundations for a vibrant information commons. After making the case for each position, I conclude by shifting attention from intellectual property law as an end to intellectual property as a means. In short, this section provides a basis for developing an instrumental view of intellectual property as a tool to secure guiding normative principles for a meaningful vision of the information commons.

Intellectual Property as Constrictive

The case that intellectual property constricts the development of the information commons follows from the status of intellectual property as a government-sanctioned right to exclude (Lessig 2001, 19–20). While the grant of a patent or a copyright to an individual establishes only the right to exclude others from imitating the subject of the patent or copyright, exclusivity gives the intellectual property owner the legal ability to restrict entry into a field of endeavor and to deny access to knowledge.

The canonical case of intellectual property exclusivity is that of pharmaceutical patents, which allow the owner of the patent to prevent a company from making cheaper, but effective generic versions of the drug. This form of exclusivity does not necessarily translate into market power, as controlled by antitrust or other competition law, since it might be possible for a company, in theory, to invent around the patent and create a noninfringing substitute for the drug. Nonetheless, patent exclusivity can be quite powerful even if it does not translate into market power in the legally recognized sense. A potential creator of a substitute for a patented drug may be inhibited from creating such a substitute because merely experimenting with the drug to discover chemical analogues can constitute patent infringement. While in the United States some limitations on patent exclusivity are enacted into law, the precise scope of these limitations is far from clear. The Patent Act does allow experimentation on patented drugs that is reasonably related to the submission of a drug application to the Food and Drug Administration, but the term "reasonably related" offers little guidance to potential competitors to patent owners. The Supreme Court has shed some light on the meaning of "reasonably related" in its 2005 *Merck v. Integra* decision, and I will discuss the implications of this case for both the constrictive view of intellectual property and the possibilities for an information commons in the market for pharmaceuticals (Merck 2005). Nonetheless, the exclusivity provided by patents in the pharmaceutical industry illustrates starkly how intellectual property can constrict the information commons.

The world of copyright also exemplifies the constrictive role of intellectual property for open access. The often-cited SunTrust case involved the attempt by the owner of the copyright in the novel *Gone With the Wind* to prevent publication of the novel *The Wind Done Gone*, a critical riff on the Scarlett O'Hara epic presented from the slave's perspective. Putting aside the aesthetic merit of either novel, the case shows that the copyright owner can have quite a bit of control over the types of information available to consumers in a free market. Once again, the absence of market power in the traditional antitrust sense is inapposite. Certainly, there are substitutes for *The Wind Done Gone* that provide insights into the slave's perspective on the "moonlight and magnolia" mythology typified by Margaret Mitchell's opus. Certainly, there are alternatives to using Margaret Mitchell's copyrighted expression, her characters, her plotting, her descriptions, in constructing a counternarrative to Southern plantation culture. But the argument is that copyright should not create minefields and should not serve as barriers to artistic and creative expression. The offensive use of copyright to prevent expression is antithetical to the goal of open access in the information commons.

Exclusivity has to have a very precise meaning for the argument that intellectual property constricts the information commons to make sense. The right to exclude in the context of personal and property rights is essential to the preservation of individual autonomy. For intellectual property, the ability to exclude use of one's creation provides the conditions for creativity and invention. Even if much artistic and scientific production is collaborative and cumulative, individualized effort is a key input to the final output of both artistic and scientific endeavors. The ability to exclude is as important for preserving individual autonomy in artistic and scientific efforts as it is for sexual activity, management of one's household, the pursuit of one's education and career, and other life choices.

However, there are key differences between exclusivity in the context of real and personal property and exclusivity in the context of intellectual property. First, with respect to intellectual property, exclusivity is almost wholly instrumental. The right to exclude serves to provide an incentive to produce and disseminate creative and innovative works. The instrumental use of the right to exclude is reflected in the duration limitations on intellectual property. While the right to exclude others from one's real or personal property is perpetual, the right to exclude others from intellectual property expires in order to ensure that the creative and innovative work becomes dedicated to the public. The balance between public access and exclusivity is also reflected in the second key difference between exclusivity in intellectual property and exclusivity in other types of property. This second difference demonstrates the potential dark side to exclusivity. In the context of intellectual property, my ability to exclude your access to my work may create impediments to your ability to create your own work. The problem is in thinking in terms of individual possession and ownership in the context of the information commons. When intellectual property constricts the information commons, our commitment to exclusivity has to give way to the need for open access.

Many of the constrictive tendencies of intellectual property can be cured through rigorous application of safety valves like fair use, the first-sale doctrine, and the First Amendment. Of course, proponents of the view that intellectual property constricts the information commons have varied programs to modernize and reform intellectual property doctrines. But it is important to recognize that this negative view of intellectual property rests on a particular legalistic view of intellectual property. Within the terms of the constriction argument, exclusivity operates through the use of the legal system, particularly a lawsuit for infringement, to prevent access to knowledge, whether embodied in a new invention or in a work of artistic expression. But intellectual property, like all legal rights, does not exist simply as an instrument of litigation and dispute. Legal rights are created not to provide a means of holding others hostage for the purposes of rent extracting. They can help define a zone of individual autonomy and social value that extends beyond the pursuit of money and privilege. The creation of patent and copyright systems validates the inventive and creative process and provides social expression of the value of artistic and scientific endeavors. While the argument for the constrictive role of intellectual property certainly recognizes these values and pursues them by fostering the information commons, the overly legalistic view of intellectual property ignores the varied role that intellectual property—specifically, and law and legal institutions more generally—plays in structuring the information commons. Consequently, the case for intellectual property as a constrictive influence overemphasizes the legalistic dimension of intellectual property and distracts from the behavioral and institutional dimensions of the information commons. Put another way, simply having better fair-use rules and a more effective First Amendment may not be sufficient or even necessary for the promotion of the information commons.

Intellectual Property as Facilitating

The case that intellectual property facilitates the information commons follows from a thought experiment. Imagine what the world would look like without intellectual property. In this world, by definition, there would be no intellectual property lawsuits, no cease-and-desist letters telling creators that their activities violate the law and may subject them to fines, and no impediments to users accessing and sharing knowledge in whatever form it might be embodied. But, proponents of the facilitation argument would suggest, there might be a handful of people who might be wary of sharing, not because they are selfish, but because they fear that someone else might appropriate their work in a way that is deemed harmful (Kitch 1977, 267–271; Kieff 2001, 701). The undesired appropriation might take many forms. It could occur through false attribution as the unscrupulous claim credit for having created a work of art or a piece of software. If markets still existed, as they most likely would even in a world without intellectual property, the unscrupulous might try to sell the misappropriated work to a willing buyer. This last possibility might still exist even without intellectual property if the work in question cannot be copied easily by the user, as with a unique sculpture or work of architecture. Users might prosper but creators may choose to opt out or seek ways to appropriate the value they feel they deserve from their work by creating limited editions or distributing through technological means that limit copying. In the case of scientific creations, such as pharmaceuticals, inventors may rely on trade secrecy, not in the form of trade-secret law (which of course would also be abolished), but in the form of professional guilds or other restrictive measures. One thinks of Leonardo Da Vinci writing in his notebook in his invented secret code or the glass makers on the Island of Murano who were required to live on the island several miles off the shores of Venice and were forced to take their glassblowing secrets to the grave. The point is that removing intellectual property has implications beyond simply giving a windfall to users, and these implications might actually be harmful to the information commons.

The elimination of the exclusivity granted by intellectual property alters the shape of institutions. While exclusivity is understood largely in legalistic terms under the constrictive vision of intellectual property, exclusivity is an important building block for the information commons under the facilitative view of intellectual property. The exclusivity of intellectual property serves as a safeguard that allows creators to disclose their work to the public without the fears of appropriation described in the previous paragraph (Ghosh 2004, 1330–1339). This disclosure in turn benefits and enriches the commons by creating a shared resource to which all members of society can have access once the term of exclusivity expires. The benefit of exclusivity to the commons needs to be gauged in terms of the alternative of secrecy. Without the ability to exclude through intellectual property, certain individuals would exclude by not disclosing at all to the detriment of society and the information commons. The challenge is to design legal institutions in a way that defines the terms of exclusivity as an attractive alternative to secrecy.

The argument does not necessarily depend on the incentive effects of intellectual property. Creators very likely would produce art and tinkerers would still invent even without intellectual property protection. The point of the argument is that there is very likely a group of creative folks who may prefer not to publicize their work and to distribute it in secret. There may also be a group of creative folks who have no problem with sharing. The problem is that we do not know which one of these groups will produce the most interesting and socially desirable works. Assuming that the distribution of talent is random, the production of socially desirable works is probably not correlated with the desire to publicize or keep the work secret. Intellectual property, properly calibrated, is designed to make it desirable for creative folks to publicize their work for the benefit of the information commons by permitting appropriation for those who seek it. For those who do not care about appropriation, intellectual property is at worst redundant. Such people can opt out of the intellectual property system, at least with respect to the works they create.

The constricting vision of intellectual property emphasizes the ways exclusivity can limit creativity and invention. By contrast, the facilitating vision emphasizes the role of exclusivity in promoting the entry of the individual, through his or her work, into the public sphere. In the simplest terms, the constricting vision sees intellectual property as an offensive tool while the facilitating vision sees intellectual property in defensive terms. More deeply, each set of arguments rests on slightly different assumptions about behavior and the design of institutions. Under the constricting view of intellectual property, exclusivity operates through formal legal processes as an impediment to creation. Under the facilitating view, exclusivity operates to shape the public sphere by creating assurances for individual creators.

Despite the differences, the constricting and facilitating views of intellectual property may lead to the same policy prescriptions. For example, both views would support limits on intellectual property that expand their respective objectives. I have pointed out that those who see intellectual property as constricting would support limits like fair use, permitting uses of intellectual property without payment, as well as the First Amendment, allowing uses of intellectual property to promote freedom of expression. Those who adopt a facilitating view of intellectual property would also advocate for similar limitations to the extent that they support the uses of intellectual property to promote disclosure. Both positions would agree that there should be duration limits on intellectual property, although proponents of each position may differ on how long is enough. It would be wrongheaded to think that either view necessarily leads to either a restrictive or an expansive agenda for intellectual property. The key difference is one of understanding how intellectual property affects the shape of the information commons.

A potential pitfall of the facilitating position is the overemphasis of market institutions in shaping the commons. Just as the constricting position may tend to overemphasize the legalistic dimensions of intellectual property at the expense of the behavioral and institutional dimensions, so the facilitating position can too readily lend support to the position that legal rights are simply servant to the market. When the facilitating view suggests that intellectual property facilitates the entry of creative output into the public arena, the arena is more often than not the marketplace. As I discuss below, the market can serve as an important institution for facilitating the information commons, particularly a market that is bolstered by competition and free entry, but it would be a grave error to equate the commons with the marketplace. Nonmarket institutions, such as the university and the household, also serve to define the commons, but the exclusivity needed for the marketplace may come into conflict with the exclusivity in the university. The conflict is essentially one of agency. If the university wants to commodify scientific research, but the professor does not, who should win? Which commons, the marketplace that facilitates the distribution of the fruits of the research, or the scientific community that facilitates the dissemination of knowledge, should be facilitated? The constricting view of intellectual property fails by relying too heavily on legalistic solutions to counterbalance exclusivity. But the facilitating view too readily ignores that the information commons consists of many different types of institutions and that intellectual property needs to be calibrated, not only to facilitate publicizing one's work but also to structure the relationship between market-based and non-market-based commons. Both approaches focus too closely on exclusivity and ignore how exclusivity should be aligned with the normative possibilities of the information commons.

Intellectual Property as Irrelevant

I have presented two views of intellectual property and have suggested that they are not satisfactory for answering the question of what the proper relationship is between intellectual property and the information commons. Before presenting my own answer to this question, I need to address the possibility that intellectual property may be irrelevant to the information commons. Given all the scholarly attention to intellectual property, this possibility seems unlikely. Nonetheless, a useful case can be made for irrelevance, and analyzing it is helpful to understanding what we mean by both intellectual property and the information commons.

The case for irrelevance rests on the precedence of informal norms and customs over formal law in defining the information commons. While patent and copyright law seemingly create a set of rules that regulate inventive and expressive activities, there are many uncertain and unanswered questions within the law. No legal system is complete and airtight, but many students of patent and copyright law tend to ignore how many holes there are in the alleged iron cage of intellectual property. For example, a basic question like ownership is far from clear. Copyright law is particularly confusing with respect to the work-for-hire doctrine, which vests ownership in the employer when the work is created under an agency relationship. While the rule in practice seems to be that copyright in a work created within an employment relationship belongs to the employer, copyright law itself establishes a multifactored balancing test taken from the common law of agency to establish when an employment relationship exists. Furthermore, copyright law is surprisingly unclear about who owns the copyright in a work that is recorded from oral expression without the authority of the speaker. Copyright is established when an original work of authorship is fixed in a tangible medium of expression and the fixation is authorized by the creator of the expression. However, when there is no authorization, technically there is no federal copyright law. As a matter of practice, this gap is filled by common-law copyright and by the custom, in some situations, of the authors making their own authorized copies. Finally, the law of joint authorship in copyright also generates legal mysteries with the requirement that each joint author contribute originality and that they agree to merge their respective creativity in a undifferentiated whole. In many situations, however, authors fail to strike an agreement, with courts having to decide which of the possible authors was the primary source of the originality and which purported authors provided only sweat of the brow. Patent law has simpler rules for determining inventorship, but puzzles still prevail. For example, an inventor must have contributed to at least one of the claims in a patent to be considered a coinventor. But it is often not until the end of patent prosecution that inventors even know what the claims of the patent will be. The point is that even on such a fundamental issue as who owns the property right, intellectual property is far from clear.

The gray areas in intellectual property law are filled in with norms and customs, in some ways more important than the formal rules of intellectual property. In the case of copyright ownership, informal customs, such as academic rules about attribution in journal articles, and the rules of professional organizations like the Screenwriters Federation of America, the Directors Guild of America, and the Screen Actors Guild, resolve attribution and ownership issues. The most important illustration of the role of informal norms and customs in intellectual property is provided by fair use in copyright and its close cousins of experimental use and repair in patent. Fair use in copyright is far from clear (and as a result, according to some, far from fair). Courts must determine fair use based on a multifactored balancing test that takes into consideration the amount taken, the nature of the work, the purpose of the use, and the effect on markets. Judicial opinions eschew simple rules like "noncommercial use is always fair" and "parody is always fair use," citing Supreme Court precedent that no one factor trumps any of the others.[2] Nonetheless, copyright practice fills in the lack of certainty in the fair-use doctrine, even if everyone may implicitly recognize that adherence to copyright practice is at one's own risk. So, in his famous study of informal settlement of disputes, Robert Ellickson points to organizational practices in the use of the photocopier as an example of how informal norms and customs help to determine what is fair use of copyrighted materials. Ellickson describes an "instructors' norm of reciprocal fair use," which permits "the unconsented copying for class use, year after year, of articles and minor portions of books." When copyright scholars hear of such practices, they invariably must offer the correction that fair use does not operate on such bright-line principles. But such practices continue, much to the chagrin of law professors and the consternation of courts. While patent law does not have a fair-use doctrine per se, unauthorized use of patented material may be excused by the experimental-use and repair doctrines. Under the experimental-use doctrine, experimenting on a patent work for the purposes of philosophical speculation is not patent infringement. Similarly, repairing a patented work is also exempted from patent infringement. But needless to say, it is not always clear what constitutes excused experimentation or repair. Once again, practices provide the certainty that the law lacks, with research labs often sharing or reusing patented equipments and materials in their day-to-day operations and tinkerers everywhere reconstituting patented machines that may often go beyond what is considered repair.

Adding further support for the irrelevance of intellectual property are the spate of organizations that manage intellectual property resources, creating their own formal rules that become incorporated into industry practice. In the previous paragraph I mentioned the Screen Actors Guild, the Directors Guild of America, and the Screenwriters Federation of America, three of the prominent professional organizations in the television and motion picture industry. Copyright has other entities, so-called copyright intermediaries, that provide private regulation of creative activities. The Copyright Clearance Center, for example, is a private organization that serves as an intermediary between those who photocopy protected materials and copyright owners. The CCC is a mainstay in most universities, providing a convenient way to put together and finance coursepacks. But while formal law makes the CCC necessary, its actual operation does not function fully within the four corners of the law. So often payments may not be made because of inefficient monitoring, especially of smaller entities. Other times, payments are made when none are necessary, such as for materials, like judicial opinions and statutes, that are not even protected by copyright law. Performance-rights organizations, like Broadcast Music, Inc. and ASCAP, that are responsible for collecting and disbursing licensing fees for performance rights for musical works also function through self-regulation. Patent law has fewer examples of these licensing organizations, partly because of the prominent role of the U.S. Patent and Trademark Office, a government agency, in administering patents. But patent pools and cross-licensing schemes serve as a form of self-regulation of patents. These schemes often police the use of patents and privately regulate the development and dissemination of patented technologies.

The case for irrelevance is largely a case for the priority of informal norms and customs over formal law. There is, however, an alternative economic formulation of the argument. In his article "The Problem of Social Cost" (1960), Ronald Coase demonstrated that in the context of nuisance disputes, formal legal rules defining property rights are irrelevant to the final allocation of resources when the transaction costs of bargaining are sufficiently low. Under his formulation, formal legal rules define initial entitlements from which affected parties can bargain to reallocate rights as long as there are no impediments to bargaining. While his argument is framed in terms of "social costs," the kind associated with polluting activities, the point extends to the "social benefits" associated with intellectual property. In the canonical problem of intellectual property, an individual has created something, a work of art, a drug, a machine, whose benefits to society exceed the benefit to the individual creator. Because the social benefits exceed the private benefit, the individual creator would lack adequate economic incentives to produce the work and distribute it to society without the ability to capture all the social benefits of the creation. Under the Coasean formulation, legal rights can be defined to internalize the externality, but in terms of the goal of efficient allocation of resources, it is largely irrelevant who has the legal rights in the creation (the creator or the public at large) as long as bargaining is allowed. Within this model, organizations like the CCC, the Screenwriters Federation of America, and the other entities discussed above can be understood as institutions to facilitate bargaining over the use of a valuable resource. If the Coasean argument is correct, formal intellectual property law is irrelevant as long as private entities can bargain to define the ways creative effort and the outputs of such effort can be allocated.

Casting the irrelevance argument in Coasean terms highlights some of the defects in the conclusion that intellectual property law is irrelevant to the information commons. The Coasean formulation of irrelevance rests on the assumption that transaction costs are low. But, as is well known in the literature, it is not clear how low transaction costs have to be in order for the conclusion of irrelevance to follow. Certainly, if transaction costs are zero, then the proposition follows as a logical matter, but a world without transaction costs is a rarefied world without friction. The operational form of Coase's argument urges policymakers to design legal rights in a way that minimizes the transaction costs of bargaining. In other words, legal entitlements are to be established in order to allow them to be traded. This directive, however, assumes the desirability of trading entitlements, and current scholarly thinking suggests that there are certain situations when it may be desirable not to let legal entitlements be easily bargained away, either for nonefficiency goals or to further the efficient allocation of contested resources. The point is that irrelevance of intellectual property, in Coasean terms, rests on being able to ascertain the level of transaction costs independent of the design of legal entitlements. As both a theoretical and a practical matter, this independence is a heroic assumption to the conclusion of irrelevance.

More importantly, there is another compelling reason to reject the irrelevance argument that does not rest on the fragility of the Coasean argument. The argument for irrelevance as I have presented it here rests on a separability between formal law and informal norms and customs. Developments in intellectual property belie this separability. For example, while fair use may rest in practice on customary behavior and organizational norms with respect to copying, the tendency has been to make fair use more lawlike, with a movement away from the interpretation of fair use as an equitable rule of reason toward the attempt to reconstitute fair use in formal doctrinal terms. Experimental use in patent law seems to be taking a similar turn, as courts narrow the scope of the exemption to a narrow protection for philosophical inquiry without protection for actual practices. In fact, the debate over experimental use is increasingly becoming one of the statutory bases for the exemption, rather than a customary one. These specific examples of the tension between formal law and informal norms and customs are symptomatic of a larger change in the background set of social and economic relations against which informal norms and customs are defined. Norms and customs are particular to specific communities, and as the shape of the communities morphs, so do the resulting informal norms and customs. The trends in intellectual property toward greater protectionism reflect the increased corporatization of the marketplace and the globalization of production and consumption. When norms and customs are defined by a market-driven, corporate culture, the case can and should be made that what we need is more formal law that protects the interests of users and consumers. Accepting the argument that intellectual property is irrelevant begs the question of what type of formal laws and informal norms and customs are desirable in order to reach the normative vision of the information commons.

Aligning the Cart and the Horse

This section addresses the question of the relationship between intellectual property and the information commons. I have addressed three possible answers to this question, which I have labeled the constrictive argument, the facilitating argument, and the irrelevance argument. Each of these arguments is uniquely flawed, but the three share a common error of assuming a particular, essentialist view of intellectual property. Each position fixes intellectual property either within a specific meaning of exclusivity or within a vision of a particular relationship between formal law and informal norms and customs. The more salient question, however, is what we want intellectual property to be in order to reach a normative vision of the information commons. While each argument alerts us to the potential problems and advantages of intellectual property for creating an information commons, none directly addresses how intellectual property is an instrument that we can fashion and utilize in designing the information commons. I now turn to this challenging task. The next section ascertains three guiding principles in designing the information commons; the following section illustrates the problems of designing an information commons through three examples.

Some Guiding Principles for Commons Design

In this section, I elaborate on three principles that should guide us in the design of the information commons: imitation, exchange, and governance. The information commons, with its assurance of open access, implements each of these principles. In turn, understanding these principles helps us grasp why the information commons is desirable. Open access facilitates imitation, which I demonstrate is important for progress in expressive and inventive activities. Open access also facilitates the exchange of information, both through market and nonmarket transactions, that fuels creation and invention. Finally, open access fosters governance structures that aid in cultural production. These three principles not only guide the design of the information commons, but also the structure of intellectual property as a means to implementing that design.

Imitation and Progress

Imitation, as the cliché states, may be the sincerest form of flattery, but within most current intellectual property regimes, imitation will often be the first step to being sued for infringement. In a famous copyright opinion concerning protection of advertising posters, Justice Oliver Wendell Holmes epitomized the traditional view of imitation within intellectual property:

Even if [the pictures] had been drawn from the life, that fact would not deprive them of protection. The opposite proposition would mean that a portrait by Velasquez or Whistler was common property because others might try their hand on the same face. Others are free to copy the original. They are not free to copy the copy. The copy is the personal reaction of an individual upon nature.[3]

Creativity is the imposition of the human imagination on nature. Creative works are a copy of nature filtered through the human mind, and intellectual property does not give the individual creator the right to copy from nature. While imitation from nature is not restricted under intellectual property, imitation from other individuals is. This view of imitation lays the foundation for intellectual property that is proprietary, including only the products of nature within the domain of the commons. My contention is that Justice Holmes has it wrong about imitation. In fact, imitation from other individuals, "copying the copy," is crucial to creativity and progress. An apocryphal story has Hunter S. Thompson learning to be a writer by typing over and over again the published work of an admired author (Menard 2005, 27). Although possibly copyright infringement, Thompson's imitation is also a common way information and knowledge are conveyed.

I am not suggesting that imitation is the only means of cultural transmission. As a couple of scholars have put it, "imitation is not sufficient for culture" (Visalberghi and Fragaszy 1996, 278). Nor am I suggesting that it is necessary. Imitation, however, is one important way cultural expressions and innovations can be propagated. Therefore, it is dangerous to categorize all imitation as actionable intellectual property infringement. Teachers, especially, should not be concerned that I am advocating plagiarism. In the production of student work, originality and attribution are important for intellectual development and social comportment in academic environments. But as a teacher, I am struck by how much learning does in fact occur through copying. As with Thompson's example, tinkering with someone else's expression can be a valuable experience in improving one's own writing. Such tinkering is analogous to experimental use in patent law, a practice currently under fire. Of course, there is a difference between copying to understand deeper structures and patterns and rote learning. But there also is a difference between imitation that should be actionable as infringement and imitation that should not be. The task is to understand those distinctions.

Research in the educational psychology literature supports my contention. For example, Elisabetta Visalberghi, a psychologist with the National Research Council in Rome, and Dorothy Fragaszy, a psychologist at the University of Georgia, identify several key influences of imitation on education and learning. First, imitation "can be a quicker way of learning than individual trial-and-error experiences" and can be "safer in some circumstances than learning on one's own" (p. 278). Second, imitation "allows the transmission of information and behaviors across individuals, a component of culture in its human form" (p. 278). Finally, imitation "is an inherently social process, involving observation of one individual (an 'expert') by another (an 'observer')" (p. 278). Although the two psychologists base their research on observing imitative behavior among monkeys and apes, they conclude that "imitative capacities and teaching in nonhuman primates do not approach those of humans" (p. 297), for whom "imitation is ubiquitous and apparent perhaps from birth" (p. 297). In short, imitation not only "aids learning new skills," but also is "used socially . . . as a probe in social interactions" (p. 297). The educational psychology literature also suggests that imitation is important for language acquisition among children and is important in kindergarten children's efforts to learn social norms and cognitive skills. The literature is careful in distinguishing among different types of imitation, identifying three categories of behavior: (1) same behavior, (2) matched-dependent behavior, and (3) copying (Rosenblith 1959, 69). The first two types of behavior have educational or cognitive content. The third can be understood as mimicking behavior and serves to transmit models of behavior and role playing.

Imitation has important pedagogical and social functions, and the design of intellectual property law should rest on a more sophisticated view of copying than that evinced by Justice Holmes. The point is quite different from the familiar argument that most creation is cumulative or collaborative. The arguments based on cumulative or collaborative creation distinguish permissible borrowing from impermissible copying— for example, in the construction of derivative works or improvements. My point, however, is that copying itself has value. The value of copying, however, does not and should not devalue copyright or other intellectual property law. Even if imitation for pedagogical purposes has a recognized purpose, it is quite a leap to suggest that there is value to someone selling or even distributing illegally obtained copies of a blockbuster movie or novel before it hits the marketplace. But the lesson from educational psychology that copying has social value has important, and often ignored, implications for intellectual property's admonition against unauthorized copying. Scholars of music appreciation and music education have shown that imitation is important to the experience and transmittal of musical meaning (Cox 2001, 196). Legal restrictions on unauthorized performances of musical works should be designed to reflect this value of imitation, and to a certain extent they do through the various exclusions under U.S. copyright law for public performances of musical and other works. Furthermore, the learning on imitation has implications for experimental use in patent law. If imitation is useful for learning how things work, whether it is social knowledge or information, then we need to reconsider patent law's restrictions on experimenting on patented subject matter. Experimental use should not be relegated to mere philosophical inquiry, but should be broadened to permit the realization of value through imitation. Finally, even though the concept of imitation is described at the level of the individual, societies too imitate each other, as some critics of globalization who decry the spread of American brand names would quickly point out. In fact, within the field of intellectual property, much of the early learning of technological improvements and legal structure were imitations of counterparts in England (Ben-Atar 2004, 113–16). Holmes's formulation of copying justifies legal protection for copies and the social sharing of originals. One interpretation of his copy-original distinction is consistent with the idea that all human expression is just an imitation, or mimesis, of nature. The theory of mimesis has come under criticism from the theory that all expression, even seemingly realistic expression, is semiotic, consisting of a series of signs that are coded by the creator, decoded by the user, and recoded by subsequent creators (Blinder 1986, 19). Both of these theories, as applied to copyright, focus on the regulation of the work under intellectual property law. The conception of imitation that I have presented in this section focuses on cognitive and behavioral processes and serves to show that imitation is important to the process of learning and socialization. For Justice Holmes, the copy of the original that is protected by intellectual property captures aspects of the human personality that should be protected from appropriation by others. However, imitation or copying is also an important way we each learn to develop that human personality.

In conclusion, the process of imitation is important for the transmission of social and cultural knowledge. This is the first principle that should guide us in structuring intellectual property as part of the design for the information commons.

Exchange and the Market Commons

Imitation forces individuals to be similar. But it is a truism that individuals, even in a commons, will vary in their interests, desires, needs, and abilities (Hirschman 1977, 10–13). These sources of heterogeneity are important for society from perspectives of both evolutionary development and sustainability. The value of heterogeneity is realized through the process of exchange and particularly from exchange coordinated through organized and well-regulated markets. The principle of exchange, as implemented through a well-regulated marketplace, is the second basis for guidance in the design of the information commons.

The phrase "well-regulated marketplace" may be dissatisfying to those concerned about the trend toward commodifying knowledge, as occurs when basic scientific ideas are allowed to be patented. But the emphasis on regulation rather than marketplace is key to the argument. The rhetorical move is not to endorse a laissez-faire approach, but to recognize that the marketplace itself is a tool of administration. The question becomes how to appropriately structure and regulate the marketplace. For intellectual property, the difficult issue is reconciling the marketplace with other institutions, such as universities, not-for-profit research communities, and public interest organizations that seek to tap invention and "promote progress."

Economist and political scientist Charles Lindbloom (2001, 258–259) captures my thoughts well with his description of the market as a "state administrative instrument." This description characterizes the market as a means and not an end in itself, and specifically a means of statecraft. His point is not to design regulation on some ideal of what a market should be, whether that ideal is the one of perfect competition that appears in economics textbooks or one of libertarianism and free contract. Rather, the market provides a mechanism through which conduct can be regulated and certain problems of resource allocation can be solved. Like all policy instruments, the use of free markets should be contested and assessed in the same way as democratic societies would assess tax policy, legislation, and economic subsidies.

Patents and copyrights fit neatly into Lindbloom's view of markets as an instrument of administration. Historically, patents and copyrights were a grant by the sovereign conveying exclusivity over certain activities, such as mining, and evolved into grants that conveyed exclusivity in the marketing of certain novel inventions (Kaufer 1989, 1–5). The Statute of Monopolies, which limited the sovereign's power to grant certain types of market exclusivity, exempted patents and copyrights (pp. 6–8). As a grant, patents and copyrights shaped the creation and development of markets. Under modern law, patents and copyrights serve as a way to administer and organize markets. When scholars speak of patents and copyrights as addressing market failures, it is clear that patents and copyrights are being described as an administrative tool. But the scope of patents and copyrights as an administrative tool has not been fully appreciated and explored. Instead, the social-contract view of patents and copyrights has reduced the patent grant to a quid pro quo: the purchase of progress in exchange for exclusivity. The view of patents and copyrights as reward emphasizes only one dimension, as compensation for invention, and ignores the role of patents and copyrights as means of regulating markets.

Critics may accuse me of projecting a particular vision of markets onto a legislative scheme, ignoring the legal context of the scheme. Paul Schwartz and William Treanor (2003, 2414) make a criticism of this type in their recent dissection of the constitutional arguments made against copyright term extension in *Eldred v. Ashcroft*. Labeling the group of scholars opposing copyright expansion "IP Restrictors," Schwartz and Treanor demonstrate that if Eldred had been successful, the resulting decision would have been another *Lochner v. New York*, the 1905 case striking down state maximum-hour legislation, which represented the bellwether of judicial activism against state economic regulation.[4] Just as the *Lochner* majority imposed a substantive vision of the economy on the due process clause that ignored economic realities and the legislative process, so the IP Restrictors, according to Schwartz and Treanor, seek to impose a substantive vision of intellectual property and competition on the copyright clause. Schwartz and Treanor (2003, 2341) conclude that it was appropriate for the Court to defer to Congress on intellectual property, just as the Court has learned to defer to economic regulation in other contexts after the jurisprudential shift away from the *Lochner* decision.

While I sympathize with Schwartz and Treanor's skepticism toward constitutional intellectual property law, I part company when they state that "from the vantage point of constitutional law, intellectual property should be treated as a form of constitutional property" (p. 2335). This is a loaded claim. Schwartz and Treanor's point is that the Court should give the same deference to the legislature in its interpretation of Article I, Section 8, Clause 8, as it does in its interpretation of the contracts clause or the due process clause. But needless to say, recognizing "constitutional property" can work in many ways. In *Dred Scott*[5] the Court recognized slaves as a form of constitutional property that justified not paying deference to congressional legislation. The *Dred Scott* decision is precisely the type of judicial activism that Schwartz and Treanor would find abhorrent. The problem is that a naked appeal to "constitutional property" ignores the kind of property and regulation at issue in a particular dispute.

The problem with *Lochner* is not so much that the Court failed to pay deference to regulation of constitutional property rights, but that the Court found that redistributive measures are categorically, as a matter of constitutional law, outside the police power of the legislature. As a result, the *Lochner* decision set the laissez-faire distribution of resources in stone. The problem was not lack of deference to the legislature but too much deference to the market. Similarly, the problem with *Eldred* is the Court's view of intellectual property in terms that considered only the rights of the creator and ignored the interests of users, follow-on creators, and institutions that depend on intellectual property, contrary to the history of the intellectual property debate. Copyright and patent serve to regulate the marketplace and should be understood not in terms of the unfettered marketplace, but in terms of the structured marketplace that facilitates innovation and creativity.

For some, my argument that the marketplace has a place in the information commons may seem contrary to the openness of the commons. The marketplace rests on exclusion and self-aggrandizement through profit seeking. The commons, by contrast, is designed to be unconstrained and open to all, at least according to one view. But this potential criticism rests on an idealized notion of the commons and an equally idealized, if dark, conception of markets (Chander and Sunder 2004, 1332). Within the commons, conflict of interest will arise. Individuals will have different conceptions of the good and will be driven to satisfy human desires and wants. The tragedy of the commons is one example of conflict among individuals in the commons. The commons will need to be regulated. My suggestion is that the market is one type of regulatory instrument, one that can serve to coordinate differences in interests and desires through exchange. As Carla Hesse (2002, 2a) has pointed out, even in much earlier periods, such as Confucian China, pre-Enlightenment Europe, and the early Islamic era, "the virtually universal proscription of private ownership in ideas . . . did not, of course, mean that ideas flowed freely." "God's agents," often in the form of state or religious institutions, would deeply control the flow of information (p. 29). The market not only provides a way to coordinate interests over contested resources, but also serves as a democratizing institution to counter concentration and control of ideas. In fact, the critics of commodification today aim their assault not at the market itself, but at the way markets are controlled by dominant corporate interests through intellectual property law (Litman 2000, 122–51). The market, therefore, is an important organizing institution for the information commons, but one that needs to be well regulated to maintain the values of open access.

Governance and Cultural Production

The well-regulated marketplace should be understood in terms of the broader democratic values that inform the commons. The third guiding principle for the construction of the commons is recognizing the importance of governance for cultural production.

Government has a role in creating the requisite institutions for democratic governance. To the extent that markets are among these institutions, the government functions of financing cultural production and facilitating sharing are relevant here. Also relevant, particularly for nonmarket institutions, are three other government functions necessary for cultural production: (1) the creation of public forums for participation, (2) the development of cultural infrastructure to facilitate autonomy and participation, and (3) the creation of open systems that permit transparency and access to cultural artifacts (Ghosh 2003, 417–418).

The creation of public forums has noneconomic values, such as providing venues for participation and the exercise of creative pursuits. I have several things in mind here. First, at the level of local government, public forums can be created by shared spaces, such as sidewalks and parks, in which open speech with minimal regulation is permitted. At the national level, First Amendment law also plays a key role in the creation of public forums through protections for certain types of speech, protections for certain speakers, and, most relevant, protection for speech in certain places through various restrictions on the regulation of the media.

The government provision of cultural infrastructure occurs in many ways, from income-distribution programs that support the arts to the creation of institutions for the collection of cultural artifacts. The Work Projects Administration (WPA) provides a unique example of the government's efforts to promote cultural production in order to redistribute income. Under the WPA, unemployed authors and mathematicians were hired to produce important cultural works, including tables of logarithms, tables of integrals, and what have been described as exemplars of premier regional writing—the WPA guides to various states, documents that recorded the history and culture of the then 48 states. While these projects could be seen as "make-work" efforts in order to move the United States out of the Great Depression, the government's involvement in creating important cultural artifacts should not be overlooked. The projects allowed unemployed authors to create works that would otherwise not have existed (Ghosh 2003, 420).

The goal of providing cultural infrastructure is also facilitated by government involvement in preserving minority cultures, such as through statutes like the Native American Grave Repatriation Act and policies to repatriate or preserve cultural artifacts. These preservationist goals are important to democratic culture in many ways. They permit the preservation and archiving of a national history that establishes an identity for citizens and a common reference point for deliberation and discussion over national issues (Ghosh 2003). For example, museum exhibits about the Japanese internment, or museums that record atrocities against Native Americans, serve as a reminder of the abuse of private and state power that can temper arguments about how to deal with minority populations in times of renewed racial and ethnic conflict. Furthermore, democratic governments have an obligation to ensure that minority populations are protected from the exercise of abuse by majorities. By supporting minority cultural production, democratic governments promote inclusiveness and allow for many interests to be voiced in the marketplace and other public forums. The point should be made that much of what I describe can take place, and in fact has taken place, through private associations. For example, the Holocaust Museum in Washington, D.C., and the Civil Rights Museums in Memphis and Birmingham were built with a mix of government and private funds. These three examples further support the argument that the government has played an important role in cultural production, developing a cultural infrastructure that protects the participation and autonomy of members of minority groups.

Finally, according to the theory of democratic governance, government can pursue the values of participation and autonomy by carrying out its function of creating open systems that facilitate transparency and access (Ghosh 2003, 421). This function entails more than creating public forums. Understanding this function requires understanding the term *cultural artifact* broadly. My examples of cultural artifacts have included items in museums, literary works, music, and other creations of the human mind, such as the WPA regional guides. Other examples of cultural artifacts would include legal rules (whether judicial opinions or code), the products of university research (whether in the humanities or the sciences), textbooks, population data, and other types of information. Including the creation of these items as cultural productions has two purposes. First, some of these items are primary cultural materials that are necessary for the operation of the other two government functions. For example, the Native American Grave Repatriation Act carries out the government function of creating cultural infrastructure. If the underlying law is inaccessible to the groups and interests that it is trying to protect, the goal of creating cultural infrastructure is undermined. Second, these items of cultural production are themselves important cultural records that can inform the creation of cultural artifacts. Records of population movements and historical records of seemingly banal items like shipping manifests can be the basis for the creation of cultural products, as any student or practitioner of history or historical fiction would attest. Open systems of recording and preserving information are important ends for the government under the theory of democratic governance.

The third principle connects with the other two. Cultural infrastructure, as described in this section, allows for the type of imitation that permits cultural learning and transmission. Cultural infrastructure also permits the well-regulated marketplace within which diverging interests can be coordinated. The vibrancy of the commons requires governance that promotes cultural production through the creation of cultural infrastructure. Governance of the commons, however, must also take into consideration the principles of imitation and the well-regulated marketplace. The three principles work together to help us construct intellectual property systems that help us achieve the open-access goals of the information commons. In the next section, two examples illustrate the application of these principles to commons construction.

File Sharing and Experimental Use: Two Illustrative Commons

I have presented three guiding principles to aid in building an information commons. These principles can be seen in action through two illustrative examples: file sharing and experimental use in the pharmaceutical industry. These examples show not only the application of the guiding principles, but also the many forms an information commons can take depending on the resources and the interests at stake.

The Technological Commons of Copying
Peer-to-peer file sharing poses a challenge to copyright law, one accepted by the U.S. Supreme Court by granting review of *MGM v. Grokster* in 2005.[6] The new technological means of copying and distributing copyrighted materials challenge not only legal doctrine but the market structure within which such materials are developed and disseminated. The three guiding principles of imitation, exchange, and governance assist in meeting the challenge by showing how to structure the information commons made possible by file sharing.

At the heart of file-sharing technologies is the ease of copying and transmitting information. Copying, however, has many means not readily captured by the term *piracy*, which is often too readily used to dismiss all applications of file sharing. Not only does the label *piracy* assume that the copyright owner has a broad exclusive right to deny access to works, but the label also ignores the various values of copying. To vest in the copyright owner the exclusive right to prevent all copying divests users of the pedagogical and interpretative values created by imitating music and other works. As noted earlier, the educational psychology literature shows that musical understanding is enriched by being able to perform and listen to music repeatedly, acts that will entail copying in most instances. The problem, of course, is that the reality of file sharing seems to be trading copyright works without charge. The uses of file sharing may not, as a consequence, serve the types of cultural goals that the psychology literature uncovers. Nonetheless, in assessing the values of file sharing, we must be careful not to paint copying and imitation with too broad a brush stroke, with the result of dismissing all activities under the questionable label of piracy. Instead, the various types of imitation should be recognized and balanced against the potential uses of file-sharing technologies.

The danger of adopting broad categories is even more salient in assessing file-sharing technologies within the framework of exchange. File sharing allows users not only to copy but also to disseminate information, and in many ways the dissemination allowed by file sharing is what copyright owners find problematic. As a mechanism of exchange, file sharing poses a threat to established markets for music, movies, and other forms of knowledge. The controversy over file sharing can be characterized as a conflict between commodified information and noncommodified information. But this characterization overstates the case. There is no question that many file-sharing systems, while operating for free or based on advertising revenue, have the potential to evolve into for-pay systems. The real question is what form the market will take. The concentrated market for music, within which distribution occurs through retailing and broadcast licensing, is tested by a decentralized mechanism that allows music to be distributed without the bundling of the conventional compact disc. The success of the iPod illustrates the viability of alternative mechanisms. The importance of market mechanisms, however, should not lead us to believe that markets will be the only form of distribution. What is at stake is the viability of new forms of exchange that file sharing makes possible when interests are unwilling to adapt existing business models.[7]

Finally, the principle of governance and cultural production also shapes file sharing. In fact, the viability of file sharing is affected by and affects the structure of the Internet. Issues of governance arise at two levels. First, the structure of file sharing is influenced by the rules of intellectual property, particularly the rules of fair use and of secondary liability. Second, file sharing allows a deconcentrated structure of the market for the transmission of information, where multiple websites potentially replace territorially spaced and branded retail outlets and information can be produced and consumed outside the boundaries of conventional media, such as books and discs. Each set of governance issues requires us to think how cultural artifacts will be produced and disseminated and what forms they will take. File sharing creates new forums and infrastructure for cultural production, and the resolution of governance issues will shape the structure of these forums.

With these three principles in mind, we can assess how file sharing should be treated in order to create an information commons founded on the value of open access. In the *MGM v. Grokster* case, the Supreme Court established the viability of the substantial noninfringing-use doctrine, articulated in 1984 in its famous *Sony* decision about the liability of VCR manufacturers for contributory copyright infringement.[8] The Court, however, also endorsed inducement as an alternative test for contributory infringement. The substantial noninfringing-use doctrine provides a legal test for liability of creators of technology that facilitate copyright infringement. The test is one of secondary liability, rather than direct liability for copyright infringement. In applying the substantial noninfringing-use test, the court will consider the uses of a technology that do not result in copyright infringement and test to see if the noninfringing uses outweigh the infringing uses. If the noninfringing uses are more substantial than the infringing uses, the maker of the copying technology is not liable for copyright infringement. For example, in the *Sony* case, the Supreme Court found that the VCR could be used for noninfringing uses, such as watching a television program at a different time than when broadcast.[9] This noninfringing use was more substantial than infringing uses of unauthorized copying of copyrighted programs, the Court concluded, and held that Sony, the maker of the VCR, was not liable for copyright infringement.

The efficacy of the substantial noninfringing-use test rests on how the words *infringing* and *substantial* are interpreted. Whether a use is infringing hinges on formal copyright law, including the meanings of infringement of fair use within the copyright statute. In its *Sony* decision, the Supreme Court held that copying to watch a program at a different time constituted fair use because the practice had a minimum effect on the market for the copyrighted work and in fact expanded the market by allowing users to watch a program when it otherwise could not.[10] In Napster, an early file-sharing case, the U.S. Court of Appeals for the Ninth Circuit held that file sharing did not constitute fair use because it adversely affected the potential market for song downloads by offering a costless alternative to users.[11] The same court, with a different panel of judges, found that the Grokster file-sharing service did constitute fair use because the technology facilitated the widespread sharing of materials that were non-copyright-protected as well as materials that were.[12] The meaning of *infringing* is fact specific as well as being informed by normative perceptions of technologies. Similarly, how substantial a use is rests on an open-ended comparison of the various ways technology can be used. In *Sony*, for example, the Supreme Court seemingly relied in part on a quantitative inquiry.[13] In *Grokster*, the Ninth Circuit gauged the potential of file-sharing technology and recognized myriad uses that would facilitate, rather than violate, copyright law.[14]

The substantial noninfringing-use test is a helpful test for assessing the liability of creators of copying technologies. By focusing on how the technology is used and taking into consideration potential noninfringing uses, the test is technology-friendly. The devil is in the details of the test's application, particularly in the meanings of *infringing* and *substantial*. The three guiding principles, however, can provide an interpretative baseline for understanding these terms. If an information commons should be formed using the principles of imitation, exchange, and governance, then substantial noninfringing use should be understood consistently with these principles. In other words, *infringing* should be understood in a way that facilitates beneficial imitation, the type of open-market exchange that generates a thriving commons, and governance structures that promote cultural infrastructure and production. What this means in practice, for example, is rejecting the notion in Napster that file sharing preempts copyright owners from developing their own download markets. Instead, the Ninth Circuit should have considered ways file sharing could create new markets and methods of distribution. Furthermore, courts are correct in considering the centralized structure of various file-sharing systems, because this dimension affects the governance systems and types of cultural infrastructure necessary for cultural production.[15]

Unfortunately, the Supreme Court's decision in *Grokster* adds more confusion to the debate over the legal treatment of file-sharing technologies. While the Court unanimously upheld the *Sony* standard, the nine justices split three ways in their clarification of the standard, with three justices (Ginsburg, Rehnquist, and Kennedy) narrowing it, three (Breyer, O'Connor, and Stevens) expanding it, and three (Souter, Scalia, and Thomas) declining to address the issue of clarification. More troubling, the nine justices also unanimously agreed that creators of technology can be held secondarily liable for copyright infringement if the technology is distributed "with the object of promoting its use to infringe copyright, as shown by clear expression or other affirmative steps taken to foster infringement." The Court stated that a trial was necessary to determine if *Grokster* would be liable under this newly articulated intent standard. The creation of this new standard will most likely turn out to be either irrelevant or unnecessarily burdensome. Its irrelevance reflects how easy it may be to avoid liability under the new standard. The creator of the technology should be advised not to do or say anything that suggests the fostering of infringement in the marketing of the technology. More troubling is the possibility that litigants and courts may use the *Grokster* decision as an invitation to more closely scrutinize the design of copying technologies. The possibility of protracted lawsuits that attempt to gauge the intent of the creators of new technologies may have a chilling effect on both the dissemination and development of innovative products and services. Instead of clarifying the *Sony* standard, which was the primary reason the Court was asked to review the case, the *Grokster* decision may hinder the promotion of the information commons based on file-sharing technologies.

Imitation and Experimentation with Pharmaceuticals

Under U.S. law, a pharmaceutical company must obtain approval of a new pharmaceutical product from the Food and Drug Administration before selling the product. The FDA will review the product for its safety and efficacy based on clinical data provided by the company. To avoid competition from knock-offs of its product, the company will also seek patent protection for the pharmaceutical. The interplay between the patent system and the system of food and drug regulation creates interesting challenges, which are the subject of *Merck v. Integra*. The requirement of clinical trials for new pharmaceutical products poses a challenge for the marketer of a generic version of a patented pharmaceutical product. In 1984, Congress enacted 35 USC § 271(e), often referred to as the Bolar Amendment in reference to the Federal Circuit decision the provision overruled. The Bolar Amendment excluded from infringement the making, using, selling, offering to sell, or importing of "a patented invention . . . solely for uses reasonably related to the development and submission of information under a Federal law which regulates the manufacture, use, or sale of drugs." The purpose of this provision was to provide generic drug manufacturers with the freedom to operate in developing the market for generic versions of patented pharmaceuticals and to limit the de facto extension of the patent term of the patented product while the generic version generates clinical trials once the patent does expire. Under the amendment, generic drug manufacturers can make, use, sell, or import the patented drug while it is still under patent to prepare the clinical trials needed for FDA approval. The issue in the pending *Merck* case is the meaning of what acts are ones "solely for uses reasonably related to the development and submission of" clinical trial data to the FDA.

The patent at stake in *Merck* is owned by Integra and covers a short peptide segment that promotes cell adhesion and growth for the benefit of wound healing and biocompatibility of prosthetic devices.[16] The promotion of cell adhesion and growth also enables blood vessels to grow new branches through controlled interactions. A researcher at Scripps discovered that key blocking receptors that play a pivotal role in Integra's patent could also be used to inhibit tumor growth. Merck, on hearing of these potential developments, hired Scripps and the particular researcher to make the "necessary experiments to satisfy the biological bases and regulatory (FDA) requirements for the implementation of the clinical trials," as stated in their written agreement. When Integra learned about the relationship between Merck and Scripps, the company offered to license its patent to the joint venturers. After rejection of the offer to license, Integra sued Merck and Scripps for patent infringement, with Merck raising, among other defenses, its rights under the Bolar Amendment. The district court found that the exemption did not apply, and the Federal Circuit affirmed. The Supreme Court subsequently reversed the Federal Circuit.

The Federal Circuit provided a fairly clear rationale for its affirmation. According to the court, "the Scripps work sponsored by Merck was not clinical testing to supply information to the FDA, but only general biomedical research to identify new pharmaceutical compounds."[17] The experimental research was characterized as "a hunt for drugs that may or may not later undergo clinical testing for FDA approval."[18] The 1984 Amendment was enacted to facilitate "expedited approval of a generic version of a drug previously approved by the FDA" and "does not globally embrace all experimental activity that at some point, however attenuated, may lead to an FDA approval process."[19] In other words, the experimental-use exception under 271(e) applies only to work required for the development of clinical trials, not for the search for new products. The Federal Circuit presents a bright-line rule for the exemption, applying it only for research activities leading to clinical trial data to be submitted to FDA review.

Judge Pauline Newman, in her concurrence/dissent, questions whether such a bright light can be applied to the research process. The early experimental stage of drug development may uncover safety or health issues that may become relevant for the FDA-required clinical trials. It may not be clear when it is too early for a researcher to seek shelter under the 1984 Amendment. In her support, Judge Newman employs the values of the patent system:

The purpose of a patent system is not only to provide a financial incentive to create new knowledge and bring it to public benefit through new products; it also serves to add to the body of published scientific/technologic knowledge. . . . The right to conduct research to achieve such knowledge need not, and should not, await expiration of the patent. That is not the law, and it would be a practice impossible to administer.[20]

With her appeal to the role of the patent system in enriching the body of scientific and technological knowledge, Judge Newman would have permitted broad experimental use of patented pharmaceuticals by generic drug manufacturers.

The three guiding principles for building an information commons provide some insight into how to interpret the confounding language of "solely for uses reasonably related to." If the goal is to create an information commons, and certainly the promotion of generic drug competition is consistent with this goal, then the reasonableness of an experimental use should be understood in terms of the values of imitation, exchange, and governance. Experimentation reflects the positive values of imitation, particularly the learning by doing that is important for the dissemination and transmission of information. Furthermore, exchange through open markets is an important dimension of the commons, and the history of the Bolar Amendment shows that the provision was designed to facilitate the entry of generic drugs into the marketplace. Finally, experimentation must also be understood in terms of the governance structure of the pharmaceutical industry. The entry of new drugs implicates not only patent law, but also food and drug law. The experimental use at issue in *Merck* entails not only the creation of new, nonobvious, and useful drugs, but also ones that are safe and effective. The Federal Circuit's bright-line test between preclinical and clinical experimentation ignores that drug research and development may not follow such a neat, linear path. Furthermore, Judge Newman's dissent, which evokes the values of patent law and the information commons quite passionately, focuses solely on the patent balance and does not expressly incorporate the issues posed by FDA review. Since drug developers must surmount two hurdles in practice, the patent obstacle and the FDA obstacle (the first by choice and market reality, the second by necessity), the Bolar Amendment should be read broadly to allow experimental uses to create safe, effective, new, and nonobvious pharmaceuticals.

The Court did endorse a broad reading of "reasonably related" in its 2005 *Merck* opinion. Specifically, a unanimous Court held that

in the vast majority of cases, neither the drugmaker nor its scientists have any way of knowing whether an initially promising candidate will prove successful over a battery of experiments. That is the reason they conduct the experiments. Thus, to construe [the Bolar Amendment], as the Court of Appeals did, not to protect research conducted on patented compounds for which an IND [investigational new drug] is not ultimately filed is effectively to limit assurance of exemption to the activities necessary to seek approval of a generic drug: One can know at the outset that a particular compound will be the subject of an eventual application to the FDA only if the active ingredient in the drug being tested is identical to that in a drug that has already been approved.

The Court's conclusion rests on a recognition of the need to experiment with patented drugs in order to promote research that may lead to the development of generic drugs. The protection of research and experimentation is consistent with the values of the information commons articulated in this chapter. Broad experimentation on patented drugs recognizes the need for copying of protected chemical compounds to understand how they work. Furthermore, experimentation is a first step in the development of generic products that can compete in the marketplace with the patented substitutes. Finally, the Court's reference to drug makers and scientists demonstrates an appreciation of the scientific culture, at least as it functions in a commercial setting. The *Merck* decision provides an example of how the information commons can be accommodated in the current atmosphere of privatization and commercialization that permeates intellectual property.

Conclusion

This chapter began with a question and ended with a blueprint for an information commons. If the argument has been successful, it should convince the reader that the question of the relationship between intellectual property and the commons is one of means and ends. The design of intellectual property systems should be undertaken with the understanding that intellectual property law is a tool for structuring the information commons. The hard question is one of developing guiding principles for building an information commons that will in turn inform intellectual property policy. I have suggested three principles—imitation, exchange, and governance—and have shown how they can be applied to two pending cases in copyright and patent law. As a scholar, I have no pretensions that my prescriptions will be adopted. But whatever direction intellectual property law takes, the holy grail of the information commons and open access may become more attainable with the understanding that intellectual property policy should recognize the importance of imitation, exchange, and governance. Whether intellectual property constricts, facilitates, or becomes irrelevant to the information commons depends on what we make of the institutions we have and the institutions that are yet to be.

Notes

1. For a survey of the literature, see Carrier 2004, 8–25; Landes and Posner 2003, 11–36.

2. See *Campbell v. Acuff-Rose Music, Inc.*, 510 U.S. 569, 584 (1994).

3. See *Bleistein v. Donaldson Lithographing Co.*, 188 U.S. 239, 249 (1903).

4. See *Lochner v. New York*, 198 U.S. 45 (1905).

5. See *Dred Scott v. Sandford*, 60 U.S. 393 (1857).

6. *MGM Studios, Inc. v. Grokster*, 125 S. Ct. 686 (2004).

7. Ghosh 2001, 572–579.

8. *Sony Corp. of America v. Universal City Studios*, 104 S. Ct. 774 (1984).

9. *Sony Corp. of America v. Universal City Studios* at 796.

10. *Sony Corp. of America v. Universal City Studios* at 794.

11. *AandM Records Inc. v. Napster*, 239 F.3d 1004, 1018 (9th Cir. 2001).

12. *MGM Studios, Inc. v. Grokster*, 380 F.3d 1154, 1159 (9th Cir. 2004).

13. 104 S. Ct. at 790–791.

14. 380 F.3d at 1162.

15. *In re Aimster Copyright Litigation*, 334 F.3d 643, 651–653 (7th Cir. 2003).

16. The facts are taken from the Federal Circuit's opinion in *Integra*, 331 F.3d at 863.

17. 331 F.3d at 866.

18. 331 F.3d at 866.

19. 331 F.3d at 866–867.

20. 331 F.3d at 873.

References

Bell, Abraham, and Gideon Parchomovsky. 2003. "Property and Anti-Property." *Michigan Law Review* 102:1–69.

Ben-Atar, Doron S. 2004. *Trade Secrets: Intellectual Piracy and the Origins of American Industrial Power*. New Haven, CT: Yale University Press.

Blinder, David. 1986. "In Defense of Pictorial Mimesis." *Journal of Aesthetics and Art Criticism* 45(1):19–27.

Carrier, Michael. 2004. "Cabining Intellectual Property through a Property Paradigm." *Duke Law Journal* 54:1–144.

Chander, Anupam, and Madhavi Sunder. 2004. "The Romance of the Public Domain." *California Law Review* 92:1331–1372.

Coase, Ronald H. 1960. "The Problem of Social Cost." *Journal of Law and Economics* 3:1–44.

Cox, Arnie. 2001. "The Mimetic Hypothesis and Embodied Musical Meaning." *Musicae Scientiae* 5(2):195–212.

Drahos, Peter, and John Braithwaite. 2003. *Information Feudalism*. Boston: Norton.

Driesen, David M., and Shubha Ghosh. 2005. "The Functions of Transaction Costs: Rethinking Transaction Costs Minimization in a World of Friction." *Arizona Law Review* 47:61–110.

Ellickson, Robert J. 1994. *Order without Law: How Neighbors Settle Disputes*. Cambridge, MA: Harvard University Press.

Frischmann, Brett M. 2005. "An Economic Theory of Infrastructure and Commons Management." *Minnesota Law Review* 89:917–1030.

Ghosh, Shubha. 2001. "Turning Gray into Green: Some Comments on Napster." *Hastings Communications and Entertainment Law Journal* 23:567–586.

Ghosh, Shubha. 2003. "Deprivatizing Copyright." *Case Western Law Review* 54:387–484.

Ghosh, Shubha. 2004. "Patents and the Regulatory State: Rethinking the Patent Bargain Metaphor After Eldred." *Berkeley Technical Law Journal* 19:1315–1388.

Hawking, Stephen. 1988. *A Brief History of Time*. New York: Random House.

Hesse, Carla. 2002. "The Rise of Intellectual Property, 700 B.C.–A.D. 2000: An Idea in the Balance." *Daedalus* (spring):26–45.

Hirschman, Albert O. 1977. *The Passions and the Interests: Political Arguments for Capitalism Before Its Triumph*. Princeton, NJ: Princeton University Press.

Kaufer, Erich. 1989. *The Economics of the Patent System*. Chur, Switzerland: Harwood.

Kieff, F. Scott. 2001. "Property Rights and Property Rules for Commercializing Inventions." *Minnesota Law Review* 85:697–751.

Kitch, Edmund. 1977. "The Nature and Function of the Patent System." *Journal of Law and Economics* 20:265–290.

Landes, William M., and Richard A. Posner. 2003. *The Economic Structure of Intellectual Property Law*. Cambridge, MA: Harvard University Press.

Lessig, Lawrence. 1999. *Code and Other Laws of Cyberspace*. New York: Basic Books.

Lessig, Lawrence. 2001. *The Future of Ideas: The Fate of the Commons in a Connected World*. New York: Random House.

Lessig, Lawrence. 2005. "Reply: Re-Marking the Progress in Frischmann." *Minnesota Law Review* 89:1031–1043.

Lindbloom, Charles E. 2001. *The Market System: What It Is, How It Works, and What to Make of It*. New Haven, CT: Yale University Press.

Litman, Jessica. 2000. *Digital Copyright*. Amherst, NY: Prometheus Books.

Menard, Louis. 2005. "Believer." *New Yorker* (March 7): 27–28.

Merges, Robert, and Richard R. Nelson. 1990. "The Complex Economics of Patent Scope." *Columbia Law Review* 90:839–914.

Ostrom, Elinor. 1990. *Governing the Commons: The Evolution of Institutions for Collective Action.* New York: Cambridge University Press.

Rosenblith, Judy F. 1959. "Learning by Imitation in Kindergarten Children." *Child Development* 30:69–80.

Schwartz, Paul M., and William Michael Treanor. 2003. "Eldred and Lochner: Copyright Term Extension and Intellectual Property as Constitutional Property." *Yale Law Journal* 112:2331–2414.

Sunstein, Cass. 1995. *Democracy and the Problem of Free Speech.* New York: Free Press.

Visalberghi, Elisabetta, and Dorothy M. Fragaszy. 1996. *Pedagogy and Imitation in Monkeys: Yes, No, or Maybe?* In David R. Olsen and Nancy Torrance, eds., *The Handbook of Education and Human Development.* Cambridge, MA: Blackwell.

9

Collective Action, Civic Engagement, and the Knowledge Commons

Peter Levine

For the most part, the other chapters of this book treat knowledge as a good. The authors advocate better ways to create, disseminate, preserve, and organize knowledge as a common resource. While I certainly share the goals of those chapters, the focus here is somewhat different. I take the *process* of creating public knowledge as an additional good, because such work builds social capital, strengthens communities, and gives people skills that they need for effective citizenship. If this is correct, then we should aim to include as many people as possible in the collaborative creation of "free" (i.e., open-access) knowledge. Not only scholars and librarians, but ordinary people should be knowledge creators.

This chapter defends a strategy for increasing opportunities to create shared knowledge. That strategy underlies some concrete work that my colleagues and I are conducting at the University of Maryland, often in collaboration with allies at other universities. Our strategy assumes that associations (not just loose groupings of people) are needed to support a knowledge commons in which ordinary citizens can be creative. Young people—above all, adolescents who are not already on track for college—must be included in these associations, or else the future of the knowledge commons will be threatened. Universities have a potentially constructive role to play, and may benefit if they work more collaboratively with the communities around them. Finally, there is a particular need for associations that create *local* knowledge: information and insights of use to places and communities.

These are the strategic assumptions that guide our work. They are consistent with a political philosophy that Harry Boyte and others call "public work"; I conclude by explaining why that philosophy is relevant.

An Example

Some University of Maryland colleagues and I are studying the geographic causes of obesity.[1] An emerging body of scientific research suggests that your health depends on your weight, and that how much you weigh depends on precisely where you live. If there are stores nearby that provide healthy produce, you will eat better. If between you and a shopping district there are streets with sidewalks, safe crosswalks, and low crime, you are likely to walk every day. But if you live in a suburban cul-de-sac with no sidewalks at all, if you are afraid of muggers in the park, or if there is a fast-food restaurant much closer to your house than the nearest greengrocer, you are more likely to become obese.[2]

We are working in a community where the majority of the population is African American or Latino, the median income is modest, and the landscape is very diverse, ranging from suburban ranch-house lanes to traditional urban grids to clusters of large apartment blocks. In general, minority people, adolescents, and those with lower socioeconomic status (SES) are disproportionately at risk for obesity and related diseases such as diabetes and hypertension; they are also relatively unlikely to lead active lifestyles.[3] However, many of the studies that have demonstrated these correlations have investigated inner-city populations. It has thus been difficult to disentangle economic and cultural factors from geographic factors such as population density.[4] We hope to get beyond the general correlation between SES and active lifestyles by identifying specific variables in the physical environment that more directly predict active-living behaviors.

So far, I have described a fairly standard social science project with policy implications. However, my own interest is not in nutrition or urban planning. Rather, my colleagues and I are constantly looking for ways to involve disadvantaged adolescents in creating sophisticated and valuable research that they can give away to the public. In our current project, college faculty and students will not conduct research alone. High school students—mostly not college-bound; all African Americans or new immigrants—will do most of the work. They will frame the research questions, collect the data in the field (using Palm Pilots to enter information), and make analytical maps for a public website.

This project is the latest in a series of informal experiments that have the goal of *engaging youth in research of public value, using new information technology*. Most recently, we worked with students at the same high school to create a deliberative website about the desegregation of their own schools. In that work, oral history rather than geography was the relevant academic discipline. Before that, we helped students interview local residents and create public maps of community assets. Once we have completed the current mapping project, we will move on to new fields.

At this point, I cannot report that engaging youth in public interest research generates powerful effects. Our own project recently began; besides, it is not well designed to measure effects on the students. (The class is small and self-selected; there is no control group.) In many other places, adolescents are engaged in original, sophisticated, community-based research. However, there are no aggregate poll data that would help us estimate the effects of research on adolescent researchers. Nor can I find any effort to assess these projects in a serious, controlled way.[5] The best available assessment presents mixed findings.[6]

This, then, is a *theoretical* discussion. For reasons described below, I believe that we should ask young people to help build a particular kind of "information commons" in partnership with professional scholars, on the World Wide Web, for their geographic communities. This kind of work will benefit the young people who are directly involved, the universities that work with them, their communities, and the polity itself.

The Associational Commons

Our current project on geography and obesity is part of a nascent organization called the Prince George's Information *Commons*. (Prince George's County, Maryland, is where the University of Maryland is located.) We have a partner in the St. Paul Information Commons, which is connected to the University of Minnesota.[7]

In their contribution to this book, Ostrom and Hess emphasize that *commons* typically involve the sharing of resources by multiple users.[8] Often, the word *commons* implies that *everyone* within some relatively broad community (even the whole globe) has the right to share the resource. This usage allows us to distinguish between a "commons" and the property of a family or corporation, which is also shared, but only by specific people who are formally connected to the owner. Peter Suber describes open-access literature as an example of a "commons" because barriers of price and permission have been completely removed (although other barriers, such as the cost of connecting to the Internet, may remain).[9]

If the shared artifact is a digital file, then many people can view it and copy it without degrading it or otherwise detracting from others' use. Nonrivalrous objects are what Ostrom and Hess call "public goods," in contrast to rivalrous "common-pool resources." It is not always easy to build or maintain a commons composed of public goods, because people may lack adequate incentives to create and share goods that others will benefit from freely. Furthermore, some may pollute a public good or use it for harmful purposes. A commons composed of common-pool resources faces the same three problems, but in addition it is threatened by overuse.[10]

Just as a village commons is composed of shared grass, a knowledge commons is composed of shared knowledge. Ostrom and Hess note that knowledge involves discrete *artifacts* (such as articles, maps, databases, and web pages), *facilities* (such as universities, schools, libraries, computers, and laboratories), and *ideas* (such as the concept of a commons itself). Thomas Jefferson already realized that ideas are pure public goods, for "he who receives an idea from me, receives instruction himself without lessening mine; as he who lites his taper at mine, receives light without darkening me."[11] Facilities are usually rivalrous, yet they can be run as commons and can house shared artifacts—as Benjamin Franklin demonstrated when he founded the first public lending library.[12] Both the library building and its collections were shared, even though they were scarce and rivalrous. In the age of networked computers, many artifacts that were rivalrous can be digitized, posted online, and thereby turned into public goods. Computer networks can themselves be seen as facilities that overcome some scarcity problems. The number of potential exchanges among people (or machines) that are linked in a network rises geometrically as the network adds members.[13] Therefore, the more users, the better the network serves *each* user as a tool for communication and research.

I admire commons such as public libraries, community gardens, the Internet, and bodies of scholarly research because they encourage voluntary, diverse, creative activity. However, I have distinguished between a libertarian commons and an associational commons.[14] In a *libertarian commons*, anyone has a right to use (and sometimes also to contribute to) some public resource. This right is de facto if no one is able to block access to the good or if no one chooses to do so. The right is de jure if it arises from a law or policy that guarantees open access. In contrast, an *associational commons* exists when some good is controlled by a group. Boyle distinguishes between the commons and the public domain, noting that the former involves rules, norms, and other restraints that are absent in the latter.[15]

There is an important category of commons that are owned by private nonprofit associations. The owner (a formal organization) has the right and power to limit access, but it sees itself as the steward of a *public* good. As such, it sets policies that are intended to maintain a commons. For example, an association may admit anyone as a member, on the sole condition that he or she protects the common resource in some specified way. (Libraries tend to function like this.) Or a group may only admit those who have special qualifications, but impose obligations on its members in order to enhance the public good. (Scientific and professional associations often use this model.) Religious congregations, universities, scientific organizations, and civic groups vary in their rules and structures, but they often have this function of protecting or enhancing a quasi-public good.

I recognize that there is a powerful limitation to such associational commons: they are only as good as the associations that manage them. Just because a group is a nonprofit does not guarantee that it is fair, responsible, transparent, or honorable. Nevertheless, there is a great tradition of banding together into voluntary groups to protect a public good. This is what Alexis de Tocqueville found exemplary in the New World. He is often seen as a theorist of free association, but what he really admired were groups that generated public goods: "The Americans make associations to give entertainments, to found seminaries, to diffuse books, to build inns, to construct churches, to send missionaries to the antipodes; in this manner they found hospitals, prisons, and schools."[16] I believe that such associational commons are the heart of "civil society" and explain a considerable part of its appeal.[17]

Furthermore, I have argued that associational commons, while hardly infallible, have several advantages over libertarian commons. First, an association can defend itself; it can litigate and lobby to protect the public good of which it is the steward. In time-honored fashion, associations give their members "selective incentives" (such as free access to the good that they control) in return for support.[18] Thus, for example, a religious congregation may own a beautiful building that creates "positive externalities" for the broader community: nice views, free concerts, tourist revenues. The congregation may allow anyone who commits to its creed and pays tithes to join. Members then gain special access to the building (for instance, reserved pews and invitations to social events). In return, the congregation gains a bank balance with which it can hire masons if the building is damaged, and lawyers if there is a legal threat. In contrast, a libertarian commons such as the ocean suffers from a classic free-rider problem. Some people and groups benefit from degrading the commons, either by taking too much of it for themselves, fencing parts off as private property, or polluting it. Many people like the commons and wish to see it defended. But no one has a sufficient incentive to pay to defend a good that benefits everyone else as well.

The Internet was born as a libertarian commons, but today it badly needs organized defenders. The free distribution of ideas online is threatened by political constraints, such as censorship and the overprotection of intellectual property; by private pollution in the form of spam, viruses, and "flaming" (abusive text); and by corporate "enclosure." For an example of enclosure, consider that if you visit a major corporate site, the source code will be hidden by technological means, and patents or copyrights may make imitation illegal. If you try to borrow Amazon's "one-click" method of purchasing goods, you could be sued for stealing the company's intellectual property, even though such "business methods" have never been patented in the past.[19] In contrast, the early web had the feel of a commons—in part—because one could always see how a site had been constructed and freely imitate its technical features. These features were public goods. Meanwhile, cable companies and other providers of high-speed Internet access are eager to drive people to particular commercial websites with which they have financial arrangements. Users who want to be able to find sites of their choice and to create and share material are engaged in a constant struggle with large corporations that want to control search engines or to discourage individuals from creating their own content.[20]

Sometimes, corporations help to create a commons. For example, with its search engine, Google has chosen to create a space with many commonslike features. Google ranks sites proportionally to the number of links from other sites. A link is a kind of gift or vote. A large number of incoming links does not indicate quality or reliability, but it does indicate popularity within the community of website owners. Google's search results mirror that popularity. To be sure, money can buy popularity, yet there are many cheap sites that have become major nodes on the web.

In theory, Google could start charging for placement (not only for the advertisements that appear on the right side of the screen, but also for basic search results). However, that would be a risky move for the company, since *its* popularity comes from its commonslike feel. Besides, Google's capacity to destroy the commons does not prove that there is no commons on its site right now. Every commons is subject to destruction and/or control. The Alaska wilderness is a commons, yet the state and federal government could suddenly decide to charge large fees for access. Thus the question is not whether Google *must* create and preserve a commons, but whether it has done so to date. In China, Google recently announced it will censor search results to conform to the government's rules. Outside of China, however, its search engine continues to be a commons.

Nevertheless, corporate power represents a constant threat to the knowledge commons. Even if some corporations find that their interests align with the norms of open access temporarily, there is always a possibility that major firms will enclose or undermine the commons. This risk requires permanent vigilance and an organized response, which only associations can provide.

Second, an association is potentially democratic. It can offer its members opportunities to deliberate about policy and to make collective decisions with fair procedures. In contrast, a libertarian commons is difficult to regulate even if the vast majority of participants feel (and feel rightly) that particular rules should be imposed. For example, we might wish that the Internet combined free speech with privacy and avoided nuisances like "spam." A commons is often most efficient and durable when "most of the individuals affected by a resource regime can participate in making and modifying [its] rules."[21] However, to the extent that the Internet is truly a libertarian commons, such regulations cannot be imposed even if they are popular and legitimate.

Third, an association can publicly articulate a comprehensive set of values. A libertarian commons is free, but liberty may be the *only* moral norm that it embodies. In contrast, a university, a religious congregation, or a professional association can declare itself the defender of a basket of values, including freedom, public access, truth, sustainability, reliability, and/or decency.[22] In some cases, a government may monitor the association to ensure that it serves its mission.

Fourth, an association can proselytize, in the best sense of the term. Any commons relies on a demanding set of norms and commitments, such as trust, reciprocity, long time horizons, optimism about the possibilities of voluntary collective action, and personal commitment. In this chapter, I will describe people as having a "civic identity" if they have internalized these norms in relation to a particular public good. People are "civic" if they see themselves as responsible for the good, and if they act accordingly.

A civic identity is unlikely to develop automatically. We have to be taught to be civic; we are not born that way. Each generation must transmit to the next a moral concern for common goods. Young people must also be given particular skills, techniques, and "operational principles" to manage shared goods.[23] As Ostrom argues, "At any time that individuals may gain from the costly action of others, without themselves contributing time and effort, they face collective action dilemmas for which there are coping methods. When de Tocqueville discussed the 'art and science of association,' he was referring to the crafts learned by those who had solved ways of engaging in collective action to achieve a joint benefit. Some aspects of the science of association are both counterintuitive and counterintentional, and thus must be taught to each generation as part of the culture of a democratic citizenry."[24]

Knowing this, successful associations recruit members with an eye to the future, looking (for example) for young people who can replace their current membership and leadership in decades to come. Associations educate their recruits—and also the general public—about collective action in pursuit of their core values. If they have narrow constituencies, they may try to broaden their appeal. If they have broad but shallow support, they may try to develop a zealous core.

Indeed, I can think of no successful historical example of a commons that arose under conditions of total individual freedom—or as a gift of nature. Even oceans only work as common fisheries if fishing communities are highly organized and self-regulated. Commons are made possible by demanding moral norms and/or enforceable agreements, hammered out in groups, taught to each rising generation, and then reinforced by hard, collaborative work.[25]

In Prince George's County, we are trying to build an independent, democratic association whose purpose is to create public goods using the new digital media. In the process, we hope to cultivate relevant skills and commitments among young people of color who are not on course to attend competitive colleges. This is a constituency that usually does not benefit from the Internet commons or have a voice in its future. We never try to persuade these young people to adopt any particular view of the Internet or the major corporate and government policies that shape it. We do not tell them, for example, that the Internet is at its best when the architecture is "open end-to-end," or that intellectual property is overprotected in the interests of Microsoft and other companies.[26] We have not even exposed them to open-source software—although that might be a good thing to do. Instead, we help kids address local problems that they care about, using the most readily available technology. (Below, I discuss the value of local knowledge.) Ultimately, we hope that their direct experiences with creativity will make them skilled and independent judges of the policies that govern the new media.

So far, the Prince George's Information Commons is not an independent, democratic association. It is a series of projects organized by a few University of Maryland colleagues, with the heavy participation of youthful volunteers. Since foundations fund these projects, the principal investigators are responsible and make many basic decisions. We decided not to start by creating a new association, because we believed that it would have been impossible to attract community members until we had created some tangible and valuable products for a public website. However, we have tried to honor associational norms by making our young participants feel that they are important members of a group, and by asking them to make as many decisions as possible. Moreover, we see ourselves as building the foundations of a robust, independent community organization. In the terms used by Ostrom and Hess, we control the *constitutional-choice* and *collective-choice* rules of the commons, although we hope to cede control to a democratic organization.[27] The day-to-day *operational rules* are already based on deliberation and consensus.

Youth Civic Development

An information commons could involve people of any age. We focus on youth because of converging evidence that people develop durable civic identities in adolescence. They either come to see themselves as efficacious, obligated, critical members of a community, or they do not. Their identity, once formed in adolescence, is hard to shake. This theory derives from Karl Mannheim, but it has considerable recent empirical support. In the 1920s, Mannheim argued that we are forced to develop a stance toward the public world of news, issues, and governments when we first encounter these things, usually around age seventeen. Our stance can be one of contempt or neglect, or it can be some kind of engagement, whether critical or conservative. Most of us never have a compelling reason to reassess this stance, so it remains in place throughout adulthood. That is why generations have enduring political and social characters, formed in their early years.[28]

Young Americans are less likely to develop civic identities today than in the past. Many ingredients of a civic identity are difficult to measure or have not been followed consistently over long spans of time. However, the percentage of young people who say they follow public affairs dropped from 24 percent in 1966 to just 5 percent in 2000.[29] Although young Americans are just as likely to say they believe in God as their predecessors were in 1976, regular attendance at religious services is down from 41 to 33 percent.[30] There are substantial declines in the percentage of high school seniors who have joined or led extracurricular groups—in school or outside.[31]

Trust correlates with associational membership, but there has been a 50 percent decline in the proportion of young people who trust their fellow human beings.[32] Wendy Rahn and John Transue explain the erosion of young people's social trust as a result of "rapid rise of materialistic value orientations that occurred among American youth in the 1970s and 1980s."[33] Eric Uslaner explains trust as a function of optimism. People who believe that the world will get better (that there will be more public goods for all) are willing to trust others and cooperate. People who believe that the pie is shrinking adopt a zero-sum, "me-first" approach.[34] Whatever the cause, a decline in trust spells danger for all forms of commons.[35]

The decline in trust and other attitudes and skills favorable to a commons is not kids' fault. I blame the failure of mediating institutions such as unions, political parties, and churches to recruit young people to help sustain public goods.[36] Ostrom notes that at any time in the early 1930s, about 4 percent of American households contained a member of a local government council or board, who might discuss issues of democratic participation and collective action with his or her children. By 1992, the raw number of board members had declined by half while the population had soared. This is just an example of the decline in participatory public institutions.

Fortunately, we know how to develop civic identities. Adolescents are more likely to become civic if they feel that they are assets, rather than potential problems; if they feel that they *matter* to a group.[37] It also helps to give them direct experience with civic or public work.[38] The value of experiential learning for citizenship has been shown in numerous studies. Partly as a result of this research, there has been a massive increase in "service learning"—that is, combinations of community service with academic work—at all levels of education from kindergarten to PhD programs.[39] At its best, service learning can be a transformational experience that develops enduring civic values and habits. However, in the context of real public schools, service learning often degenerates into tutoring younger children or cleaning a park—and then talking about the experience. This happens for two reasons. First, developing more ambitious service projects is difficult and time consuming. And second, public schools court controversy whenever their students engage in political advocacy and/or "faith-based" community action. Yet forbidding politics and religion drastically narrows the range of discussion and action; as a result, service learning often becomes trivial.

Many of the best programs are found in Catholic high schools, where service experiences are connected to a challenging normative and spiritual worldview: post–Vatican II Catholic social thought. There is no evidence that these programs cause their graduates to agree with the main doctrines of Catholic theology, but students do develop lasting engagement with their community.[40] However, this model cannot be replicated in public schools, which must be more normatively neutral and respectful of pluralism.

As an alternative, it seems promising to involve young people in *public interest research using the new digital media*. Conducting research is consistent with the express purposes of public schools, so it is less controversial than political action. Yet research on public issues can be deeply motivating; it can influence identities and attitudes, not just knowledge. By asking students to study their own communities, we can help them to experience and prize the values of public service, empirical rigor, and critical inquiry.

Using research for civic education has always been possible, but the Internet helps in two ways. First, it cuts the costs of conducting research and then disseminating results. For example, ten years ago, it would have required tremendous investments of skilled time and equipment to help adolescents to create reliable and original maps of their community. If they did create excellent maps—say, of pollution levels—disseminating their work to the community would have been expensive and difficult.

Today, GIS software can assist a class in making professional maps, which they can place on a website at almost no cost.

Besides, the Internet has an appeal to adolescents. Many people born after 1970 view computers as exciting and accessible; they are more likely to address civic issues by creating a website than by joining a labor union or a fraternal organization. We have often been able to recruit youth with the promise of working with computers. The Pew Internet and American Life Project has identified a group of "Power Creators" who each create online material in an average of two different ways: for instance, maintaining a personal site and also posting on other sites. This group has a median age of twenty-five. Since the youngest people surveyed were eighteen, the real median is certainly lower.[41]

On the other hand, adolescents are not automatically facile with computers just because they were born after the release of Windows 1.0. Many students with whom we have worked have spent little time in front of computers; they have only been taught "keyboarding" in school (this is typing, but with a word processor); and they have fairly low confidence in their own abilities.

In fact, young adults are not the most active age group online; people in their thirties and forties are more likely to create or contribute to websites. Content creators also tend to be well educated: just 6 percent are adults without high school diplomas, and almost half hold college degrees.[42]

Subtle forms of inequality arise even when students have equal access to computers. Analysis of the National Education Longitudinal Study (NELS) by Jianxia Du and James Anderson reveals that consistent use of computers in schools is correlated with higher test scores for white and Asian students and for those who take advanced courses. Presumably, they are using computers to enrich their studies and to do creative, challenging work. But there is no positive correlation for young people in other racial and ethnic groups or for those of any background who take less challenging courses, possibly because "disadvantaged children tend to utilize computers for routine learning activities rather than for intellectually demanding applications."[43] In fact, disadvantaged students who take computer courses perform *worse* on standardized tests than other students, other things being equal.

Mark Warschauer has compared two schools in Hawaii that intelligently integrate computers into their science courses. In both schools, teams of students use computers to conduct scientific research, guided by teachers from several disciplines. But one school serves an affluent and selective student body, 97 percent of whom go straight to four-year colleges, while the other serves a neighborhood with a per capita income under $10,000. At the selective private school, teachers have experience in graduate-level scientific research. They teach students to collect field data using handheld devices, download the data to computers, and then intensively analyze them (with help from the calculus teacher). Meanwhile, the students at the Title One public school take boats to outdoor locations, learn to grow seaweed, and then use computers to publish a newsletter.

Both activities are worthwhile; both teach skills and knowledge and engage students in creative teamwork. But there is a fundamental difference in the kinds of skills taught and the overall purpose of the exercise. As Warschauer notes, "One school was producing scholars and the other school was producing workers. And the introduction of computers did absolutely nothing to change the dynamic; in fact, it reinforced it."[44] Teachers at the public school are very conscious that they need to give their students the skills demanded by employers today—collaboration, responsibility, and teamwork—whereas the private school tries to place its graduates in demanding college programs where they will be expected to show independence, originality, and sheer intellectual excellence.

It is not easy for teachers to overcome this gap, even if they possess sophisticated research skills themselves. Many of the students in our project write English at an elementary school level (although they may be bi- or even trilingual) and have limited skills for searching the web or reading text. It is hard to move them a long distance in a single course, and hard to set high expectations when their academic self-confidence seems fragile and they are far from achieving precollege work. We began our current project with high hopes that students might find statistical correlations between their home locations and behavior relevant to obesity (such as exercise and eating fast food). But that relationship proved complicated and subtle. We will need a great deal more high-quality data before we have a chance of finding statistically significant results. So far, our students' most successful and prominent public product has been a short online video about the changes in food consumption that they experienced when they immigrated to the United States. It is far easier to notice the difference between food in Sudan versus Prince George's County, Maryland, than to calculate the effects of living on a street with a continuous sidewalk. But the latter research would teach much more advanced academic skills.

Educators (including ourselves) are always tempted to settle for merely teaching responsibility, teamwork, and presentation skills. After all, these attributes help high school graduates in the workplace. This is one reason that African-American and Hispanic students are most likely to use computers in school for games, for drill and practice, or at best to create simple websites with text and pictures, whereas white and Asian students are most likely to use them for "simulations and applications."[45] By and large, minority students are being prepared for service jobs. To give them a shot at professional occupations, we are going to need much better curricula and pedagogical methods for youth-led research. First, teachers should develop a set of serious community research projects that kids can handle effectively, and then it would be extremely useful to collect these ideas in textbooks for youth-led research.

The Engaged University

Many people are rightly concerned about how well higher education serves its core purposes, which are to educate college students and to produce public goods in the form of knowledge, debate, and cultural artifacts.[46] But I think that universities should also use their faculty and student expertise and technical resources to benefit nearby communities. This is partly a matter of fairness; universities should be responsible citizens, sharing their enormous advantages. Engagement is also a way to address a sense of alienation that many professors feel. They enter the profession with idealistic motivations, but find that they only contribute incrementally to the knowledge of fellow specialists, with whom they interact sporadically at conferences or by e-mail. Engaging with their local communities can be profoundly rejuvenating for some faculty.

The most common way to "engage the public" is to provide technical assistance: in other words, to advise people on how to address a public problem. This kind of work can be valuable. However, it does not tap the knowledge and energy of people outside the academy. Nor does it increase their capacity to address their own problems. The application of expertise can even *reduce* public capacity if people become overly reliant on, or deferential to, experts.

Furthermore, technical assistance cannot settle normative conflicts, since no one is an expert on matters of value. Yet sometimes expert opinion can *suppress* normative debates. For example, economists may appear to resolve a debate when they claim that one policy is most efficient, and lawyers may claim to settle a controversy when they assert that one side has more support in the law. But neither discipline exhausts the range of considerations that citizens should consider.[47]

Technical assistance is either expensive (in which case it is out of the reach of poor communities) or else it is a gift from experts. A gift does nothing to challenge the basic power imbalance. If anything, it may make residents feel indebted to the university.

Finally, technical assistance tends not to be highly challenging for professors. For many scholars, public service research is "normal science," a routine application of their methods to some local problem. For junior faculty, this is a diversion on the road to tenure (and inadvisable). For senior faculty, it is pro bono—something that they do out of generosity but without a close link to their core work.

I am much more interested in research that contributes important new methods and knowledge to a discipline *as a result of* close engagement with communities. For example, I doubt that Elinor Ostrom and her colleagues at Indiana University could have made crucial contributions to the theory of collective action if they had not worked closely with people who manage "common-pool resources" (forests, fisheries, irrigation systems, and grazing lands) on several continents. They have drawn advice and inspiration from these people even as they have provided technical assistance and derived generalizable lessons.[48] Likewise, Jane Mansbridge's discovery of regular norms in consensus-based democratic organizations arose from her close and collaborative work with such groups.[49] Such engaged research projects are not only interesting (and useful for the populations studied); they also create models within the academy. Professors and graduate students can see that community engagement is not extracurricular or optional; rather, it is the *only* way to make progress on certain important questions.

Academics are strongly influenced by policies regarding funding, hiring, promotion, and tenure. Often universities that compete internationally for academic prominence do not reward applied research—let alone service—despite rhetoric to the contrary. Even if they want to promote and retain faculty who serve their communities, they are constrained by measures of reputation (like the *U.S. News and World Report* rankings) and by other universities' hiring decisions.[50] At best, there are two tiers of faculty: the most prominent scholars who do advanced research, and their lower-status colleagues who provide "public service," perhaps to improve the university's relations with its neighbors.

Fortunately, universities do reward scholars who break new ground in their disciplines by working with communities. Thus a strategy of using community engagement to achieve genuine scholarly insight is better suited to the existing academic marketplace than a strategy based on "service."

However, there is at least one respect in which existing policies and priorities probably need to change. Academic departments tend to prefer research that will interest a national or international audience within their own disciplines. Thus scholars are best rewarded for work that belongs within a single field but generalizes across a large geographic area. While such results are useful, there is also a need for *local* knowledge. Communities differ; they have their own problems, traditions, and assets. Scholarly research can contribute to important discussions and decisions at the community level. Therefore, I believe it would be very useful to create interdisciplinary publications or websites devoted to metropolitan areas. An example is San Diego Dialogue (www.sandiegodialogue.org), which the University of California at San Diego supports by providing sophisticated research studies. Such work can be peer-reviewed and highly selective. Nevertheless, I think almost all academic departments would prefer that their faculty publish in single-discipline journals of national or international scope. This is a bias that is difficult to defend on intellectual or normative grounds, but it is reinforced by the way the faculty labor market works.

Community-based research should go beyond description and include tough-minded analysis. I have attended many meetings and events at which young people or poor people "document" an asset, problem, or activity in their environment. But academics and other professional researchers "document" things only as a first stage in research (if they do it at all). Their real interests are comparing, assessing, and explaining phenomena, not merely listing or portraying them. I understand why disadvantaged people often make do with description; it requires fewer skills and resources. But much more power comes with assessment and explanation. Too often, the rich do research while the poor get documentation. The solution is to try to involve young people, poor people, and other disadvantaged people in real research, whenever possible.

Our work in Prince George's County is hardly a model. We are unlikely to break new ground in geography or urban planning, since I am the principal investigator and I am no expert in these fields. However, we are committed to working in the vicinity of our university, and we see this local engagement as a strength. For faculty, local work connects their professional research to their citizenship; it allows them to contribute to their *own* communities while doing serious professional work. It is thus an antidote to a certain kind of alienation that is common in the age of jet-set academia. At the same time, focusing on a defined geographic community is a good way to create a commons—for reasons described in the next section.

Local Roots

An association can be local and face to face or else dispersed, even global. This is particularly true on the Internet, which lowers the costs of identifying fellow travelers in faraway places and communicating with them. Often the results are beneficial. For instance, people with shared stigmas are able to find one another at long distance and thereby escape the oppression of their hostile local communities. Boyle observes that very large aggregations of people can build amazingly good compendiums of information.[51] Global networks make such aggregation possible.

Nevertheless, I believe it is especially important to build associational commons with roots in geographic communities. There are four major reasons for this conclusion.

First, many people care deeply about their own localities, so a local or regional focus will encourage them to participate in the commons. As a general rule, people are more likely to contribute to voluntary associations that work locally, because it is expensive to move, and therefore a household's welfare is tied to the common welfare of the place.[52]

Second, geographic communities (especially whole counties and metropolitan areas) are *diverse*. This is evidently true of Los Angeles, New York—and Prince George's County—but it is also the case in many ethnically homogeneous areas, which still contain ideological, religious, and other forms of diversity that are typically absent when people associate voluntarily. Some observers argue that the Internet encourages narrow discussions and segmentation into small, like-minded groups. We can too easily escape from people unlike ourselves by going online.[53] However, a geographically defined commons will encourage us to interact with people who are different.

Third, local governments make important decisions, so we need a healthy democracy at the local level. Democracy requires not only good institutions, but also active publics that can deliberate, organize, and act.

Public work with the Internet can help to form such geographically defined publics. In Prince George's County, for example, most people are confused by the overlapping layers of government authority exercised by towns, school boards, regional planning bodies, the three branches of county government, and the state. They are also largely indifferent to this structure, which means that they do not vote in local elections, deliberate about local policies, or lobby local politicians. Power thus falls into the hands of organized special interests that have the resources to master local politics: especially developers, police unions, and chambers of commerce. But even teenagers with very ordinary academic skills who participate in the Prince George's Information Commons quickly encounter political issues that have to be addressed through local law. And so they develop both knowledge and interest in local government.

Finally, much research suggests that online interactions are most meaningful and satisfying when they are accompanied (at least occasionally) by face-to-face contact. This is partly because being known and seen discourages outrageous and offensive behavior, which is common in anonymous online settings.[54] However, it is very expensive to add face-to-face contact to an Internet group—unless all the participants live nearby.

Thus there are important benefits from local associations. But they are not thriving online, as evidenced by the shortage of compelling websites produced by voluntary groups for specific localities. People want the chance to do collaborative public work, to represent and experience their distinctive local cultures, and to engage in sustained dialogue—but no one has found ways to make money from hosting such activities. Commercial sites intended for geographic communities are full of advertising and generic news and entertainment, but they have few public contributions. Neighborhood associations, voluntary organizations, religious congregations, and other groups that do public work within geographic communities have benefited from establishing web pages. But most of the actual sites these groups have created amount to simple online brochures, no more valuable to their visitors than printed posters would be.

A 2001 survey by the Pew Internet and American Life Project found that, of those Americans who communicated online with other members of a group, just 15 percent contacted people in their "own local communities"—compared to 43 percent who contacted others "all over the country." Asked whether "the Internet [is] more useful for becoming involved in things going on in your local community, or things going on outside of your local community," just 9 percent chose the first option. And only a fifth of those who had used the Internet to communicate with fellow members of a group had ever met those people face to face.[55] It is great to be able to participate at low cost in national or international associations and to communicate with people one will never be able to meet in person. But if local associations have an important civic and social role, we need to take deliberate action to support them online.

Public Work

By now it should be obvious that there is a political agenda behind our projects in Prince George's County, but the nature of this agenda could easily be misunderstood. My own political orientation derives from Harry Boyte's concept of "public work."[56] Boyte and his colleagues argue that ordinary citizens have enormous capacity to make things of public value by working together outside of a market. For example, citizens can create public goods by recycling, starting associations, revitalizing their culture, or fighting crime. By creating new institutions and projects, people also gain political power that they can use to claim rights and benefits.

Our response to obesity illustrates Boyte's ideas. In March 2004, the Centers for Disease Control announced that excessive body weight will soon be the leading cause of death in the United States.[57] The next day, the House of Representatives passed the "Personal Responsibility in Food Consumption Act" (H.R. 339) to block "civil liability actions . . . against food manufacturers, marketers, distributors, advertisers, sellers, and trade associations for claims of injury relating to a person's weight gain, obesity, or any health condition associated with weight gain or obesity." The press dubbed this legislation the "Cheeseburger Bill" and gave it considerable coverage.

There are legal academics and lawyers who advocate "an onslaught on the fast-food industry as a whole, in which it would be made to pay its share of responsibility for type-two diabetes, sclerotic arteries, heart attacks and strokes."[58] Those in favor of the "Cheeseburger Bill" reply that we should be personally responsible for our behavior and should not sue McDonald's because we are fat. "Look in the mirror, because you're the one to blame," said F. James Sensenbrenner Jr. (R-WI).[59] I disagree in part: a rapid increase in the obesity rate is a social problem with political solutions. However, I agree that lawsuits are not the right response. There are much more constructive, positive, participatory responses to obesity. For example, a community can work to make its streets safe and walkable, to identify and publicize existing assets, and to provide new food and exercise options.

As a matter of fact, just two days before the CDC released its report on obesity as the leading killer in America, forty-five high school students had spent the day with us discussing the local causes of obesity and planning their mapping project. They talked about harmful advertising and their own lack of willpower. But we also encouraged them to ask whether there are local causes of the problem that may be more tractable. For example, in the areas around Hyattsville, Maryland, there are no full basketball courts. This is a political issue (the authorities do not want young black men hanging around, so they do not build courts), and it may affect adolescents' body weight. It shows the limits of conservative arguments. You cannot exercise if there are no sidewalks, no basketball courts, and no grassy spaces. If the only place that lets you hang out at 10 p.m. is McDonald's, then you are going to eat a lot of fries. Still, that does not mean that lawyers will ever solve the problem by suing McDonald's on behalf of the American people. Communities have the power to take their fate into their own hands.

Every community, no matter how poor and embattled, has assets that its residents can use for their common benefit.[60] Whereas leftists might say that the only solution to the afflictions of an inner-city neighborhood is government aid, proponents of public work stress people's capacity to improve their *own* communities by acting together. Poor people do need outside resources—both capital and government assistance—but they are unlikely to get such help unless they have first organized themselves as a powerful political force. The best way to organize is to address tangible local problems, even before powerful outsiders offer aid. And if residents are used to working together, are confident and experienced, and have created their own institutions, then they can handle an influx of cash without being overwhelmed by corruption or manipulative outsiders.

At bottom, both the Left and the Right believe that all things of value are created either by companies and entrepreneurs or else by governments. They assume that markets and states produce a pool of goods that citizens fight over. This struggle is what we conventionally call "politics." It is a zero-sum game, hence largely unpleasant. In contrast, the public-work approach suggests that citizens can make new goods—expand the pie—by cooperating.

Unfortunately, opportunities for ordinary citizens to do public work have shrunk over the last century. This is partly because professionals and experts have taken over many traditional duties of citizens, from managing towns to setting educational policy to lobbying. And it is partly because many civic functions have been privatized. For example, Americans often pay companies to provide neighborhood security or to watch their small children. All that is left for citizens to do is to complain, vote, and volunteer. Volunteering can be valuable, but it is usually squeezed between work and family time. Moreover, conventional volunteering tends to mean direct, face-to-face service that does not change policies or institutions or grant much power to those who participate. A national survey of Americans conducted in 2002 found that many volunteered, at least occasionally, but only 20 percent of the volunteers (and 10 percent of young volunteers) described their participation as a way to address a "social or political problem."[61] In a qualitative study of Minnesota citizens completed in 2000, respondents said that volunteering often consigned them "to positions of mediocrity with the assumption that they lacke[ed] the capacity to work on big issues that impact the community."[62] At its best, public service is demanding, creative, responsible, serious business.

In modern America, we prize expertise as perhaps never before in human history. And nowhere is the admiration for specialized intelligence greater than in fields connected to computers, where nerds rule. It is good news that young people without high social status or formal education can rise quickly in this world. However, most people remain unable to perform important tasks or to make significant decisions, because only technical experts are competent. Thus, for anyone attracted to the general idea of public work, it is crucial to find projects that are genuinely valuable, that involve the new information technologies, and that can be accomplished by ordinary people.

Conclusion

The Internet was born as a commons, as a particular kind of public resource. A commons can be beneficial for civil society and democracy, mainly because it permits people to be creative as citizens—to contribute things of value to the commonwealth. It is an antidote to consumerism and to passive forms of citizenship.

While there is value to the very low-cost products that we see on the Internet (personal web pages, e-mail lists, and blogs), we also need fairly expensive and elaborate products such as moderated deliberations, maps linked to databases, streaming videos, online newspapers with original reporting, historical archives, and photo essays—to name just a few. Young people can contribute such products, thus exercising their creativity in the public interest. This is especially important since many young people are otherwise alienated from public and civic life.

The Internet commons is threatened by state regulation, but more seriously by corporate control. Corporations can increase their profits by restricting access to the commons and by treating Internet users as consumers, not coproducers. Since the Internet commons is threatened, and since the most valuable public products are expensive and elaborate, worthwhile uses of the Internet require *organizations* and constituencies.

College faculty, students, and staff have a special opportunity to help communities use the Internet for public purposes, thereby developing a political constituency for the commons and also creating models and templates that can be used elsewhere in civil society. Such work is not only beneficial to the public; it can also make scholarly work more satisfying and multidimensional.

These premises have encouraged us to create an experimental "commons" attached to the University of Maryland. We would welcome collaborations with anyone involved in similar efforts.

Notes

1. We are working under the aegis of the Engaged University Initiative of the Democracy Collaborative. For the broad strategy of this initiative, see Gar Alperovitz and Ted Howard, "The Next Wave: Building a University Civic Engagement Service for the Twenty-First Century," in *Journal of Higher Education Outreach and Engagement* 10/2 (spring/summer 2005): 141–157. Our current funding comes from the National Geographic Education Foundation. There are eight colleagues and graduate students involved in the project, but I would especially like to acknowledge Margaret-Morgan Hubbard, Associate Director of the Democracy Collaborative, and Carrie Donovan, formerly Youth Director of CIRCLE. They have done as much as I to create the Prince George's Information Commons; nevertheless, the views expressed in this chapter are mine alone. I would also like to thank the Workshop in Political Theory and Policy

Analysis at Indiana University for the invitation to write this chapter and for feedback on an earlier draft.

2. Frank L. D. Engelke, "How Land Use and Transportation Systems Impact Public Health: A Literature Review of the Relationship between Physical Activity and Built Form," *ACES Working Paper*, no. 1; S. A. French, M. Story, and R. W. Jeffery, "Environmental Influences on Eating and Physical Activity," *Annual Review of Public Health* 22 (2001): 309–325 (review article); B. Giles-Corti and R. J. Donovan, "The Relative Influence of Individual, Social and Physical Environmental Determinants of Physical Activity," *Social Science and Medicine* 54(12): 1793–1812.

3. P. Gordon-Larsen, R. G. McMurray, and B. M. Popkin, "Determinants of Adolescent Physical Activity and Inactivity Patterns," *Pediatrics* 105 (2000): 83–91.

4. J. F. Sallis, A. Bauman, and M. Pratt, "Environmental and Policy Interventions to Promote Physical Activity," *American Journal of Preventive Medicine* 15/4 (1998): 379–397 (review article).

5. The following report notes the lack of such studies: Education Development Center, Inc., *Self-Evaluation in Youth Media and Technology Programs: A Report to the AOL Time Warner Foundation* (Newton, MA: Education Development Center, Inc., September 2003).

6. Earthforce is an excellent program that involves students in environmental research and political action. It was evaluated by Alan Melchior and Lawrence Neil Bailis in 2001–2002, using pre/post student questionnaires, teacher questionnaires, and focus groups (but no comparison groups or testlike assessments). See "2001–2002 Earth Force Evaluation: Program Implementation and Impacts," www.earthforce.org/resources.cfm. There were many positive changes in self-reported skills, knowledge, and attitudes over the course of the program, and teachers were favorable. However, the participants became *less* likely over the course of the program to say, "I believe I can personally make a difference in my school or community," "I believe that people working together can solve community problems," "It is important to listen to people on all sides of a community issue if we want to find a solution that will work," "I think it is more important to look for ways to help the environment for a long time than to do something that will just make a difference for a few days," and "I pay attention to local environmental issues when I hear about them." These are civic attitudes, supportive of commons. The evaluators conclude: "One possible explanation is that the decline reflects an increased understanding on the part of participants of how slow and difficult change can be, and that participants are both more realistic and in some cases discouraged by the challenges they face in addressing issues in their communities."

7. For the origins and goals of these projects, see Peter Levine, "Building the Electronic Commons" (April 2002), www.democracycollaborative.org/publications/reports/; Harry Boyte and Paul Resnick, with Peter Levine, Robert

Wachbroit, and Lew Friedland, "White Paper: Civic Extension for the Information Age" (draft of July 23, 2001), www.si.umich.edu/~presnick/papers/civicextension/.

8. Ostrom and Hess, chapter 3, this volume.

9. Suber, chapter 7, this volume.

10. Ostrom and Hess, chapter 3, this volume.

11. Jefferson to Isaac Mcpherson [sic], August 13, 1813; quoted in Lawrence Lessig, *Code and Other Laws of Cyberspace* (New York: Basic Books, 1999), 132.

12. See Kranich, chapter 4, this volume.

13. For a good statement of Metcalfe's law (the value of a network is proportional to $\frac{n(n-1)}{2}$, where n is the number of users) and Reed's Law (the value is even higher, because of the potential number of n-person *groups*, each of which can potentially communicate with other groups within the network), see http://216.36.193.92/ec/n3.html.

14. Peter Levine, "A Movement for the Commons?", *Responsive Community* 13/4 (fall 2003): 28–39; "Building the E-Commons," *Good Society* 11/3 (2003): 1–9.

15. Boyle, chapter 5, this volume.

16. See Alexis de Tocqueville, *Democracy in America*, translated by Henry Reeve and others (New York: Vintage Books, 1954), vol. II, book II, chap. v, p. 114.

17. I connect "civil society" talk to the idea of a commons in "Civic Renewal and the Commons of Cyberspace," *National Civic Review* 90/3 (fall 2001): 205–211.

18. Mancur Olson, *The Logic of Collective Action: Public Goods and the Theory of Groups* (Cambridge, MA: Harvard University Press, 1971).

19. David Bollier, *Public Assets, Private Profits: Reclaiming the American Commons in an Age of Market Enclosure* (New York: New America Foundation, 2001), 58.

20. Jeffrey Chester, "The Death of the Internet: How Industry Intends to Kill The 'Net as We Know It," TomPaine.com (October 24, 2002).

21. Elinor Ostrom, "Collective Action and the Evolution of Social Norms," *Journal of Economic Perspectives* 14/3 (summer 2000): 150.

22. See Ostrom and Hess's section on "Evaluative Criteria," chapter 3, this volume.

23. Ostrom, "Collective Action and the Evolution of Social Norms," 151.

24. Elinor Ostrom, "The Need for Civic Education: A Collective Action Perspective," Working Paper W98-26 (Indiana University, Bloomington, Workshop in Political Theory and Policy Analysis, 1998).

25. Ostrom, "Type of Goods and Collective Action" (unpublished paper delivered at the University of Maryland, 2002): "Groups of individuals are consid-

ered to share communal property rights when they have *formed an organization* that exercises at least the collective-choice rights of management and exclusion to some defined resource system and the resource units produced by that system. In other words, all communal groups have established some means of governing themselves in relationship to a resource" (italics added).

26. Points made persuasively in Lawrence Lessig, *The Future of Ideas: The Fate of the Commons in a Connected World* (New York: Random House, 2001).

27. Ostrom and Hess, chapter 3, this volume.

28. Karl Mannheim, "The Problem of Generations" (1928), in Paul Kecskemeti, ed., *Essays on the Sociology of Knowledge* (New York: Oxford University Press, 1952), 276–322, especially p. 300. Mannheim says: "Even if the rest of one's life consisted in one long process of negation and destruction of the natural world view acquired in youth, the determining influence of these early impressions would still be predominant" (p. 298). For a good summary of recent literature, see Constance Flanagan and Lonnie R. Sherrod, "Youth Political Development: An Introduction," *Journal of Social Issues* 54/3 (fall 1998): 447–456. The period between age fourteen and twenty-five is identified as crucial in R. G. Niemi and M. A. Hepburn, "The Rebirth of Political Socialization," *Perspectives on Political Science* 24 (1995): 7–16.

29. Of Americans age seventeen to twenty-four, 24.6 percent said they paid attention to public affairs in 1966; just 5.1 percent said so in 2000 (American National Election Study, author's tabulation).

30. Monitoring the Future data analyzed by Child Trends (http://www.childtrendsdatabank.org/family/school/32ReligiousServices.htm).

31. M. Kent Jennings and Lara Stocker, "Generations and Civic Engagement: A Longitudinal Multiple-Generational Analysis" (unpublished paper, 2001).

32. In 1976, 31.6 percent said that most people could be trusted; the figure was 17.3 percent in 1995 (Monitoring the Future data as analyzed in Wendy M. Rahn and John E. Transue, "Social Trust and Value Change: The Decline of Social Capital in American Youth, 1976–1995," *Political Psychology* 19/3 (1998): 548).

33. Rahn and Transue, "Social Trust and Value Change: The Decline of Social Capital in American Youth, 1976–1995," *Political Psychology* 19/3 (1998): 545–565.

34. Eric M. Uslaner, "Trust as a Moral Value" (forthcoming in Dario Castiglione, ed., *Social Capital*), www.bsos.umd.edu/gvpt/uslaner/uslanerexeter.pdf.

35. Ostrom, "The Need for Civic Education," 1–2.

36. The claim that association life has declined is complicated by the fact that some organizations (e.g., professional associations) have grown while others have shrunk. It is my view that the net change has been negative, because organizations that confer power and skills on disadvantaged and marginalized people are the most likely to have declined. See William A. Galston and Peter Levine, "America's Civic Condition: A Glance at the Evidence," *Brookings Review* 15/4 (fall 1997): 23–26.

37. Constance Flanagan, "Developmental Roots of Political Engagement," *PS: Political Science and Politics* 36/2 (April 2003): 257–261.

38. See, for example, the literature review in Miranda Yates and James Youniss, "Community Service and Political Identity Development in Adolescence," *Journal of Social Issues* 54 (fall 1998): 495–512.

39. Almost half of U.S. high schools offer service-learning programs. See U.S. Department of Education, National Center for Education Statistics, *Service Learning and Community Service in K–12 Public Schools* (Washington, DC: September 1999), table 1. Since the term was coined about 1990, it is difficult to measure the increase since the 1980s, but it appears to be very dramatic.

40. Yates and Youniss, "Community Service and Political Identity Development in Adolescence"; David E. Campbell, "Bowling Together: Private Schools, Serving Public Ends," *Education Next* 1/3 (2001): 55–62.

41. Amanda Lenhart, John Horrigan, and Deborah Fallows, *Content Creation Online* (Washington, D.C.: Pew Internet and American Life Project, February 29, 2004).

42. Lenhart, Horrigan, and Fallows, *Content Creation Online*.

43. Jianxia Du and James D. Anderson, "Technology and Quality of Education: Does Technology Help Low-Income and Minority Students in Their Academic Achievements?", *Illinois Journal of Law, Technology, & Policy* (spring 2003): 1–34 (quote on 7).

44. Mark Warschauer, "Technology and School Reform: A View from Both Sides of the Track(ing)," revised version of Warschauer, "Technology and School Reform: A View from Both Sides of the Track," *Education Policy Analysis Archives* 8/4 (2000), epaa.asu.edu/epaa/v8n4.html.

45. National Assessment of Educational Progress (NAEP) Mathematics Assessment, 1996, analyzed by Harold Wenglinsky, *Does It Compute? The Relationship between Educational Technology and Student Achievement in Mathematics* (Princeton, NJ: Educational Testing Service, 1998): 22–24. At the eighth grade, students who use computers primarily for drill and practice are half a grade level behind their peers with similar demographic characteristics, while students who use computers for "simulations and applications" are nearly half a grade ahead of the mean (p. 30).

46. For the mission, see Harry Boyte and Elizabeth Hollander, "Wingspread Declaration on the Civic Responsibilites of Research Universities" (Providence, RI: Campus Compact, 1999; www.compact.org/civic/Wingspread/Wingspread .html) and Carnegie Foundation for the Advancement of Teaching and CIRCLE, "Higher Education: Civic Mission and Civic Effects" (College Park, MD, 2006; http://www.civicyouth.org/research/areas/higher_ed.htm). For the criticism of current practice, see, e.g., Eyal Press and Jennifer Washburn," The Kept University," *Atlantic Monthly* 285/3 (March 2000): 39–54.

47. Peter Levine, "Public Intellectuals and the Influence of Economics," *Higher Education Exchange*, Dayton, Ohio, 2001, pp. 43–51; "The Idea of an Engaged

University," an interview of me by David Brown, *Higher Education Exchange*, Dayton, Ohio, 2003, pp. 31–41.

48. I am referring to the Workshop in Political Theory and Policy Analysis and the Center for the Study of Institutions, Population, and Environmental Change (CIPEC) and to such products as a database of 127 common-pool irrigation systems in Nepal (see Elinor Ostrom and Roy Gardner, "Coping with Asymmetries in the Commons: Self-Governing Irrigation Systems Can Work," *Journal of Economic Perspectives* 7/4 (fall 1993): 101).

49. Jane Mansbridge, *Beyond Adversary Democracy* (Chicago: University of Chicago Press, 1983), and subsequent work.

50. Matthew Hartley and Elizabeth L. Hollander, "The Elusive Ideal: Civic Learning and Higher Education," in Susan Fuhrman and Marvin Lazerson, eds., *Institutions of American Democracy: The Public Schools* (New York: Oxford University Press, 2005), 252–276.

51. Boyle, chapter 5, this volume.

52. Ostrom claims, on the basis of studies from around the world, that communal ownership arrangements generally work best when "participants plan to live and work in the same area for a long time (and in some cases, expect their offspring to live there as well) and, thus, do not heavily discount the future" ("Type of Goods and Collective Action," 27).

53. In *Republic.com* (Princeton, NJ: Princeton University Press, 2001), Cass Sunstein claims that the Internet allows people to choose news and opinion that already interest them, while filtering out views and facts that they find uncongenial. As a result, the population splits into small communities of like-minded people who reinforce their shared views. Another predicted result is a widening gap between those who have a lot of interest in public issues and those who are not interested. Motivated citizens benefit from all the news and opinion online. Unmotivated ones can ignore the broader world in a way that was more difficult back when they relied on TV for entertainment and the newspaper for want ads and crossword puzzles. Whether they liked it or not, they saw news on television and on the front page of the newspaper.

Sunstein's book was mostly based on his theory of democracy and some experimental evidence about deliberation in narrow groups. His empirical evidence about the Internet was relatively weak. Thus many reviewers criticized him and offered anecdotes about the web as a place for diverse public deliberations. Even Sunstein seemed to back off from his own claims in the face of these criticisms. Yet I never thought he was proved wrong.

If Sunstein were right, those who started off uninterested in politics would be less informed, and therefore less likely to participate, once they gained Internet access. Recently, Markus Prior has demonstrated that Internet access correlates with a lower probability of voting among people who start with a low interest in the news. (In other words, these people are more likely to vote if they do *not* have Net access.) Prior's article is titled "Liberated Viewers, Polarized Voters: The Implications of Increased Media Choice for Democratic Politics," *Good Society* 11/3 (2002): 10–16.

I still think the best theoretical account of "cyberbalkanization" is Marshall van Alstyne and Erik Brynjolfsson, "Electronic Communities: Global Village or Cyberbalkans? (1997; see web.mit.edu/marshall/www/papers/CyberBalkans .pdf). They predict that the Internet will help people who are so inclined to increase the range and diversity of their information and contacts. They also predict that the Internet will allow people to "filter" out unwelcome ideas or contacts and to form narrow, exclusive groups. So the technology will not determine the outcome; people's motives will. And clearly, people have varying motives. Some prefer diverse ideas and serendipitous encounters; others want to shun people who are different and simply confirm their own prejudices.

I am fairly pessimistic about the cyberbalkanization problem, not because of the technology, but because of cultural trends in the United States. Niche marketing has become highly sophisticated and has divided us into small groups. There is more money to be made through niche programs than by creating diverse forums for discussion. Meanwhile, people have developed consumerist attitudes toward news, looking for "news products" tailored to their private needs. And broad-based organizations have mostly shrunk since the 1950s. In this context, the Internet looks like a means to more balkanization. In a different context, such as contemporary Saudi Arabia, it may have a much more positive impact.

54. See, for example, A. Joinson, "Causes and Implications of Disinhibited Behavior on the Internet," in J. Gackenbach, ed., *Psychology and the Internet: Intrapersonal, Interpersonal, and Transpersonal Implications* (San Diego: Academic Press, 1998), 43–57.

55. Pew Internet and American Life Project, Online Communities Survey (2001), available from www.pewinternet.org.

56. Boyte is a former field secretary in the civil rights movement, a University of Minnesota professor, and codirector of the University's Center for Democracy and Citizenship. See, for example, Harry C. Boyte and Nancy N. Kari, *Building America: The Democratic Promise of Public Work* (Philadelphia: Temple University Press, 1996).

57. Rob Stein, "Obesity Passing Smoking as Top Avoidable Cause of Death," *Washington Post* (March 10, 2004): A01; citing Ali H. Mokdad, James S. Marks, Donna F. Stroup, and Julie L. Gerberding, "Actual Causes of Death in the United States, 2000," *Journal of the American Medical Association* 291/10 (2004): 1238–1245.

58. Andrew Gumbel, "The Man Who Is Taking FAT TO COURT," Sydney *Morning Herald* (July 14, 2002): Sunday Life, p. 16; cf. Kate Zernike, "Lawyers Shift Focus from Big Tobacco to Big Food," *New York Times* (April 9, 2004): A15.

59. Maureen Dowd, "The Politics of Self-Pity," *New York Times* (March 14, 2004): sec. 4, p. 13.

60. See the work of the Asset-Based Community Development (ABCD) Institute at Northwestern University and articles by ABCD faculty John Kretzmann and John L. McKnight.

61. Molly Andolina, Scott Keeter, Cliff Zukin, and Krista Jenkins, *Civic and Political Health of the Nation: A Generational Portrait*, available from CIRCLE at www.civicyouth.org.

62. Dean Mohs, *Celebrating and Encouraging Community Involvement of Older Minnesotans: A Snapshot of Current Minnesota Baby Boomers and Older Adults*, Minnesota Board of Aging, April 2000, p. 6; quoted in Boyte, "Information Age Populism," May 28, 2002, p. 11.

10

Free/Open-Source Software as a Framework for Establishing Commons in Science

Charles M. Schweik

In his article "High Noon: We Need New Approaches to Global Problem-Solving, Fast," Rischard (2001, 507) emphasizes that "the current setup for solving global problems doesn't work" and that we need new approaches to solving these problems at a much faster pace. In this chapter I argue that the collaborative ideals and principles applied in Free/Libre and Open Source Software (FOSS) projects could be applied to any collaboration built around intellectual property (not just software) and could potentially increase the speed at which innovations and new discoveries are made. In other words, we can conceive of a future where such "knowledge commons" are built not around software, but more generally any kind of work or "content." This chapter attempts to make this argument in the context of enhancing global scientific collaboration. It also tries to outline important issues that will need to be addressed to make this idea a reality.

Let me begin with a little history. The core theme of this book— "knowledge as a commons"—has its underpinnings in the idea and norms of "open science" that emerged beginning in the sixteenth and seventeenth centuries. David (2005) describes open scientific inquiry as a social, rather than an individual, process propelled by the principles of full disclosure of findings and methods, systems of peer review with skeptical mindsets, and processes of verification in the quest to build "reliable knowledge." Of course, the invention of the printing press in the sixteenth century was central to the advancement of these ideals. Mass printing technologies, the formation of professional societies, and the development of "networks of correspondence" provided the opportunity for greatly expanded peer-review processes for validation and support of new knowledge (David 2005; Ziman 1969; Johns 2001; Kronick 1990). This led to great advances in knowledge during periods such as the

Scientific Revolution in the seventeenth century, the post–World War II era of the twentieth century, and up until the current day.

Clearly, the Internet, as a technological advance, is as important a "structural change" to the way scientific advances are communicated and collaborated on as was the printing press. Digital storage has become so cheap that many treat the saving of a file on a hard disk as nearly cost-less. Advances like the web and e-mail software have greatly reduced the costs or skills required to access information on the Internet. Over the last five to ten years, the Internet has moved from a domain utilized primarily by high-skilled computer scientists, engineers, or others in the high-tech industries, to a system utilized by scientists and scholars in all disciplines. We are now in a shake-up period where traditional organizations chartered with the management of scientific information (e.g., libraries, publishers) are developing new organizational models and missions built around computer database and connectivity issues (see, for example, chapters 4 and 11 in this book). This environment, where digital files can be copied and transferred globally in an instant and at very little cost, makes it much easier to treat information or knowledge as a global public good. But as other contributors to this book describe, these advances in technology are directly at odds with other societal trends and developments in intellectual copyright law that are pushing to treat information and other digital products as private goods for monetary gain (see chapters 5 and 7).

Computer scientists and engineers invented Internet technologies and have been actively using them since the 1960s. It is only natural, then, that this class of Internet users would continue to innovate using this tool and develop new approaches for global collaboration to promote open-science principles, broadly defined. While we do not always consider computer programming a scientific endeavor, indeed, the development of software is one form of science, and software, as a product, is a form of intellectual property. The innovation I am referring to is the emergence over the last twenty years of FOSS as a form of "software commons." One popular FOSS website, Sourceforge.net, hosts over 200,000 such projects (Sourceforge.net 2006). While there are or will be many failures in this collaborative domain, there are some major success stories (measured in terms of growth in software use or "market share"), with prominent ones being the Linux operating system, Apache Web Server, Php (an open-source scripting language), MySQL (a FOSS relational database), Firefox (web browser), OpenOffice (office software), and others.

To promote the argument made in the opening paragraph of this chapter—that the collaborative ideals and principles applied in FOSS projects are potentially applicable to any collaboration built around intellectual property—I first provide an overview and summary of the FOSS software "movement" and describe some critical project components. I use the Institutional Analysis and Development Framework described in chapter 3 to help guide the description of these projects. Next, I provide more detail on the argument that the FOSS collaborative principles and approaches can extend more broadly to scientific research in general. At this juncture, I introduce the more recent innovation of "open-content" licensing. Using a short example in the scientific field of land-use change modeling, I then provide a discussion of some critical issues that will need to be addressed in order to transfer the collaborative principles of FOSS software commons to scientific-commons endeavors.

An Overview of Free/Libre and Open-Source Software (FOSS) Commons

The primary innovation in FOSS projects is a combination of a new approach to software licensing coupled with Internet-based collaborative tools. This resulted in a new form of Internet-based collaboration that represents a form of "commons" (see chapter 1; also Dietz, Ostrom, and Stern 2003), but one that differs slightly from the environmental commons that most readers are familiar with (Hardin 1968; Ostrom 1990). In FOSS commons, groups of people act collectively to produce a public good (the software), rather than overappropriate the resource (e.g., Hardin 1968). In other words, the challenge in FOSS commons is how to achieve collective action to create and maintain a commons or public good rather than the issue of protecting an existing commons from destruction (a public bad).

Importantly, FOSS projects produce this public good through a *common-property regime* (Benkler 2002; Boyle 2003)—one form of commons. In environmental-commons literature, the phrase "common property" is defined as a resource (e.g., a forest, a fishery, a body of water, and so on) where members of a defined group possess a set of legal rights, including the ability to exclude nonmembers from using that resource (Ostrom et al. 1999; Hess and Ostrom, chapter 1, this volume). Some readers unfamiliar with FOSS software may be surprised to hear that there are property rights (copyright) and ownership issues involved (McGowan 2001). But as a result of FOSS licensing (described more in the "Rules-in-Use" section below), some individuals involved in the project do indeed have legal rights to the code (the resource), have control over what goes into future versions of the software, and can exclude others from submitting new code to a new release (Schweik 2005).

Let me now turn to a description of major components of FOSS projects as common-property regimes. To do so, I utilize the "Institutional Analysis and Development Framework" (chapter 3, figure 3.1) presented by Ostrom and Hess (referred from now on as the "Framework)". It is important to note that this Framework captures a dynamic system with feedback over time.

Central to Ostrom and Hess's Framework is the focus on individual actors in "action situations" who are making decisions related to their actions in a commons or common-property-regime situation. In FOSS settings, actors tend to be computer programmers (but can also be end users of software) who contribute, either voluntarily or because they are paid to do so, toward the further production of FOSS-licensed software (elaborated on below). The action situation these programmers face is whether, at some point in time, it is worth their while to continue to contribute to the development of this software. The interactions of programmers working collaboratively over the Internet result in some kind of outcome that may change over time (see figure 3.2).

Schweik and Semenov (2003) presented a three-stage trajectory of these commons, going through an initiation stage, followed by a "going-open" stage, and then a more mature stage. This last stage can be categorized as "high growth" (in terms of software use, participation, or both) or "stabilization," where the project continues with generally the same participants (often small groups), or project death or stagnation. High-growth projects can be measured in terms of project participation or software use (Crowston, Annabi, and Howison 2003; Crowston et al. 2004; Stewart 2004). Stabilized but smaller projects are ones that maintain a small group of participants but satisfy the needs of this community. Dead projects are obviously ones where participation ceases to exist (Capiluppi, Lago, and Morisio 2003). Recent studies of FOSS projects have shown that it is rare for projects to reach high growth (measured in terms of programmer participation), and in many cases they involve only a small number of individuals (Ghosh and Prakash 2000; Ghosh, Robles, and Glott 2002; Dempsey et al. 2002; Krishnamurthy 2002; Healy and Schussman 2003; Capiluppi, Lago, and Morisio 2003). But it could be that some do achieve high growth in terms of end users even if the development team is small.

Key, then, to the success of FOSS common-property regimes is the willingness of a programmer to contribute to the collaborative effort (the action in the Framework), and the cumulative efforts of at least small teams of actors to collectively produce and maintain software (an outcome). As the Framework shows, this decision depends on the configuration of three groups of attributes: (1) the design and structure of rules in use, (2) the (human) community participating in FOSS, and (3) the physical or material environment.

Rules-in-Use: "Copyleft," FOSS Licensing, and Project Governance

As I stated earlier, the primary innovation that led to FOSS commons was an innovation in software licensing that occurred in the mid-1980s. At that time Richard Stallman, a programmer at MIT developing a PC-based Unix operating system called "GNU," initiated the Free/Libre software movement. Stallman (1999, 2001) has argued that the digital properties of software (e.g., easy copying and distribution) make it possible to treat it as a public rather than a private good, and as a result, users of software should be provided the *freedom* to use, distribute, and modify the software in any way they might desire. The emphasis here is on free as in freedom rather than free in the monetized sense (http://www.gnu.org/philosophy/free-sw.html). This philosophy led Stallman to consider how he could ensure that these freedoms could be intertwined, in a sense, with the software. His major advance was to devise a way of working within copyright law to provide an alternative to the traditional proprietary, full-copyright approach to software licensing.

Most readers will be quite familiar with the "traditional" method of software licensing. While specifics will vary, in general, proprietary software licensing usually limits the user in the number of installations on computers he or she can undertake, and the software itself is distributed in binary, compiled, or executable form. For example, in the case of

Microsoft's Office suite, the end user or person with programming skills can run Word but cannot "look under the hood" to see the internal logic or computer source code that the Word executable program is built on.

Stallman felt this approach of distributing software in compiled form infringed on end-user freedoms, and he did not want the software he was developing, the GNU operating system, to be hampered by such restrictions. This brings us to the major advance—Stallman's principle of "Copyleft"—which harnesses copyright law to provide users of the software the right to (1) access and read the program logic or source code, (2) copy and redistribute the software, and (3) make modifications to the source code (Stallman 1999). Copyleft is a critical innovation, for it differs from traditional software licensing in how it allocates the entitlements in copyright, rather than being a replacement of copyright law itself.

A Copyleft-type software license may also be "viral" in nature; it stipulates that any new derivation of the software automatically inherits the licensing principles of its "parent" software. Stallman implemented these Copyleft principles by creating the "GNU General Public License" (GPL; http://www.gnu.org/licenses/licenses.html), and to promote these freedom ideals, Stallman created the "Free Software Foundation" or FSF (http://www.gnu.org/).

Over time a social movement around these principles of software freedom emerged, and other programmers joined in. The ideas were embraced not only in Stallman's GNU project but also in other software-development projects, and the Free/Libre software movement emerged. However, there was a concern by some that the freedom principles were hindering the development and use of certain software, such as Linux, in the business world (Perens 1999). Consequently, the concept of open-source licensing emerged, with the intention to tone down the attention to the "freedom" issue, and to make a better connection to industry. In other words, the primary distinction between Free/Libre and open-source licensed software has to do with other restrictions provided in the license. For example, some open-source licenses allow software under their jurisdiction to be used in proprietary software packages—a practice that the Free Software Foundation rejects.

The open-source software movement was led in part by software developers Bruce Perens and Eric Raymond, who created the Open Source Initiative (OSI, http://www.opensource.org) and worked to develop an "Open Source Definition" (OSD)—a set of rules that can be used to determine whether a piece of software can be officially OSI certified. In general, open-source certified licenses follow the same general principles as the Free/Libre GPL: free redistribution, readable source code, derived works permitted, and viral licensing. However, in effect, OSD establishes a set of "moral rights" that open-source software developers must adhere to in order to have their work officially sanctioned by OSI. For example, related to the "derivative-works" component of OSD, there are rules regarding how to keep original authors' source code intact to protect these authors from having new derivatives represent them in a poor fashion. (Author attribution will be an important issue extending the FOSS idea to scientific commons later.)

Stallman's GPL can be considered the "parent" of over fifty Open Software Initiative–approved licenses (Perens 1999; http://http://www .opensource.org/licenses/), which all satisfy the general conditions of open-source software but have variations in the rights provided to software users. These variations demonstrate that software authors have a more complicated decision to make when considering how to license their software. It is not a question of choosing between the two extremes of full copyright ("all rights reserved," the default condition) or no copyright at all ("public domain"). What Copyleft and FOSS licenses reveal is that authors of software have a set of rights that they can retain or give away (for comparisons of various FOSS licenses, see Perens 1999 or http://www.gnu.org/licenses/license-list.html).

The Copyleft licensing innovations are "rules-in-use" (figure 3.2) that contribute to the motivation of computer programmers to take action in FOSS commons. And it is important to note that because these software products are copyrighted—they are not treated as public domain, but rather authors keep some of their intellectual property rights and relinquish others through the licensing. FOSS software are governed, as I have said earlier, by a common property regime. The principles of Copyleft create such a regime.

Another "rules-in-use" component of FOSS commons has to do with the governance of such projects. In environmental-commons settings it is well understood that governance is the central issue in maintaining a commons (Dietz, Ostrom, and Stern 2003). Weber (2004, 189) noted the importance of governance structures in the context of FOSS when he stated: "The open source process is an ongoing experiment. It is testing an imperfect mix of leadership, informal coordination mechanisms, implicit and explicit norms, along with some formal governance

structures that are evolving and doing so at a rate that has been sufficient to hold surprisingly complex systems together."

Scant literature exists that analyzes governance structures of a broad
group of FOSS commons, and consequently this attribute is poorly
understood (Schweik and Semenov 2003). But such a governance structure might include: (1) prioritizing features to include in new versions of
the software; (2) defining rules and procedures on how production will
proceed and how new submissions are evaluated and chosen for inclusion in software releases; (3) assigning or managing tasks; and (4) assisting in the resolution of disputes between team members. For example,
Sharma, Sugumaran, and Rajgopalan (2002, 13) note that open-source
communities create and abide by sets of rules that are modified over time
as the project matures. And studies such as Divitini et al. 2003 and
Shaikh and Cornford 2003 provide examples of conflict in open-source
software settings.

Community Attributes of FOSS Commons
In chapter 3, Ostrom and Hess characterize the community in scholarly
commons as consisting of information users, information providers, and
information decision makers or policymakers. In FOSS settings, the community is composed of users of software and software providers (programmers). Recent studies of FOSS have emphasized the volunteer
nature of these types of commons, usually focusing on high-profile,
success-story examples like the Linux operating system project, Apache
Web Server, and a few others (e.g., Raymond 1998a, 1998b; Feller and
Fitzgerald 2002). Indeed, the volunteer nature still is a factor in many
FOSS projects and this phenomenon has puzzled economists and sociologists, who have asked why these programmers freely contribute their
time and effort (Lerner and Tirole 2002; Ghosh 2003; Lee, Moisa, and
Weiss 2003).

Analyses show that there are different types of motivations, which can
be organized under three categories: "technological," "sociopolitical,"
and "economic" (Feller and Fitzgerald 2002; Lakhani et al. 2002;
Schweik and Semenov 2003). One of the main technological reasons for
someone to participate in a volunteer capacity is that there is a need for
software that is unavailable or too expensive, and the individual realizes
he or she cannot develop it working alone. A main sociopolitical motivation in FOSS settings is because the programmer believes in a social
or political movement (e.g., the "software should be free" philosophy of

the Free Software Foundation, or the motivation to take on a perceived software monopoly), or has a desire to participate in a broader community with a shared interest. "Passion" is another social attribute that is an important driver of volunteer participation. Projects need to be interesting to attract other developers and survive into the future (Raymond 1998a; Hissam et al. 2001; Van Wendel de Joode, de Bruijn, and van Eeten 2003). Hissam et al. 2001 reports that factors contributing to the failure of one FOSS project included an inability to gain a critical mass of eager volunteer programmers, and a lack of financing to pay for participants (discussed more below).

Economic explanations of volunteer participation in FOSS projects include the goal of (1) building human capital through learning by reading existing software code and through the process of peer review for code submissions (Hann et al. 2002; Voightmann and Coleman 2003); and (2) signaling one's abilities as an expert, which might then lead to future job opportunities. Giving credit to authors of code is a key norm in FOSS projects (Lerner and Tirole 2002). In this regard, volunteer participation in FOSS is seen by participants as an investment in their future (Lerner and Tirole 2002; Johnson 2002; Lee, Moisa, and Weiss 2003) and as a way of establishing a reputation (Sharma, Sugumaran, and Rajgopalan 2002).

But while the early hype over FOSS was about the promise of large groups of participants (e.g., Raymond 1998a), in reality, most FOSS projects have only a handful of participants (Ghosh, Robles, and Glott 2002; Dempsey et al. 2002; Krishnamurthy 2002; Healy and Schussman 2003). Even in some very large projects (measured by numbers of people associated with them), only a small percentage of participants appear to be performing the work (Warsta and Abrahamsson 2003). However, in recent years, firms in the software industry have invested human and organizational resources to support FOSS software believed to reflect strategic interests (e.g., IBM, Hewlett-Packard, and so on; see Lerner and Tirole 2002; Goldman and Gabriel 2005). One study of FOSS projects reports that nearly one-third of the developers surveyed were directly paid by employers to participate (Ghosh, Robles, and Glott 2002). Wichmann's (2002) study of twenty-five firms active in one FOSS project, the Linux operating system, found that self-interest was the key motivating factor for firms' participation—for example, product standardization, cost savings, strategies to weaken competition, and efforts to make their own products compatible with FOSS products. And some government agencies are starting to place more emphasis on the use and possible support for FOSS as well (Hahn 2002).

The participation of firms and governments—or more specifically the financial support these organizations bring—may be a key critical "community-attribute" success factor for FOSS projects, at least for high-profile, "enterprise" FOSS projects like Linux, OpenOffice (a rival office suite to Microsoft Office), and others. There are skeptics of the viability of an all-volunteer FOSS effort, and indeed, how critical it is to have a financial base to support a FOSS effort is a question requiring further research. But to summarize, FOSS project communities either consist of a group of passionate (volunteer) developers and users, or programmers who are paid by some organization to participate, or some combination of both.

Physical Attributes of FOSS Commons
Even though FOSS projects operate in a digital environment, there are characteristics of the project that could be considered physical attributes (see figure 3.2). At least three important "physical" subcategories exist in FOSS settings: (1) the utility of the software, (2) the design or structure of the software, and (3) the collaborative infrastructure that helps to coordinate and manage production.

Studies in other commons settings have found that in order for people to engage in commons-related activities, they must perceive a benefit for doing so (Ostrom et al. 1999). Moreover, for users to see major benefits, the resource must not be perceived as of little value (Ostrom et al. 1999, 281). In FOSS commons, the "resource" is the software, and to extend these ideas to this type of commons is straightforward: it is doubtful that programmers or firms will devote valuable time and resources to the development of software that is deemed to have little utility.

In addition to the utility attribute of the software, studies of FOSS development practices have emphasized clean software logic and modularity as important factors contributing to the success of the projects (O'Reilly 1999; Manley 2000; Hissam et al. 2001). Modularity is an important physical attribute promoting the idea of parallel work: the efficiency of multiple people working on different (or possibly the same) components of the code at the same time. The early days of the development of the Mozilla web browser provide an example of a project with problems, where there was a "tangled mess" of code that caused difficulties in the collaborative efforts (Hissam et al. 2001). Alternatively, the original authors of the highly successful Linux operating system and the Perl open-source programming language have stated that part of the success of their creations is that they made early design decisions, including modularity, which made it easier for others to contribute (O'Reilly 1999).

In addition to physical characteristics of the software, FOSS collaborations, regardless of participant-group size, require some form of Internet-based infrastructure to help coordinate the cooperative effort (Shaikh and Cornford 2003). In FOSS projects, group collaboration is supported through web-based communication and version-control systems. For example, the FOSS project-management website www.sourceforge.net provides group communication functions and software version-control systems based on the "Concurrent Versioning System" or CVS (Fogel 1999). CVS and other version-control systems

1. Archive versions of software

2. Allow for the retrieval of modules

3. Allow for new submissions and protect against the problem of over-writing and errantly eliminating the work of others

4. Document change history and participant contributions over time (author tracking)

5. Provide analysis functions to identify differences between module versions

6. Provide functions to e-mail subscribers when project components are moved, updated, or deleted

This kind of infrastructure works in conjunction with established rules-in-use to provide a system or process for new work to be conducted, a system for submissions of new or revised modules to be received, and a system for peer review of these modules for possible inclusion in subsequent releases of the software. Moreover, CVS and other version-control systems actually dictate and enforce some rules-in-use by controlling who can check in and check out code, who has over-write authority, and so on. In other words, the CVS system actually articulates some of the project's operational rules and enforces them.

In short, FOSS projects evolve over time as a result of their configurations of rules-in-use (e.g., licensing, governance structures), community attributes (e.g., motivated volunteers and users or paid programmers), and physical attributes related to the structure of the software to ease collaboration and effective tools for team coordination and content management. We believe these components provide the foundation for a new paradigm in collaborative scientific research: a FOSS-like science commons.

Extending the FOSS Collaborative Paradigm to Create a Science Commons

Software is one form of digital intellectual property, not all that different from others, such as a research paper or a dataset. Indeed, the argument has been made that the FOSS development approach is similar to the traditional method of submitting and publishing papers in refereed journals (Bezroukov 1999). But there are some important differences, which we believe provide additional support that this collaborative paradigm should be considered an option to create a science commons (Schweik and Semenov 2003). First, in FOSS collaboration settings, the entire research product (software) is shared with the community, including the "research process" (software development), rather than just the final results (e.g., the software release). For example, CVS and other systems provide the ability to roll back to an earlier update via the system archives. A history of the development of the software is kept, and one can recover older versions of the code and see how code evolved over time. This is different from the traditional publishing model in most scientific journals, where length (e.g., word-count) restrictions limit what can be provided to the community. In most traditional publishing contexts, what is published is all that is available. There is no real way to review history to, for example, see the data processing conducted that led to a passage or a statistical table in the published text. Second, the open-access nature of FOSS projects provides an opportunity for others outside of organizational lines to participate; this differs from most traditional scientific research projects that are usually tightly controlled and usually limit participation to people associated with one or a handful of organizations. Third, the rights provided in many FOSS licenses to freely duplicate and distribute copies of the intellectual property (software) are very different from the policies of many scientific journals, which hold full copyright and require the reader to obtain permission before duplication can be made—an important point that connects to other chapters in this book (e.g., see Suber, chapter 7). Fourth, FOSS collaboration over the Internet potentially increases the speed at which innovations can be published, compared to that in standard paper-based publishing. Systems of peer review in FOSS contexts might take similar amounts of time compared to that of traditional peer-review processes in scientific journals, but the act of publishing the results (e.g., improvements to a program module) can be dramatically increased—in fact, they can be nearly immediate—after the peer-review process is completed.

Transferring the FOSS collaborative paradigm to the scientific research domain shifts the focal "actor" in Ostrom and Hess's Framework (figure 3.3) from the computer programmer to a professional scientist, or academic. Central to this shift will be considerations of the rules-in-use and the physical and community attributes established, for it is these sets of attributes together that create the incentive structure or "action situation" that will either encourage academics and professional scientists to participate in such collaborations, or discourage them from doing so.

A Science-Commons Example: Land-Use Change Modeling

To give the reader a better understanding of what I am proposing, let me briefly provide an example of an area in need of better mechanisms for sharing scientific advances: land-use change modeling. This is a field of scientific research that focuses on understanding how the landscape in a particular area of the world has changed over time or is expected to change in the future. It is an area that can involve scientists from a variety of disciplines, including geography, ecology, regional planning, economics, political science, and others. Over the last decade, a variety of modeling approaches have been developed to understand and predict change, including statistical and econometric-based models, geographic information system–based models, and models that integrate a variety of techniques (Briassoulis 2000). But during a recent effort inventorying existing land-use change models for the USDA Forest Service that I was involved in, (e.g., Grove et al. 2002; Agarwal et al. 2002), it became apparent that most of the advances in a particular modeling approach were being produced by the same developers themselves or people closely tied to the original developers. One explanation for this is because in some instances the models are not readily available for others to use. Another reason is because these models require substantial technical and interdisciplinary knowledge to work with them, and the transaction costs for a scientist to learn a model and possibly build on it is not trivial. Finally, the traditional method of publishing modeling results in standard academic journals with length limitations poses additional barriers to knowledge sharing across organizational lines.

But in some respects, land-use change modeling projects can be quite similar to FOSS projects in that they involve computer programming or some technical procedures that are similar to programming (and this is true in a number of scientific fields). For example, the UrbanSim model for simulating urban land-use, transportation, and environmental impacts (Waddell 2002) consists of a number of modules written in the computer programming language Java (Freeman-Benson and Borning 2003). These modules involve econometric analysis (e.g., logistic regression) and spatial analysis and dynamic modeling using geographic information system–based tools. UrbanSim, and other land-use change models, demonstrate the need for participants with technical skills to undertake future enhancements to such models.

This short discussion of land-use change modeling is included in this chapter to demonstrate that many areas of science are not all that different from programming situations. They require people with technical expertise writing about a subject in some kind of language, whether it be a formal computer programming language, statistical functions, a set of analytic procedures, or even theoretical ideas documented using natural languages such as English.

But what is different between scientific projects and FOSS projects is that in the FOSS setting the types of people typically involved can be categorized as either programmers or end users of software. But in the case of land-use change modeling research (or other scientific endeavors), there are a variety of different participant types. These include modelers (e.g., the technical people described above); theoreticians, who write about the important drivers of such models (e.g., Geist and Lambin 2002); data providers, who create datasets needed for input to these models; and policy analysts and decision makers, who ultimately want to utilize these models.

The central question turns to how the FOSS paradigm would operate in scientific collaboration situations like the land-use change modeling case above, and what set of incentives would need to be created to encourage scientists, academics, policy analysts, and other decision makers to participate in such an intellectual commons. For instance, in the land-use modeling context above, the argument could be made that given the investment necessary for a scientist to learn or develop a model, allowing open access to their contributions and knowledge might reduce

the value of these contributions. Given this, four areas need critical attention: (1) how to license digital "content" that is not computer software,
(2) how to work within the existing norms and incentive structures faced
by most scientists and academics in their workplace today, (3) how to
govern such a collaboration, and (4) how to finance such an endeavor.
The rest of this chapter is devoted to these issues.

The Licensing of Scientific Digital Content

Utilizing the FOSS collaborative paradigm to create a scientific commons
requires broadening Stallman's Copyleft idea so that it applies not only
to software but to any form of intellectual property. And although the
Copyleft principle has been around for two decades, this licensing innovation has only recently been applicable to other intellectual property or
"content" (Bollier 1999; Schweik and Grove 2000; Stallman 2001;
Weber 2004).

Naturally, the first extension of Copyleft beyond software was also
advanced by Stallman, who felt his "freedom philosophy" not only
needed to apply to software, but also to accompanying user guides, technical documentation, and so on. In this context, he developed the GNU
Free Documentation License or GFDL (http://www.fsf.org/copyleft/
fdl.html), which governs the use, modification, and distribution of
GNU software documentation. The GFDL specifies the sections of
the document that must remain unmodified from version to version
(such as the original author's copyright notice) and the terms of distribution, and requires a list of previous authors to be maintained
(Stallman 1999).

But around the year 2001, a new set of licenses following similar principles was developed by people associated with the nonprofit organization CreativeCommons.org that can be applied to works of music, art,
video, text, and educational lesson plans (CreativeCommons.org 2004a).
These licenses allow the author of a work to keep the copyright but still
allow others to copy and distribute their work as long as credit is given
to the original author (CreativeCommons.org 2004b). Creative
Commons provides a series of questions to allow authors to choose
between particular rights they wish to retain versus rights they would
like to relinquish. Key questions include: (1) Can readers freely copy and
distribute this intellectual property? (2) Are users permitted to create
derivative works based on the digital content? If so, should new derivatives fall under the same license as the parent work (a "viral" licensing

scheme; Pavlicek 2000), or can they be distributed under a different licensing scheme? And (3) is author attribution required?

An important innovation made by the people at Creative Commons is that they offer a suite of license types, or, in other words, they provide a kind of modularity to their licenses. This means that authors of various works can craft, through the answers to the above questions, a license that holds "some rights reserved" and relinquishes others (Stix 2003). And it is important to note that people connected with Creative Commons have recently initiated a "Science Commons" project focusing on three areas: (1) promoting open access to scientific publications, (2) developing standard licensing models to facilitate wider access to scientific information, and (3) exploring ways to increase the sharing of scientific data (Science.CreativeCommons.org 2005). While it is too early to make definitive statements about the connection between the Science Commons effort and the ideas proposed here, clearly their efforts in all three areas will inform this discussion.

In this chapter, scientific work communicated in a form other than software (e.g., a paper, for example) and assigned a GNU Free Documentation or Creative Commons license, will be referred to generally as "open content." These licenses follow the lead of open-source software licensing but, when applicable to other forms of content, provide a critical step toward scientific collaboration following FOSS principles. This means that in the context of scientific commons or collaborations, licensing principles from FOSS can now be applied to all types of content or work produced by participants. For example, in the land-use change modeling example discussed earlier, each type of project output (e.g., model modules, model usage documentation, empirical papers, theoretical papers, and datasets) will need to be assigned some kind of FOSS or Creative Commons license. In other words, whatever form or technology the land-use model utilizes (e.g., a computer program, a statistical script, and so on), it should be placed under some license that allows the free copying of the model, requires the model "source" to be readable, and permits the development of new derivative components of the model or other products related to the model. In some instances, the model developers might decide to make all related products (e.g., the model modules, their documentation, data, and even theoretical papers) fall under these conditions. However, there will be situations where more restrictive licensing is warranted. For instance, empirical papers describing a particular application of a model would probably be licensed with a "no derivative work" component, because these types of papers report findings from a particular study at a particular time.

Open-content licensing of theoretical papers presents a particularly interesting and potentially difficult problem. Consider the hypothetical situation where someone writes a theoretical paper on the drivers of land-use change for some city or region of the western United States. Suppose another scientist decides to build on this (digital) paper to create a new derivative work on the drivers of land-use change in a city or region in the eastern United States. Under a Creative Commons licensing situation where derivative works are permitted, the result would be two separate theoretical papers, the east coast version and the original west coast version. This differs from the traditional approach to publishing research, because the second version of the paper may have substantial sections of text taken verbatim from the first paper, with new text added. (This is similar, of course, to what might occur in a software-documentation update situation under the GNU Free Documentation License described earlier.) This situation treads dangerously close to the issue of plagiarism. And if the licensing for the research paper permits new derivative works, the situation exists where someone could download a paper, make trivial revisions, and then add their name as an additional author. While this latter case might be protected by the license (e.g., copyright infringement due to inadequate attribution of the original author), the overall idea of tracking various work contributions in a science-commons situation could be relatively complicated.

While I cannot profess to have all the answers to the question of the appropriate licensing to use for various contexts in a science-commons environment, I can propose some general thoughts to address the plagiarism concern. A conservative approach might be to utilize no-derivative-work licensing for academic or scientific papers in general, but still promote other licensing options such as the free copying and distribution of these papers, which served over the Internet will promote open access worldwide and will likely lead to a more rapid evolution of the field. Other project outputs, such as distance-learning materials, might be licensed with "derivative works OK" to promote more rapid improvements to such materials. Finally, the development of technical solutions for the tracking of author contributions is critical here (I return to this issue more fully in the next section).

Working within the Norms of the Academy: A "Next-Generation" E-Journal

The idea of placing scientific work on the Internet and making it open access and available on the web is a central issue in this book. The key question at this juncture is whether, if some foundational material in some scientific domain is made available under an open-content license that permits new derivative work and mandates that new derivatives are given back, scientists or academics would be motivated to contribute. What incentives would be required, under the existing norms and institutions of academia and science, to make this happen?

Earlier I discussed the motivations of FOSS programmers, highlighting the fact that there were philosophical motivations in some camps (e.g., the Stallman "freedom" principles). There are also legitimate economic incentives, including a desire to signal one's skills and build human capital through the reading of other people's source code and by contributing new source code and going through a peer-review process. I also noted that more recently firms and government agencies have been paying people to participate in FOSS projects deemed important to their mission.

Schweik and Semenov (2003) compared the incentives driving what (1) FOSS programmers and (2) academics and scientists do and found them to be quite similar. First, as exemplified by some of the papers in this book referring to the open-access movement (e.g., chapters 3, 4, 5, and 7), many in science and academia are advancing a social movement not unlike that of Stallman. People participating in these camps feel that scientific knowledge is a public good and that institutions should be designed and developed that encourage the continued construction and maintenance of that public good. Second, long before FOSS emerged, academics and scientists had been honing their skills through the reading of published and other material and through the peer-review process of scholarly publishing. Certainly many in science and academia (graduate students, junior or even senior faculty) would be willing to sharpen their skills through the distance-learning components of reading "source" (e.g., models, papers, and so forth) and through peer review with feedback. Third, like FOSS programmers, academics and scientists have the motivation to signal their abilities to others interested in a scientific domain. This is particularly important in the case of junior scientists who are searching for a job or trying to gain prestige prior to tenure. For example, in the context of land-use modeling, one modeler said in a workshop we had on these open-source and open-content collaborative ideas (Schweik, Evans, and Grove 2003): "Had I known about it, I would have gladly licensed my model as open source in graduate school. That way others might have used it and it would have gotten my name more widely known."

If the idea of an open-content-based scientific commons can gain sufficient traction, scientists (particularly junior scientists) will probably be motivated to participate for the signaling and learning reasons described above. But in order to signal one's abilities by posting intellectual property, one's name needs to be associated, over time, with that submission. Consequently, a key desideratum in open-content scientific commons will be a mechanism for author attribution, and for tracking and archiving submissions, over time. The same issue arises in FOSS settings, where it has been, to some degree, addressed. The GPL, for example, mandates that authors of a new program place at the start of the source code a short copyright notification designating them as the original author of the work and providing additional information specifying where the full notice can be found. The GPL also requires that (1) the copyright statement stay with all future derivative works based on that original code and (2) authors of new derivative works update the software comments with a prominent notice that changes were made, giving their name and the date of the change (Free Software Foundation 2004).

Extending this same logic to the open-content-based scientific-commons idea, scientists will be more likely to contribute new research content if they are able to maintain the copyright over their original work in the same way a programmer does using the GPL. This means that mechanisms will need to be developed that attach similar copyright information (perhaps a Creative Commons license) to any research product (e.g., a paper, a dataset, an analytic module of some sort). This is easily accomplished for content that takes the form of text documents and could be done by specifying the copyright information or update histories in metadata documentation for other components like datasets. In short, the infrastructure built to support an open-content collaboration in science (discussed further below) will need to include a good historical record of how someone contributed over time to a new model module, to a new derivative paper on land-use change theory, to empirical findings, or to other project content. And it would be beneficial if in the design of an open-content collaborative infrastructure there were some design for how to measure contributions based on the author-attribution information stored in the system (e.g., citation counts). For example, in the context of computer-based modeling, measures of the importance of a contribution might be the number of subsequent derivative modules or amount of new code that utilized that module, or how often comments in model software code refer to a particular paper.

But perhaps the most significant detriment to what I am proposing in science or academia is the fear that if a scientist makes his or her analytic products (e.g., models) or even data available in an open-source or content-licensed way, he or she might be "scooped" by someone else who utilizes this material in a paper published in a peer-reviewed journal or book. This is a critical issue from the standpoint of pretenured academics. Consequently, central to making this idea work in the context of the current scientific and academic culture is connecting open-source and open-content contributions to the *refereed publication process*. In other words, we need to move toward what I call a "next-generation e-journal."

This connection to peer-reviewed publishing is important from the perspective of the participants and most of their employers and relates to the point in FOSS contexts where organizations are paying employees to contribute. For many scientists, regardless of whether they are employed by government agencies, private firms, or universities, having their work published in high-quality, refereed journals is an important measure of their success and is used by their employer as a metric for job promotion. Consequently, for any viable open-content scientific commons to succeed, at least in the short term, it must be compatible with the current evaluation systems in place in universities and scientific research organizations. Again, this points to the importance of conceptualizing the communication component of the open-content scientific commons as a scientific e-journal that incorporates peer review in the submission process.

I refer to this idea as a "next-generation e-journal" because there would be the need to publish traditional peer-reviewed "final" content (e.g., papers on theory or results of empirical studies), but also other work including new or revised versions of complete models or subcomponent modules and new distance-learning material (such as to assist people in learning or applying a land-use change model, for example). In some open-content science commons, even datasets might be "published" after some level of peer review (such as a dataset on economic projections for a country that might be utilized in another application of a land-use change model). In short, all components of model development or application could be published in this e-journal, broadly defined. This journal would need to include many if not all of the "content-management" functions described in the section on "Physical Attributes of FOSS Commons" above. This is vastly different from the maximum thirty or so pages that most journals (even most e-journals) currently accept.

Admittedly, this idea is radical and is at loggerheads with current scientific or academic norms and practices. It requires a change in mindset related to what we consider publishable. And there are other hurdles to overcome with this idea, such as establishing a system of peer review where not only papers but also other scientific products are reviewed. Scientists certainly are busy enough reviewing traditional papers, so there might be resistance to establishing a peer-review system for other scientific products. But computer programs (e.g., model modules) would get reviewed through their use. And what specifically gets peer-reviewed or not could be opened up to an editorial board to decide.

Even with these challenges, both computer scientists and librarians have recognized that this change in the way science is shared is needed; there is subtle evidence toward a shift from publication as product to publication as process (see, for example, Lougee's chapter 11 in this volume). And increasingly, there are open-source software tools available to use as the scaffolding on which to build the e-journal infrastructure required for such an effort.[1]

Financing an Open-Content Science Commons

The "rules-in-use" component of the Hess and Ostrom Framework (figure 3.2) involves not only the choice of open-content licensing described above but also other rules that govern day-to-day activities of participants, as well as how these rules are modified over time and who is eligible to change them (Ostrom, Gardner, and Walker 1994). These elements could be generally referred to as "commons governance structures."

Some studies of FOSS projects have hinted at the existence of such structures (Bezroukov 1999; Weber 2004), although currently little is known about how these structures are designed (Schweik and Semenov 2003). The majority of FOSS projects studied by Ghosh, Robles, and Glott (2002) are led by a single "lead developer" who maintains a centralized decision-making structure. Studies of perhaps one of the largest (in terms of participation) open-source projects, the Linux operating system, report that the lead developer acted as a "benevolent dictator" who would work with a team of "trusted lieutenants" with expertise in a particular domain (Shaikh and Cornford 2003; Moody 2001; Sharma, Sugumaran, and Rajgopalan 2002; Goldman and Gabriel 2005). In some FOSS projects, would-be developers work their way up the decision-making hierarchy by first working at boundaries of the project (e.g., offering bug reports) and then, over time, contributing more to actual source-code maintenance or development. Other FOSS projects have a different approach to management. For example, Jorgensen's (2001) study of the FreeBSD project found that an elected nine-member team of developers made the operational decisions about the project. And some other early studies suggest that decisions related to FOSS project direction are reached by consensus (Fielding 1999; Markus et al. 2000; Mockus, Fielding, and Herbsleb 2000). Operationally, established systems of rules, shared norms of behavior, voting systems, and monitoring and sanctioning systems appear to be important in some FOSS projects (Sharma, Sugumaran, and Rajgopalan 2002). Many projects have established norms of behavior that members must follow (Bonaccorsi and Rossi 2003).

Lessons from other settings (e.g., environmental commons) have shown that the design of governance structures is a critical factor in determining whether the commons can be "long-enduring" (Ostrom 1990; Dietz, Ostrom, and Stern 2003). This may be less of an issue in commons settings with very low participation rates (e.g., many FOSS projects with a handful of participants), but could be a critical issue in FOSS projects with numerous participants. Consequently, an important issue in extending the FOSS paradigm to scientific research collaboration will be considerations about the design and composition of the system of rules that govern operational practices as well as how those rules are changed over time, who has the authority to make such changes, and how conflicts are resolved. It is conceivable that an open-content science commons communicating through a "next-generation e-journal" infrastructure may ultimately need a governance body that combines components of how professional journals today are run and organized (e.g., an editor and editorial board) and how FOSS projects are organized.

Financing an Open-Content Science Commons

I have found that some are very skeptical of the viability of an all-volunteer model of FOSS development—and it is a reasonable concern.

I mentioned earlier that a number of studies reveal that the majority of FOSS projects involve a small number of participants (Ghosh and Prakash 2000; Ghosh, Robles, and Glott 2002; Dempsey et al. 2002; Krishnamurthy 2002; Healy and Schussman 2003; Capiluppi, Lago, and Morisio 2003). One major concern with an all-volunteer model is what happens if a key individual decides to stop contributing to the commons? This issue led one FOSS practitioner to comment at a meeting in UNESCO Paris on science and public-domain issues (Esanu and Uhlir 2004) that the *only* way FOSS projects will succeed (in terms of longevity and high growth) is if they are sponsored by a national government agency. While clearly national government support is not the only way a FOSS project might succeed, the important point is that it is highly likely that (at least for major projects) some level of financial support will be required.[2] This probably explains why, at lease in part, some of the larger FOSS software projects have incorporated and established foundations (O'Mahony 2005).

And in fact, in the open-source software domain, projects can be found that fall under a variety of different financial-support schemes—not just government support—including (1) the government-subsidy model (Hahn 2002), (2) philanthropic funding, (3) corporate consortia (Hildebrand 2004), (4) corporate investment (Webb 2004), (5) venture capital/investment banking, (6) donations from participants or users, or (7) a hybrid/mix of these. One could hypothesize that the long-term success of some of the high-profile FOSS success stories is a result of the commitment by firms like IBM or Sun Microsystems, which pay people in their organization to contribute to these endeavors (Ghosh, Robles, and Glott 2002).

The same question about financing will be raised in the context of moving to an open-content scientific commons. To what degree is financial support required and what are the different funding approaches that could be considered? As with FOSS projects, there are at least two dimensions of this: (1) the financial support for participants' time and energy in contributing to the commons and (2) the financial support for the administrative or collaborative infrastructure that makes the commons available and helps to coordinate activities.

Considering the issue of paid participants, in the domain of science and academia, this may already be addressed to a large degree in the way academia operates. Most universities expect or demand that their faculty undertake research that contributes to a larger research program found in the global society, and faculty are often evaluated in their annual faculty reviews in the context of how much service they have provided to a broader professional community. If a faculty member wanted to participate in a virtual open-content scientific commons as part of his or her research program, most universities would be supportive of this so long as the individual continued to meet traditional measures of scholarship and productivity (such as publications in refereed outlets). This point underscores the importance of designing the open-content science commons as a refereed e-journal, for it is likely that this approach would greatly enhance the number of researchers willing to contribute. The problem that may loom on the horizon related to this strategy is the trend on the part of universities to treat ideas generated by their faculty as private or toll goods that can be capitalized on in a market.

This leads to the second dimension of financing: the question of how the communicative infrastructure (e.g., a next-generation e-journal) and the administrative apparatus needed to support it might be financed. This issue is discussed in some depth in several chapters in this book (see, for example, chapter 7). Traditionally, scientific journals tend to be published by academic or professional societies or by commercial publishers. While I do not have reliable estimates of the costs of administering and supporting a traditional paper journal or current e-journal publications, I found one estimate of an e-journal costing approximately $20,000 for the editorial work involved in publishing a 1,000-page journal per year (Open Journal Systems 2004). This estimate does not include the additional cost of maintaining the computer server that their (free) software could be installed on. This estimate is almost certainly on the low end, for there is a sizable cost involved for administration (e.g., editorial support, management of the peer-review process), final printing costs (if there is a paper version as well), backup, archiving, and so on, perhaps even reaching the hundreds of thousands of dollars. Moving from a paper-based journal to a web-based e-journal may save some money (e.g., for printing), but the peer-review structure in an open content–based science commons where the submissions to be evaluated are larger in scope (e.g., models and model documentation, theoretical and empirical papers, data, and distance-learning documents) will certainly increase the time investment required by reviewers and various component editors and raise the costs of these activities.

It is an open question whether traditional journal publishers following a "user-pays" subscription model and taking an "all rights reserved" philosophy would be willing to move toward an open-content licensing strategy. In traditional subscriber-pays publishing, the content—a set of manuscripts—is treated as a toll good, and this is how these firms gain revenue. The idea of open access and free distribution via open-content licensing directly contradicts this model. But this issue is quite similar to the question of why a firm like IBM might decide to participate in open-source projects. In a FOSS software domain, what is it that brings in revenue and makes this a viable business model? While I have no references to support this, after discussing this with some in the industry, my sense is some of the viability is moving away from software as a product and moving toward more of a software support or service role. This raises the question: Could an alternative e-journal publishing model be created that would support an open-content-based scientific commons and that would also provide some services to bring in revenue? For example, some proprietary software companies are offering online distance-learning programs (e.g., in the context of geographic information systems, see http://campus.esri.com) to earn additional revenue and promote the use of their software. Could similar distance-learning services be established to provide registration-based courses on the particular science-commons subject matter, with some of the revenues being used to help support the administration of the project?

As other contributors to this book have noted, other financing models are being explored to promote more open access to scientific information, such as the "author-pays-to-publish" model with open access to the journal, and the model where academic institutions or research libraries take on the publishing of disciplinary e-journals as part of their mission (Shortliffe 2004; chapters 4 and 7, this volume). Another possibility is for professional scientific societies to take this on through their subscriptions and support an open-content science commons as part of their mission. These examples suggest alternative financing models that might make the administration of an open-content science commons viable.

I cannot claim to have a solution to the financing issue, other than to say that experiments in alternative e-journal funding to promote open access are emerging. A sizable number of FOSS packages are available (e.g., wiki's, Drupal, DSpace, and other content-management systems; see opensourcecms.com) with some of the needed functionality to support open-content collaboration, which may reduce some of the software-development costs. Professional societies, foundations, or government agencies (e.g., national science agencies) could potentially invest in the development of the next-generation e-journal infrastructure needed for these efforts and provide this infrastructure under a FOSS license for other groups to use. Other financing will surely be necessary to support such e-journals, possibly using the "author-pays" model or, in the case of specialized research areas, perhaps through support as part of a research-library mission at a particular institution. Whatever approach is taken, clearly, financing is an issue that will need to be carefully considered in order for the ideas outlined here to work.

Conclusion

A common thread in the chapters in this book is that the Internet provides a mechanism to treat scholarly or scientific information as a public good or commons, rather than as a private or toll good. The argument made in this chapter is that for nearly twenty years, the groups that developed the Internet—computer scientists and engineers—have also developed new approaches to collaboration using the Internet as the communication platform and through innovative licensing built around the principle of Copyleft. The result is the creation of FOSS projects, common-property regimes, or commons—whatever name you want to give them. The FOSS collaborative paradigm has produced a large number of successful collaborative experiments. Enough interest has been generated—including industry and government interest—to attest to its potential as a new collaborative venture. At the same time, one only needs to be aware that thousands of FOSS projects have failed to realize that this collaborative paradigm is no panacea. Further research on FOSS commons is required to identify the critical success factors in collaboration that lead to the success stories (Schweik and Semenov 2003; Weber 2004).

Awareness is growing that the FOSS collaborative paradigm is not limited to software (e.g., Bollier 1999; Schweik and Grove 2000; Stallman 2001; CreativeCommons.org 2004a; Schweik and Semenov 2003; Weber 2004) and that it can potentially be applied in any domain that requires a team of thinkers to tackle a problem. The licensing advances made by the people at CreativeCommons.org are important components of this idea. However, extending the FOSS paradigm to scientific commons requires not only attention to these licensing innovations, but also the development of Internet-based infrastructure to support it (what I term the "next-generation e-journal") and, most importantly, ways of fitting this idea within the norms and incentives that currently exist in the academy. Successful FOSS projects are ones that have licensing and collaborative infrastructure in place and that somehow establish a situation where participants and/or organizations are willing to devote time, energy, and resources to building these commons. The same will be true in open-content science commons.

Like their software counterparts, open-content collaborations will require experimentation, and some will undoubtedly fail. But the possibility is there that this innovation in collective action, applied to globally important scientific problems and questions, has the potential to lead to more rapid progress than is possible within the existing structure of scientific research and publication.

Notes

I am grateful to Robert English and an anonymous reviewer for helpful comments on an earlier version of this chapter. Support for work related to the chapter was provided by the USDA Forest Service's Burlington Laboratory (4454) and Southern and Northern Global Change Programs; the Cooperative State Research Extension, Education Service, U.S. Department of Agriculture, Massachusetts Agriculture Experiment Station, under project MAS00847; the Center for Policy and Administration and the Department of Natural Resources Conservation at the University of Massachusetts, Amherst, and the Center for the Study of Institutions, Population and Environmental Change at Indiana University (NSFSBR 9521918). Additional support was provided by the U.S. National Science Foundation (NSFIIS 0447623). Finally, this chapter benefited from discussions with participants at a workshop on open-source development of land-use/landcover change models (see http:www.lulc.org/bcworkshop_2003/os_lulc_workshop_report_2003.pdf) sponsored by the NSF Biocomplexity Program (grant NSFSBR 0083744). However, the recommendations and opinions expressed are mine and do not necessarily reflect the views of the funding agencies.

1. For example, as noted on the Public Knowledge Project's website (http://pkp.ubc.ca/ojs/other_OJS.html), various kinds of open-source e-journal management software are available, such as the "Open Journal Systems" (http://www.pkp.ubc.ca/ojs/), the "Article System" (http://artsys.sourceforge.net/), and efirst XML (http://www.openly.com/efirst/). There are also other open-source tools, such as Zope for developing general content-management systems and Internet portals (http://zope.org).

2. However, it remains an open question as to when such funding is absolutely needed for a project to survive versus when a FOSS project can exist solely through a volunteer base. One hypothesis might be that for FOSS projects that are "large" in scale—that is, projects like office-support software, geographic information systems, and the like—some financial support is critical. But in

smaller, more specialized software used in smaller circles (some bioinformatics analysis software, for example), it could be that an all-volunteer-based effort is sufficient.

References

Agarwal, C., G. M. Green, J. M. Grove, T. Evans, and C. M. Schweik. 2002. *A Review and Assessment of Land-Use Change Models: Dynamics of Space, Time, and Human Choice*. CIPEC Collaborative Report No. 1. USFS Publication NE-GTR-297 Joint Publication by the Center for the Study of Institutions, Population and Environmental Change at Indiana University–Bloomington and the USDA Forest Service. Burlington, VT: USDA Forest Service Northeastern Forest Research Station. http://www.fs.fed.us/ne/newtown_square/publications/technical_reports/pdfs/2002/gtrne297.pdf.

Benkler, Y. 2002. "Coase's Penguin, or Linux and the Nature of the Firm." *Yale Law Journal* 112(3):369–446.

Bezroukov, N. 1999. "A Second Look at the Cathedral and the Bazaar." *First Monday* 4(12). http://firstmonday.org/issues/issue4_12/bezroukov/.

Bollier, D. 1999. "The Power of Openness: Why Citizens, Education, Government, and Business Should Care about the Coming Revolution in Open Source Code Software." http://h2oproject.law.harvard.edu/opencode/h2o/.

Bonaccorsi, A., and C. Rossi. 2003. "Why Open Source Software Can Succeed." *Research Policy* 32(7):1243–1258.

Boyle, J. 2003. "The Second Enclosure Movement and the Construction of the Public Domain." *Law and Contemporary Problems* 66(1–2):33–75.

Briassoulis, H. 2000. *Analysis of Land Use Change: Theoretical and Modeling Approaches*. The Web Book of Regional Science. Morgantown, WV: Regional Research Institute, West Virginia University. http://www.rri.wvu.edu/WebBook/Briassoulis/contents.htm.

Capiluppi, A., P. Lago, and M. Morisio. 2003. "Evidences in the Evolution of OS Projects through Changelog Analyses." In J. Feller, B. Fitzgerald, S. Hissam, and K. Lakhani, eds., *Taking Stock of the Bazaar: Proceedings of the 3rd Annual Workshop on Open Source Software Engineering*. http://opensource.ucc.ie/icse2003.

CreativeCommons.org. 2004a. http://creativecommons.org.

CreativeCommons.org. 2004b. "Creative Commons Licenses" http://creativecommons.org/licenses.

Crowston, K., H. Annabi, and J. Howison. 2003. "Defining Open Source Project Success." In *Proceedings of the 24th International Conference on Information Systems (ICIS 2003)*. Seattle: Association for Information Systems.

Crowston, K., H. Annabi, J. Howison, and C. Masango. 2004. "Towards a Portfolio of FLOSS Project Success Measures." In J. Feller, B. Fitzgerald, S. Hissam, and K. Lakhani, eds., *Collaboration, Conflict and Control: The Proceedings of the 4th Annual Workshop on Open Source Software Engineering*, Edinburgh, Scotland, May 25.

David, P. A. 2005. "From Keeping 'Nature's Secrets' to the Institutionalization of 'Open Science.'" In Rishab Aiyer Ghosh, ed., *CODE: Collaborative Ownership and the Digital Economy*. Cambridge, MA: MIT Press.

Dempsey, B., D. Weiss, P. Jones, and J. Greenberg. 2002. "Who Is an Open Source Developer?" *CACM* 45:67–72.

Dietz, T., E. Ostrom, and P. C. Stern. 2003. "The Struggle to Govern the Commons." *Science* 302 (December 12): 1907–1912.

Divitini, M., L. Jaccheri, E. Monteiro, and H. Traetteberg. 2003. "Open Source Processes: No Place for Politics?" In J. Feller, B. Fitzgerald, S. Hissam, and K. Lakhani, eds., *Taking Stock of the Bazaar: Proceedings of the 3rd Annual Workshop on Open Source Software Engineering*. http://opensource.ucc.ie/icse2003.

Esanu, J., and P. Uhlir, eds. 2004. *Proceedings of the International Symposium on Open Access and the Public Domain in Digital Data and Information for Science*. Washington, DC: National Academies Press.

Feller, J., and B. Fitzgerald. 2002. *Understanding Open Source Software Development*. London: Addison-Wesley.

Fielding, R. Y. 1999. "Shared Leadership in the Apache Project." *Communications of the ACM* 42(4):42–43.

Fogel, K. 1999. *Open Source Development with CVS*. Scottsdale, AZ: Coriolis Group.

Freeman-Benson, B., and A. Borning. 2003. "Experience in Developing the UrbanSim System: Tools and Processes." Paper presented at the Conference on Object Oriented Programming Systems and Languages, Anaheim, California, October 26–30.

Free Software Foundation. 2004. "GNU General Public License" http://www.fsf.org/copyleft/gpl.html.

Geist, H. J., and E. F. Lambin. 2002. "Proximate Causes and Underlying Driving Forces of Tropical Deforestation." *BioScience* 52(2):143–150.

Ghosh, R. A. 2003. "Cooking Pot Markets: An Economic Model for the Trade of Free Goods and Services on the Internet." *First Monday* 3(3). http://www.firstmonday.org/issues/issue3_3/ghosh/.

Ghosh, R. A., and V. V. Prakash. 2000. "The Orbiten Free Software Survey." *First Monday* 5(7). http://firstmonday.org/issues/issue5_7/ghosh/.

Ghosh, R. A., G. Robles, and R. Glott. 2002. *Free/Libre and Open Source Software: Survey and Study*. Technical report. University of Maastricht, The Netherlands: International Institute of Infonomics, June. http://www.infonomics.nl/FLOSS/report/index.htm.

Goldman, R., and R. P. Gabriel. 2005. *Innovation Happens Elsewhere: Open Source as a Business Strategy*. Amsterdam: Elsevier.

Grove, J. M., C. M. Schweik, T. P. Evans, and G. M. Green. 2002. "Modeling Human-Environmental Dynamics." In K. C. Clarke, B. E. Parks, and M. P. Crane, eds., *Geographic Information Systems and Environmental Modeling*, 160–188. Upper Saddle River, NJ: Prentice Hall.

Hahn, R. W., ed. 2002. *Government Policy toward Open Source Software.* Washington, DC: Brookings Institution Press.

Hann, I., J. Roberts, S. Slaughter, and R. Fielding. 2002. "Why Do Developers Contribute to Open Source Projects? First Evidence of Economic Incentives." Paper presented at the 2nd Workshop on Open Source Software Engineering (ICSE 2002). http://opensource.ucc.ie/icse2002/HannRobertsSlaughterFielding. pdf.

Hardin, G. 1968. "The Tragedy of the Commons." *Science* 162:1243–1248.

Healy, K., and A. Schussman. 2003. "The Ecology of Open-Source Software Development." http://opensource.mit.edu/papers/healyschussman.pdf.

Hildebrand, J. D. 2004. "Hidden Agendas in Linux Land." *Software Development Times.* http://www.sdtimes.com/cols/opensourcewatch_015.htm.

Hissam, S., C. B. Weinstock, D. Plaksoh, and J. Asundi. 2001. *Perspectives on Open Source Software.* Technical Report CMU/SEI-2001-TR-019. Pittsburgh: Carnegie Mellon University. http://www.sei.cmu.edu/publications/documents/01 .reports/01tr019.html.

Johns, A. 2001. "The Birth of Scientific Reading." *Nature* 409:287–289.

Johnson, J. P. 2002. "Economics of Open Source Software." *Journal of Economics and Management Strategy* 11(4):637–662.

Jorgensen, N. 2001. "Putting It All in the Trunk: Incremental Software Development in the FreeBSD Open Source Project." *Information Systems Journal* 11(4):321–336.

Krishnamurthy, S. 2002. "Cave or Community? An Empirical Examination of 100 Mature Open Source Projects." *FirstMonday* 7(6).

Kronick, D. 1990. "Peer Review in 18th Century Scientific Journalism." *Journal of the American Medical Association* 263(10):1321–1322.

Lakhani, K. R., B. Wolf, J. Bates, and C. DiBona. 2002. "The Boston Consulting Group Hacker Survey, Release 0.73." http://www.osdn.com/bcg/bcg-0.73/ BCGHackerSurvey0-73.html.

Lee, S., N. Moisa, and M. Weiss. 2003. "Open Source as a Signaling Device: An Economic Analysis." In J. Feller, B. Fitzgerald, S. Hissam, and K. Lakhani, eds., *Taking Stock of the Bazaar: Proceedings of the 3rd Annual Workshop on Open Source Software Engineering.* http://opensource.ucc.ie/icse2003.

Lerner, J., and J. Tirole. 2002. "Some Simple Economics of Open Source." *Journal of Industrial Economics* 52:197–234.

Manley, M. R. 2000. "Managing Projects the Open Source Way." http://www.welchco.com/02/14/01/60/00/10/3101.htm.

Markus, M. L., B. Manville, and C. E. Agres. 2000. "What Makes a Virtual Organization Work?" *Sloan Management Review* 42(1):13–26.

McGowan, D. 2001. "Legal Implications of Open Source Software." *University of Illinois Review* 241(1):241–304.

Mockus, A., R. Fielding, and J. Herbsleb. 2000. "A Case Study of Open Source Software Development: The Apache Server." *Proceedings of the 2000 International Conference of Software Engineering (ICSE 2000)*. Limerick, Ireland: Association of Computing Machinery.

Moody, G. 2001. *Rebel Code: Linux and the Open Source Revolution*. Cambridge, MA: Perseus Press.

O'Mahony, S. 2005. "Nonprofit Foundations and Software Collaboration." In J. Feller, B. Fitzgerald, S. Hissam, and K. Lakhani, eds., *Perspectives on Free and Open Source Software*. Cambridge, MA: MIT Press.

Open Journal Systems. 2004. "Open Journal Systems" http://www.pkp.ubc.ca/ojs/.

O'Reilly, T. 1999. "Lessons from Open-Source Software Development." *Communications of the ACM* 42/4 (April): 33–37.

Ostrom, E. 1990. *Governing the Commons: The Evolution of Institutions for Collective Action*. New York: Cambridge University Press.

Ostrom, E., J. Burger, C. B. Field, R. B. Norgaard, and D. Policansky. 1999. "Revisiting the Commons: Local Lessons, Global Challenges." *Science* 284(5412):278–282.

Ostrom, E., R. Gardner, and J. K. Walker. 1994. Rules, Games, and Common-pool Resources, Ann Arbor: University of Michigan Press.

Pavlicek, R. C. 2000. *Embracing Insanity: Open Source Software Development*. Indianapolis, IN: SAMS.

Perens, B. 1999. "The Open Source Definition." In C. DiBona, S. Ockman, and M. Stone, eds., *Open Sources: Voices from the Open Source Revolution*. Sebastopol, CA: O'Reilly and Associates.

Raymond, E. 1998a. "The Cathedral and the Bazaar." *First Monday* 3/3 (March). http://firstmonday.org/issues/issue3_3/raymond/.

Raymond, E. 1998b. "Homesteading the Noosphere." *First Monday* 3(10). http://www.firstmonday.dk/issues/issue3_10/raymond/index.html.

Rischard, J. F. 2001. "High Noon: We Need New Approaches to Global Problem-Solving, Fast." *Journal of International Economic Law* 4(3):507–525.

Schweik, C. M. 2005. "An Institutional Analysis Approach to Studying Libre Software 'Commons.'" *Upgrade: The European Journal for the Informatics Professional* (June): 17–27. http://www.upgrade-cepis.org/issues/2005/3/up6-3Schweik.pdf.

Schweik, C. M., J. Evans, and J. M. Grove. 2003. "Initiating an Open Source\Content Landcover Change Modeling Effort." http: //www.lulc.org/bcworkshop_2003/os_lulc_workshop_report_2003.pdf.

Schweik, C. M., and J. M. Grove. 2000. "Fostering Open-Source Research via a World Wide Web System. *"Public Administration and Management* 5(3). http://www.pamij.com/5_4/5_4_2_opensource.html.

Schweik, C. M., and A. Semenov. 2003. "The Institutional Design of 'Open Source' Programming: Implications for Addressing Complex Public Policy and Management Problems." *First Monday* 8(1). http://www.firstmonday.org/issues/issue8_1/schweik/.

Science.CreativeCommons.org. 2005. "welcome to Science Commons" http://science.creativecommons.org/.

Shaikh, M., and T. Cornford. 2003. "Version Management Tools: CVS to BK in the Linux Kernel." In J. Feller, B. Fitzgerald, S. Hissam, and K. Lakhani, eds., *Taking Stock of the Bazaar: Proceedings of the 3rd Annual Workshop on Open Source Software Engineering.* http://opensource.ucc.ie/icse2003.

Sharma, S., V. Sugumaran, and B. Rajgopalan. 2002. "A Framework for Creating Hybrid–Open Source Software Communities." *Information Systems Journal* 12(1):7–25.

Shortliffe, E. H. 2004. *Electronic Scientific, Technical and Medical Journal Publishing and Its Implications: Report of a Symposium.* Washington, DC: National Academies Press.

Sourceforge.net. 2006. "Sourceforge.net" http://www.sourceforge.net.

Stallman, R. M. 1999. "The GNU Operating System and the Free Software Movement." In C. DiBona, S. Ockman, and M. Stone, eds., *Open Sources: Voices from the Open Source Revolution.* Sebastopol, CA: O'Reilly and Associates.

Stallman, R. M. 2001. "The Free Universal Encyclopedia and Learning Resource." In C. Werry and M. Mobray, eds., *Online Communities: Commerce, Community Action, and the Virtual University.* Upper Saddle River, NJ: Prentice Hall.

Stewart, K. 2004. "OSS Project Success: From Internal Dynamics to External Impact." In J. Feller, B. Fitzgerald, S. Hissam, and K. Lakhani, eds., *Collaboration, Conflict and Control: The Proceedings of the 4th Annual Workshop on Open Source Software Engineering*, Edinburgh, Scotland, May 25.

Stix, G. 2003. "Some Rights Reserved." *Scientific American* (March).

Van Wendel de Joode, R., J. A. de Bruijn, and M. J. G. van Eeten. 2003. *Protecting the Virtual Commons: Self-Organizing Open Source and Free Software Communities and Innovative Intellectual Property Regimes.* The Hague: Asser Press.

Voightmann, M. P., and C. P. Coleman. 2003. "Open Source Methodologies and Mission Critical Software Development." In J. Feller, B. Fitzgerald, S. Hissam, and K. Lakhani, eds., *Taking Stock of the Bazaar: Proceedings of the 3rd Annual Workshop on Open Source Software Engineering.* http://opensource.ucc.ie/icse2003.

Waddell, P. 2002. "UrbanSim: Modeling Urban Development for Land Use, Transportation and Environmental Planning." *Journal of the American Planning Association* 68(3):297–314.

Warsta, J., and P. Abrahamsson. 2003. "Is Open Source Development Essentially an Agile Method?" In J. Feller, B. Fitzgerald, S. Hissam, and K. Lakhani, eds., *Taking Stock of the Bazaar: Proceedings of the 3rd Annual Workshop on Open Source Software Engineering.* http://opensource.ucc.ie/icse2003.

Webb, C. L. 2004. "IBM's Open Source Lovefest." *Washington Post* (September 13). www.washingtonpost.com/wp-dyn/articles/A17842-2004sept/3.html.

Weber, S. 2004. *The Success of Open Source.* Cambridge, MA: Harvard University Press.

Wichmann, T. 2002. *Firm's Open Source Activities: Motivations and Policy Implications.* FLOSS Final Report Part 2. Berlin: Berlecon Research. http://www.berlecon.de/studien/downloads/200207FLOSS_Activities.pdf.

Ziman, J. 1969. "Information, Communication, Knowledge." *Nature* 224: 318–324.

11

Scholarly Communication and Libraries Unbound: The Opportunity of the Commons

Wendy Pradt Lougee

The world in which ideas and information are created, shared, and documented—the world of scholarly communication—is undergoing some of the most phenomenal transformations in the history of recorded knowledge. One can point to pivotal events in the history of these centuries-old traditions (whether it is the invention of the printing press, or the establishment of scientific societies), but more recent technologies have enabled a sea change of unusual scale and impact. While technology has prompted new venues and models for communication, it has also motivated the various stakeholders in the scholarly communication arena in both subtle and not-too-subtle ways.

This chapter explores the changes underway and in particular the new ways in which the research library's role as *archive* or *steward* of information goods is being transformed as a *collaborator* and potentially a *catalyst* within interest-based communities. The thesis presented here acknowledges that the trends of distributed computing and open paradigms for scholarly exchange have relaxed the boundaries between stakeholders, allowing more permeable and overlapping roles. Content once fettered by physical constraints has been loosened. The conventions of scholarly communication have been stretched and opened to a wider audience. The products of publication have become more processlike. The roles of libraries have also changed to embrace new opportunities for facilitating and shaping content, communication, and collaboration.

While this discussion is not focused on the concept of a commons per se, a central premise of this analysis involves the interplay of stakeholder roles within the scholarly information commons. The intent is to provide a review of key themes and a practical exploration of roles, including potential opportunities for libraries in the future.

Hess and Ostrom's (2004) organizing framework for the 2004 work-shop notes the convergence of forces within the commons, citing the *hyperchange* brought about by "linear, exponential, discontinuous, and chaotic change." The exploration here includes instances of linear change (extrapolation from past models) as well as discontinuous change (inno-vation) and will suggest that the fundamental social norms and con-straints of discipline communities explain a good deal of the variability in the adoption of new scholarly-communication models. Further, while research libraries have the potential to affect change, sensitivity to context—to the prevailing norms—will be absolutely key. This focus also poses significant challenge and potentially significant cost for the library.

The future roles of libraries are presented as a range of possible roles, drawing from historical and well-established functions but also inspired by opportunities for new levels of engagement. While there is no one certain path, the possibilities are presented in archetypal form to bring distinct characteristics of each model into sharper relief.

To understand the contemporary environment, I will first address the traditional conventions of scholarly communication and the traditional stewardship role of libraries in that environment. Then, to set the stage for an analysis of new, more engaged and collaborative roles for libraries, the transformations underway in content and communication processes will be pursued with attention to discipline-based history and culture. With this investigation as a backdrop, I can then explore library engage-ment within discipline communities and in shaping scholarly communi-cation processes.

Communication Conventions in the Commons

Borgman (1990, 13–14) has provided a useful definition of scholarly communication and of the critical social aspects of the processes:

By *scholarly communication* we mean the study of how scholars in any field (e.g., physical, biological, social, and behavioural sciences, humanities, technology) use and disseminate information through formal and informal channels. The study of scholarly communication includes the growth of scholarly information, the relationships among research areas and disciplines, the information needs and uses of individual user groups, and the relationships among formal and informal methods of communication.

We can identify generic stages in the scholarly-communication process (e.g., moving from concept to documentation and dissemination) as well as venues for communication that exist in the majority of disciplines (e.g., conferences, books, journals, or reviews). However, disciplines have also developed significant domain-specific practices and expectations. Hyland's (2000, 11) analysis of discourse within disciplines differentiates the common practices (such as acknowledging sources, testing, intellectual honesty) from activities that evolve as the result of community-specific consensus:

The ways that writers choose to represent themselves, their readers and their world, how they seek to advance knowledge, how they maintain the authority of their discipline and the processes whereby they establish what is to be accepted as substantiated truth, a useful contribution and a valid argument are all culturally-influenced practical actions and matters for community agreement. . . . Disciplinary communicative practices involve a system of appropriate social engagement with one's material and one's colleagues. The [types of] writing that disciplines produce, support and authorise . . . are representations of legitimate discourses which help to define and maintain particular epistemologies and academic boundaries.

"Appropriate social engagement with one's material and one's colleagues." This phrase captures the core dynamic that has fueled scholarship. The interaction of ideas, typically represented in some tangible form, and individuals has been the primary context for advancing knowledge within a discipline. These interactions occur through both formal and informal means. The so-called invisible college—informal groups and networks of interested parties—has played a critical role in advancing knowledge within disciplines.

In her pre-Internet analysis of invisible colleges, Crane (1972) captures the defining characteristics of these informal networks. The exact boundaries are difficult to define. Members are geographically separated and each is aware of some, but not all, members. Interaction rarely involves the entire group in a physical context, but typically is indirect or mediated through intervening parties. Central figures, rather than leaders, are evident.

Crane's analysis raises a number of interesting possibilities for revolution within disciplines. She notes, for example, that central figures and some of their associates are often "closely linked by direct ties and develop a kind of solidarity that is useful in building morale and maintaining motivation among members" (p. 139). In addition, the multiple affiliations of individuals enable communication and potentially innovation to move between groups, possibly advancing new ideas, paradigms, or methods.

There are, of course, obvious parallels to be drawn and understood between the notion of invisible colleges and the asynchronous communications and links among interested parties in today's world of electronic communication, although Internet applications may provide for broader participation than might have occurred in a pre-network era.

The evolution of twentieth-century scholarship shows evidence of increasing specialization within disciplines, growth of informal networks, and also growth of another stakeholder group, namely, professional societies and associations. These organizations began publications, and concurrently universities initiated systems of publishing (often subsidized) through institutional presses. Articulated systems of peer review took hold within communities as a primary mechanism for designating quality. As these organizations took shape, the research library also matured, its role focusing primarily on collecting the *valued* publications of the community. Driven largely by demand for specific types of publications, the library operated relatively independently from the informal circles of communication. Collecting tangible, recorded knowledge—primary and secondary sources—was the library's focus.

The profession of librarianship also took shape, developing systems of access through cataloging and classification. These systems generally were undifferentiating and unintrusive—that is, all materials were treated with the same descriptive systems, and the library's actions had little effect on the functionality or the structure of the published works. In general, the library emerges in the twentieth century as an organization serving all disciplines with similar tools, providing broad and generalized access to its collections. Stewardship of resources is a defining characteristic and this responsibility is manifest in roles that acquired, organized, preserved, and mediated the products of scholarship. The twentieth-century library exists largely as an institution separate from the processes of scholarly communication, with its role distinct from other stakeholders.

Distributed, Open Trends

If we fast-forward to the late twentieth century, we see several emerging trends that provided a significant catalyst for changing relationships among the stakeholders.[1] The growth of distributed technologies and the World Wide Web brought democratic access. The capability to disseminate ("publish") and collect information (build "libraries") now existed on the individual desktop. As standards emerged for creating, structuring, and disseminating digital content, libraries and other content-rich organizations were able to move away from proprietary methods of information access and management. The standards and tools offered libraries new opportunities for more robust services—for example, to add functionality to content or to deliver content differently for different audiences, or to sustain digital collections over time. Intelligent tools and systems also enabled information inquiry and analysis that were previously impossible.

A second critical trend is evident in the emergence of "open" paradigms—that is, models for processes and products that are often broadly accessible and in which collaboration stimulates development. Programs to adopt these open models took shape, sometimes with both a practical and political agenda. Efforts such as the Open Knowledge Initiative to share learning technologies offered an alternative to more formal or commercial means of sharing resources. The Open Archives Initiative was launched in response to community concerns about the constraints of commercial journal publishing. The resulting technical protocols for information exchange and initiatives to implement these protocols created new conventions for freely distributing content, such as e-print archives. Similarly, open-access publishing models have taken shape with an expressed purpose of creating alternative mechanisms for funding and conveying rights associated with the dissemination of intellectual goods.

As control and access to information become more distributed and open models of exchange become more common, another critical trend is taking shape. There is, in these open trends, evidence of a shift from publication as *product* to publication as *process*. Computer scientist Hal Berghel (2001, 18) has forecast that this shift will become increasingly prominent:

By 2100, our current view of electronic publications as copyright-able artifacts will be viewed primarily as a historical allegiance to a pre-participatory, non-interactive, essentially dull and lifeless era of publishing—an era in which one thought of digital libraries . . . as a collection of linked "things" rather than articulated processes and procedures. The current digital publication will be a relic, an obscure by-product from the horse and buggy age of digital networks.

This notion of "articulated processes and procedures" provides a quite different context in which to think about scholarly communication. The potential for dynamic and cumulating exchange not only affects scholars, but other stakeholders as well. The library's historic focus on tangible products (with associated rights) is significantly affected by this new paradigm. How will libraries describe or provide durable access to dynamic publications? What role can or should libraries play?

In this new context, libraries are challenged not only to harness the potential offered by distributed and open models, but to sustain and possibly enhance the library's longstanding traditions of bringing order, access, permanence, and trust to the information commons. The question remains, however: Can these traits be translated to an environment where process, not product, is king? Are control and management possible in this context, or will some new role for libraries emerge?

Transformation: Content and Publication

Evidence of changes in publication—the products of scholarship— reflects considerable variability. In some cases we have examples that merely replicate traditional structures as digital equivalents of print publications. Except for additional search capability, these e-versions are otherwise as fixed and "conventional" as their print counterparts. At the other end of the spectrum, we see new models that "push the envelope" in experimenting with new constructs that are more organic, more dynamic, and more a process than product.

These new forms of publication reflect innovation on a number of dimensions. Working papers and e-print services now abound, allowing access to early instances of publication, often outside of the peer-review process. While widely used in some disciplines (e.g., physics), their centrality within other disciplines varies (e.g., RePEc in economics has evidenced slower adoption).[2] In some domains, large-scale services such as the Social Science Research Network combine working papers and published articles, bringing together diverse publication types for a community of disciplines.

Examples are emerging that introduce the concept of dynamic publication. For example, *Living Reviews* is an online-only model created by the Max Planck Institute, incorporating peer review and tools to support ongoing revision of each article by the author. *Living Reviews* articles are truly "living" in their cumulating presentation. Related models exist whereby fixed articles might be complemented by ongoing commentary and dialogue. And, of course, the concept of blogs has introduced a whole new genre of cumulating commentary (see, for example, *Into the Blogosphere*).[3]

AAAS's Signal Transduction Knowledge Environment (STKE) challenges the boundaries of a publication. Rather than a singular product, STKE incorporates the functions of journal, current awareness, community dialogue, and analytic tools in a compound and interrelated environment of different media.[4] In a similarly compound mode, the Civil War historical site *The Valley of the Shadow* conceived by University of Virginia's Ed Ayers provides a rich environment of primary sources and tools. While the idea began as a proposed monograph, according to its creators it now has characteristics that more resemble a library than a book.

The point of this highly selective set of examples is that models are diverse and may vary along dimensions of peer review, stability or "fixity," incorporation of associated data or media, and tools and capabilities for communication and analysis. Publication is no longer of singular form nor are publications necessarily the final product in the communication process. Rather, technology has increased access, added functionality, and enabled interaction. These are significant steps in unbinding or unbundling traditional modes of scholarly communication.

Transformation: Disciplines

The themes of distributed technologies and open paradigms have had a transforming effect on the products and processes of communication within disciplines. Since disciplines have evolved with different practices and expectations about scholarly communication, it is no surprise that the impact of new technologies has played out differentially within each community. Kling and McKim (2000) remind us of the misguided, deterministic assumption that "sooner or later everyone will catch on" and that disciplines will converge on a stable set of electronic vehicles such as e-prints, e-lists, and e-journals. Rather, the unique characteristics of disciplines will prevail in shaping the future of scholarly discourse and communication within each disciplinary culture. A variety of factors are salient, including the role of scholarly/professional societies, the degree of collaboration and coauthorship, established norms for informal communication, methods for conveying recognition, and the existence of dominant publishers within a domain.

The field of physics has been the focus of study from a variety of perspectives to understand the culture and to analyze the success of the arXiv e-print environment. Anthropologist Sharon Traweek's (1988,

122) analysis of the high-energy physics community paints a picture of a well-bounded group, characterized by large research projects, focuses on shared instrumentation, and a critical distinction between the roles of informal (gossip) and formal (publication) communication:

Acquiring the capacity to gossip and to gain access to gossip about physicists, data, detectors, and ideas is the final and necessary stage in the training of a high energy physicist. Losing access to that gossip as punishment for violating certain moral codes effectively prevents the physicist from practicing physics. . . .

If gossip is a means of producing physics, physicists, and their culture, then written materials, articles and preprints, are the commodities the physicists produce in their turn. Articles represent the consensus, the "facts," data with the noise removed. The authors of these written accounts own the information in the account. Any subsequent users of that new information must pay royalties to the authors in the form of homage or credit, thereby increasing the accumulating reputations of the authors. In talk physicists rarely give credit to others. Scientific writing keeps track of the results of these debates. It is a record-keeping device, a spare ledger of credits and debits.

This dichotomy that existed in the pre-Internet culture of physicists (i.e., informal sharing within distinct research groups and the highly valued "ledger" role of the published literature) sheds significant light on what has transpired with the phenomenal success of the arXiv e-print service.

Physics offers an interesting case study of change. The critical role of central figures (as Crane has suggested about invisible colleges) is evident in this community, namely, the critical role of creator Paul Ginsparg. Interestingly, however, the high-volume, high-use, and rapid dissemination of e-prints has not entirely diminished the importance of traditional journals in physics. The need for the "ledger of credits and debits" remains. At least one recent analysis (Brown 2001) suggests that the citation of top-tier physics journals has not decreased despite the concurrent rise in citation of e-print literature. In the world of physics, the prevailing cultural norms have been sustained while exploiting the tools of the digital age.

Other disciplines offer similar examples of community culture shaping the adoption of new modes of communication. The influential work of Garvey and Griffith (1971) in psychology, for example, depicts a well-established sequence of scholarly communication that reinforces distinct roles for conferences, preprints, journal articles, citation, and review articles. They also identify the critical role of the highly structured professional societies. They note that "the most crucial point in the process of dissemination of *scientific* information is the transfer of information from the informal to the formal domain" (p. 358). Garvey and Griffith's commissioned analysis concluded with concern about the emerging emphasis on speeding up the flow of informal scientific information: "Such mechanisms would change the norms governing these processes and confuse the mechanisms concerned with evaluating and integrating knowledge" (p. 360). Not surprisingly, the American Psychological Association journals exhibited similar caution in initially prohibiting publication of manuscripts previously posted on the web.[5]

Chemistry is another discipline where the strong role of the primary society publisher, the American Chemical Society, has constrained widespread adoption of e-print technologies through policy restrictions on self-archiving or prepublication distribution. In contrast, the Association for Computing Machinery had been more open about preposting and has been liberal in policies with respect to the retention of author rights, suggesting a more enabling role of the professional organization.

The picture in the humanities is, not surprisingly, quite different. Stone (1982, 303–304) depicts the humanist:

He works differently in terms of time-scale, approach to his material, the age and form of material required, and the extent of immediate contact with other researchers. He is rather disadvantaged in terms of the development of secondary services and is very dependent on a well-stocked library with open access. The literature he uses tends not to become obsolete, though frequency of use of some important items may be low. The importance in humanities of criticism and analysis—including personal observation and opinion—marks a fundamental difference from the literature of science, and the subjective interaction between the humanist and his material is a unique feature.

Here we see the prominence of the "lone scholar" and the intimate interaction between the scholar and his or her targeted materials. While initially the publications of scholarly associations served to create a distinctive identity for humanistic disciplines and to define practice, over time these publications became the disseminators of stable (and archivable) authoritative scholarship as well (Tomlins 1998).

Learned societies play a unique role in the humanities, since they help establish connections between scholars who might otherwise remain separate due to the solitary nature of their work. Some have argued that societies such as the American Council of Learned Societies should help validate and organize scholarly resources, and there is evidence they have indeed played such a role through pilot efforts to incorporate digital technologies in publication and dissemination (Bennett 1997). The challenge in creating responsive digital environments for humanists may well lie in bringing aggregations of content and highly functional tools to the individual scholar rather than attempting to create a more collaborative culture of communication. While the traditional vehicles for disseminating scholarship have largely resisted change, there is evidence of new arenas for dialogue (e.g., H-Net in History) and for coalescing resources of interest. Unsworth (2003) perhaps best captures the tension experienced by the humanities in a digital era, tension between the reward structures, the technology, and the desire for connection:

What matters, in the humanities, is brilliance usually measured in citation—that is, reputation—not (frankly) efficacy, or proof, or any other outcome. These network discussion groups—which are really communities of interest—make it possible for people to break out of their underfunded, undercapitalized, underrecognized institutional contexts, and become recognized for their own contributions to the community. This provides a kind of access and even mobility that formal publication would not, precisely because of the weakness of the peer review system in the humanities.

The distinction between formal and informal venues for communication may remain distinct for humanities disciplines for the foreseeable future.

Transformation: Libraries

A shared assumption of many of the contributions to this book has been the utility of an ecological analysis of the information commons—that is, an understanding of the stakeholders, the dynamics between and among them, the norms of behavior, and the structure of incentives and disincentives that advance knowledge. Kranich, for example, chronicles the distinct and shared roles of institutions, organizations (such as SPARC), libraries, and authors in stimulating change. Similarly, Waters offers a series of models for digital archiving that present varying relationships between producers, archives, and consumers.

The analysis presented here has focused on the context within disciplines, within communities of common interest. The changes that are evident, fueled by distributed technologies and open models of exchange, have played out uniquely within each discipline's context. The selected examples suggest constraints that obtain in some disciplines as well as the natural progressions to new media in others. In some cases, new venues or new types of publication have been more readily adopted and valued within a community. In other cases, true innovation is at the margins. As the library seeks to adapt and transform itself in this emerging environment, sensitivity to context—to these prevailing forces within each discipline context—is critical.

There are numerous examples of library experimentation and investment in new roles in the scholarly-communication environment. The majority of research libraries have assumed responsibilities for digital content that modestly extend existing core functions (e.g., creation of metadata for intellectual access or digital reformatting for preservation). A much smaller number of libraries have become significant players in advancing new systems and tools that fundamentally change scholarly-communication practices. Rather than inventorying here the many projects underway, the overview that follows will highlight three models of library activity, each reflecting different characteristics and degrees of library engagement within the scholarly-communication process.

The Library as Control Zone

Libraries lack the strategic position in the distribution chain that publishers, commercial or non-commercial have. . . . And although they are often an important part of the chain, their role is not exclusive.
—Brian Kahin (1995)

The traditional focus of libraries as stewards of the products of scholarship places the library in a relatively fixed role within the commons. Authors and publishers also hold distinct and separate roles within the traditional, linear sequence of scholarly communication. Libraries typically serve as agent, as intermediary between publisher and user, acquiring and managing content that had been conceived by the author and produced by the publisher. We see evidence in early digital libraries of this role continuing, with e-content being brought into the library environment either by locally managing the bits or through a sustained access relationship (license) with the publisher. Libraries acquire, manage, describe, and preserve the digital content much as they handle traditional media.

Early in the evolution of digital libraries Cornell's Ross Atkinson (1996), in fact, proposed that a critical task for libraries was the creation of a "control zone" that would be "technically and conceptually separate from the open zone" (the "open zone" representing the unfettered and free arena on the Internet). His proposal adds a critical aspect of creating the zone, namely, the *explicit* transfer of digital content into a context in which the library would guarantee the quality and accessibility of that object indefinitely. Control, in this sense, is the library exercising direct responsibility for stewardship of digital bits. Further, this "modest proposal" suggests that the academy could seize the oversight over the control zone to assume responsibility for publications intended for a scholarly audience, leaving more general-interest and broader market information resources within the commercial sector. Atkinson's assertion maintains that the enclosed or bounded library remains the "ultimate and quintessential research instrument."

The emergence of institutional repositories is, in some respect, consistent with this notion of the control zone, with the important distinction that institutional repositories currently can embody a range of information types, from informal to more formal. As libraries become engaged in such services (e.g., DSpace or the California Digital Library), the potential exists for involvement earlier in the communication and dissemination process. We see, for example, the possibility of libraries working actively with a community to ensure the creation of content employing standards-based methods, or perhaps educating stakeholders about options with respect to rights and dissemination. While the shift is perhaps subtle, the library's stewardship role has expanded to embrace a broader arena of content and to work with a community to ensure the sustainability of the archive.

There are also instances where libraries have created roles further "upstream" in the scholarly communication process, serving as formal distributors of publications. In these models, libraries support electronic dissemination services, while publisher partners sustain the editorial functions, although there are variations on this theme. For example, Stanford's HighWire Press works in cooperation with major society publishers to fulfill a distribution role. The University of Michigan's Scholarly Publishing Office and Cornell's Digital Consulting and Production Services offer examples where expertise and tools are brought to the table for creators and authors in a service-bureau environment.[6] Michigan's services for the ACLS History E-Book project, for example, demonstrate a focused production role, while the Cornell library's Project Euclid reflects more of a partnership with publishers in order to codevelop an interoperable environment for theoretical and applied statistics.

In these examples, the library's role is still largely as steward, but is now involved in direct interaction with the authors and content providers. The content management, archival, and dissemination functions coexist in the "library."

A reasonable question to be raised about these services is "why the library?" Surely other entities have expertise in structuring content for dissemination, technology services to provide access, or incentives to ensure longevity? However, the library may be uniquely or strongly positioned to uphold principles of cost-effective or low-barrier access. Also, libraries bring other important characteristics associated with integrity, authenticity, and trust. Each of these characteristics has been evident in the library's traditional roles, but takes on new importance and dimensions in the digital context. Cliff Lynch (2000, 2001) has explored the fundamental values represented by these characteristics— for example, the determination of provenance of an object, assurance that the digital object is what it purports to be, and codification of the version or instance of an object. These functions, which may have been largely handled through description (e.g., cataloging of fixed objects) in the print arena, now take on new proportions in the more dynamic digital context. While capabilities exist to capture information about these basic characteristics, more robust systems will be essential in the future. And, as Lynch (2001) suggests, the development of a technology framework to establish trust within a community may actually pose dangers of censorship and control, requiring that the system mechanisms that differentiate content be sufficiently transparent to users.

Equally important will be the codification of responsibilities in ensuring long-term access through sustainable archives. As Waters points out elsewhere in this book, there may be risks associated with consumer- or producer- (publisher) driven archives. Libraries may be uniquely motivated to ensure the longevity of the cultural record, yet are also constrained by legal and economic forces.

In the models described here as "control zone," the library role remains relatively well bounded—that is, typically acting on behalf of or in response to the needs of the client group. While new forms or methods of scholarly communication may result, the motivating forces remain largely within the discipline community and its associated publishing organizations.

The Library as Systems and Services

As digital libraries have evolved, there have been concurrent developments in technology applications. These developments have included progress in creating structure and functionality of content, in the intelligence of systems of description and retrieval, and in interoperable architectures to enable federation of distributed resources. Libraries have made considerable investment in these areas, often in partnership with technology or research organizations.[7] As these investments mature, libraries have shifted emphasis from management of digital products of scholarship to understanding content, its use, and associated users in order to develop more robust and useful digital environments. These explorations reflect a second model for library roles—that is, more engaged in adding value, in harnessing the potential of content and systems for particular user communities, and in creating tools for more complex exploitation of content by individual scholars and communities of scholars.

The Digital Library Federation's Aquifer project reflects this next level of engagement.[8] With more structured content and protocols for dissemination, the potential exists to share richer digital masters of content and thereby enable local manipulation, analysis, and new capabilities for research. A key element in the Aquifer plan is the essential repurposing of content for multiple uses and users with a goal of nurturing new scholarship and new forms of scholarship. Through Aquifer, libraries will be developing the protocols for this deeper sharing and establishing the interlibrary and interinstitutional rules of repurposing content.

Other examples of libraries attending to the use dimensions of digital content include instances where socially based cues (e.g., collaborative or social filtering, and recommender systems) or semantic structures are incorporated in information systems. Here we see the library taking on a more overt role in shaping the discovery environment through complex associative and interpretive structures. These structures, in turn, enable associations between digital objects and potentially between resources of different disciplines. The semantic web, as specified, would bring together metadata and a framework of relationships between digital terms and objects. W3C's Semantic Web lead developer Eric Miller (2003) notes that a semantic framework will enable collaboration by creating the structure to document the flow of data, information, and knowledge: "the steps, social and automatic, by which the associated information evolved." This articulation of relationships is an important step for libraries in addressing issues associated with communication processes versus the products of scholarship.

In an analysis of ontologies and their potential for new forms of library service, Atkinson (2003) describes capabilities for specifying the relationship among multiple metadata descriptions through an articulation of the *events* in a resource's life cycle. This would enable interoperability among different metadata schema that serve different disciplines and purposes—in other words, that could stimulate interdiscipline connections. Events, as specified in the ontology, might include actions on content such as modification, compilation, extraction, or derivation. This framework allows tracking a work to its origins, but tracking variations in the history of the work, too. Such a framework should also allow a user to trace the evolution of a concept over time. Atkinson further explores two types of library service that might be created, an analytic service (to essentially identify the origin and integrity of a work) and a synthetic service (to allow the user to combine the contents of different objects and create new contexts for them):

The synthetic service is therefore in some ways the exact opposite of the analytical one. The analytical service is more observational, seeking not to disturb objects, but to observe them, so to speak, in their natural habitat—rather like a delicate archaeological dig. The synthetic service, on the other hand, has the potential to pull objects to pieces, recombining parts of them into new forms, disregarding in some cases even the intentions of their original creators. In the synthetic service, the purpose of objects is to serve as building blocks for new user creations.

A certain amount of "damage" to a personal database could be done in the course of the kind of recontextualization made possible by such a synthetic service. One role the library plays, therefore, is the same as that for the analytical service—to serve as the protected space to which the user can always return to find the original intact. (p. 169)

This description captures a significant and complex role (which, it should be noted, is proposed rather than operational) wherein the library provides the capacity to document processes of scholarly communication *and* enable the repurposing and transformation of scholarship over time. In this case, the library role in explicating and enabling scholarly communication proceeds in tandem with the communication itself. For example, the DLF Aquifer project would facilitate reuse of digital content in ways that transform the object into a new manifestation. That repurposing could be captured and described so as to document the processes for future scholarship.

The model reflected in these examples presents the library as facilitator of scholarship and potentially of new forms of scholarship. Often acting in partnership with disciplines, the goal is adding value or utility to the content and, in the future, the processes. An important characteristic that emerges in the event-based example is the library's role in *capturing* the communication process and, in so doing, playing a much more integrated role in that process.

Library as Catalyst

New models of collaboration are evident as discipline communities exploit technologies and the possibilities technology affords for informal and formal exchange. The University of Virginia, for example, has advanced the concept of *information communities* as part of the library's overall strategic planning framework. Each information-community project brings together distributed content, distributed content providers and organizations, and relevant communication and analytic tools to serve a particular discipline community. The community may include students, faculty, researchers, librarians, information specialists, and citizens with a common interest in a particular thematic area. Examples include an American Studies information community and a Tibetan and Himalayan community, each with diverse participants and users.

The information community includes content resources built by faculty and the library based on local and remote collections, online finding aids for physical library collections, and digital objects licensed for campus use. Tools might include software to create concordances, translation capabilities, or geographic resources, depending on the community need. "Features" promote research themes, events, and activities involving or of interest to the community's members. An e-mail list and an online discussion forum are incorporated to stimulate dialogue and collaboration. The capability exists to allow participants to register their own digital projects and tools.

The University of Virginia describes these information communities as "learning and teaching environments" developed around a particular subject domain, with the expressed goal of fostering interdisciplinary and collaborative research and publication. Perhaps most significant, the system and services are explicitly designed to serve a social role as catalyst for an interdisciplinary community. This is a far more intrusive role for the library than its traditional role.

This integration of content, services, data, and tools begins to mirror the construct of a *collaboratory* for focused research communities. Collaboratories have been defined as "tool-oriented computing and communication systems to support scientific collaboration."[9] For example, the Space Physics and Aeronomy Research Collaboratory provides an online knowledge environment for atmospheric scientists worldwide.[10] This collaboratory incorporates the ability to control remote instrumentation, to review and collaboratively analyze observational data of atmospheric events, to create and archive vast amounts of research data, and to use tools to manipulate the data. These types of robust information environments are also envisioned in the recent NSF Cyberinfrastructure report.

While libraries have not been players in research-collaboratory development, the Virginia concept suggests a potential role. In this capacity, the library is called on to comprehend and engage the needs of a community, knitting together content, technology, tools, and people. This is a critical *social* role and has the potential to motivate change within a community. One could also imagine these online environments incorporating the interpretive and semantic functions described above to enhance the utility of content and to document processes over time.

This model of "library as catalyst" reflects two key elements. The library works in collaboration with other stakeholders (scholars, publishers, organizations) and potentially serves as an agent of change in the context of the newly created scholarly communication environment. Library functions are fully part of the overall process of scholarly activity within the environment; in fact, it may be difficult to define what is "library" within the online-community context. The imperative, however, is gauging and engaging the discipline and its norms for communication and interaction.

In this model, the library's role builds on distributed technologies and open paradigms, but it is also fully engaged in the processes of communication within the community. The boundaries between traditional stakeholders are permeable, enabling interactions between creators, producers, libraries, and users of resources. Unlike the "control zone" and "systems and services" models, the library's role extends beyond acting *on* scholarly products and processes to working *within* the processes. The outcome of such engagement is a library that is a useful and purposeful collaborator within the discipline.

Concluding Remarks

The exploration of library roles in the scholarly information commons suggests there is no one model that will emerge in the foreseeable future. Since disciplines vary in terms of the degree of *openness to change*, the potential for libraries to engage within these communities will vary as well. Characteristics of each discipline, including existing norms of communication and publication, may inhibit adoption of new models within a community or enable a willing response to new opportunities. Existing control of communication processes by scholarly/professional organizations and publishers also carries significant weight, as do more general legal and economic constraints.

I have discussed the forces that are prompting change, including the technology and social forces enabling traditional products and processes to be unbound, to be enabled for change. This exploration of three archetypal models for library engagement—a focus on "control," on systems and services, or as a catalyst for change—also suggests several core challenges for the future.

The library community has already invested in significant experimentation, and partnerships with the research community have yielded important new capabilities to further development. However, one area for attention that has been largely absent from research agendas is further exploration of academic cultures in general and discipline cultures in particular. As described, this is a critical element in the comprehension, design, and catalyzing of new models of scholarly communication. Analyses similar to the anthropological work of Traweek that shed light on a community's communication norms could inform the development of more agile and community-sensitive information environments. A number of Mellon Foundation–sponsored projects explore dimensions of these issues. Scholarly communication institutes have brought together scholars (e.g., in the field of practical ethics), technologists, and librarians to explore new venues for publishing. The University of California at Santa Barbara has received support to investigate informatics research needs and behaviors on campus as background for developing data-intensive services and archives.[11] A recent award to the University of Minnesota Libraries will similarly enable assessment of research behaviors and preferences in order to design programs that better integrate expertise, technology, content, and specialized facilities for particular disciplines.[12]

In a recent address, Cliff Lynch (2005) describes the increasingly specialized interests of disciplines for academic technologies and the resulting distribution (fragmentation) of campus services. Lynch notes that these emerging needs require "a set of expertises that are more common in disciplinary informatics, in library and information science, in archives, in records management, in knowledge management, and a whole complex of fields. . . . One of our challenges perhaps is how to align our organizations to deliver these kinds of services." Analyses of emerging discipline-based technologies and of the requisite expertise to develop and sustain these tools and systems will be critical in shaping future contexts for scholarly activity.

A second obvious arena for research and investment involves the development of the semantic and interpretive structures and tools that will enable libraries and scholarly communities to create the systems to document and potentially manage scholarly-communication processes. As the emphasis on process takes greater shape, existing schema and tools will prove inadequate. Existing formal schema may also be enhanced by new methods of social computing, enabling user input as well.

A third area for focused investment involves the necessary structure(s) to coalesce library resources and expertise. Organizations such as the Digital Library Federation have brought attention to the variability and distribution of library capacity—that is, technology infrastructure, expertise, and potential for expanded effort. Coordinating resources and leveraging investments require a new framework for federated governance of multiple library partners. These challenges are magnified further as groups of libraries pursue collaboration with communities and associated organizations.

Understanding communities, developing new interpretive systems, and framing interorganizational models for collaboration are three critical areas where collective attention could make a difference in facilitating collaboration in the commons.

In closing, consider the following question from OCLC's (2003) Environmental Scan report:

What if libraries . . . and all the other players in the world of structured access to information erased the organizational charts, the artificial separations of content, the visible taxonomies, and the other edifices real or otherwise built to bring order and rationality to what we perceive as a chaotic universe? What if we built an infosphere rich in content and context that was easy to use, ubiquitous and integrated, designed to become woven into the fabric of people's lives; people looking for answers, meaning and authoritative, trustable results?

This question underscores the key themes. The future roles for libraries are associated both with traditional roles of content stewardship and increasingly with shaping community-based digital contexts for inquiry. The overarching challenge is to create the ubiquitous and integrated information communities that will serve scholars of today and at the same time enable the products and processes of scholarly communication for tomorrow. In so doing, attention to community norms and emerging interests is essential. Libraries have a critical role to play in exercising control, in adding value, and—increasingly—in catalyzing change.

Notes

1. See Lougee 2002 for an exploration of the impact of distributed computing and open models on classic functions of libraries: collection development, access, and service.

2. Information about RePEc can be found at http://www.repec.org/.

3. http://blog.lib.umn.edu/blogosphere/.

4. Additional information and analysis of STKE can be found at http://stke .sciencemag.org/.

5. The decision on prepublication posting shifted to the discretion of individual APA journal editors.

6. In these examples, the library's expertise with respect to content, technology, and users is brought to bear in designing new products and distribution systems. The library role is largely in service to the production of products conceived or developed by other stakeholders.

7. While the initial NSF Digital Library Initiatives had modest library involvement, over time library presence has been increasingly evident and the research projects have moved from testbeds to more operational settings.

8. See http://www.diglib.org/aquifer/.

9. National Research Council Committee on a National Collaboratory, *National Collaboratories* (Washington, DC: National Academy Press, 1993).

10. Information on SPARC can be found at http://www.windows.ucar.edu/ sparc/.

11. See "UCSB Campus Informatics: Collaboration for Knowledge Management," http://www.cni.org/tfms/2004a.spring/abstracts/PB-ucsb-pritchard.html.

12. See http://www.lib.umn.edu/about/mellon/.

References

Atkinson, Ross. 1996. "Library Functions, Scholarly Communication, and the Foundation of the Digital Library: Laying Claim to the Control Zone." *Library Quarterly* 66/3 (July):239–265.

Atkinson, Ross. 2003. "Toward a Rationale for Future Event-Based Information Services." In Patricia Hodges, Maria Bonn, Mark Sandler, and John Price Wilkin, eds., *Digital Libraries: A Vision for the 21st Century*, 154–175. Ann Arbor: University of Michigan Library Scholarly Publishing Office. http://name.umdl .umich.edu/bbv9812.

Bennett, Douglas C. 1997. *New Connections for Scholars: The Changing Missions of a Learned Society in an Era of Digital Networks*. American Council of Learned Societies Occasional Paper No. 36. http://www.acls.org/op36.htm.

Berghel, Hal. 2001. "Digital Village: A Cyberpublishing Manifesto." *Communications of the ACM* 44/3 (March):17–20.

Borgman, Christine L. 1990. In C. L. Borgman, ed., *Scholarly Communication and Bibliometrics*, 10–27. Newbury Park, CA: Sage.

Brown, Cecelia. 2001. "The E-volution of Preprints in the Scholarly Communication of Physicists and Astronomers." *Journal of the American Society for Information Science and Technology* 52(3):187–200.

Crane, Diana. 1972. *Invisible Colleges*. Chicago: University of Chicago Press.

Garvey, William D., and Belver C. Griffith. 1971. "Scientific Communication: Its Role in the Conduct of Research and the Creation of Knowledge." *American Psychologist* 26:349–362.

Hess, Charlotte, and Elinor Ostrom. 2004. "A Framework for Analyzing Scholarly Communication as a Commons." Workshop on Scholarly Communication as an Information Commons, Bloomington, Indiana, March/April.

Hyland, Ken. 2000. *Disciplinary Discourses: Social Interactions in Academic Writing*. New York: Longman.

Kahin, Brian. 1995. "Institutional and Policy Issues in the Development of the Digital Library." *Journal of Electronic Publishing* (January). http://www.press .umich.edu/jep/works/kahin.dl.html.

Kling, Rob, and Geoffrey McKim. 2000. "Not Just a Matter of Time: Field Differences and the Shaping of Electronic Media in Supporting Scientific Communication." *Journal of the American Society for Information Science* 51(14): 1306–1320.

Lougee, Wendy Pradt. 2002. *Diffuse Libraries: Emergent Roles for the Research Library in the Digital Age*. Washington, DC: Council on Library and Information Resources.

Lynch, Clifford. 2000. *Authenticity and Integrity in the Digital Environment: An Exploratory Analysis of the Central Role of Trust*. Council on Library and Information Resources Report 92. http://www.clir.org/pubs/abstract/pub92abst .html.

Lynch, Clifford. 2001. "When Documents Deceive: Trust and Provenance as New Factors for Retrieval in a Tangled Web." *Journal of the American Society for Information Science and Technology* 52(1):12–17.

Lynch, Clifford. 2005. "ECURE 2005 Keynote Address, Arizona State University, March 2005." http://www.asu.edu/ecure/2005/keynote.

Miller, Eric. 2003. "Enabling the Semantic Web for Scientific Research and Collaboration." NSF Post Digital Library Futures Workshop, Chatham, Massachusetts, June. http://www.sis.pitt.edu/~dlwkshop/paper_miller.html.

National Research Council Committee on a National Collaboratory. 1993. *National Collaboratories: Applying Information Technology for Scientific Research.* Washington, DC: National Academy Press.

OCLC. 2003. *The 2003 OCLC Environmental Scan: Pattern Recognition.* Dublin, OH: OCLC Online Computer Library Center. http://www.oclc.org/membership/escan/default.htm.

Seaman, David. 2003. "Deep Sharing: A Case for the Federated Digital Library." *Educause Review* (July/August). http://www.educause.edu/ir/library/pdf/erm0348.pdf.

Stone, Sue. 1982. "Humanities Scholars: Information Needs and Uses." *Journal of Documentation* 38(4):292–313.

Tomlins, Christopher L. 1998. *Wave of the Present: The Scholarly Journal on the Edge of the Internet.* American Council of Learned Societies Occasional Paper No. 43. http://www.acls.org/op43.htm.

Traweek, Sharon. 1988. *Beamtimes and Lifetimes: The World of High Energy Physicists.* Cambridge, MA: Harvard University Press.

Unsworth, John. 2003. "The Humanist: 'Dances with Wolves' or 'Bowls Alone'"? *Scholarly Tribes and Tribulations: How Tradition and Technology Are Driving Disciplinary Change.* Washington, DC: Association of Research Libraries, October 17. http://www.arl.org/scomm/disciplines_program.html.

12

EconPort: Creating and Maintaining a Knowledge Commons

James C. Cox and J. Todd Swarthout

Public and academic libraries are traditionally designed and run by librarians and information specialists. The advent of the World Wide Web, however, gave the capacity to build useful libraries to anyone with subject knowledge and information-technological expertise. This chapter focuses on an open-access digital library of microeconomics for students, teachers, researchers, and the general public. This digital library, Econ-Port (http://www.econport.org), is a new knowledge commons.

EconPort was created, beginning in 2002, by a team from the Economic Science Laboratory (http://www.econlab.arizona.edu) and the Artificial Intelligence Lab (http://www.ailab.arizona.edu) at the University of Arizona, under a grant from the National Science Digital Library (http://www.nsdl.org) initiative of the National Science Foundation. The goal of the project was to provide microeconomics educational resources to the public, with a particular focus on the use of microeconomics experiments in learning, teaching, and research. Although the use of microeconomics experiments in teaching had increased significantly during the previous several years, most instructors still faced formidable difficulties when trying to use an array of experiments in their classes. It is this problem, widely shared at other educational institutions, and the experience of creating and using experiments for both teaching and research at the Economic Science Laboratory (ESL), that led the ESL team and other colleagues at the University of Arizona to undertake the creation of EconPort.

Two developments in public policy provided supporting conditions for the creation of EconPort. One was passage by direct democracy of Proposition 301, an initiative by Arizona voters in which they implemented a twenty-year increase in the state sales tax with revenues earmarked to support technology education (at all levels, including K through 12 and the state universities). The other policy development was the National Science Foundation's digital library initiative. In response to the need to develop a plan for spending its part of Proposition 301 funds, the dean of the Eller College of Management at the University of Arizona appointed a faculty committee with responsibility to make recommendations to the dean "on the use of Proposition 301 funds" and on ways to promote collaborative work involving information technology researchers and researchers from more traditional disciplines, including economics. The committee included among its members James Cox (coauthor of this chapter) from the Department of Economics and Hsinchun Chen from the Department of Management Information Systems. Cox is an experimental economist and Chen is an information technologist specializing in databases and digital libraries. Following their interaction on the dean's committee, Cox and Chen led a group of colleagues in the Eller College—including Todd Swarthout (coauthor of this chapter)—that submitted a successful proposal to NSF's digital library initiative to create a microeconomics digital library named Econ-Port. The incentives of the team members for creation and maintenance of EconPort differed depending on their academic disciplines; they are discussed below.

This chapter describes the content of EconPort and the educational philosophy that underlay its creation. However, the main focus of the chapter is the use of EconPort as a case study of the effectiveness of incentives for creation, maintenance, and utilization of a specific type of knowledge commons.

Microeconomics and Experiments

Microeconomics is the study of individual economic agents such as consumers and firms; how those individual agents interact with each other in markets; the properties of different kinds of markets such as perfectly competitive markets, monopolies, and imperfectly competitive markets; and how distinct markets are aggregated to form an economy. The study of microeconomics dates at least as far back as Adam Smith's (1776) classic work. Throughout much of its history, microeconomics has followed Smith's (1776) lead in seeking to explain how, and under what conditions, markets can harness the motivating drive of economic self-interest to promote the common good. In more recent decades, some areas of microeconomics have adopted the approach of game theory (von Neumann and

Morgenstern 1947; Nash 1950), which models the interaction of economic agents in terms of each agent adopting a strategy that is the best reply to the strategies of competing agents. Recently there has been a return to an even earlier theme of Adam Smith's (1759), in the development by experimental economists of a body of data to guide creation of models of agents characterized by a richer set of motivations that includes trust, reciprocity, and altruism (see, for examples, Cox 2004; Cox, Friedman, and Gjerstad forthcoming), in addition to the economic self-interest focused on in Smith's (1776) more widely quoted, later book.

Experimental economics involves the design and implementation of experiments involving human agents in order to study economic behavior and the properties of economic institutions, such as markets of various types, under controlled conditions. Economics experiments are run both in laboratories, such as the Economic Science Laboratory, and recently in field environments, including naturally occurring markets such as eBay. The use of controlled experiments makes it possible to test theoretical models and thereby facilitate the development of microeconomics as an empirical science.

Experimental methods in microeconomics were developed for research, but it was recognized fairly early that experiments could be valuable as a teaching and learning method. For many years, economists using experiments in teaching could cite only their own experience to support the conclusion that class experiments are an effective teaching method. There is now better support for that conclusion.

Microeconomics Experiments as a Teaching Method

The benefits of using experiments in teaching economics have been reported in several articles in professional journals (see Emerson and Taylor 2004), as well as widely discussed informally at professional gatherings. There are several reasons to expect even better learning outcomes with computerized market experiments than with typical hand-run experiments (see Bergstrom and Miller 2000 for a textbook presentation of several hand-run experiments). One advantage is that trades are faster with computerized experiments. Faster trades mean that more trades per session are possible, which promotes better convergence to theoretically predicted outcomes and thereby better learning from market participation by the students. Another advantage is that computerized experiments can graphically represent trades relative to the underlying market conditions (supply and demand) and automate analysis of market performance measures, such as price convergence and market efficiency. With sharper convergence to predicted outcomes and built-in graphics and analysis, the ability of instructors to describe experiment outcomes and relate outcomes to economic models is greatly enhanced. Computerized laboratory market experiments have a twenty-year history of use in experimental economics laboratories. By bringing such experiments to the Internet, and by integrating experiment software into a large array of other types of educational material, EconPort is a culmination of a decades-long development of experimental economics laboratories.

Experimental Economics Laboratories as Information Facilities

EconPort is a unique addition to the economics knowledge commons. As a digital library and archive, it is distinctive in that among the artifacts that it incorporates are multiperson interactive experimental economics software packages. These software packages support experiments involving human subjects. Such software is used both for research experiments and for teaching experiments designed to support student learning of economics. EconPort is also a unique experimental economics laboratory and an epistemic repository, which is described in more detail below. The historical development of experimental economics laboratories has distinct stages associated with the evolution of information technology.

Historical Development of Experimental Economics Laboratories

Edward Chamberlin is credited with running the first economics experiments while teaching economics at Harvard in the late 1940s. He subsequently published an article (Chamberlin 1948) reporting these experiments using the form of market now known as a double auction, which is a market institution (using New York Stock Exchange trading rules) that provides robust convergence of price and quantity outcomes consistent with economists' model of a perfectly competitive market. These experiments, preceding the invention of modern information technology, were conducted with students in classrooms using paper, pencil, and chalkboard. Subsequent early double-auction experiments were also conducted with paper, pencil, and chalkboard by Vernon Smith (1962), but general use of experimental markets in either research or teaching came much later.

In 1977, researchers at the University of Arizona developed the first computerized market experiments. Creating experimental economics software was an important step, since it allowed for the experiments to be run much more efficiently, and also provided the foundation to create more complex types of experiments than could realistically be conducted by paper, pencil, and chalkboard. The computer technology of the day relied on mainframe computers and "dumb" terminals connected by telephone line because this preceded the development of personal computers and local area networks. The use of this technology was both costly and fragile, and because of this, no other laboratories of this type were in existence.

In response to the above limitations and taking advantage of the increased availability of personal computers in the 1980s, the University of Arizona's Economic Science Laboratory (ESL) was created in 1985 as both an administrative unit of the university and a dedicated physical laboratory containing a local area network of personal computers. ESL first used DOS-based software for running experiments. Development of specialized software packages for experiments and increasing use of these artifacts required a dedicated laboratory facility and staff for efficient running of research and teaching experiments.

Beginning in 1995 there was a gradual shift from DOS-based to Windows software for running experiments. Because the DOS-based and Windows software was designed to run on a local area network, it constituted a common educational resource only for the community of scholars physically in residence at the University of Arizona. The very local nature of the public-good elements of the resource made it relatively easy to solve the free-rider problem. However, this also limited use of the resource, which was a problem that was only marginally ameliorated by a few transfers of software to other dedicated laboratories.

The growth of the Internet has provided the foundation for building a twenty-first century virtual laboratory that could be used in research and education in economics anywhere in the world on the favored side of the digital divide. EconPort is a response to this opportunity to develop a new type of facility. There are a variety of other Internet economics facilities, none of which provide experiment software that is integrated with a wide array of other educational material.

Challenges in Creating an Economics Common Resource

Two types of challenges were encountered in the effort to construct Econ-Port: pedagogical challenges and technological challenges. The pedagogical challenges included the need to locate, evaluate, and select from the huge amount of microeconomics material available on the World Wide Web the artifacts that would be archived and organized by topic in EconPort. Another critical challenge was to find ways to make it easier for people to use microeconomics experiments, especially people with no prior experience with experiments.

The technological challenges that had to be overcome were related to creating new software systems needed for the site to function, including

• An *archive* of microeconomics artifacts that was Open Archives Initiative (OAI)-compliant so that it could be a component of the National Science Digital Library.

• A framework that makes experimental economics software easy to use over the Internet. This was a challenge because these software resources are not self-contained information but rather networked software that requires many simultaneous users to connect with one another. This was a significant challenge with regard to the typical types of information stored in a digital library. The EconPort framework does not just host program files that people download; instead this system handles almost all of the software-connection issues present when one is attempting to connect multiple computers to each other when they may be dispersed over the Internet.

• A software interface that allows additional external software to be easily added into the EconPort framework. Software technology inevitably changes over time, so we created an Applications Program Interface that allows externally created software artifacts to be incorporated into the EconPort facility, independent of programming language or paradigm.

EconPort: A Digital Library for Microeconomics Education

EconPort provides a wide variety of content and services for instructors and students.

An Online Experimental Economics Laboratory

EconPort's software packages can be used in both dedicated experimental economics laboratories and in distance/decentralized online experiments in which participants are located in their dormitory rooms, apartments, coffeehouses, student computer laboratories, or a variety of other locations with Internet connectivity.

The insider-created software is programmed such that when an experiment is actually running, it does so independently of EconPort, thus creating no additional processing load on the EconPort server. This substantially ameliorates the congestion problems from use of the common educational resource. Use of the Java language for the experiment software provides cross-platform support and eliminates the need for any client or server software installation other than a one-time installation of the free Java software. EconPort currently provides software for running standard experiments used in teaching economics, including double auctions, extensive form games, normal form games, and one-sided auctions such as English, Dutch, first-price sealed-bid, and second-price sealed-bid auctions. New software is added whenever possible.

In addition to the actual experiment software, EconPort offers an infrastructure that simplifies configuring and running experiments. This infrastructure provides many "premade" configurations that can greatly reduce the time required to set up an experiment; these configurations are designed to illustrate and bring to life economic and game-theoretic principles. Also, experiment management tools and postexperiment analysis tools are provided to better support experiments originating on EconPort. Data from teaching and research experiments are archived on both EconPort and local machines used by experimenters. Users can archive their experiment data on the site.

An Underlying Educational Method

Advocacy of the use of the experiment software in EconPort for teaching economics is premised on published research that supports the effectiveness of this approach in teaching economics to undergraduates. EconPort supports this interactive approach by providing instructional material and an experimental economics software infrastructure. In addition to experiment software, EconPort incorporates an extensive array of created and collected artifacts, including the following.

A Searchable Portal

EconPort provides a searchable portal to existing online economics material. This gives users a central access point to instructional material for economics experiments, including economics content and motivation for the use of experiments in teaching, in addition to parameter sets designed to demonstrate specific economic principles. EconPort makes it easier to locate and use experimental software contained in EconPort and other facilities and to evaluate the relative merits of different software packages.

A Substantive Handbook

EconPort organizes much of its content by way of a handbook. The goal of the handbook is not simply to discuss economic concepts, but also to (1) provide a better understanding of the rationale for using economics experiments; (2) make it easier for users to select, understand, and use existing experimental tools; and (3) provide knowledge of how to interpret the results. The handbook is divided into major economics topic areas. Each handbook topic section provides (1) introductory concepts, (2) more advanced discussions, (3) experimental research in the area, (4) citations and suggested additional reading, and (5) related online resources.

A Glossary of Economics Terms

EconPort contains a glossary of economics terms. The glossary provides definitions of terms written by both the EconPort insider team and outside contributors. Outsider-provided artifacts include "Econterms"— a glossary of over 1,300 economics terms—and the "Experimental Economics Glossary" created by the University of Mannheim Experimental Economics Laboratory. The glossary is easy to search and linked to the handbook.

Other Collections

As a digital library, EconPort collects many types of artifacts created by outsiders. EconPort collects information on hundreds of economics resources found on the Internet, including off-site experiment software, interactive online tutorials, and essays on a variety of economics topics. EconPort provides (1) a single web portal to access these resources, (2) comprehensive search capabilities, (3) exposure to the National Science Digital Library, and (4) concept integration from these collected artifacts to the EconPort handbook.

EconPort as a (Globally Consumable) Local Public Good

EconPort is freely available on the Internet to every person in the world. In practical terms, this means that the economics educational content of EconPort can be consumed at a price of zero by anyone who reads and understands English and has access to a modern computer, with a browser, that is connected to the Internet. Furthermore, consumption of the central educational content of the experiment software requires the existence of a group of individuals, in communication with each other, each of whom satisfies the preceding qualifications and also has an interest in and ability to coordinate the use of the interactive experiment software to implement an economics experiment. Thus EconPort, even more than typical digital libraries without interactive content, is a public good available to be consumed only by some communities of users. In that sense, it is a local public good, albeit one that can be consumed by local communities that might possibly exist worldwide, or at least in all parts of the world with institutions of higher education.

EconPort as an Associational Knowledge Commons

As explained above, looked at from the demand or consumption side, EconPort is a local public good. We will now examine the supply side of EconPort. As is typical of digital libraries, the supply side of EconPort is best understood as a knowledge commons. Explanation of the particular type of commons that is characteristic of a digital library is helped by the distinction between a *libertarian* commons and an *associational* commons that is drawn by Levine in his contribution to this book. Open-source software is a supply-side example of a libertarian commons in that anyone is free to contribute content. In contrast, the supply side of a digital library such as EconPort is an example of an associational commons, albeit one subsidized by taxpayers through the National Science Foundation.

The effort to develop EconPort began with the writing of a grant proposal to the National Science Foundation by faculty and staff of the Economic Science Laboratory and the Artificial Intelligence Lab at the University of Arizona with an author of this chapter (Cox) as principal investigator. The motivations for creating EconPort of the economists associated with the Economic Science Laboratory differed from the motivations of the information technology specialists associated with the

Artificial Intelligence Lab. These distinct motivations created difficulties that had to be overcome during the initial development phase of Econ-Port and, more importantly, have implications for the sustainability of EconPort that provide a specific example of a problem generic to digital libraries.

The information technologists' primary motivation was to create an OAI-compliant infrastructure for a digital library that was capable of supporting the "active objects" that constitute software for running experiments and that would provide a constituent part of the most recent stage in the development of the National Science Digital Library. This motivation implies a primary interest in the information technology content of the digital library and a possibly continuing interest in its further development that is *conditional* on the availability of funding for further work in information technology applications. The economists' principal motivation was to create a state-of-the-art experimental economics facility that would provide the early twenty-first century stage in the historical development of experimental economics laboratories examined above. This motivation implies a primary interest in the economics content of the digital library and an *unconditional* continuing interest in its further development and use.

The artifacts contained in the EconPort facility have been explained above. Some of these artifacts were created by economists from the Economic Science Laboratory, while other artifacts were collected and archived by those insider economists. The collected artifacts were, of course, created by "outsiders"—other economists not formally associated with the Economic Science Laboratory. These outsiders contribute content to EconPort by allowing its collection, but they exercise little control over the facility itself and were not originally motivated to create content for a specific digital library.

Incentives for ESL Insiders to Create EconPort

Funding of the initial grant allowed the ESL a way to showcase and offer its expertise over the Internet to outsiders. Traditionally, the costs associated with packaging and providing the expertise possessed by a research facility may be too high to do it solely for the free benefit of outsiders. Previous NSF projects have focused on funding the development of specific types of software. In contrast, we saw an advantage not to develop software, but instead a framework that can host and offer a menu of software made by the ESL, as well as others. This framework can then function as a virtual facility offering many different types of experimental economics software resources on the Internet.

Incentives for ESL Insiders to Continue Supporting EconPort

Since the ESL sees EconPort as a showcase product and a way to increase awareness of what ESL has always done, there is an incentive to support the project even after the period of initial funding. This arrangement of a research facility backing such a project may not be typical, because not all research facilities may possess the technical computer skills needed to maintain such a site. However, there is a definite advantage in terms of sustainability of having a research facility invest its resources in such a project—in this case, there is likely to be continued interest in the project even if direct funding for digital libraries is no longer available.

Further, we see the site as a resource we will indeed actively use within our facility, and not just an archive created for the general public. This gives us the incentive to not only work on the site while we are supported by the NSF, but also after the funding period. Obviously, the level of external support we receive will indeed influence the amount of support we are able to provide in the future.

Incentives for ESL Insiders to Provide Software to Outsiders

ESL has made available many of its software applications over the years. In the past, this practice was only marginally successful, because the technical knowledge required to make full use of the software was relatively costly. This led to relatively little incentive for the ESL to actively share our software, since the support during and after the transfer was costly.

The people in the past most able to make use of our software tools were those at one of the few other experimental economics labs, because there was sufficient in-house technical and experimental economics knowledge. However, there were likely reasons why some labs had an incentive not to use software developed by others—the recipient lab perhaps would not want to give the impression that it was unable to create its own software.

With the development of EconPort as a platform from which experiment software can be run, the marginal cost of offering experiment software is now much lower—both for the ESL and for other developers. EconPort was designed to allow new pieces of experiment software to be easily added. Experiment software need not even reside on the

EconPort server; instead, EconPort can simply serve as an organizer and portal for the integrated software.

Incentive for the Artificial Intelligence Lab to Work on the Project

The incentive for this group, which is likely a very similar incentive for most groups taking on such a project, is the existence of grant funding. Additionally, the AI team was motivated by the challenge created by the technological problems of providing a framework for experiments, or providing a digital library for nonstandard digital resources such as experiment software. However, the AI team does not use the EconPort facility in its teaching or research, in contrast to the economists on the ESL team, who do use this facility in their continuing professional work. Thus the AI team does not have an incentive for maintenance and further development of EconPort, as an end in itself, in contrast to the ESL team, which has a professional self-interest in sustaining the facility.

Incentives for Outsiders to Contribute Software

Some owners of artifacts have contributed them to be hosted by EconPort—for example, the economics glossaries now fully integrated into the facility. In contrast, outsiders have not been contributing software to EconPort to date, even though there have been invitations to contribute—and given that the Application Program Interface makes the facility accommodating to a variety of software programming languages. This problem in expanding the association of contributors could be caused by several factors, such as potential contributors fearing that their work would become disassociated from their identities when the material is integrated into EconPort. Also, potential contributors could fear that EconPort will not be sustained, and that associating with such a site would not be wise—a likely problem for any collection activity, especially when the project is in its earlier stages.

To encourage contributions, we promise to give accreditation to contributors and preserve identification of artifacts with their creators. Examples of this are provided by the glossaries EconPort hosts. Given the, to date, limited success of this approach, we employ a secondary method to collect material that does not require the content to be hosted on EconPort—we collect pointers to the location of the information elsewhere on the Internet, and provide extra classification information with the pointer. This allows us to virtually collect information across the

Internet without the requirement to host the material on the EconPort server. Subsequently, EconPort serves as a central gateway for a variety of annotated links covering microeconomics and relays this information. Additionally, this classification information is OAI-compliant, meaning that OAI harvesting engines (such as NSDL and Yahoo) can collect it and repackage it within search engine databases.

Sustainability: Fostering a User Community and Workshop Dissemination

Fostering and supporting a user community is a strategy that will help to ensure success of the facility. This process can encourage development of a group of scholars who care about the site and thus become potential contributors of artifacts. We can identify users that have a particularly strong interest in the site, and thus target invitations to contribute. EconPort tracks users in two general ways. Professors must register to make use of the experiment software, because this allows us to keep their information private and available only to them via a login procedure. As of June 2006, over 500 people have registered to use the EconPort software. Since we began tracking site usage in February 2005, EconPort has averaged over 300 sessions per day (a session consists of all the pages viewed by a user on a single visit to a website).

One way that we will strive to foster more informed users is by holding a series of workshops funded by a new NSF national dissemination grant. The planned national dissemination consists of a series of workshops during 2006–2009, a few at our home university and more in association with professional conferences. The workshops will teach invited faculty how to use the online educational resources of EconPort in teaching economics at their home universities. Workshop participants who are interested will be invited to contribute data measuring effectiveness of the use of experiments in teaching, as measured in matched sections taught with and without experiments, similar to the 2004 Emerson and Taylor study.

We are currently developing additional resources on EconPort to allow our users to interact as an online community. We are considering several options to aid us in this, including

• Forum software to allow our users to interact with us and one another on discussion boards on our site.

• Tools to allow users to build and annotate custom sets of resources on our site, and then share these sets with one another. These information sets could cover a specific topic used in a classroom, a specific type of experiment, and so on.

• Creation of a better way for users to contribute materials to the site. Currently, we have a feedback mechanism that allows anyone to suggest new information for the site, but we would like to expand and automate this procedure, to make it easier and less costly to add new information that site users identify. The difficulty with doing this is obviously quality control.

Conclusion

The development of the Internet has made many types of resources available to large numbers of people—often for free. In academia, many projects have been undertaken to digitize, archive, and present information artifacts in ways that ease access to these resources. Such projects often face sustainability problems, however, when initial funding has ended. By engaging in a large-scale project to create and maintain a digital library for microeconomics education, the EconPort team at the Economic Science Laboratory applied its expertise in microeconomics, experimental economics, and information technology in a way that was consistent with its professional self-interest. Having professionals associated with a research institution such as the Economic Science Laboratory create and maintain such an information commons may be an important factor in sustainability, especially if the professionals affiliated with the facility actively use the resource in their normal activities.

As discussed in many of the earlier chapters, sustainability of digital libraries is a serious problem once initial funding by external granting agencies has been fully utilized. As evidenced by recent developments with the EconPort team, universities are not always willing to allocate sufficient funds to ensure the long-term sustainability of knowledge commons, even when they have been evaluated highly. In response to severe budget cuts at the Eller College of the University of Arizona, the authors of this chapter have relocated to the Andrew Young School of Policy Studies (AYSPS) at Georgia State University. Responsibility for maintenance and development of EconPort will remain with the authors and next be housed at the new Experimental Economics Center (http://excen.gsu.edu) at AYSPS, ensuring the continuing provision of

EconPort for the near future. We will be working with colleagues at other universities on the central issues of long-term sustainability beyond the professional lives of the creators of this knowledge commons. We hope that we can report in the future that we have developed an effective strategy to make this digital library sustainable for the long run.

References

Bergstrom, Theodore, and John Miller. 2000. *Experiments with Economic Principles: Microeconomics*. New York: McGraw-Hill.

Chamberlin, Edward H. 1948. "An Experimental Imperfect Market." *Journal of Political Economy* 56:95–108.

Cox, James C. 2004. "How to Identify Trust and Reciprocity." *Games and Economic Behavior* 46:260–281.

Cox, James C., Daniel Friedman, and Steven Gjerstad. Forthcoming. "A Tractable Model of Reciprocity and Fairness." *Games and Econimic Behavior*.

Emerson, Tisha, and Beck Taylor. 2004. "Comparing Student Achievement across Experimental and Lecture-Oriented Sections of a Principles of Microeconomics Course." *Southern Economic Journal* 70:672–693.

Nash, John. 1950. "Equilibrium Points in N-Person Games." *Proceedings of the National Academy of Sciences, U.S.A.* 36:48–49.

Smith, Adam. [1759] 1976. *The Theory of Moral Sentiments*. Indianapolis: Liberty Classics.

Smith, Adam. [1776] 1937. *The Wealth of Nations*. New York: Modern Library.

Smith, Vernon L. 1962. "An Experimental Study of Competitive Market Behavior." *Journal of Political Economy* 70:111–137.

von Neumann, John, and Oskar Morgenstern. 1947. *Theory of Games and Economic Behavior*. Princeton, NJ: Princeton University Press.

Glossary

All glossary references are in chapter 3.

Adaptive systems Human systems that exhibit capacities to learn from experience and improve structure and outcomes over time.

Anticommons The potential *underuse* of scarce scientific resources caused by excessive intellectual property rights and overpatenting in biomedical research.

Archives Organizations dedicated to the mission of collecting, storing, preserving, and providing access to cultural, historical, scientific, and other kinds of records.

Artifacts Physical-resource units—discreet, observable, namable representations of ideas.

Associational commons Exists when some good is controlled or managed by a group.

Collaboratories Tool-oriented computing and communication systems to support scientific collaboration.

Collective action Two or more individuals needed to work together in order to accomplish an outcome.

Commodification Alternatively, *commoditization*; originally a Marxist term, the turning of a noncommercial object into a market commodity; related to *commercialization* and *corporatization*.

Common-pool resource One of four types of economic goods. CPRs are either natural or human-made, where one person's use subtracts from another's and where it is difficult to exclude users.

Common property A legal regime; a jointly owned legal set of property rights.

Commons A general term that refers to a resource shared by a group of people and often vulnerable to social dilemmas.

Commons-based production When no one uses exclusive rights to organize an effort or capture its value, and when cooperation is achieved through social mechanisms other than price signals or managerial directions. Large-scale instances of such cooperation include *peer production* (Benkler 2004).

Design principles   Characteristics of robust, long-enduring common-pool resource institutions (Ostrom 1990).

Efficiency   Production, management, and use of a resource involving the greatest net benefits.

Enclosure   Originally from the European Enclosure Movement, which privatized common agricultural fields and grazing pastures used by peasants and frequently put them in the hands of the elite.

Equity   Appropriation from, and contribution to, the maintenance of a resource that is considered just by those involved.

Facilities   Resource systems that store artifacts and make them available.

Framework   A theoretical scaffolding helping to organize a research process, rather than a model or a theory. It helps researchers know which questions to ask.

Free riding   Occurs when one person seeks their self-interest at the expense of others by not contributing to a joint effort when the person will benefit from the contributions of others.

Hyperchange   Rapid, exponential, discontinuous, and chaotic change (Barrett 1998).

Ideas   Nonphysical resource flow units: coherent thoughts, mental images, creative visions, and innovative information.

Incentives   Benefits, or reduced costs, that motivate a decision maker in favor of, or against, a particular choice. http://www.wwnorton.com/stiglitzwalsh/economics/glossary.htm

Institutional analysis   The analysis of how institutions are formed, how they operate and change, and how they influence behaviors and outcomes (Ostrom 2005).

Institutional repositories   Archives of a university, research center, or other educational, cultural, or scientific organization that aim to collect, store, preserve, and provide access to the digital products of its members.

Institutions   Rules affecting two or more persons that specify who decides what in relation to whom (Oakerson and Walker 1995).

Intellectual property rights   Legal rights to intangible property—patents, trademarks, copyrights, and trade secrets. http://usinfo.state.gov/products/pubs/intelprp/

Libertarian commons   Where anyone has a right to use (and sometimes also to contribute to) some public resource.

Mertonianism   From Robert Merton's *On the Social Structure of Science*; generally used to describe a process of free, open inquiry, without crippling secrecy norms or major property claims, strongly reliant on the process of peer-reviewed publication and citation to drive hypotheses closer to an underlying objective reality.

Nestedness   Layered clusters of actions and arenas.

Open access   *Of land and tangible property*: Free entry to all without effective rules or restrictions.

Of knowledge and information: Free, online access to information without most copyright and licensing restrictions.

Path dependency   Originally from new institutional economics, the phenomenon of outcomes being shaped by a previous sequence of decisions—that is, when outcomes are strongly affected by their past history.

Polycentricity   Decentralized, alternative areas of authority—with multiple levels of rule and decision making.

Preservation   A process that requires institutional commitment, technical ability, and economic means of ensuring that designated resources are available to future generations.

Prisoner's dilemma   A formal model of the tragedy of a social dilemma. A classic game with two players in the roles of criminals being interviewed separately by police. If either gives information to the police, the other will get a long sentence. Either player can Cooperate (with the other player by being silent) or Defect (by giving information to the police). The game illustrates the problems of collective action and irrational group behavior when trust and reciprocity have little opportunity to develop and be expressed.

Property rights   Legally sanctioned rules that affect the use of resources and the corresponding assignment of costs and benefits. (Libecap 1989, 229)

Public domain   The realm of material—ideas, images, sounds, discoveries, facts, texts—that is unprotected by intellectual property rights and free for all to use or build on. (Boyle, http://www.law.duke.edu/cspd/about.html)

Public goods   A good that is available to all and where one person's use does not subtract from another's use.

Reciprocity   Where an individual contributes to the welfare of others with an expectation that others will do likewise, but without a fully contingent quid pro quo (Oakerson 1993).

Repository   An organizational or epistemic digital archive that collects, stores, and usually distributes its contributors' documents.

Resource Systems   See *Facilities*

Resource Units   See *Ideas* and *Artifacts*

Rules   Formal and informal prescriptions for what one must do, must not do, or may do. Rules are nested in constitutional, collective-choice, and operational levels.

Scholarly communication   How scholars in any field (e.g., physical, biological, social, and behavioral sciences, humanities, technology) use and disseminate information through formal and informal channels.

Self-governance   The ability of people to exercise and control the prerogatives of rulership in a society, requiring both knowledge and will on the one hand, and supporting and consistent institutional arrangements on the other hand.

Social capital   The collective value of social networks (i.e., who people know) and the inclinations that arise from these networks to do things for each other (i.e., the norms of reciprocity) (from Putnam 2000).

Stewardship   Taking on the care and responsibility of a resource to preserve it for future generations.

Subtractability   Where one person's use subtracts from the available benefits for others (alternatively, *rivalrousness*).

Sustainability   The persistence of the integrity and structure of any system over time (from Costanza et al. 2001).

Tragedy of the commons   Metaphor based on Garrett Hardin's eponymous 1968 *Science* article has come to symbolize the degradation of the environment that is expected whenever many individuals use a scarce resource in common without accepted and enforced rules to limit their use.

Index

Action arena, 16, 44, 45, 49, 53–57, 289
Academic journals. *See* Journals
Adaptive systems, 64, 66, 68. *See also* Robust Systems
definition, 349
Advocacy, 32, 86, 102, 193–194, 257
Alienability, 29, 33, 52–53
Amazon.com, 99, 196–197, 252
one-click method, 252
search Inside the Book, 196
American Anthropological Association, 95–96
American Library Association, 91, 101–102
Anderson, James, 258
Andrew W. Mellon Foundation, the, ix–x, 96, 100, 107, 148, 156, 160, 161, 328
AnthroCommons, 95
AnthroSource, 95
Anticommons, 11, 61. *See also* Enclosure; Overpatenting; Patents; Tragedy of the Commons
definition, 349
Apache Web Server, 278, 284
Aquifer Project, 324–325
Archives, 18, 20, 100, 106, 108, 140, 149–156, 159–60, 311. *See also* arXiv.org; Digital Libraries; Libraries; Self-archiving

community-based archives, 155–159, 161
consumer, 155, 323
costs, 173
definition, 159–160
digital, 315
disappearing act, 161
global archives, 54
Internet Archive, 148, 151
libraries as, 312
open access archives, 187–188, 190–192
Open Archives Initiative, 48, 97, 160, 173, 315, 338
organizational, 152–153
preservation, 322–323
producer, 153–155, 157, 323
repositories, 190
specialist archives, 133–134, 140
Artifacts, 46–48, 53–54, 64, 106, 127, 149, 232–234, 236, 250, 260, 336–340, 342, 344–346
definition, 47–48, 350
Artificial Intelligence Lab, 333, 341, 342, 344
ARTstor, 161
ArXiv.org, 98, 110, 317–318
Ashcroft, John, 90
Association of College and Research Libraries (ACRL), 102
Association of Research Libraries (ARL), 102

Associational Commons, 19, 50,
    249–251, 263, 341
  definition, 251, 349
Atkinson, Ross, 321–322, 324–325
Attributes of the community. *See*
    Community attributes
Authors (as information providers)
    13, 18, 21, 45, 52–53, 55, 59,
    64–66, 93, 98–99, 102,
    107–109, 153–154, 174–178,
    182, 184, 186–196, 222–223,
    247, 283, 285, 287, 293, 295,
    319–322. *See also* Copyright
    (holders); Faculty; Scholarly
    communication
Attribution, 295

Baen Free Library, 196–197
Barnes, Peter, 31
Benkler, Yochai, 13, 93, 128
Berghel, Hal, 315
Berlin Declaration, 56–57
Berry, Wendell, 34
BioMed Central (BMC), 96, 107,
    183
  BMC's *Journal of Biology*, 192
BioOne, 96–97
Biophysical characteristics, 45–48,
    286–287
Blog, 36, 61, 105, 316
Bolar Amendment, 239–241
Bollier, David, xiii, 15, 93
Borgman, Christine, 312
Boundaries, 5, 7, 11, 20, 45–46, 98,
    100, 104, 106, 124, 128, 152,
    236, 298, 311, 313, 317, 327
Boyle, James, ix, xi, 12, 17, 30, 102,
    105, 109, 251, 263
Boyte, Harry, 247, 265
Brown, Pat, 96
Brown, Sheridan, 187, 192
Buck, Susan, 31
Budapest Open Access Initiative
    (BOAI), 96, 136, 171
Bush, George W., 91

Caesar, Julius, 45
Card, Andrew, 91
Carson, Rachel, 30
Center for the Public Domain, 103
Chamberlin, Edward, 336
Chemistry, 319
Chen, Hsinchun, 334
Children's Internet Protection Act,
    90, 102
Citizenship, x–xi, 16, 19, 86, 93,
    247, 254, 257, 263, 268
Civil society, 112, 251, 267–268
Club goods (includes toll goods), 9,
    159, 162, 300, 302
Coalition for Networked Information
    (CNI), 97
Coase, Ronald, 222–224
Code (computer), x–xi, 13, 51, 252,
    280, 282, 285–288, 294–295,
    298
Collaboration, x–xi, 18–19, 34–35,
    59, 66, 94–97, 99, 101,
    103–106, 147, 215, 247, 259,
    264, 277–281, 286–292, 295,
    298–299, 301–303, 311–312,
    315, 317, 320, 324, 326–327,
    329, 334. *See also* Peer
    production
Collaboratories, 13, 20, 326
  definition, 349
Collective Action, 5–6, 10–11,
    13–15, 18, 21, 43, 52, 58, 86,
    93, 100, 103, 105–106, 108,
    110, 146, 247, 254, 256, 261,
    280, 303
  definition, 349
  organizations, 206
Committee on Institutional
    Cooperation (CIC), 108
Commodification, 4–5, 12, 14, 28,
    49, 61, 194, 219, 229, 232, 235
  definition, 349
Common good, 5, 8, 18, 94, 105,
    109, 184, 254, 334. *See also*
    Public good

Common Information Environment
Group, 99
Common Pool Resources, 5–7, 9–10,
15–16, 43, 62, 95, 100, 146,
149, 250, 261. *See also* Club
goods; Commons; Design
principles; Public goods
definition, 349
Common Property, 5–6, 87, 94, 182,
279–281, 283, 302
definition, 349
Commons. *See* Anticommons;
Associational Commons;
Common Pool Resources;
Cornucopia of the Commons;
Digital Commons; Global
Commons; Financing the
Commons; Libertarian
Commons; Public goods,
Tragedy of the Commons
definition, 349
Commons-based production, 13, 35,
93, 129
definition, 349
Commons history, 4–7, 10–13, 28,
87, 130, 231, 278
Communication Decency Act (CDA),
102
Community attributes, 284–286, 287,
289
Community-based archives,
155–157
Complexity, 5, 9, 59, 66–68
Compliance, 57, 61, 66–67, 188. *See
also* Noncompliance
Concurrent Versioning System (CVS),
287–288
Conflict, 4, 43, 59, 61, 66, 67, 219,
231, 260, 284
Conflict resolution, 7, 11, 298
Congestion, 4, 28, 47, 339
Conservation Commons, 27, 98
Consumers, 89, 94, 129, 140,
151–158, 162, 212, 214, 224,
268, 274, 320, 323, 335

Consumerism, 268
Copyleft, 281–284, 291, 302. *See
also* Stallman, Richard
Copyright, 13, 16, 17, 18, 48, 52,
53, 99, 102, 110, 125–127, 129,
134, 139, 154, 161, 172,
175–182, 187, 188, 194,
211–216, 221–222, 225–237,
242, 252, 280–283, 288, 295,
316, 350, 351. *See also* Copyleft;
Copyright Term Extension Act;
Digital Millennium Copyright
Act (DMCA); Fair Use; First
Sale; Intellectual Property Rights;
Patent Law; Trademark Law
holders, 125, 174, 176, 179–182,
188, 197, 214, 221–222, 235,
238, 291
industry, 90
infringement, 236–238, 293
law, 35, 47, 51, 52, 86, 89–90, 96,
97, 111, 125–127, 159, 161,
176, 193, 209, 211–216,
220–222, 228, 235–237, 242,
278, 281–282
protection, 17, 36–37, 149
restrictions, 17, 136, 171
terms, 10, 89, 97, 125–127, 137,
230
transfer agreements, 191, 235
Copyright Clearance Center, 222
Copyright Term Extension Act, 13,
89
Cornell University, 98, 107
Cornucopia of the Commons,
34
Cost-benefit analysis, 33, 196
Costs, 44, 55, 59, 64–65, 107,
132–133, 136, 162, 182, 257,
263, 278, 301, 342. *See also*
Digitization, costs of; Peer
review, costs of; Price barriers;
Publication costs; Subscriptions;
Transaction costs
Cox, James, xi, 21, 334

Crane, Diana, 313, 318
Creative Commons, 37, 52, 53,
    102–103, 291–293, 295
Creativity, 226. *See also* Innovation
Cronin, Blaise, 57
Customs, 213, 220, 221, 222,
    224–225

Da Vinci, Leonardo, 217
Davenport, Thomas H., 8
David, Paul A., 277
Degradation, 5, 28, 61
Democracy (includes democratic
    systems), 13, 30, 49, 85–86,
    92–93, 104, 105–106, 140, 229,
    232–234, 253–256, 261, 263,
    267, 314, 334. *See also*
    Citizenship; Governance; Self-
    governance
  discourse, 95, 111
  libraries role in, 16, 85, 93, 109,
    111
  participation (*see* Participation, in a
    democracy)
  processes, x–xi
  principles, 86
  values, 38, 232
Design Principles, 7, 68, 124,
    135–136, 138–139
  definition, 350
Diffuse Libraries, 103
Digital Commons, 13, 14, 49, 60
Digital Divide, 61, 65, 92, 183
Digital libraries, xi, 20, 65, 97,
    98–99, 106, 321–324, 329,
    333–334, 336, 338, 340–344,
    346–347. *See also* Archives;
    Repositories; Libraries
  ArXiv.org, 98, 110, 317–318
  Baen Free Library, 196–197
  Digital Library of the Commons,
    ix, 31, 59, 98
  EconPort, 333–347
  eScholarship, 97
  Public Library of Science (PLoS),
    96, 183, 192

Digital Library of the Commons, ix,
    31, 59, 98
Digital Millennium Copyright Act
    (DMCA), 13, 51, 89
Digital Opportunity Investment Trust
    (DO IT), 99
Digital Promise Project, 99
Digital Rights Management (DRM),
    37, 51, 86, 89, 96, 182
Digitization, 87
  costs of, 172
Directors Guild of America, 221–222
DISPUTE, 97
Distance learning, 110, 293, 294,
    296, 300, 301. *See also* Teaching
Distributed Open Digital Library
    (DODL), 99
Dred Scott Decision, 230
DSpace, 56, 64, 97, 153, 301, 322
Du, Jianxia, 258

eBay, 28, 335
Economic efficiency. *See* Efficiency
Economic goods, 5, 8–10, 16, 34, 52,
    94, 146, 149, 151, 159, 182,
    211, 250–251, 254, 256–260,
    265–267, 278, 300, 311, 315.
    See also Club goods; Common-
    pool resources; Private goods;
    Public goods
Economic Science Laboratory, 333,
    335, 337, 341, 342, 346
Economics. *See* Economic goods;
    Experimental economics;
    Microeconomics
EconPort, 20, 27, 333–347
EconWPA, 98
Education, 49, 57, 339, 161, 162,
    215. *See also* Distance learning;
    Engaged university; Teaching;
    Universities
  civic, 257
  higher, 42, 88, 156, 360–363
  institutions, 109
  policy, 267
  public, 38

Educational psychology, 226–227, 235

Efficiency, 3, 6, 62, 64–65, 182, 211, 223, 286, 336
definition, 350

Eisen, Michael, 96

Eldred v. Ashcroft, 89, 230–231

Electronic journals, 14, 294–297, 300, 317. *See also* Journals
preservation of, 148–163 (*see also* LOCKSS; Portico)
vs. traditional journals, 318

Ellickson, Robert, 221

Emrich, Frederick, 112

Enclosure, 4, 5, 12, 32, 38, 60–61, 85–112, 181, 188, 252. *See also* Anticommons; Second Enclosure Movement; Tragedy of the Commons
definition, 350

Encryption, 36, 89

Encyclopaedia Britannica, 129

Engaged university, 260–263

Eprints Open Source Software, 57

Equity, 6, 29, 43, 61–62, 64–66, 95
definition, 350

Érudit, 97

eScholarship, 97

Ethics of Memory, 163

Evaluative criteria, 62–66

Exclusion, 213–219, 224, 229–230

Executive order 13233, 91

Experimental economics, 335–343, 346

Facilities, 47, 103, 106, 250, 328
definition, 350
information, 336
provision of, 65

Faculty, 10, 54–58, 61, 63, 85, 92, 97–98, 101–108, 110, 153–154, 185–187, 189–190, 192–194, 248, 260–263, 268, 294, 299–300, 341, 345. *See also* Authors; Teaching

Fair use, 37, 51, 89, 93, 102, 110, 176, 177, 178, 182, 215, 216, 218, 221, 224, 236–237. *See also* Copyright; First Sale

File sharing, 89–90, 212, 234–238. *See also* Peer-to-peer

Film, 37, 124–127

Filters, 90, 102, 183

First amendment, 110, 215–216, 218, 232

First sale doctrine, 37, 177, 178, 182, 215. *See also* Copyright; Fair use

Fiscal equivalence, 62, 65–66

Flickr, 36

Food and Drug Administration, 214, 239

Fragaszy, Dorothy, 226–227

Fragmentation, 328

Framework. *See* Institutional Analysis and Development Framework
definition, 350

Franklin, Benjamin, 182, 250

Free/Libre and Open Source Software (FOSS), 15, 19–20, 34–35, 43, 48, 97, 128, 131, 134–135, 138–139, 153, 173, 195, 225, 277–303. *See also* Code (computer); Concurrent Versioning System (CVS); Intellectual property rights, and software; Linux; GNU; Stallman, Richard
collaboration, 277–281, 286–292, 295, 298–299, 300, 301–303 (*see also* Collaboration)
financing, 298–302
licensing, 280, 281–284
management of, 297–298
as a model for the science commons, 288–302
volunteerism in the development of (*see* Volunteerism, and open source software)

Free market, 27, 35, 214, 229

Free riding, 4–5, 10, 33, 58, 129, 131, 150, 159, 186, 252, 337
    definition, 350
Freedom of Information Act, 90
Freedom principles, 282, 294
Frischmann, Brett, 210–211

Game theory, 11, 334, 339. *See also* Prisoner's dilemma
    non-zero-sum game, 11
    zero-sum game, 267
Genetic information, 28, 33
Ghosh, Shubha, 13, 147
Ginsparg, Paul, 98, 318
GIS, 258
Global commons, 4, 10, 13, 32, 41
GNU, 35, 281–282. *See also* Free/libre and Open Source Software (FOSS); Linux
    Free Documentation License (GFDL), 291–293
    Public License (GPL), 282–283, 295
Gone with the Wind, 214
Goods. *See* Common-pool resources; Economic goods; Private goods, Public goods
Google, 108, 124, 129, 134, 184, 252–253
Google Print, 99
Gordon and Betty Moore Foundation, the, 96
Governance, 5, 7, 15, 19, 29, 33, 36, 43, 51, 66–67, 86, 94, 95, 104–106, 110, 211–212, 225, 232–238, 241–242, 284, 297–298, 329. *See also* Self-governance
    democratic, 106, 232–235
    local, 256, 263–264, 282
    project, 281, 283–284, 287
Governing the Commons, 31
Government, 11, 16, 17, 32, 62, 86, 87, 102, 111, 151, 183, 232–234, 253, 255, 263–264,

266, 286. *See also* Governance; Self-governance
    funding, 87, 136, 149, 150, 180, 187–188, 232, 266, 294, 299, 301
    information, 13, 14, 86, 87, 90–94, 100, 102, 177, 234
    property, 53
    publications, 87, 91, 100
    restrictions, 91, 183, 213, 253
Grafton, Anthony, 145–146, 148
Gray literature, 177
Greenpeace, 30
Greenstein, Daniel, 99
Grokster, 89. *See also MGM vs. Grokster*

Hardin, Garrett, 10–11, 13, 15, 32, 92, 95, 150–151. *See also* Tragedy of the commons
Harnad, Stevan, 56, 98
Heller, Michael, 11
Hess, Charlotte, ix, xi, 28, 94–95, 106, 147, 249–250, 255, 280, 284, 289, 297, 312
Hesse, Carla, 231
Hewlett-Packard Labs, 97
Hissam, S. et al., 285
Hobbes, Thomas, 150
Holmes, Justice Oliver Wendell, 225, 226, 227–228
Holocaust Museum, 233
Humanities, 99, 124, 172, 174, 234, 319–320
Hyland, Ken, 313
Hyperchange, 9, 59–60, 312
    definition, 350

IAD framework. *See* Institutional analysis and development framework
Ideas, 7, 8, 9, 47–48, 94, 106, 112, 232, 250, 260, 290, 311, 313
    access to, 85, 96
    and copyright, 17, 229
    definition, 350

exchange of, 18, 93, 102, 103, 105, 109, 111, 211
free flow of, 102, 231, 252
preservation of, 103, 105
as private goods, 300
Imitation, 235
and the creation of the knowledge commons, 211–212, 225, 237
and the creation of knowledge, 226–228, 234
and intellectual property rights, 19, 225–226, 227, 228, 238, 252
and pharmaceutical research, 239–242
Incentives, 11–12, 50, 64, 108, 138, 163, 182, 184, 192, 210, 250–252, 290–291, 294, 334, 342–344. *See also* Motivation
and copyright, 125–126, 129, 149, 176
definition, 350
and free riding, 150 (*see also* Free-riding)
and intellectual property rights, 215, 217, 223
and journal submissions, 18, 174, 176, 182, 185, 186, 189, 191–192 (*see also* Journals)
and the market, 158–159
nonmonetary, 134, 174, 176
and open access, 55–56, 59, 189, 192, 210, 294 (*see also* Open access (OA); Repositories)
for preservation, 147, 152, 154, 158–159, 163, 323
structures, 138, 289, 291, 320
Indiana University, 57, 101, 261. *See also* Workshop in Political Theory and Policy Analysis
Informatics, 328
Information Industry Association (IIA), 87
Information provision, 59, 61, 64, 65, 95, 128, 130, 132, 149

Infrastructure, x–xi, 47, 66–68, 92, 107, 152, 211, 286–287, 295, 297–303, 329, 339, 342
cultural, 232–234, 236, 238
Ingelfinger, Franz, 191
Ingelfinger Rule, 191
Innovation, 93, 217, 288, 312, 313, 316, 321
stimulation of, 35, 38, 85, 94, 154, 231
thwarting of, 91
Institutional Analysis, 41–42
definition, 350
Institutional Analysis and Development (IAD) Framework, 41–68, 279–280
Institutional change, 68
Institutional repositories. *See* Repositories
definition, 350
Institutions, ix, 7, 41–42, 46, 57, 67, 103–104, 163, 217–218, 232, 256, 263, 265–267, 294, 335. *See also* Design principles; Norms; Rules
definition, 350
Intellectual property rights, x, xi, 10, 11, 52–53, 175, 176, 209–242, 252, 280, 283. *See also* Copyright; Fair Use; First Sale; Patents; Overpatenting
absence of, 138
and copyleft, 283, 291
definition, 350
digital, 139, 161
education about, 255
expansion of, 10, 11, 12, 52, 230
legislation, 13, 14, 161
relinquishing of in royalty-free literature, 175, 176
as rules, 52–53
and software, 277, 278–279
theory of, 138
intellectual public domain. *See* Public domain

Interdisciplinarity, ix, 4–6, 9, 12, 41,
    59, 61, 247, 262, 289, 325–326
International Association for the
    Study of Common Property
    (IASCP), 6, 31
Internet, 90, 132, 138–139, 236,
    252, 267. *See also* World Wide
    Web
  access to, 91–92
  as a commons, 30, 35
  as a shared resource, 4
Internet Archive, 99
Interoperability, 13, 61–62, 325
Invisible Colleges, 313–314, 318
iPod, 246
Irving, Larry, 92
Ithaka, 156

Java, 290, 339
Journals, 262, 288–289, 315. *See
    also* Electronic journals; Peer
    review; Publication costs;
    Publishing Industry;
    Subscriptions
  censorship of, 91
  humanities, 319–320
  open access, 55, 56–57, 95–97,
    136–137, 171–197
  scientific, 88, 90–91, 317–319
  and self-archiving, 98
  subscription costs of, 16, 88, 36–37,
    87–88, 107–108, 195
JSTOR, 156, 161, 162

Kahle, Brewster, 148, 151
KaZaA, 89
Keynes, John Maynard, 27, 31
Kling, Rob, 317
Knowledge
  advancement of, 175, 313, 320
  definition, 7–9
  dissemination of, 56, 58, 62, 86, 98,
    100, 104, 106, 147, 210, 219,
    258, 313, 322, 324, 333, 340
  ecosystem, x, 3, 14–15, 109
  indigenous, x, 8, 62

  local, 58, 247, 255, 262
  management, 211, 329
  public, 91, 247
  reliable, 129, 131, 146, 155, 257,
    277
  as a resource, 3, 5, 7–10, 49, 65,
    101, 110, 147, 247
  scientific, 55, 62, 278, 292,
    301–302, 319, 327
Knowledge commons history, 3–4,
    12, 15, 18, 20, 28, 34, 134, 139,
    231, 277
Kranich, Nancy, xi, 13, 16, 48, 57,
    60, 147, 320

Land-use change modeling, 289–294,
    296–297
Lavoie, Brian, 151
Lawrence, Steve, 186
Learned societies, 96, 193, 319
Leopold, Aldo, 30
Lessons learned, x, 43–44, 62, 67,
    68, 98, 111, 138, 261, 264, 298,
    303
Lessig, Lawrence, 102, 161
Levine, Peter, xi, 49–50
Lexis/Nexis, 14, 88
Libertarian commons, 19, 250–253,
    341
  definition, 350
Librarians, 56, 59, 85–86, 105–106,
    109–110, 133–134, 184, 190,
    193, 314, 328, 333. *See also*
    American Library Association
  as stewards, 13, 92, 94–95, 98,
    101–105, 111, 190–191
Libraries, x–xi, 4, 13, 36, 46, 47, 61,
    64, 65, 126, 139, 156–157, 173,
    193, 250. *See also* Archives;
    Digital libraries; Repositories
  access to, 251
  as catalysts, 20, 311, 326–327
  as control zones, 321–323
  as cornerstones of democracy, 16,
    85, 93, 109, 111 (*see also*
    Democracy)

public, 90
research, 27, 85–86, 87, 88–89,
101, 103–108, 147, 153–154,
173–174, 301, 311–312
as systems and services,
323–326
Library of Congress, 124–126, 128,
139, 156
LibLicense-L, 154–155
Licenses, 14, 37, 51, 88–89, 100,
102, 107, 147, 157, 160, 240,
280, 282–283, 291–296, 302,
321, 326. *See also* Creative
Commons; LibLicense-L
Click Through, 37
Open-Content, 279, 292
restrictions, 17, 88, 96, 110
Shrink-Wrap, 37, 88
software, 281
Lindbloom, Charles, 229
Linux, 35, 278, 284, 285, 286, 287,
298
Litman, Jessica, 128, 129
Living Reviews, 316
Lochner v. New York, 230–231
LOCKSS, 100, 157–159
Logic of Collective Action, 10
Lougee, Wendy Pradt, xii, 103–104,
147
Ludwig von Mises Institute, 196
Lynch, Clifford, xii, 61, 97, 103,
154, 323, 328

Machlup, Fritz, 8
Mannheim, Karl, 255–256
Mansbridge, Jane, 261
Margalit, Avishai, 163
Massachusetts Institute of
Technology, 56, 64, 97, 107,
153, 281. *See also* DSpace
McKim, Geoffrey, 317
Medline, 136
Merck v. Integra, 214, 239–242
Merton, Robert, 17, 124
Mertonianism, 123–124, 135
definition, 350

MGM v. Grokster, 235–238
Microeconomics, 20, 333–335, 338,
345–347
Microsoft, 99, 255, 286
Mitchell, Margaret, 214
Models, 11, 134, 136, 150, 162–163,
223, 257, 261, 268, 311–312,
315, 320. *See also Commons*;
Tragedy of the commons;
Prisoner's dilemma
business, 156–157, 159,
161–163, 172–174, 192, 236,
300–302
economic, 334–336
vs. frameworks, 42
land-use change, 279, 289–291,
296–297 (*see also* UrbanSim)
of library activity, 321–327 (*see
also* Libraries, as catalysts;
Libraries, as control zones;
Libraries, as systems and
services)
open-source, 298–300
organizational, 151–157, 278,
329
publishing and distribution, 174,
185, 192, 288, 291–293, 301,
315–317, 328
Monitoring, 7, 10, 21, 63, 67–68,
110, 222, 253, 298. *See also*
Sanctioning
Motivation, 157, 283–285, 294, 313,
335, 340–342. *See also*
Incentives
Musgrave, Richard A., 8
Music, 8, 36–37, 52, 89–90, 109,
124–125, 127, 137, 174–175,
180–181, 197, 222, 227–228,
233, 235–236, 291

Napster, 89, 237–238
National Academies Press, 196
National Education Longitudinal
Study (NELS), 258
National Institutes of Health (NIH),
97, 136

National Science Digital Library
(NSDL), 99, 333, 334, 338, 340,
342
National Science Foundation (NSF),
99, 333, 341
Native American Grave Repatriation
Act, 233–234
Neighborhood Associations, 264
Nested enterprises, 7, 264
Nestedness, 7, 44, 49, 351
definition, 351
Networked Digital Library of Theses
and Dissertations, 98
Networks, 13, 34, 88, 103, 105, 277,
313–314
digital, 30, 35–36, 47, 87, 92, 94,
127, 128, 137, 156, 197, 250,
315, 337–338
social, 6, 9, 35 (*see also* Social
capital)
New commons, 4, 15, 28
New England Journal of Medicine,
191
Newman, Judge Pauline, 240–241
Noncompliance, 50, 58, 61. *See also*
Compliance
Nonrivalry (includes
nonsubtractability), 5, 13, 34,
47, 48, 180–181, 183, 186, 188,
210–211
Norms, 6, 15, 29, 224

Oakerson, Ronald, 41, 42
O'Donnell, James, 155
Olson, Mancur, 10
Open access (land), 11, 13
Open access (OA) (information), 10,
13–14, 48, 53, 95, 149,
171–197, 210
definition, 351
for publishing, 37, 55–56
Open Archives Initiative (OAI), 48,
97, 160, 315
metadata harvesting protocol of the,
172–173, 315, 338
Open Content Alliance (OCA),
99

Open content licenses, 294. *See also*
Licenses
Open Knowledge Initiative, 315
Open science, 13, 55, 61, 277, 278,
292
Open Society Institute, 96, 107
Open source definition (OSD),
282–283
Open Source Initiative (OSI),
282–283
Open source software. *See* Free/Libre
and Open Source Software
(FOSS)
Ostrom, Elinor, ix, xii, 7, 28, 31,
94–95, 106, 130, 147, 249–250,
254, 255, 256, 261, 280, 284,
289, 297, 312
Outcomes, 5, 13, 59–62
Overharvesting, 5, 28, 47
Overpatenting, 4, 10, 11, 14, 61,
350. *See also* Anticommons
Overpricing, 14
Overuse, 4, 201, 250
Oxford Text Archive, 98

Participation, 7, 36, 57, 61–62, 67,
86, 93–95, 99–100, 133, 137,
140, 158–159, 195–196,
232–233, 267, 286–288, 314,
339. *See also* Collective Action;
Incentives; Motivation
in the commons, 28, 34, 94, 253,
263–265, 281, 289–290, 295,
299
incentives for, 55–56, 149, 159,
162, 284–285
in democracy, 93–94, 104–105, 112,
256
low, 59, 298–299
paid, 299
project, 280–281, 285, 294, 301,
303
public, 93
as a right, 52
in rule-making, 50–51, 53–54,
148–149
standards of, 62, 64

Participatory media, 36
Patent Act, 214
Patent Law, 13, 212, 216, 220,
    221–222, 224, 226, 228,
    241–242
Patents, 13, 18, 28, 35, 52, 210–214,
    220, 222, 228–230, 239–242,
    252. *See also* Anticommons;
    Intellectual Property Rights;
    Overpatenting
Path dependency, 41
  definition, 351
Patriot Act, 13, 90, 102
Patterns of interaction, 44, 49, 50,
    53, 57–59
Pay-per-view, 99
Peer production, 35–36, 93,
    349
Peer-to-peer (file sharing), 35,
    235
Peer review, 18, 98, 107, 123, 128,
    172, 177, 277
  alternatives to, 130–132
  costs of, 172–174
Perens, Bruce, 282
Pew Internet and American Life
    Project, 258, 264
Philosophers' Imprint, 174
PhilSci Archive, 98
Physics, 98, 172, 316–318, 326
  journals, 88
Piracy, 235
Plagiarism, 161, 179, 183, 226,
    293
Pluralism, 257
Pollution, 4, 5, 28, 30, 33, 61, 223,
    250, 252, 257
Polycentricity, 55
  definition, 351
Pope, Carl, 32
Pornography, 90
Portico, 100, 156–159
Precautionary principle, 32
Preservation, x–xi, 8, 9, 10, 14,
    17–18, 20, 21, 48, 61, 63–64,
    89, 97, 105, 145–163, 183, 233,
    321

community-based, 100, 103, 105,
    156–159 (*see also* LOCKSS;
    Portico)
  definition, 351
Price barriers, 171, 183. *See also*
    Costs; Digitization, costs of; Peer
    review, costs of; Publication
    costs; Subscriptions
Prisoner's Dilemma, 11, 42
  definition, 351
Private goods, 4, 8–9, 52, 159, 182,
    278, 281, 300, 302. *See also*
    Economic goods
Private property, 28, 33, 38, 138,
    182, 231, 251–252
Privatization, 11, 12, 32, 38, 86, 87,
    92, 150, 242, 267
Project Gutenberg, 137
Property rights, 5, 6, 15, 28, 32–33,
    43, 52–53, 129, 138, 211, 215,
    222, 231. *See also* Copyright;
    Fair use; First sale; Intellectual
    property rights; Patent law;
    Patents
  bundles of, 52–53
  definition, 351
  regimes, 5, 6, 129, 211
  and the Tragedy of the Commons,
    32, 129
Proposition, 301, 333–334
Prusak, Laurence, 8
Public Access to Science Act,
    179
Public citizen, 32
Public data, 91
Public domain, 15, 17, 36–37, 48,
    88–89, 92, 95, 99, 102, 123,
    125, 138, 171, 177–182, 197,
    251, 283, 299. *See also* Center
    for the Public Domain
  definition, 351
Public goods, 8–10, 13, 16, 29, 48,
    52, 58, 129, 146, 149, 151, 157,
    159, 162, 182, 186, 211,
    250–252, 254, 256, 260, 278,
    279, 294, 302, 337, 341. *See
    also* Club goods; Common good;

Public goods (cont.)
  Common-pool resources;
  Economic goods; Private goods
definition, 351
Public Library of Science (PLoS), 96,
  183, 192
Publicnews.com, 36
Public policy, 38, 86, 90–91, 93,
  101–102, 105, 110, 137, 177,
  218, 223, 229, 242, 248, 251,
  253, 261, 267, 333–334
Public trust doctrine, 32
"Public work," 247, 257, 264,
  265–267. *See also* Boyte, Harry
Publication costs, 65, 132, 172–173,
  300. *See also* Journals;
  Subscriptions
  Authors-pay model for, 66, 96, 107,
    173, 301–302
  Institutions-pay model for, 107,
    173–174, 301–302
  User-pays model for, 300–301
Publishing industry, 16, 21, 37, 86,
  88, 94, 99, 100, 102, 104,
  107–110, 129, 148, 154–155,
  162–163, 191–192, 193–194,
  196, 300, 315, 317–320,
  321–323. *See also* Electronic
  Journals; Journals; Publication
  costs; Reed Elsevier
PubMed Central, 97

Random House, 99
Raymond, Eric, 195, 282
Reciprocity, 6, 11, 12, 43, 61, 94,
  104, 106, 254, 335
  definition, 351
Reed Elsevier, 107–108, 154–155,
  194
Religious congregations, 251, 264
Removal, 52–53, 154–155
Repositories, 10, 16, 18, 21, 37, 45,
  51, 50–67, 97–98, 104,
  105–106, 140, 153–156, 157,
  160, 172, 186, 187, 190, 322,
  336. *See also* Archives; Digital

Libraries; Digital Library of the
  Commons; Dspace; EconPort;
  Libraries
definition, 351
Research, 16, 85, 240, 288
  collaborative, 59, 95, 131, 190,
    279, 298, 302, 326–327,
    334
  funding (*see* Government, funding)
  medical (includes biomedical), 11,
    37, 136–137, 174, 191, 240
  process, 36, 42–43, 55, 60, 94, 136,
    194, 234, 257–259, 288,
    299–300, 336–337, 339
  products, 10, 47–48, 54–55, 58, 64,
    85, 98, 129, 173–176, 196, 288,
    293, 295
  projects, 42, 248, 260–261, 318
  questions, 21, 66, 86, 129, 138,
    248–249, 289
Resource system, 5, 6, 47, 52, 65
Resource unit, 46, 47
Rischard, J. F., 277
Rivalry, 9, 28, 47, 211
Robust systems, 14, 298, 323
Robustness, xi, 7, 10, 15, 34, 49, 66,
  68, 146, 154, 255–257, 298,
  315, 324, 327, 336, 350
RoMEO Project, 98
Rose, Carol, 109
Rowling, J. K., 125
Royalties, 174–175
Royalty-free literature, 18, 174–197
Rules, 7, 10, 11, 12, 15–16, 28, 29,
  33, 37, 41–42, 46–52, 53, 58,
  64, 67, 94–95, 104, 106, 177,
  221, 236, 251, 253, 282–283,
  284, 297, 324, 350, 351, 352.
  See also Compliance;
  Institutional analysis; Intellectual
  property rights; Norms; Patterns
  of behaviors
  collective-choice, 50, 255
  constitutional, 50, 255
  definition, 351
  evolution of, 64, 284, 297

formal, 42, 53, 212, 216, 220–222, 234, 236
informal, 42
operational, 50, 52, 255, 287, 298
in use, 7, 19, 43, 45–46, 49–52, 280–281, 283, 287, 289, 297

Sabo, Martin, 179
Safe-harbor principles, 161
Samuelson, Paul, 8
Sanctioning, 7, 36, 50, 67, 298. *See also* Monitoring
San Diego Dialogue, 262
Scholarly communication, ix–xi, 18, 20, 27, 34, 61, 86, 94–95, 108–109, 123–124, 130, 132, 138–139, 146, 152, 163, 311–330
crisis in, 102, 105
definition, 351
process, 104
Scholarly Publishing and Academic Resources Coalition (SPARC), 95–96, 102, 153
Schwartz, Paul, 230–231
Schweik, Charles, xii, 19–20, 57, 280, 294
Science Commons, 292
Science Direct, 88, 154
Scientific knowledge. *See* Knowledge, science
Scientific revolution, 278
Screen Actors Guild, 221–222
Screenwriters Federation of America, 221–222
"Second Enclosure Movement," 12. *See also* Boyle, James
Self-archiving, 53, 56–57, 64, 98, 155, 319. *See also* Archives
Self-governance, 6, 14, 106
definition, 352
Semantic web, 324
Semenov, Andrei, 280, 294
September 11, 2001, 15, 91, 100
Shulenburger, David, 56
Sierra Club, 32

Smith, Adam, 334–335
Smith, Vernon, 336–337
Social benefits, 154, 222–223
Social capital, 5, 6, 56, 61, 94, 106, 131, 247. *See also* Reciprocity
definition, 352
Social costs, 222
Social dilemmas, 4, 5, 13
Social networks, 6, 9, 35
Social norms, 29, 32, 33, 227, 312
Social Science Research Network, 316
Software Freedom Law Center, 35
Sourceforge.net, 278, 287
Space Physics and Aeronomy Research Collaboratory, 226–227
Spam, 61, 210, 252, 253. *See also* Pollution
Stallman, Richard, 281–283, 291, 294
Standards, 51, 61, 62, 64, 66, 95, 96, 98–99, 315, 322
metadata, 54
Stanford University, 11, 100, 107, 157, 158, 322
Statute of Monopolies, 229
Stewardship, 13, 106, 147, 251, 311–312, 314, 321–322, 329
definition, 352
Stone, Sue, 319
Suber, Peter, xii, 13, 96, 147, 249
Subscriptions, 9, 16, 36–37, 61, 65, 87–89, 100, 103, 107–108, 134, 154–155, 195, 300. *See also* Electronic journals; Journals; Publication costs; Publishing Industry
history of, 87–88, 103
Subtractability, 5, 9. *See also* Rivalry
definition, 352
Supreme court. *See* U. S. Supreme Court
Sustainability, ix, 5, 6, 7, 10, 11, 14, 16–17, 29, 32, 43, 49, 53, 62–63, 94, 100, 105–107, 229,

Sustainability (cont.)
  256, 315–316, 322, 323,
  342–347. *See also* Preservation
  definition, 352
  of ecological systems, 63
  funding models for, 149, 156, 157,
    161–163, 172–173
  of the knowledge commons, 64,
    86, 89, 94–95, 101, 103, 107,
    112
  of scholarly communication, 85, 329
Swan, Alma, 187, 192
Swarthout, J. Todd, 20, 334

Task Force on Archiving of Digital
  Information, 150
Teaching, 20, 49, 94, 98, 99, 101,
  103, 107, 146, 147, 154, 227,
  258–260, 326, 333, 335–337,
  339–340, 344–345
Technology, 46, 51, 67, 92, 101, 111,
  139, 149, 236–238, 278, 311,
  317, 320, 323–324, 326, 328,
  333, 337–338, 241–342
  history of, 133–134, 136
Tenner, Edward, 155
Thompson, Hunter S., 226
Thorin, Suzanne, 99
Tocqueville, Alexis de, 45, 251, 254
Toll goods. *See* Club goods
Trademark law, 35
Tragedy of the Commons, 10–11, 12,
  15, 18, 32, 92, 106, 129, 130,
  138, 150, 180, 183, 210,
  230–231. *See also* Enclosure;
  Tragic depletion; Tragic
  stalemate
  definition, 352
Tragic depletion, 183. *See also*
  Tragedy of the Commons
Tragic stalemate, 183. *See also*
  Tragedy of the Commons
Transaction costs, 3, 222–223, 225,
  289. *See also* Costs
Transboundary commons, 4
Traweek, Sharon, 317–318, 328

Treanor, Willliam, 230–231
Tribalism, 59
TRIPS, 13
Trust, 11, 12, 43, 56, 59, 104, 106,
  129, 146, 210, 254, 256, 316,
  323, 335. *See also* Patterns of
  Behavior; Reciprocity
Tucker, A. W., 11
Two-sided market, 158–159

Underuse, 11, 58. *See also*
  Anticommons
Universities, 10, 16, 21, 37, 59,
  65–66, 88, 92, 95, 97–98,
  106–108, 148, 153, 185–187,
  191–192, 247, 260–262,
  299–300, 314, 346
University of Arizona, 101, 333, 334,
  337, 341, 346
University of California at San Diego,
  262
University of California at Santa
  Barbara, 328
University of Maryland, 19, 247,
  248, 249, 268
University of Minnesota, 249, 328
University of Southampton, 57
University of Virginia, 317, 326
UrbanSim model, 290
U.S. Congress, 85, 89–90, 213, 230,
  239
  members of, 160
U.S. Constitution, 89, 111, 159, 161,
  187, 213, 230, 231
U.S. Information Security Oversight
  Office, 90
U.S. Patent and Trademark Office,
  222
U.S. Supreme Court, 89–90, 214,
  221, 235–238, 240–242

Vaidhyanthan, Siva, 89
Van Houweling, Douglas, xii
Vanishing act, 154–155, 157
Varmus, Harold, 96
Visalberghi, Elisabetta, 226

Visibility, 186, 190
Voluntary associations, 13, 159, 263
Volunteerism, 132, 139, 192, 195, 255, 267, 280, 299
and the Internet, 127, 128, 138 (*see also* Internet)
and open source software, 134, 284–286, 287, 298–299 (*see also* Open source)

Warschauer, Mark, 258–259
Waters, Donald, xii, 48, 100
Westlaw, 134
Wikipedia, 36, 131
Wind Done Gone, The, 214
Work Projects Administration (WPA), 232–234
Workshop in Political Theory and Policy Analysis, ix, 16, 31
World Summit on the Information Society (WSIS), 49
World Wide Web, 87, 128, 249, 314, 333, 338. *See also* Internet

Yahoo.com, 99, 184, 345

Zurkowski, Paul, 87